CIGARETTE CARD VALUES

2004 Catalogue

other Tra

"My catalogue is long, through every passion ranging"
W. S. Gilbert (The Mikado)

Compiled and published by

MURRAY CARDS (INTERNATIONAL) LIMITED
51 Watford Way, Hendon Central, London NW4 3JH
Tel: (020) 8202 5688
Fax: (020) 8203 7878
E-mail: murraycards@ukbusiness.com
Web site: http://www.murraycard.com/
For International Calls dial (011) 44208 202 5688

Opening hours — 9am-5pm, Monday-Friday

Watford Way is the A41 road into London, and is one mile from the end of the M1 Motorway. It can be reached via Hendon Central Underground Station (Northern Line), which is 100 yards away, and is also served by a number of bus routes and Green Line.

ISBN 0-946942-25-0

HEAD OFFICE AND MAIN RETAIL SHOWROOM

When in London, why not pay us a visit?

* Fast, courteous service.
* Odds lists filled while you wait.
* Sample albums of cards arranged thematically.
* New Issues and additions to stock.
* Monthly Special Offers.
* Unlisted lines always available.
* Albums without postal charges.
* Second hand books and albums.
* Complete framing service.
* Packets, playing cards and other ephemera.
* Spot cash for purchases.

Murray Cards (International) Limited

51 Watford Way, Hendon Central, London NW4 3JH

Opening hours 9.00 a.m. to 5.00 p.m., Monday-Friday

Watford Way is the A41 road into London, and is one mile from the end of the M1 Motorway. It is 100 yards from Hendon Central Underground Station (Northern Line), and is also served by a number of bus routes and Green Line. Private parking bay available for customers.

Introduction

In the past year Congestion charging and increased transport costs together with the inability (through lack of space) to store and display our ever-increasing range of cards have persuaded us to transfer our Cecil Court business to Hendon from 5th January 2004. Only 30 minutes (and then 100 yards by foot) by underground from Central London, our Hendon store provides more comfortable viewing facilities, off-street parking, and access to our complete range of stock. Cecil Court regulars and all other visitors can be assured of a friendly welcome and expert help with their requirements. As an incentive we are offering to pay the fare between the two locations – £4.50 to **all** callers at Hendon who spend at least £25, from January 5th 2004 (and the Travelcard can be used for all journeys for the remainder of the day). The Cecil Court branch will close for business on December 24th 2003, and from November 1st until that date the prices of all remaining stock of sets, albums and frames (not books) will be reduced by 25% to avoid having to transfer them to Hendon.

Card prices have all, as usual, been considered on an individual basis. In the case of many we have been able to avoid any increases at all, because of a number of substantial purchases. We have however taken the decision to increase the price of many of our reprint issues, and some of our original productions. It is now 20 years since we produced the first reprint – Wills Cricketers 1896 – and the selling price had remained the same since then! We are therefore increasing the price of all sets at £7.50 by £1.00, with some increases elsewhere; but all small sets of 25 remain at £6.00. And use of the special voucher on Page 311 could more than make up for any increases.

A new feature this year in the Catalogue is a selection of sets on thematic subjects, both original and reprints at very substantial discounts. These all appear on Page 6, and are well worth a look.

One new publication this year, which we did predict in our last Catalogue, is the British Tobacco Issues Handbook. This first revision for over 50 years lists or illustrates all unnumbered series to enable collectors to identify their missing cards, and ranges in time from the earliest of Player and Taddy issues right up to series by Doncella and Rothman. Issues by Ogden, Wills and the Godfrey Phillips group are not included, since these will be the subject of individual books, but all other issues are comprehensively covered. There are 369 pages and over 2,600 cards illustrated, and at a price of £23.50 including inland postage this book cannot be recommended too highly. It is essential reference for all serious collectors, for even if one does not wish to obtain the cards, one can at least see what many of them, including some of the very rarest, look like.

HOW TO USE THE CATALOGUE

The Catalogue is in three parts.

Part I contains all known issues by British-based tobacco companies. Thus all cards by the firm W. D. & H. O. Wills, which was located in Bristol, are shown, even though they may have been issued in a Wills brand abroad. Issues from the Channel Islands and the Republic of Ireland are included in this part. Excluded are most post cards and larger non-insert items.

Part II contains tobacco issues by most of the major manufacturers in the English-speaking world, and a selection of other series, including all the sets readily available to collectors.

Part III comprises series issued with commodities other than tobacco (commonly known as "trade cards"). Although mainly British issues, there are a number of overseas sets included. Each issuer's name is followed by the commodity with which the cards were issued; where the set was not given away free, but produced in order to be sold, the issuer is described as "commercial".

Parts I and III commence with an index of brand names, and the issuer's name under which that item appears. Series are listed in alphabetical order of series title under the issuing firm, regardless of country of origin. Where the issuer was not normally located in the United Kingdom the country of origin is given. In the case of certain larger issuers series have been listed in logical groups so that they may be more readily found.

For each set the following information is given:–

(1) **Size information.**Cards are assumed to be standard size unless otherwise stated. Sizes used generally correspond to the page sizes used for our plastic albums (see separate notice) i.e. when a letter is used it may be assumed that at least one dimension is greater than the size shown by the previous letter. Abbreviations used are:–

K	smaller than standard.	51 x 41 mm.
M	medium size.	80 x 52 mm.
L	large size.	80 x 71 mm.
T	Typhoo/Doncella size.	106 x 52 mm.
X	extra large size.	80 x 113 mm.
P	postcard size.	165 x 110 mm.
G	cabinet size.	228 x 165 mm.
E	too large for albums.	
D	dual (more than one) size.	
S	stereoscopic series.	
F	photographic production.	

(2) **Number of cards in set.** When there are several rare numbers in a set the quantity normally available is shown. Thus 35/37 means that the series consists of 37 cards, but that only 35 are usually obtainable.

(3) **Series title.** Where the set has no name, then the title accepted by common usage is given. Sect. = sectional series. Silk = silk, satin or canvas. P/C = playing card. When a dimension is shown this may be compared on the ruler printed on page 312.

(4) **Year of issue.** This is approximate only, and should in no way be considered to be binding. Particularly in the case of overseas and pre-1900 issues the date should be treated as merely an indication of the era in which the set was produced.

(5) **Price of odd cards.** Because of high labour costs and overheads it is not an economic proposition to offer odd cards from many post-1945 series. Where

shown the price is that of normal cards in the set. End numbers (e.g. numbers 1 and 50 from a set of 50 cards) are DOUBLE the price shown. Known scarce subjects from a series, and also thematic subjects from general series (e.g. cricketers from general interest series) would be more expensive than the price shown here.

Where no cards from a series were actually in stock at the time of compilation the price is shown in *italics.* It must be borne in mind that many of these prices are only approximate, since the discovery of just a few cards from a scarcer series could greatly affect the price.

(6) **Price of complete sets.** Prices shown are for sets in clean, undamaged condition. Where mint sets are specified (and available) there will be a premium of 50% extra for sets post 1919, and 100% for pre 1920 sets. Where no set price is quoted we had no complete sets in stock at the time of compilation; however, when available these will be sold at prices based on the odds figure. *With each pre 1940 set the appropriate Nostalgia album pages are presented FREE!*

UNLISTED SERIES

Because our stocks are constantly changing we always have in stock a large number of series which are unlisted. In particular we can presently offer an excellent selection of German sets, loose or in their special albums and also a good choice of Australian trade issues. If you require a specific item please send us a stamped addressed envelope for an immediate quotation.

ALIKE SERIES

There are many instances where affiliated companies, or indeed completely independent groups issued identical series, where the pictures are the same, and only the issuer's name is altered. Examples are Fish & Bait issued by Churchman, I.T.C. (Canada) and Wills; British Cavalry Uniforms of the Nineteenth Century issued by Badshah, Browne, Empson, Rington and Wilcocks & Wilcocks; or even Interesting Animals by Hignett or Church & Dwight. If wishing to avoid duplication of pictures, please state when ordering which series you already **have.**

THEMATIC SPECIAL OFFERS

A mixture of Original and Reprinted Sets

AVIATION	6 different sets Catalogue value £34+ Includes Player – Aircraft of the RAF *reprint* Doncella – Golden Age of Flying	**£18.50**
BIRDS	6 different sets Catalogue value £32 Includes C.W.S. – Parrot Series *reprint* Imperial Publishing – Birds of Britain	**£17.50**
BOXING	6 different sets Catalogue value £41 Includes Churchman – Boxing Personalities *reprint* Ideal Albums – Boxing Greats	**£22.00**
CRICKET	10 different sets Catalogue value £49+ Includes Wills – Cricketers 1896 *reprint* Cecil Court – Ashes Winning Captains	**£26.00**
ENTERTAINMENT	11 different sets Catalogue value £72 Includes Player – Film Stars Third Series *reprint* Mister Softee – Pop Stars (shaped)	**£38.00**
FLORA AND FAUNA	8 different sets Catalogue value £62+ Includes Wills – Roses, A series *reprint* Grandee – Britain's Wayside Wildlife	**£33.00**
FOOTBALL A	13 different sets Catalogue value £76 Includes Ogdens – A.F.C. Nicknames *reprint* Rothmans – Football International Stars	**£40.00**
FOOTBALL B	13 different sets Catalogue value £71+ Includes Taddy – Manchester United *reprint* Topps – Saint & Greavsie	**£37.50**
GOLF	8 different sets Catalogue value £71 Includes Churchman – Prominent Golfers (50) *reprint* Birchgrey – Panasonic European Open	**£37.50**
MILITARY	13 different sets Catalogue value £71 Includes Player – Military Series *reprint* Victoria Gallery – Uniforms of the War of Independence	**£37.50**
NAVAL	9 different sets Catalogue value £56 Includes Player – Old Naval Prints *reprint* Swettenham – Evolution of the Royal Navy	**£30.00**
ROAD TRANSPORT	10 different sets Catalogue value £62+ Includes Lambert & Butler – Motorcycles *reprint* Doncella – Golden Age of Motoring	**£33.00**
RUGBY UNION	7 different sets Catalogue value £44 Includes Smith – Prominent Ruby Players *reprint* Rugby Football Union – English Internationals	**£23.50**

THE NOSTALGIA CLASSIC COLLECTION

Limited Edition reprints of 50 rare sets
Only 1000 of each set printed

THIS IS A UNIQUE OPPORTUNITY TO ACQUIRE SETS THAT FEW PEOPLE HAVE SEEN

P4	Adkin – Games by Tom Browne	£4.00
9	Allen & Ginter (U.S.A.) – Women Baseball Players	£3.00
X50	Allen & Ginter (U.S.A.) – The World's Champions, Second Series	£17.50
35	Ardath – Hand Shadows	£7.50
25	A. Baker – Star Girls	£6.00
20	Bradford – Boer War Cartoons	£5.00
L16	Brigham – Down the Thames	£6.50
25	B.A.T – Beauties, Blossom Girls	£6.00
T6	Cadbury – Sports Series	£3.00
10	Chappel – British Celebrities	£3.00
30	Clarke – Cricketer Series	£7.50
P7	Cope – The Seven Ages of Man	£6.00
6	Empire Tobacco – Franco British Exhibition	£2.00
25	Faulkner – Beauties (Coloured)	£6.00
25	Globe Cigarette Co. – Actresses - French	£6.00
17	Goode (Australia) – Prominent Cricketer Series	£5.00
8	Hall (U.S.A.) – Presidential Candidates & Actresses	£2.00
P12	Huntley & Palmer – Aviation	£7.50
M20	James & Co. – Arms of Countries	£7.50
50	Kimball – Champion of Games and Sports	£10.00
15	Kinnear – Australian Cricket Team	£4.00
50	Kriegsfield – Phrases & Advertisements	£10.00
25	Kuit – Principal British Streets	£6.00
50	Lacey's – Footballers	£10.00
20	Lambert & Butler – International Yachts	£5.00
20	J. Lees – Northampton Town Football Club	£5.00
X6	Liebig (France) – Famous Explorers (S.1094)	£5.00
25	Lusby – Scenes from Circus Life	£6.00
15	Marburg (U.S.A.) – Beauties, "PAC"	£4.00
35	Mayo (U.S.A.) – Prizefighters	£7.50
13	National (Australia) – English Cricket Team 1897-8	£4.00
50	Ogden – Cricketers & Sportsmen	£10.00
X16	Old Calabar – Sports and Games	£7.50
40	Orlando Cigarette Co. – Home & Colonial Regiments	£8.50
30	Godfrey Phillips – Beauties, Nymphs	£7.50
20	Godfrey Phillips – Russo Japanese War Series	£5.00
20	Richmond Cavendish – Yachts (White Back)	£5.00
6	E. Robinson & Sons – Medals & Decorations	£2.00
25	E. Robinson & Sons – Regimental Mascots	£6.00
16	S.D.V. Tobacco – British Royal Family	£4.00
30	Salmon & Gluckstein – Music Hall Stage Characters	£7.50
50	Singleton & Cole – Footballers	£10.00
25	F. & J. Smith – Advertisement Cards	£6.00
50	F. & J. Smith – Champions of Sport (Unnumbered)	£10.00
10	Spiro Valleri – Footballers	£3.00
12	Spratt – Prize Dogs	£3.50
5	Taddy – English Royalty	£2.00
20	Taddy – Royalty, Actresses & Soldiers	£5.00
10	United Tobacconists – Actresses, "MUTA"	£3.00
22	Henry Welfare – Prominent Politicians	£6.00

CIGARETTE CARD AUCTIONS

Our auctions are the largest and most successful in the world!

Every month about 469 interesting lots are sold. These include rare sets and type cards, cheaper sets and mixtures, sets in excellent to mint condition, literature, overseas and trade cards not recorded in our Catalogue and highly specialised collections such as Guinea Golds and silks. Lots are submitted to us from other dealers, collectors disposing of their unwanted cards, estates, overseas sources and antique dealers.

Highlights of recent years have included:–

Sets: Taddy Clowns & Circus Artistes, Actresses with Flowers, V.C. Heroes (125).
Wills Waterloo, Soldiers & Sailors, Cricketers 1896.
Players Military Series, Old England's Defenders.
Smith Races of Mankind, Boer War Series.
Ogden Guinea Golds 1-1148 complete.
Fairweather Historic Buildings of Scotland.
Cope Golfers.

Odds: Players, Wills, Smith Advertisement Cards, Clarke Tobacco Leaf Girls, Kinnear Cricketers, Edwards Ringer & Bigg Eastern Manoeuvres, Taddy Wrestlers, etc.

But there is something for everyone each time, from beginner to advanced collector, as the more than 200 participants every month will attest.

You do not have to attend in order to bid. Most of our clients bid by post, knowing that their instructions will be dealt with fairly and in confidence.

How do you bid? Just assess each lot that interests you. Then tell us the maximum amount that you are prepared to pay for it. We will then obtain it (if there are no higher bids) for the cheapest price possible — if for example your bid is £30 and the next highest received is £20 then you will obtain the lot for just £21. If you wish to put a ceiling on your total spending in any auction we can accommodate this too.

How do you obtain Auction Catalogues? Send £1.50 (£2.00 Overseas) for a sample, or else £15.00 (£20.00 Overseas) will cover the cost of all 12 Catalogues for 2004 including Prices Realised Lists. £1.00 is refundable to subscribers who bid successfully and pay promptly, each month. Auctions are held on the third Sunday of every month and Catalogues are sent out at least three weeks before sale date.

TERMS OF BUSINESS

All previous lists are cancelled.

Cash with order. Any unsatisfactory items may be returned for credit or refund within seven days of receipt.

Overseas payments can only be accepted by sterling cheque drawn on a British bank, or by Credit/Debit Card.

Credit Cards. We can accept payment by American Express, Access, Eurocard, Mastercard and Visa at no extra charge. Just quote your card number and expiry date, and we will complete the amount of items actually sent. This is particularly useful for overseas customers, saving bank and currency conversion problems. Minimum credit card order — £5.00.

Condition. All prices are based on cards in clean, undamaged condition. Where available mint sets post 1919 will be at a premium of 50% above the normal price, and mint sets pre 1920 and all mint odd cards will be an extra 100%.

Minimum Order. We are unable to accept orders totalling less than £2.00. For payments of less than £2, in conjunction with credit notes, we can only accept stamps and postal orders, not cheques.

Postage. Inland second class or parcel delivery, which is now a guaranteed next week-day delivery, is included in all prices quoted. Overseas letter post is sent free by surface mail. Overseas parcels and air mail are charged at cost. Overseas orders will be sent by air unless otherwise specified.

Value Added Tax at the rate current on publication is included. Customers outside the E.E.C. should deduct $\frac{7}{47}$ (approx 15%) from everything except books.

When ordering cards please quote the issuer's name, the name of the set, the date of issue, and the price. This will enable us to identify the precise series.

Odd Lists must be submitted on a separate sheet of paper with the name and address clearly shown; this will be returned with the cards for checking if sent in duplicate. Remember that end cards are double the normal price. Please write all the numbers required, e.g. NOT "17-20" but 17, 18, 19, 20. If the cards are required to complete an unnumbered set, and you do not know the missing titles, we can supply them provided that you list all the cards that you HAVE in alphabetical order. Please note we cannot accept telephone orders for odd cards.

Alternatives. Although this catalogue is based upon current stocks, these are bound to fluctuate. Therefore, whenever possible give alternatives.

Credit Notes. When items are out of stock a credit note is normally sent. This may be utilised or encashed at any time, but MUST be returned when so doing.

Unlisted series. We are always pleased to quote for series unlisted, or unpriced.

Purchasing. We are always pleased to purchase or exchange collectors' unwanted cards. Please write with full details before sending cards.

Enquiries. We are always pleased to offer our advice on all collectors' queries. Please enclose a stamped addressed envelope with all enquiries.

Callers. Our shop is open from 9.00 a.m. to 5.00 p.m. each Monday to Friday, and collectors are always welcome to select from our complete range of cards and accessories. Watford Way is at Hendon Central (Underground, Northern Line), and is served by a number of buses, including Green Line. Private parking bay available for customers.

Fax Machine/E-mail/Web site. Our machines are always on. They can be used to place orders (including odd cards) when a credit card number and expiry date are quoted, and also for Auction bids. The Fax number is 020-8203-7878 (International 011-44208-203-7878) E-mail is murraycards@ukbusiness.com Web site: www.murraycard.com

Answering machine. For the convenience of customers an answering machine is in operation whenever the shop is closed. Just leave your message, or order with Credit Card number and expiry date, and it will be dealt with as soon as we re-open. Please note we cannot accept telephone orders for odd cards.

No Hidden Extras. Remember that all prices shown include postage, packing, insurance and (where applicable) V.A.T. And that with every pre-1940 set we include Nostalgia pages *absolutely free!*

CARTOPHILIC SOCIETY REFERENCE BOOKS

A number of the earlier Reference Books have been unavailable for some years. However we are now pleased to be able to offer the following paper backed reprints at exceptionally low cost.

No. 1 Faulkner.
No. 2 Hill.
No. 4 Gallaher.
No. 5 Abdulla, Adkin & Anstie.
No. 6 Ardath.
No. 7 Directory of British Cigarette Card Issuers (16 cards illustrated).
No. 8 Glossary of Cartophilic Terms (27 cards illustrated).
No. 9 Lambert & Butler (25 cards illustrated).
No. 10 Churchman (29 cards illustrated).
No. 12 Taddy (30 cards illustrated).
No. 13 Phillips (225 cards illustrated).
No. 17 Player (26 cards illustrated).

ONLY £3.50 Per Booklet!

The following reprints have been combined in hard cover. The information contained cannot be found elsewhere, and each book represents excellent value. Each contains lists of unnumbered series, illustrations of untitled cards, and background information to most sets.

The Cigarette Card Issues of Wills and The B.A.T. Book. New combined volume. Over 500 pages, 2518 cards illustrated. **PRICE £20.00**

The New Tobacco War Reference Book. Complete re-write with 236 pages and 2330 cards illustrated. Essential information. **PRICE £20.00**

THE WORLD TOBACCO ISSUES INDEX

Published by the Cartophilic Society of G.B. Ltd., the **revised** edition was published in 2001. This is an index of series only, with minimal illustrations, and is in two volumes. The text is completely revised, with a large number of additions and amendments, completely integrated. This is an essential work for all keen collectors.

Volume I Introduction and Issues A-K **PRICE £22.50**

Volume II Issues L-Z and Anonymous **PRICE £22.50**

The **original** volumes of the World Index are still available, except Part 1. The information in them concerning lists of subjects and illustrations will not be updated for at least several years, so they still form a basic reference library.

Part II. 452 pages, with 3,600 cards illustrated. Many U.S. listings. **PRICE £15.50**

Part III. 504 pages, 66 cards illustrated. Includes lists of many U.S. non-insert cards, blankets and pins. **PRICE £25.00**

Part IV. 688 pages. Lists of U.S. Photographic and Maltese cards. **PRICE £18.50**

Part V. 552 pages, 1,329 cards illustrated. **PRICE £18.50**

SPECIAL OFFER – Parts III, IV and V for only £45.00

OTHER LITERATURE

GENERAL WORKS

The Story of Cigarette Cards by Martin Murray, Hardback, 128 pages, including 32 in colour. **£7.25**

Operation Red Poppy by Jack Nickle Smith. A spy thriller featuring a cartophilist. Hard cover. 158 pages. **Now Only £5.00**

Collecting Cigarette & Trade Cards by Gordon Howsden. 152 large pages. An excellent work with 750 cards illustrated in colour. **£17.00**

REFERENCE BOOKS

Smith Cigarette Cards. 36 pages with illustrations. Lists all known series, including back varieties. **£3.50**

British Trade Index, Part I. Series up to 1940. 216 pages, many illustrations. **£10.00**

British Trade Index, Part II. 232 pages. Additions to Part 1 and also issues 1945-1968 **£10.00**

British Trade Index, Part III. 400 pages, many illustrations. Additions to Parts I and II, with new issues to the end of 1985. **£12.50**

British Trade Index, Part IV. 411 pages, many illustrations. Additions to Parts I, II and III with new issues to the end of 1994. This well printed book includes an Index to the three previous volumes. **£20.00**

Typhoo Tea Cards. 36 pages with illustrations. Lists of back varieties. **£3.50**

A. & B.C. Gum Cards. Revised Edition. 42 pages with illustrations. Many lists. **£3.50**

British Silk Issues by Dorothy Sawyer. 2nd Edition. Many illustrations, 65 pages with details of all known British Tobacco and Trade silk issues. Essential reading for silk collectors. **£5.00**

Lawn Tennis Cards by Derek Hurst. 90 pages, including 4 pages of illustrations. Combined listing of Tobacco and Trade Cards. **£8.45**

Half Time (Football and the cigarette card 1890-1940) by David Thompson. 104 pages, listing every tobacco issue. Revised June 2001. **£9.50**

Errors & Varieties, British Cigarette Cards by W. B. Neilson. Lists of all known varieties, corrected or uncorrected. **£7.50**

Errors & Varieties, British Cigarette Cards, Part 2 by W. B. Neilson. 37 pages. Additions to Part 1, plus Guinea Golds, Tabs. **£3.00**

Errors & Varieties, British Trade Cards by W. B. Neilson. Revised 2002 edition. Many illustrations. **£3.00**

Huntley & Palmers Catalogue of Cards by E. Vansevenant. 63 pages, paper back, many cards illustrated. **£10.00**

Peek Frean Catalogue of Cards. 76 pages, many illustrations. **£13.50**

Cricket Cigarette & Trade Cards by Derek Deadman. The definitive work. 254 pages, 16 pages of illustrations. Comprehensive list of all titles known until the end of 1984. 'Monumental'. **£10.95**

Cricket Cigarette & Trade Cards. A further listing by Alan Harris and Geoff Seymour. 143 pages, 16 pages of illustrations. Lists all cards issued since the Deadman book and updated information. **£7.50**

A Century of Golf Cards by Bruce Berdock and Michael Baier. 126 pages, 18 pages of mostly coloured illustrations. List all known golf cards — an essential reference book. **£19.50**

Seconds Out, Round One by Evan Jones. 172 pages, over 700 illustrations. Lists all known English language boxing cards (except recent commercial issues). A well researched book with interesting biographical information. **£14.50**

Brooke Bond Picture Cards 'The First Forty Years' by A. L. Waterhouse. A reference book of all Issues in Great Britain and Overseas. 72 pages with many illustrations. **£7.25**

The Price Guide to Golf Cards Part 1: Tobacco Cards by Philip Smedley & Bruce Berdock. 108 pages. All cards individually priced, illustrations from each series, including singles. **£9.00**

FOREIGN CARDS

Australian & New Zealand Index. Published by Cartophilic Society. Over 300 pages — 600 cards illustrated. Lists all tobacco and trade cards. Published 1983. **£10.50**

LIEBIG CARDS

Liebig Catalogue in English. Ninth Edition. See page 253 for full details. **£4.95**

Sanguinetti Liebig Catalogue. 1991 Edition. 431 pages, listing all titles from 1,974 sets and menus, Italian text, illustrations of 1,308 series. Indices in various languages. **£20.00**

Liebig Menu and Table Cards by L. De. Magistris. 118 page listing of all known Table and Menu cards, plus printing varieties. Colour illustrations of each series. **£20.00**

Unificato Liebig Catalogue, 2002. Second Edition. Hardback Ring Binder with over 400 pages. Published by CIF Italy. Complete listing of Chromos, Menus and Table cards in Fada sequence. Two coloured illustrations from each chromo series and one from other series. Prices in Euros and details of different languages. A magnificent achievement. **£35.00**

MISCELLANEOUS

Picture Postcard Values, 2004. Numerous updates. 24 page colour section (Available December 2003). **£9.95**

Golf on Old Picture Postcards by Tom Serpell. 64 pages heavily illustrated in both black and white and colour. **£5.50**

Jacobs Famous Picture Cards from History. 32 colour reproductions from 32 sets dealing with Transport & Natural History, together with an album including details of each card and a general introduction to card collecting. **£2.00**

Sweet Cigarette Packets by Paul Hart. 50 pages including 5 pages of illustrations. A most useful book for sweet cigarette packet collectors. **£6.50**

THE BRITISH TOBACCO ISSUES HANDBOOK

This long awaited new book replaces and updates considerably the old L.C.C.C. Handbooks Parts 1 and 2. It comprises 369 pages, and over 2,600 cards are illustrated.

The following British tobacco issues are included:

1. Lists of known captions of all unnumbered series.
2. Illustrations of subjects known of all unnumbered series without captions.
3. Collation of identical or similar series issued by more than one firm, whether GB tobacco, GB trade or overseas.
4. Illustrations of specimen cards from certain rare series, which might not otherwise be accessible.
5. Lists of particularly complicated printing varieties by the same firm.

Many additional new features, too numerous to mention. AVAILABLE NOW **£23.50**

FRAMING SERVICE

The last few years have seen a big upsurge in the framing of cigarette cards, both originals and reprints. We can offer an individual framing service for a favourite set or a specific interest.

Standard sets can be accommodated in the kits detailed on page 14, but if you have a horizontal Gallaher set, or a non-standard set please enquire.

FRAMING KITS

Best materials — Competitive prices
Easy to do-it-yourself — Cards positioned without damage
— Backs can be read —

MOUNTING BOARDS

(Can be used horizontally or vertically)
(Most available in Black, Brown, Green and Maroon)

	A	To hold	25	Standard sized cards.	259 x 421 mm
**	B	To hold	50	Carreras Black Cat cards.	470 x 421 mm
	C	To hold	24	Large cards.	383 x 469 mm
	D	To hold	10	Large cards.	259 x 421 mm
	E	To hold	25	Large cards.	383 x 469 mm
	F	To hold	50	Standard sized cards.	470 x 421 mm
	G	To hold	12	Large sized cards.	259 x 421 mm
**	H	To hold	15	Standard sized cards.	278 x 289 mm
**	J	To hold	20	Large sized cards.	348 x 502 mm
	K	To hold	10	Standard sized cards.	251 x 202 mm
	L	To hold	6	Liebig cards.	278 x 289 mm
	M	To hold	10	Extra large cards.	315 x 310 mm
	N	To hold	12	Faulkner Cartoon cards.	251 x 202 mm
	P	To hold	16	Large cards.	315 x 388 mm
*	Q	To hold	48	Vertical Gallaher cards.	470 x 421 mm
**	R	To hold	15	Large cards.	300 x 526 mm
	S	To hold	7	Large cards.	278 x 289 mm
	T	To hold	3	Standard sized cards.	127 x 174 mm
	W	To hold	6	Large sized cards.	251 x 223 mm
**	X	To hold	12	American Gum sized cards	259 x 421 mm

* = Available in Green only ** = Available in Black only

PRICES

POSTAL – minimum quantity of 6 – can be assorted sizes
PERSONAL CALLERS – no minimum quantity

Boards	A, D, G, M, X	£2.00
Boards	B, C, E, F, J, P, Q	£3.50
Boards	H, L, S	£1.35
Boards	K, N, W	£1.00
Board	R	£2.70
Board	T	£0.50

COMPLETE KITS

Comprising frame, glass, mounting board, spring clips, rings and screws.

PRICES (Now Post Free!)

A, G, X	£22.00 each	H, L	£16.50 each
B, C, E, F, J, Q	£35.00 each	K, W	£14.00 each

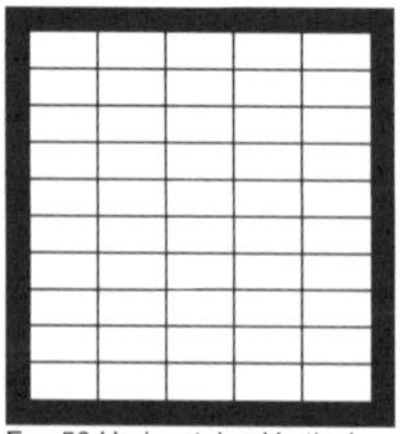

F — 50 Horizontal or Vertical

"NOSTALGIA" REPRINTS

An exciting concept for collectors. Reproductions of Classic card sets, all of which are almost impossible to obtain, at a price that everyone can afford.

These cards are of the highest quality, and the latest technology has been used to recreate as closely as possible the beauty of the originals. They have received universal acclaim in the cigarette card world, and are indeed becoming collector's items in their own right.

Because of the difficulty of distinguishing our reproductions from the originals each reprint has 'A Nostalgia Reprint' printed on the back of the card.

TITLES CURRENTLY AVAILABLE

Faulkner – Cartoon Series

Cricket Terms Football Terms 1st Series Football Terms 2nd Series
Golf Terms Grenadier Guards Military Terms 1st Series
Military Terms 2nd Series Nautical Terms 1st Series
Nautical Terms 2nd Series Policemen of the World Police Terms
Puzzle Series Sporting Terms Street Cries

ONLY £2.50 per set

Taddy 1908 County Cricketers – 16 Counties Available
ONLY £2.50 per County, or all 238 cards for £32.00

Taddy Prominent Footballers – 15 Cards per Set

Aston Villa Chelsea Everton Leeds City Liverpool Manchester United
Middlesbrough Newcastle United Queens Park Rangers Sunderland
Tottenham Hotspur West Ham United Woolwich Arsenal

ONLY £2.50 per Club

Allen & Ginter	50	American Indian Chiefs	**£8.50**
Allen & Ginter	50	Fruits	**£8.50**
Berlyn	25	Humorous Golfing Series	**£6.00**
C.W.S.	25	Parrot Series	**£6.00**
Cope	50	Cope's Golfers	**£8.50**
Cope	50	Dickens Gallery	**£8.50**
Duke	25	Fishers	**£6.00**
Ellis	25	Generals of the Late Civil War	**£6.00**
Gabriel	20	Cricketers Series	**£3.50**
Jones Bros.	18	Spurs Footballers	**£2.50**
Kinney	25	Leaders	**£6.00**
Player	50	Military Series	**£8.50**
Taddy	20	Clowns and Circus Artistes	**£6.00**
Taddy	25	Natives of the World	**£6.00**
Thomson	24	Motor Bike Cards	**£6.00**
Thomson	20	Motor Cycles	**£6.00**
U.S. Tobacco	28	Baseball Greats of the 1890's	**£6.00**
Wills	50	Cricketers 1896	**£8.50**
Wills	25	National Costumes	**£6.00**

A specially designed frame, is available for Taddy Clowns priced at £30 (to include special mounting board, glass and set).

THE "NOSTALGIA" ALBUM

We believe our album to be the finest on the market — yet now it is even better. Our pages are now being made from a material which contains no potentially harmful plasticiser and has a crystal-clear appearance. Only available from Murray Cards (International) Ltd. and approved stockists. Note also the following features:–

★ ★ Album leaves are made from clear plastic, enabling the entire card to be examined easily without handling!

★ ★ Cards easily removed and inserted!

★ ★ Wide margin enables pages to be turned in album without removing retention clip!

★ ★ A planned range of page formats allows most cards to be housed in one cover. Eight different pages now available!

★ ★ Handsome loose leaf PVC binders for easy removal and insertion of pages. Matching slip cases. Four different colours available.

★ ★ Black or coloured interleaving to enhance the appearance of your cards.

★ ★ Binder with 40 pages ★ ★

1 — £12.00 each

2-4 — £11.00 each

5 + — £10.00 each

Matching slipcase (only supplied with binder) £3.00

Extra pages — 15p each

Pastel interleaving	75p per 8	Black interleaving	£3.00 per 40
Binders	£6.00 (2 or more – £5 each)	Tweezers	£1.75 each

Pages sizes available:–

K.	holds 15	cards smaller than standard.	Size up to 51 x 41 mm.
A.	holds 10	standard size cards.	Size up to 80 x 41 mm.
M.	holds 8	medium size cards.	Size up to 80 x 52 mm.
L.	holds 6	large size cards.	Size up to 80 x 71 mm.
T.	holds 6	Doncella/Typhoo cards.	Size up to 106 x 52 mm.
X.	holds 4	extra large size cards.	Size up to 80 x 113 mm.
P.	holds 2	post card size cards.	Size up to 165 x 110 mm.
G.	holds 1	card cabinet size.	Size up to 228 x 165 mm.

Binders, size 303 x 182 x 60 mm., are available in blue, gold, green or red.

Nostalgia – Collect with Confidence!

NOSTALGIA ALBUMS

Preserve the best of the past in the best of the present. See opposite page for details.

National Flags & Flower-Girls
American Tobacco Co.,
Daniel, Johnson

Highwaymen – Frameability

Dogs – Pascall

Star Trek
Weetabix

Ferrari 1950's and 1960's – Golden Era

THE "HENDON" ALBUM

For Postcards, trade cards, and all printed ephemera.

* Page in crystal clear material, free of plasticiser.
* 7 different page formats.
* Handsome loose leaf binders, in choice of blue, brown, green or red.
* Matching slip cases.
* Big enough for BIG cards, small enough for small muscles.

Pages available

1. Pocket. Cards size 294 x 214mm.
2. Pockets. Cards size 143 x 214mm. Ideal for banknotes.
3. Pockets. Cards size 93 x 214mm. Ideal for banknotes.
4. Pockets. Cards size 143 x 105mm. Especially for postcards.
6. Pockets. Cards size 92 x 105mm.
8. Pockets. Cards size 67 x 105mm. Ideal for Gum cards, XL cigarette cards and phone cards.
9. Pockets. Cards size 94 x 68mm. Suitable for playing cards.

Binder with 25 pages	**£15.00**	(including postage).
Extra pages	**35p**	each.
Matching slip case	**£3.50**	(must be ordered with binder).
Black interleaving, full page size	**£3.00**	per 25.
Black inserts for postcard pages	**£2.00**	per 100.

COLLECTORS' AIDS

Cleartex strips, for wrapping standard size sets	**200 for £2.80**
large size sets	**200 for £3.20**
extra large sets	**200 for £3.50**
Tweezers, fine quality, with plastic sheath	**£1.75**
Magnifying Glasses, 2½" diameter	**£5.00**
4" diameter	**£9.00**
Printed wants lists, numbered 1-50 on thin card	**30 for 75p**
Plastic Wallet. Pocket size with 10 postcard size pages. Ideal for carrying odds (and ends)	**£1.75**
Postcard pockets, thin PVC	**100 for £3.50**

INDEX OF BRANDS (Tobacco)

These appear on cards without the Manufacturer's name (see also Information opposite Page 49)

GREYS TOBACCO — See Drapkin (Part 1)
GUARDS CIGARETTES — See Carreras (Part 1)

HAVELOCK CIGARETTES — See Willis (Part 1)
HAWSER Etc. — See Wholesale Tobacco Co. (Part 1)
HEARTS DELIGHT CIGARETTES — See Pritchard & Burton (Part 1)
HERBERT TAREYTON CIGARETTES — See American Tobacco Co. (Part 2)
HOFFMAN HOUSE MAGNUMS — See American Tobacco Co. (Part 2)
HONEST LONG CUT — See Duke or American Tobacco Co. (Part 2)
HUDAVEND CIGARETTES — See Teofani (Part 1)
HUSTLER LITTLE CIGARS — See American Tobacco Co. (Part 2)

ISLANDER, FAGS, SPECIALS, CLUBS — See Bucktrout (Part 1)

JACK ROSE LITTLE CIGARS — See American Tobacco Co. (Part 2)
JERSEY LILY CIGARETTES — See Bradford (Part 1)
JUNIOR MEMBER CIGARETTES — See Pattreiouex (Part 1)

KENSITAS CIGARETTES — See J. Wix (Part 1)
KONG BENG — See American Tobacco Co. (Part 2)

LENOX CIGARETTES — See American Tobacco Co. (Part 2)
LE ROY CIGARS — See Miller (Part 2)
LEVANT FAVOURITES — See B. Morris (Part 1)
LIFEBOAT CIGARETTES — See United Tobacco Co. (Part 2)
LIFE RAY CIGARETTES — See Ray (Part 1)
LITTLE RHODY CUT PLUG — See Geo. F. Young (Part 2)
LOTUS CIGARETTES — See United Tobacco Co. (Part 2)
LUCANA CIGARETTES — See Sandorides (Part 1)
LUCKY STRIKE CIGARETTES — See American Tobacco Co. (Part 2)
LUXURY CIGARETTES — See American Tobacco Co. (Part 2)

MAGPIE CIGARETTES — See Schuh (Part 2)
MANIKIN CIGARS — See Freeman (Part 1)
MASCOT CIGARETTES — See B.A.T. (Part 2)
MATTOSSIANS IMPORTED EGYPTIAN CIGARETTES — See Henly & Watkins (Part 1)
MAX CIGARETTES — See A. & M. Wix (Part 1)
MAYBLOSSOM CIGARETTES — See Lambert & Butler (Part 1)
MECCA CIGARETTES — See American Tobacco Co. (Part 2)
MILLBANK CIGARETTES — See Imperial Tobacco Co. (Canada) (Part 2)
MILLS CIGARETTES — See Amalgamated Tobacco Corporation (Part 1)
MILO CIGARETTES — See Sniders & Abrahams (Part 2)
MINERS EXTRA SMOKING TOBACCO — See American Tobacco Co. (Part 2)
MOGUL CIGARETTES — See American Tobacco Co. (Part 2)
MOTOR — See American Tobacco Co. (Part 2)
MURAD CIGARETTES — See American Tobacco Co. (Part 2)

NASSA CIGARETTES — See Policansky Bros. (Part 2)
NEBO CIGARETTES — See American Tobacco Co. (Part 2)

OK CIGARETTES — See Hartleys T.C. (Part 2)
OBAK CIGARETTES — See American Tobacco Co. (Part 2)
OFFICERS MESS CIGARETTES — See African Tobacco Mfrs. (Part 2)
OLD GOLD CIGARETTES — See American Tobacco Co. (Part 2)
OLD JUDGE CIGARETTES — See B.A.T. or Goodwin (Part 2)
ONE OF THE FINEST — See Buchner (Part 2)
ORACLE CIGARETTES — See Tetley (Part 1)
OUR LITTLE BEAUTIES — See Allen & Ginter (Part 2)
OXFORD CIGARETTES — See American Tobacco Co. (Part 2)

PALACE CIGARETTES — See Teofani (Part 1)
PAN HANDLE SCRAP — See American Tobacco Co. (Part 2)
PEDRO — See American Tobacco Co. (Part 2)
PETER PAN CIGARETTES — See Sniders & Abrahams (Part 2)
PHAROAH'S DREAM CIGARETTES — See Teofani (Part 1)
PIBROCH VIRGINIA — See Fryer (Part 1)
PICCADILLY LITTLE CIGARS — See American Tobacco Co. (Part 2)
PICK-ME-UP CIGARETTES — See Drapkin & Millhoff (Part 1)
PIEDMONT CIGARETTES — See American Tobacco Co. (Part 2)
PINHEAD CIGARETTES — See British American Tobacco Co. (Part 2)
PINNACLE — See G. Phillips (Part 1)
PIONEER CIGARETTES — See Richmond Cavendish (Part 1)
PIRATE CIGARETTES — See Wills (Part 1)
POLO MILD CIGARETTES — See Murray (Part 1)

Part 1

BRITISH TOBACCO MANUFACTURERS

(Including Channel Islands, Eire, and Overseas Issues
by British-based firms)

ABDULLA & CO. LTD.

24 Page Reference Book (with Anstie & Adkin) — £3.50

Qty		*Date*	*Odds*	*Sets*
50	Beauties of To-Day	1938	£3.40	£170.00
L1	Bridge Rule Cards (Several Printings)	1936	—	£12.50
25	British Butterflies	1935	£1.20	£30.00
F52	Cinema Stars	1932	£3.75	£195.00
30	Cinema Stars (Brown Back)	1932	£5.00	—
30	Cinema Stars (Black Back)	1933	£3.60	£108.00
32	Cinema Stars (Brown Glossy Front)	1933	£2.50	£80.00
32	Cinema Stars (Hand Coloured)	1934	£2.50	£80.00
30	Cinema Stars (Hand Coloured)	1934	£3.25	—
P2	Commanders of the Allies	1914	£70.00	—
25	Feathered Friends	1935	£1.00	£25.00
50	Film Favourites	1934	£3.60	£180.00
50	Film Stars	1934	£6.25	—
P24	Film Stars (Series of Cards)	1934	£7.00	—
P24	Film Stars (Series of 24 Cards)	1934	*£7.25*	—
P24	Film Stars, 2nd (25-48)	1934	£7.00	—
M3	Great War Gift Packing Cards	1916	£70.00	£210.00
18	Message Cards (Blue Printing)	1936	£11.00	—
18	(Green Printing)	1936	*£12.50*	—
18	(Orange Printing)	1936	*£12.50*	—
K18	Message Cards(Two Wordings)	1936	*£11.50*	—
25	Old Favourites	1936	80p	£20.00
L1	Princess Mary Gift Card	1914	—	£17.50
40	Screen Stars (No "Successors"Clause)	1939	£1.40	£56.00
40	(With Successors Clause)	1939	£2.25	£90.00
50	Stage and Cinema Beauties	1935	£3.25	—
30	Stars of the Stage and Screen (Black and White)	1934	£4.00	—
30	(Hand Coloured)	1934	£4.50	—

GERMAN ISSUES

M150	Autobilder Serie I	1931	£1.40	—
M150	Autobilder Serie II	1932	£1.40	—
M160	Im Auto Mit Abdulla Durch Die Welt	1930	£1.00	£160.00
M110	Landerwappen-Sammlung	1932	90p	—
M110	Landerwappen-Sammlung Serie II	1932	90p	—
M150	Landerwappen-Sammlung Serie III	1932	80p	£120.00
M200	Nationale und Internationale Sport Rekorde	1931	£2.40	—
M50	Soldatenbilder Europaischer Armeen	1928	£2.25	—
X80	Wappenkarten	1928	80p	£64.00

ADCOCK & SON

11/12	Ancient Norwich	1928	£3.25	£36.00

ADKIN & SONS

24 Page Reference Book (with Anstie & Abdulla) — £3.50

25	Actresses-French	1898	*£165.00*	—
12	A Living Picture (Adkin & Sons Back)	1897	£6.50	£78.00
12	(These Cards Back)	1897	£7.00	£84.00
P12	A Living Picture	1897	£90.00	—
12	A Royal Favourite	1900	£11.50	£138.00
15	Beauties "PAC" (7 Brands)	1898	*£240.00*	—
50	Butterflies & Moths	1924	£1.80	£90.00

ADKIN & SONS — cont.

Qty		*Date*	*Odds*	*Sets*
12	Character Sketches (Black Back)	1897	£7.00	£84.00
12	(Green Back)	1897	£7.00	£84.00
P12	Character Sketches	1897	£85.00	—
P4	Games by Tom Browne	1909	*£200.00*	—
25	Notabilities	1915	£4.40	£110.00
12	Pretty Girl Series (Actresses)	1897	£55.00	£660.00
12	Pretty Girl Series (12 Calendar Backs)	1900	£60.00	—
12	(6 Verse Backs)	1900	£35.00	—
12	(32 Other Backs)	1900	£30.00	—
	Soldiers of the Queen			
24	("Series of 50, Issued Exclusively with")	1899	£22.50	—
50	("Series of 50")	1900	£5.00	£300.00
59	("Series of 60")	1900	£4.25	£255.00
31	Soldiers of the Queen & Portraits	1901	£5.50	£165.00
30	Sporting Cups & Trophies	1914	£16.50	£500.00
25	War Trophies	1917	£4.00	£100.00
50	Wild Animals of the World	1923	£1.60	£80.00

AIKMAN'S (Tobacconist)

30	Army Pictures, Cartoons, etc	1916	*£100.00*	—

H. J. AINSWORTH (Tobacconist)

30	Army Pictures, Cartoons, etc	1916	*£100.00*	—

ALBERGE & BROMET

25	Boer War & General Interest			
	(Brown Bridal Bouquet)	1900	*£100.00*	—
	(Green Bridal Bouquet)	1900	*£100.00*	—
	(Green La Optima)	1900	*£100.00*	—
40	Naval & Military Phrases (Bridal Bouquet)	1904	£90.00	—
40	(La Optima)	1904	*£90.00*	—
30	Proverbs	1903	*£95.00*	—

PHILLIP ALLMAN & CO. LTD.

50	Coronation Series	1953	70p	£35.00
12	Pin Up Girls, 1st Series			
	(Numbered)	1953	£4.50	£54.00
	(Unnumbered, "Ask For Allman-Always")	1953	£3.00	£36.00
	(Unnumbered, "For Men Only")	1953	£2.75	£33.00
L12	Pin Up Girls, 1st Series	1953	£3.75	£45.00
12	Pin Up Girls, 2nd Series	1953	£3.50	£42.00
L12	Pin Up Girls, 2nd Series	1953	£3.75	£45.00
24	Pin Up Girls, Combined Series			
	(Numbered "First Series of 24")	1953	*£7.00*	—

AMALGAMATED TOBACCO CORPORATION LTD. (Mills)

Qty		*Date*	*Odds*	*Sets*
25	Aircraft of the World	1958	75p	—
25	A Nature Series	1958	—	£2.50
25	Animals of the Countryside	1958	—	£5.00
25	Aquarium Fish	1961	—	£2.50
25	Army Badges-Past and Present	1961	—	£25.00
25	British Coins and Costumes	1958	—	£7.50
25	British Locomotives	1961	—	£7.50
25	British Uniforms of the 19th Century	1957	80p	£20.00
25	Butterflies and Moths	1957	—	£5.00
25	Cacti	1961	—	£12.50
25	Castles of Britain	1961	—	£25.00
25	Coins of the World	1961	—	£3.50
25	Communications	1961	—	£20.00
25	Dogs	1958	—	£17.50
25	Evolution of the Royal Navy	1957	—	£16.00
M25	Famous British Ships, Series No.1	1952	—	£4.00
M25	Famous British Ships, Series No.2	1952	—	£4.00
25	Football Clubs and Badges	1961	£1.00	£25.00
25	Freshwater Fish	1958	—	£6.00
25	Guerriers a Travers Les Ages (French)	1961	—	£15.00
25	Histoire De L'Aviation, Première Série	1961	—	£3.50
25	Histoire De L'Aviation, Seconde Série	1962	—	£25.00
25	Historical Buildings	1959	—	£17.50
M25/50	History of Aviation	1952	—	£5.00
M50	History of Aviation	1952	—	£45.00
25	Holiday Resorts	1957	—	£2.50
25	Interesting Hobbies	1959	—	£8.00
25	Into Space	1959	—	£7.50
25	Kings of England	1954	£1.40	£35.00
25	Les Autos Modernes (French Text)	1961	—	£9.00
25	Medals of the World	1959	—	£5.00
25	Merchant Ships of the World	1961	—	£12.50
25	Merveilles Modernes (French Text)	1961	—	£7.50
25	Miniature Cars & Scooters	1958	—	£25.00
25	Naval Battles	1959	—	£8.00
25	Ports of the World	1959	—	£2.50
25	Propelled Weapons	1953	—	£4.50
25	Ships of the Royal Navy	1961	—	£10.00
25	Sports and Games	1958	—	£25.00
25	The Wild West	1960	—	£25.00
25	Tropical Birds	1958	—	£25.00
25	Weapons of Defence	1961	—	£25.00
25	Wild Animals	1958	—	£5.00
25	World Locomotives	1959	80p	£20.00

THE ANGLO-AMERICAN CIGARETTE MAKING CO. LTD.

20	Russo-Japanese War Series	1904	*£250.00*	—

ANGLO CIGARETTE MANUFACTURING CO. LTD.

36	Tariff Reform Series	1909	£26.50	—

ANONYMOUS ISSUES — TOBACCO

Qty		*Date*	*Odds*	*Sets*
PRINTED BACKS				
?33	Beauties "KEWA" ("England Expects"Back)	1899	*£100.00*	—
25	Boer War and General Interest (Design Back)	1901	£37.50	—
41	V.C. Heroes	1916	£7.00	£285.00
50	War Portraits	1915	£24.00	—
PLAIN BACKS				
25	Actors & Actresses "FROGA"-C	1900	£10.00	—
?9	Actresses "ANGLO"	1896	*£70.00*	—
?23	Actresses "ANGOOD" (Brown Front)	1898	£30.00	—
?23	(Green Front)	1898	£40.00	—
?26	(Grey Front)	1898	£22.00	—
20	Actresses "BLARM"	1900	£8.50	£170.00
50	Actresses "DAVAN"	1902	*£32.50*	—
26	Actresses "FROGA A" (Brown)	1900	£9.00	£235.00
26	(Coloured)	1900	£10.00	—
25	Actresses "HAGG"	1900	£7.50	—
25	Beauties "BOCCA"	1900	£13.50	—
50	Beauties "CHOAB" (Brown)	1902	£9.00	—
50	(Coloured)	1902	£10.00	—
50	Beauties "FECKSA"	1903	£8.50	—
24	Beauties "FENA"	1899	£45.00	—
25	Beauties "GRACC"	1898	£15.00	£375.00
26	Beauties "HOL"	1900	£9.50	—
?14	Beauties “KEWA”	1898	£30.00	—
20	Beauties "PLUMS"	1898	£40.00	—
25	Boer War & General Interest	1901	£25.00	—
20	Boer War Cartoons	1900	£13.50	—
20	Boer War Generals "CLAM"	1901	£11.50	—
12	Boer War Generals "FLAC"	1901	£12.50	—
25	Boxer Rebellion-Sketches	1904	£9.00	—
M108	British Naval Crests	1916	£3.00	—
16	British Royal Family	1902	£8.50	—
F12	Celebrities of the Great War	1915	£16.00	—
50	Colonial Troops	1902	£7.50	—
M108	Crests & Badges of the British Army	1916	£3.00	—
20	Cricketers Series	1902	*£225.00*	—
50	Dogs (as Taddy)	1900	*£25.00*	—
30	Flags & Flags with Soldiers (Draped)	1902	£7.00	—
15	Flags & Flags with Soldiers (Undraped)	1902	£7.50	—
24	Flags Arms & Types of Nations	1904	£6.00	£144.00
40	Home & Colonial Regiments	1900	£8.00	—
2	King Edward & Queen Alexandra	1902	£17.50	£35.00
1	Lord Kitchener	1915	—	£16.50
40	Naval & Military Phrases	1904	£7.50	—
F30	Photographs (Animal Studies)	1935	£1.65	£50.00
?42	Pretty Girl Series "BAGG"	1898	£15.00	—
12	Pretty Girl Series "RASH"	1899	£13.00	—
30	Proverbs	1901	£10.00	—
19	Russo Japanese Series	1904	£13.50	—
20	Russo Japanese War Series	1904	£17.50	—
25	Star Girls	1900	£8.50	—
20	The European War Series	1915	£6.00	£120.00
25	Types of British & Colonial Troops	1900	£17.00	—
25	Types of British Soldiers	1914	£8.00	£200.00
?22	Views and Yachts	1900	£12.50	—

E. & W. ANSTIE

24 Page Reference Book (with Abdulla & Adkin) — £3.50

Qty		*Date*	*Odds*	*Sets*
25	Aesop's Fables	1934	£2.40	£60.00
16	British Empire Series	1904	£11.50	£180.00
10	Clifton Suspension Bridge (Sect.)	1938	£2.50	£25.00
M36	Flags (Silk)	1915	£1.60	—
X10	Flags (Silk)	1915	£10.00	—
40	Nature Notes	1939	£7.00	—
50	People of Africa	1926	£3.00	£150.00
50	People of Asia	1926	£3.00	£150.00
50	People of Europe	1925	£2.70	£135.00
40	Places of Interest (Matt Front)	1939	£3.00	—
40	(Varnished Front)	1939	£1.00	£40.00
8	Puzzle Series	1900	£140.00	—
25	Racing Series (1-25)	1922	£3.50	£87.50
25	Racing Series (26-50)	1922	£5.50	£137.50
60/85	Regimental Badges (Silk)	1915	£1.75	—
M5	Royal Mail Series	1900	*£225.00*	—
X5	Royal Standard & Portraits (Silk)	1915	£13.50	—
2	Royal Portraits (Silk)	1915	£50.00	—
50	Scout Series	1923	£2.80	£140.00
10	Stonehenge (Sect.)	1936	£2.50	£25.00
10	The Victory (Sect.)	1936	£2.75	£27.50
50	The World's Wonders	1924	£1.30	£65.00
20	Wells Cathedral (Sect.)	1935	£1.90	£38.00
40	Wessex	1938	£1.40	£56.00
20	Wiltshire Downs (Sect.)	1935	£2.00	£40.00
10	Windsor Castle (Sect.)	1937	£2.75	£27.50

HENRY ARCHER & CO.

51	Actresses "FROGA" (Vari-Backed)	1900	*£65.00*	—
50	Beauties "CHOAB" (Brown)	1900	£27.00	£1350.00
25	Beauties "CHOAB" (Vari-Backed)	1900	*£70.00*	—
20	Prince of Wales Series	1912	£26.50	—

ARDATH TOBACCO CO. LTD.

28 Page Reference Book — £3.50

50	Animals at the Zoo (Descriptive Back)	1924	£2.00	£100.00
50	(Double Ace Back)	1924	£12.50	—
F54	Beautiful English Women	1930	£3.25	—
25	Big Game Hunting (Descriptive Back)	1930	£4.00	—
25	(Double Ace Back)	1930	*£12.50*	—
L30	Boucher Series	1915	£3.00	£90.00
50	Britain's Defenders	1936	70p	£35.00
50	British Born Film Stars	1934	£1.50	£75.00
M50	British Born Film Stars	1934	£2.60	£130.00
X1	Calendar 1942	1941	—	£2.50
X1	Calendar 1942-3	1942	—	£3.50
X1	Calendar 1943	1942	—	*£10.00*
X1	Calendar 1943-4	1943	—	£2.00
X1	Calendar 1944	1943	—	£2.00
P2	Calendars (Silk)	1937	*£65.00*	—
MF36	Camera Studies	1939	£1.25	£45.00
LF45	Camera Studies	1939	£1.00	£45.00

ARDATH TOBACCO CO. LTD. — cont.

Qty		*Date*	*Odds*	*Sets*
L8	Christmas Greeting Cards (Folders)	1943	£2.25	£18.00
X25	Champion Dogs	1934	£1.80	£45.00
X?97	Contract Bridge Contest Hands	1930	*£20.00*	—
50	Cricket, Tennis & Golf Celebrities (Brown, N.Z. Issue)	1935	£2.20	£110.00
50	(Grey, G.B. Issue)	1935	£1.40	£70.00
X25	Dog Studies (State Express etc.)	1938	£5.00	£125.00
X25	(Firm's Name Only, N.Z.)	1938	*£11.50*	—
25	Eastern Proverbs	1932	£1.60	£40.00
48	Empire Flying-Boat (Sect.)	1938	£1.50	£72.00
50	Empire Personalities	1937	65p	£32.50
50	Famous Film Stars	1934	90p	£45.00
50	Famous Footballers	1934	£1.50	£75.00
25	Famous Scots	1935	£1.30	£32.50
X25	Fighting & Civil Aircraft	1936	£2.20	£55.00
50	Figures of Speech	1936	80p	£40.00
50	Film, Stage and Radio Stars	1935	£1.00	£50.00
X25	Film, Stage & Radio Stars (Different)	1935	£1.40	£35.00
PF?7	Film Stars (State Express)	1938	*£25.00*	—
PF?10	Film Stars (Straight Cut)	1938	*£25.00*	—
M50	Flags 4th Series (Silk)	1914	*£40.00*	—
M50	Flags 5th Series (Silk)	1914	*£40.00*	—
M25	Flags 6th Series (Silk)	1914	*£45.00*	—
L40	Franz Hals Series (No Overprint)	1916	£12.50	£500.00
L40	(2.5 Cents Overprint)	1916	*£15.00*	—
X50	From Screen and Stage	1936	£1.00	£50.00
L30	Gainsborough Series (Multi-Backed)	1915	£2.50	£75.00
L30	Girls of All Nations	1916	£16.50	—
50	Great War Series	1916	£4.50	—
50	Great War Series "B"	1916	£5.00	—
50	Great War Series "C"	1916	£5.50	—
35	Hand Shadows	1930	*£22.50*	—
X25	Historic Grand Slams	1936	*£25.00*	—
L25	Hollandsche Oude Meesters (4 Backs)	1916	£13.50	—
L25	Hollandsche Oude Meesters (26-50)	1916	£14.00	—
X48	How to Recognise the Service Ranks	1940	£5.00	—
X2	Industrial Propaganda Cards (Black)	1943	£6.00	—
X4	Industrial Propaganda Cards (Coloured)	1943	£6.00	—
X11	Industrial Propaganda Cards (White)	1943	£4.50	—
X?171	Information Slips	1940	£3.00	—
L24/25	It all depends on ME	1940	£1.25	£30.00
50	Life in the Services (Adhesive)	1938	80p	£40.00
50	(Non-adhesive N.Z.)	1938	£1.20	£60.00
96	Modern School Atlas	1936	£1.50	£144.00
50	National Fitness (Adhesive)	1938	50p	£25.00
50	(Non-adhesive N.Z.)	1938	90p	£45.00
50	New Zealand Views	1928	£2.20	£110.00
L1	On the Kitchen Front	1942	—	£2.50
50	Our Empire	1937	£1.25	£62.50
LF110	Photocards "A" (Lancs. Football Teams)	1936	£1.50	£165.00
LF110	Photocards "B" (N.E. Football Teams)	1936	£1.70	—
LF110	Photocards "C" (Yorks. Football Teams)	1936	£1.40	£154.00
LF165	Photocards "D" (Scots. Football Teams)	1936	£1.10	£180.00
LF110	Photocards "E" (Midland Football Teams)	1936	£1.50	£165.00
LF110	Photocards "F" (Southern Football Teams)	1936	£1.30	£143.00
LF99	Photocards "Z" (Sport & General Interest)	1936	70p	£70.00
LF11	Photocards "Supplementary"	1936	£3.60	£40.00

Qty		*Date*	*Odds*	*Sets*
LF22	Photocards Group "A" (Sports)	1937	£1.00	£22.00
LF21/22	Photocards Group "B" (Coronation, Sports)	1937	65p	£13.50
L22	Complete Set	1937	—	£34.00
LF21/22	Photocards Group "C" (Lancs. Celebrities)	1937	£1.00	£21.00
L22	Complete Set	1937	—	£41.00
LF22	Photocards Group "D" (Irish Celebrities)	1937	£1.30	£28.50
LF22	Photocards Group "E" (Films, Sports)	1938	85p	£18.50
LF22	Photocards Group "F" (Films, Sports)	1938	£1.25	£27.50
LF11	Photocards Group "G" (Cricketers)	1938	£17.50	—
LF66	Photocards Group "GS" (Various)	1938	£2.40	—
LF22	Photocards Group "H" (Films, Sports)	1938	85p	£18.50
LF22	Photocards Group "I" (Films, Various)	1938	£1.00	£22.00
LF22	Photocards Group "J" (Films, Various)	1939	£1.10	£24.00
LF22	Photocards Group "K" ("KINGS" Clause)	1939	80p	£18.00
LF22	(No Clause)	1939	£1.60	—
LF44	Photocards Group "L" (Various)	1939	60p	£26.00
F45	Photocards Group "M" (Films, Various)	1939	80p	£36.00
LF45	Photocards Group "M" ("KINGS" Clause)	1939	85p	£38.00
LF45	(No Clause)	1939	80p	£36.00
F45	Photocards Group "N" (Films)	1939	85p	£38.50
LF45	Photocards Group "N" (Films)	1939	60p	£27.00
LF66	Photocards Views of the World	1938	85p	£56.50
25	Proverbs (1-25)	1936	£1.40	£35.00
25	Proverbs (26-50)	1936	£2.60	£65.00
L30	Raphael Series	1916	£2.80	£84.00
LF45	Real Photographs Group "O" (Films)	1939	50p	£22.50
F45	Real Photographs 1st Series	1939	90p	£40.00
XF18	Real Photographs 1st Series (Views)	1937	£2.25	£40.50
F54	Real Photographs 2nd Series	1939	90p	£48.00
XF18	Real Photographs 2nd Series	1937	£2.25	£40.50
XF18	Real Photographs 3rd Series (Views)	1937	£2.25	£40.50
XF18	Real Photographs 4th Series	1938	£2.25	£40.50
XF18	Real Photographs 5th Series (Views)	1938	£2.25	£40.50
XF18	Real Photographs 6th Series	1938	£2.25	£40.50
LF44	Real Photographs Series 1-GP1	1939	85p	£37.50
LF44	Real Photographs Series 2-GP2	1939	50p	£22.00
LF44	Real Photographs Series 3-GP3	1939	£3.00	—
LF44	Real Photographs Series 3-CV3 (Views)	1939	75p	£33.00
LF44	Real Photographs Series 4-CV4 (Views)	1939	35p	£15.00
XF36	Real Photographs Series 7	1938	65p	£22.50
XF54	Real Photographs Series 8	1938	50p	£27.00
LF54	Real Photographs Series 9	1938	75p	£41.00
XF54	Real Photographs Series 9	1938	55p	£30.00
LF54	Real Photographs Series 10	1939	60p	£32.50
XF54	Real Photographs Series 10	1939	80p	£42.50
LF54	Real Photographs Series 11	1939	50p	£27.00
XF54	Real Photographs Series 11	1939	£1.00	£54.00
LF54	Real Photographs Series 12	1939	55p	£30.00
LF54	Real Photographs Series 13	1939	50p	£27.00
LF36	Real Photographs of Famous Landmarks	1939	£3.00	—
XF36	Real Photographs of Famous Landmarks	1939	£1.50	£54.00
LF36	Real Photographs of Modern Aircraft	1939	£4.00	—
XF36	Real Photographs of Modern Aircraft	1939	£3.00	£108.00
L30	Rembrandt Series	1914	£3.50	—
L40	Ditto (Splendo Cigarettes)	1914	£15.00	£600.00
X30	Rembrandt Series	1914	£5.00	£150.00

ARDATH TOBACCO CO. LTD. — cont.

Qty		Date	Odds	Sets
L30	Rubens Series	1916	£2.75	£82.50
L30	Ditto ("N.Z." at Base)	1916	*£15.00*	—
L30	(Splendo Cigarettes)	1916	*£15.00*	—
L30	(Winfred Cigarettes)	1916	*£15.00*	—
100	Scenes from Big Films	1935	£1.75	£175.00
M100	Scenes from Big Films	1935	£4.00	—
X20	Ships of the Royal Navy (Package)	1953	*£10.00*	—
50	Silver Jubilee	1935	65p	£32.50
50	Speed Land Sea & Air (State Express)	1935	£1.30	£65.00
50	("Ardath"-N.Z.)	1935	£1.90	£95.00
X25	Speed Land Sea & Air (Different)	1938	£1.40	£35.00
50	Sports Champions (Title In 1 Line)	1935	£1.10	£55.00
50	(Title In 2 Lines-N.Z.)	1935	£1.80	£90.00
6	Sportsmen (Double Ace)	1953	*£4.00*	—
50	Stamps Rare & Interesting	1939	£1.25	£62.50
50	Swimming Diving and Life-Saving	1937	£1.70	£85.00
50	Tennis	1938	£2.00	£100.00
X?3	Theatre Actresses Smoking (2 Sizes)	1915	*£25.00*	—
L?	The Beauty of State Express (Circular)	1928	*£70.00*	—
9	The Office of Chief Whip	1955	£3.00	—
48	Trooping the Colour (Sect.)	1939	£1.75	£84.00
L?12	Types of English Manhood (Circular)	1935	*£40.00*	—
X12	Types of Smokers	1914	*£40.00*	—
M1	Union Jack Folder	1943	—	£7.50
L30	Velasquez Series	1916	£3.50	£105.00
X30	Velasquez Series	1916	£5.00	—
50	Who is this? (Film Stars)	1936	£2.00	£100.00
X?25	Wonderful Handcraft	1935	*£30.00*	—
X24/25	World Views (2 Printings)	1937	35p	£8.50
50	Your Birthday Tells Your Fortune	1937	65p	£32.50

ASSOCIATED TOBACCO MANUFACTURERS

25	Cinema Stars (5 Backs)	1926	*£25.00*	—

ATKINSON (Tobacconist)

30	Army Pictures, Cartoons, etc	1916	*£100.00*	—

AVISS BROS. LTD.

40	Naval & Military Phrases	1904	*£110.00*	—

J. A. BAILEY

40	Naval & Military Phrases	1904	*£150.00*	—

A. BAKER & CO. LTD.

25	Actresses, 3 Sizes	1901	£26.00	£650.00
L25	Actresses, 3 Sizes (Different)	1901	£45.00	—
P25	Actresses, 3 Sizes (As Small)	1901	*£225.00*	—

A. BAKER & CO. LTD. — cont.

Qty		Date	Odds	Sets
20	Actresses "BLARM" (Back Design 58mm Long)	1900	£27.50	—
20	(Back Design 64mm Long)	1900	£27.50	—
10	Actresses "HAGG"	1900	£27.50	£275.00
41	Baker's Tobacconists Shops			
	(Cigar etc. Manufacturers)	1901	£115.00	—
	(Try Our 3½d Tobaccos)	1901	*£175.00*	—
25	Beauties of All Nations (Albert Baker)	1898	£17.00	£425.00
25	(A. Baker)	1899	£12.00	£300.00
16	British Royal Family	1902	£45.00	—
20	Cricketers Series	1902	*£250.00*	—
25	Star Girls	1898	*£150.00*	—

BAYLEY AND HOLDSWORTH

26	Flag Signalling Code Series	1912	£160.00	—

THOMAS BEAR & SONS LTD.

50	Aeroplanes	1926	£4.00	—
50	Cinema Artistes, Set 2	1936	£3.00	—
50	Cinema Artistes, Set 4	1937	£3.50	—
50	Cinema Stars "BAMT" (2 printings)	1928	£2.50	—
50	Do You Know?	1923	£1.60	£80.00
270	Javanese Series (Blue)	1925	£1.35	—
100	Javanese Series (Yellow)	1925	*£6.50*	—
50	Stage and Film Stars	1926	*£3.50*	—

E.C. BEESTON

30	Army Pictures, Cartoons, etc	1916	*£100.00*	—

BELFAST SHIP STORES CO. LTD.

?10	Dickens Characters Burlesqued	1893	*£300.00*	—

J. & F. BELL LTD

10	Actresses "HAGG"	1900	£70.00	—
25	Beauties (Scotia Back)	1897	£100.00	—
25	(Three Bells Back)	1897	£100.00	—
25	Colonial Series	1901	£35.00	—
30	Footballers	1902	£55.00	—
60	Rigsvaabner	1925	£25.00	—
25	Scottish Clan Series	1903	£12.50	£365.00
60	Women of All Nations (Printed Back)	1925	£25.00	£1500.00
60	(Plain Back)	1925	£15.00	—

R. BELLWOOD

18	Motor Cycle Series	1913	*£90.00*	—

RICHARD BENSON LTD.

L23/24	Old Bristol Series	1925	£3.00	£69.00
X24	Old Bristol Series (Re-Issue)	1946	£2.00	£48.00

BENSON & HEDGES LTD.

Qty		Date	Odds	Sets
1	Advertisement Card, Original Shop	1973	—	£2.00
48	Ancient & Modern Fire Fighting Equipment	1947	£5.50	£265.00
L10	B.E.A. Aircraft	1958	£8.50	—
50	Friendly Games	1970	*£1.20*	—
X?12	"Oxford" University Series	1912	*£25.00*	—

FELIX S. BERLYN

25	Burline Mixture (Golfers Blend) Series	1910	*£350.00*	—
P25	Burline Mixture (Golfers Blend) Series	1910	*£500.00*	—

BERRY'S

20	London Views	1904	*£175.00*	—

BEWLAY & CO.

6	Comic Advertisement Cards (7 Backs)	1909	£150.00	—
P6	Comic Advertisement Cards	1909	£85.00	£500.00
12	War Series (Portraits, Multi-Backed)	1915	£11.50	£138.00
12	(Portraits, Plain Backed)	1915	£10.00	—
25	War Series (Scenes, Modern Man Cigarettes)	1915	£12.00	£300.00
25	(Scenes, Modern Man Mixture)	1915	£12.00	£300.00
25	(Scenes, Two Great Favourites)	1915	£12.00	£300.00

W. O. BIGG & CO.

37	Flags of All Nations (Horizontal Back)	1904	£7.50	—
37	(Vertical Back)	1904	£7.50	—
50	Life on Board a Man of War	1905	£10.00	£500.00

JAS BIGGS & SON

26	Actresses "FROGA A" (Brand In Black)	1900	*£50.00*	—
26	(Brand In White)	1900	£35.00	—
26	Actresses "FROGA B"	1900	£50.00	—
25	Beauties "BOCCA" (Black Back)	1900	£65.00	—
25	(Blue Back)	1900	*£65.00*	—
25	Beauties "CHOAB" (Blue Back)	1902	*£70.00*	—
50	(Black Overprint)	1902	*£62.50*	—
30	Colonial Troops	1901	£30.00	—
30	Flags & Flags with Soldiers	1903	£27.50	—
25	Star Girls	1900	*£175.00*	—

J. S. BILLINGHAM

30	Army Pictures, Cartoons, etc	1916	*£100.00*	—

R. BINNS

?15	Halifax Town Footballers	1924	£125.00	—

BLANKS CIGARETTES

Qty		*Date*	*Odds*	*Sets*
50	Keystrokes in Break-building	1910	*£250.00*	—

BOCNAL TOBACCO CO.

25	Luminous Silhouettes of Beauty & Charm	1938	£2.50	£62.50
25	Proverbs Up-to-Date	1938	£2.00	£50.00

ALEXANDER BOGUSLAVSKY LTD.

P12	Big Events on the Turf	1924	£42.50	—
25	Conan Doyle Characters (Black Back)	1923	£6.80	£170.00
25	(Green Back)	1923	£6.50	£162.50
25	Mythological Gods and Goddesses	1924	£2.40	£60.00
25	Sports Records (1-25)	1925	£1.60	£40.00
25	Sports Records, 2nd Series (26-50)	1925	£1.80	£45.00
25	Winners on the Turf (Name no Serifs)	1925	£3.20	£80.00
25	(Name with Serifs)	1925	£5.00	—
L25	Winners on the Turf	1925	£5.20	£130.00

R. & E. BOYD LTD.

25	Places of Interest	1938	*£50.00*	—
M25	Places of Interest	1938	*£50.00*	—
L25	Wild Birds at Home	1938	*£50.00*	—

WM. BRADFORD

50	Beauties "CHOAB"	1902	£30.00	—
?7	Beauties, Jersey Lily	1900	*£250.00*	—
20	Boer War Cartoons	1901	*£95.00*	—

THOS. BRANKSTON & CO. LTD.

30	Colonial Troops (Golf Club Mixture)	1901	£30.00	—
30	(Red Virginia)	1901	£27.50	—
30	(Sweet as the Rose)	1901	£27.50	—
12	Pretty Girl Series "RASH"	1900	*£200.00*	—

BRIGHAM & CO.

L16	Down the Thames from Henley to Windsor	1912	£120.00	—
16	Reading Football Players	1912	*£200.00*	—
X3	Tobacco Growing in Hampshire, England	1928	£15.00	£45.00

BRITANNIA ANONYMOUS SOCIETY

?29	Beauties & Couples	1914	*£75.00*	—

BRITISH & COLONIAL TOBACCO CO.

25	Armies of the World	1900	*£125.00*	—

Old Naval Prints
Player. Also reprint

National Motor Museum
Quaker Oats

Cunard in the 1950's
Rockwell

British Aircraft
Carreras – Turf Slides

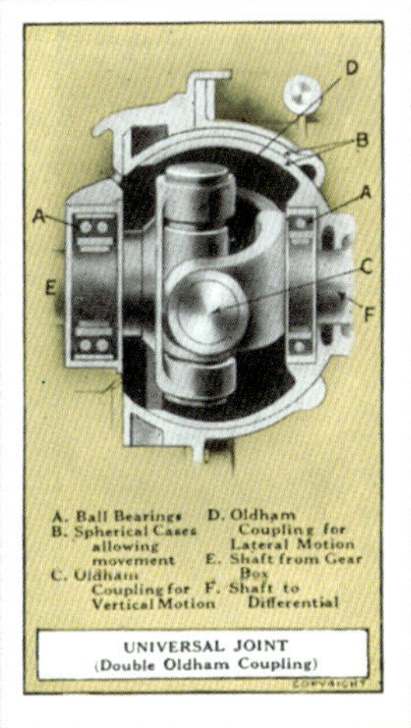

Motor Series
Morris

Vintage Tractors – Wilson

British Warships
Stephen Mitchell

Aeroplanes (Plain Back)
Amalgamated Press

The Story of the Locomotive
Kellogg

Modern Motor Cars of the World
Gaycon, Kane

Conquest of Space
Weetabix

Famous Ships
Thomson

J. M. BROWN

Qty		Date	Odds	Sets
30	Army Pictures, Cartoons, etc.	1916	£90.00	—

JOHN BRUMFIT

50	The Public Schools Ties Series (Old Boys)	1925	£3.50	£175.00

BUCKTROUT & CO. LTD. (Channel Isles)

M416	Around The World/Places of Interest	1924	50p	£210.00
24	Birds of England	1924	£3.00	£72.00
50	Cinema Stars, 1st	1926	£1.80	£90.00
50	Cinema Stars, Second Series	1927	£2.00	£100.00
M50	Football Teams	1928	£2.80	£140.00
L22	Football Teams of the Bailiwick	1927	90p	£20.00
123	Guernsey Footballers (Multi-Backed)	1923	£2.40	—
20	Inventors Series	1924	£1.00	£20.00
25	Marvels of the Universe Series	1919	£2.50	£62.50
M54	Playing Cards	1930	75p	£40.00
25	Sports & Pastimes	1926	£4.00	£120.00

G. A. BULLOGH (Tobacconist)

30	Army Pictures, Cartoons, etc.	1916	*£95.00*	—

BURSTEIN ISAACS & CO. LTD.

50	Famous Prize Fighters (Names in Capitals)	1923	£6.50	—
50	(Mixed Lettering)	1923	£5.75	£287.50
F27/28	London View Series	1922	£3.50	£100.00

BYRT WOOD & CO.

?30	Pretty Girl Series "BAGG"	1900	£115.00	—

CABANA CIGAR CO.

40	Home & Colonial Regiments (C.C.C.)	1901	*£225.00*	—
M1	Little Manturios Advertisement Card (4 Types)	1904	—	*£200.00*

PERCY E. CADLE & CO.

20	Actresses "BLARM"	1900	£32.50	—
26	Actresses "FROGA" (Brown, Printed Back)	1900	£35.00	—
26	(Brown, Stamped Back)	1900	*£125.00*	—
26	Actresses "FROGA" (Coloured)	1900	*£45.00*	—
?12	Boer War & Boxer Rebellion Sketches	1901	£45.00	—
10	Boer War Generals	1901	£65.00	—
20	Footballers	1904	£55.00	£1100.00

CARRERAS LTD.

F24	Actresses and their Pets (2 Printings)	1926	£4.25	£102.00
50	A Kodak at the Zoo, A Series	1924	60p	£30.00

Qty		Date	Odds	Sets
50	A Kodak at the Zoo, 2nd Series	1925	60p	£30.00
48	Alice in Wonderland (Round Corners)	1930	£1.50	£72.00
48	(Square Corners)	1930	£3.00	£144.00
L48	Alice in Wonderland	1930	£1.80	£90.00
X1	Alice in Wonderland (Instructions)	1930	—	*£13.00*
50	Amusing Tricks & How To Do Them	1937	£1.00	£50.00
22	Battle of Waterloo	1934	£1.40	—
L15	Battle of Waterloo	1934	£2.50	—
M1	Battle of Waterloo (Instructions)	1934	—	*£11.00*
M50	Believe It Or Not	1934	60p	£30.00
50	Birds of the Countryside	1939	90p	£45.00
200	Black Cat Library	1913	£11.50	—
50	Britain's Defences	1938	65p	£32.50
25	British Costumes	1927	£1.10	£27.50
L25	British Costumes	1927	£1.20	£30.00
F27	British Prime Ministers	1928	£1.50	£40.00
1	Calendar	1934	—	£22.50
50	Celebrities of British History	1935	£1.00	£50.00
25	Christie Comedy Girls	1928	£1.80	£45.00
30	Cricketers	1934	£3.30	£100.00
50	Cricketers (A Series of 50, Brown)	1934	£3.20	£160.00
50	(A Series of 50, Black)	1934	*£35.00*	—
F50	Dogs & Friend	1936	40p	£20.00
50	Do You Know?	1939	30p	£15.00
50	Famous Airmen & Airwomen	1936	£1.60	£80.00
25	Famous Escapes	1926	£1.30	£32.50
L25	Famous Escapes	1926	£1.40	£35.00
P10	Famous Escapes	1926	£2.75	£27.50
96	Famous Film Stars	1935	£1.20	£116.00
48	Famous Footballers	1935	£1.40	£70.00
24	Ditto (25-48 Redrawn)	1935	£1.75	£42.00
25	Famous Men	1927	£1.30	£32.50
LF24	Famous Naval Men	1929	£1.75	£42.00
X6	Famous Posters (St. Dunstans)	1923	£24.00	—
LF12	Famous Soldiers	1928	£5.25	£63.00
F27	Famous Women	1929	£1.00	£27.00
25	Figures Of Fiction	1924	£1.80	£45.00
F54	Film & Stage Beauties	1939	50p	£27.00
LF54	Film and Stage Beauties (2 Printings)	1939	60p	£32.50
LF36	Film and Stage Beauties (2 Printings)	1939	90p	£32.50
XF36	Film and Stage Beauties	1939	£1.50	£54.00
50	Film Favourites	1938	£1.30	£65.00
F54	Film Stars, A Series	1937	80p	£43.00
F54	Film Stars, 2nd Series (3 Printings)	1938	50p	£27.00
LF54	Film Stars (as 2nd Series)	1938	£1.00	£54.00
XF36	Film Stars (Different)	1936	£2.75	£100.00
XF36	Film Stars, Second Series (Different)	1936	£2.50	£90.00
XF36	Film Stars, Third Series	1937	£2.50	£90.00
XF36	Film Stars, Fourth Series	1938	£2.50	£90.00
50	Film Stars (by Desmond)	1936	90p	£45.00
72	Film Stars (Oval, Half-Tone)	1934	£1.40	£100.00
F72	(Oval, "Real Photos")	1934	£2.40	—
60	Flags of all Nations	Unissued	—	£32.50
28	Flag Dominoes (Unissued)	1926	£11.00	£308.00
K6	Flags & Arms (Circular)	1915	£50.00	—

Qty		Date	Odds	Sets
K7	Flags of the Allies (Shaped)	1915	£45.00	—
K?6	Flags of the Allies (Pin as Mast)	1915	£95.00	—
50	Flowers	1936	50p	£25.00
75	Footballers (Large Titles)	1934	£2.00	£150.00
75	(Small Titles)	1934	£1.75	£132.00
36	Fortune Telling (Card Inset)	1926	30p	£10.50
36	(Head Inset, Black No.)	1926	25p	£9.00
36	(Head Inset, Brown No.)	1926	75p	—
L36	Fortune Telling (Card Inset)	1926	30p	£10.50
L36	(Head Inset)	1926	35p	£12.00
X1	Fortune Telling (Instructions)	1926	—	£11.00
F54	Glamour Girls of Stage and Films	1939	60p	£32.50
LF54	Glamour Girls of Stage and Films	1939	70p	£38.00
LF36	Glamour Girls of Stage and Films	1939	£1.20	£43.00
XF36	Glamour Girls of Stage and Films	1939	£1.50	£54.00
M50	Gran-Pop	1934	60p	£30.00
L50	Gran-Pop	1934	50p	£25.00
M16	Guards Series (Sectional)	1970	50p	£8.00
M8	Guards Series (Full Length)	1970	65p	£5.00
M4	Guards Series (Mugs)	1971	75p	£3.00
48	Happy Family	1925	25p	£12.00
L48	Happy Family	1925	25p	£12.00
25	Highwaymen	1924	£2.20	£55.00
50	History of Army Uniforms	1937	£1.25	£62.50
50	History of Guards Uniforms	Unissued	*£5.00*	—
50	History of Naval Uniforms	1937	90p	£45.00
25	Horses and Hounds	1926	£1.80	£45.00
L20	Horses and Hounds	1926	£1.80	£36.00
P10	Horses and Hounds	1926	£3.75	£37.50
50	Kings & Queens of England	1935	£1.50	£75.00
L50	Kings & Queens of England	1935	£2.30	£115.00
L?79	Lace Motifs	1915	£6.50	—
P?15	Lace Motifs (Double Size)	1915	£35.00	—
G?7	Lace Motifs (Quadruple Size)	1915	*£65.00*	—
F27	Malayan Industries	1929	80p	£21.50
F24	Malayan Scenes	1928	£2.75	—
LF24	Malayan Scenes	1928	75p	£18.00
7	Millionaire Competition	1971	£1.75	—
K53	Miniature Playing Cards	1934	20p	£8.50
50	Notable M.P.s	1929	£1.20	£60.00
L50	Notable M.P.s	1929	60p	£30.00
F25	Notable Ships Past & Present	1929	£1.20	£30.00
24	Old Staffordshire Figures	1926	£1.00	£24.00
P12	Old Staffordshire Figures	1926	£2.75	£33.00
L24	Old Staffordshire Figures (Different)	1926	£1.35	£32.50
24	Orchids	1925	£1.25	£30.00
L24	Orchids	1925	£1.10	£26.50
P24	Orchids	1925	£3.25	£78.00
50	Our Navy	1937	£1.20	£50.00
50	Palmistry	1933	50p	£25.00
F27	Paramount Stars	1929	£1.75	£46.00
25	Picture Puzzle Series	1923	£1.30	£32.50
52	Playing Cards	1926	£1.10	—
52	Playing Cards & Dominoes (Numbered)	1929	20p	£8.00
52	(Unnumbered)	1929	20p	£10.00

Qty		Date	Odds	Sets
L26	Playing Cards & Dominoes (Numbered)	1929	50p	£13.00
L26	(Unnumbered)	1929	70p	£18.00
48	Popular Footballers	1936	£1.25	£60.00
72	Popular Personalities (Oval)	1935	90p	£65.00
10	Irish Subjects (1-10)	1935	£16.00	—
E12	Premium Silks (Assorted Subjects)	1914	£160.00	—
25	Races-Historic & Modern	1927	£2.20	£55.00
L25	Races-Historic & Modern	1927	£2.40	£60.00
P12	Races-Historic & Modern	1927	£5.00	£60.00
50	Radio & Television Favourites	Unissued	£8.00	—
140	Raemaekers War Cartoons (Black Cat)	1916	85p	£120.00
140	(Carreras)	1916	£3.50	—
25	Regalia Series	1925	40p	£10.00
L20	Regalia Series	1925	50p	£10.00
P10	Regalia Series	1925	£2.00	£20.00
L50	Round the World Scenic Models	1925	75p	£37.50
50	School Emblems	1929	80p	£40.00
L40	School Emblems	1929	75p	£30.00
P20	School Emblems	1929	£2.25	£45.00
M20	Sport Fish (Canada)	1986	*£3.20*	—
L216	Sportsman's Guide-Fly Fishing (Canada)	1950	£1.25	—
48	Tapestry Reproductions of Paintings (Sect.)	1938	50p	£24.00
52	The Greyhound Racing Game	1926	20p	£10.00
L52	The Greyhound Racing Game	1926	20p	£10.00
X1	The Greyhound Racing Game (Instructions)	1926	—	£11.50
M5	The Handy English-French Dictionary	1915	£20.00	—
50	The Nose Game	1927	40p	£20.00
L50	The Nose Game	1927	40p	£20.00
X1	The Nose Game (Instructions)	1927	—	£12.50
50	The Science of Boxing (Black Cat)	1914	£2.40	£120.00
50	(Carreras)	1914	£4.00	—
50	Tools and How to use Them	1935	£1.50	£75.00
80	Types of London	1919	£1.25	£100.00
F27	Views of London	1929	50p	£13.50
F27	Views of the World	1927	70p	£19.00
M15/20	Wild Animals (Canada)	1985	35p	£5.25
25	Wild Flower Art Series	1923	£1.20	£30.00
50	Women on War Work	1916	£6.00	£300.00

TURF SLIDES (Cut to Size)

50	British Aircraft	1953	60p	£30.00
50	British Fish	1954	30p	£15.00
50	British Railway Locomotives	1952	70p	£35.00
50	Celebrities of British History	1951	60p	£30.00
50	Famous British Fliers	1956	£2.00	£100.00
50	Famous Cricketers	1950	£2.50	£125.00
50	Famous Dog Breeds	1952	80p	£40.00
50	Famous Film Stars	1949	£1.30	£65.00
50	Famous Footballers	1951	£2.00	£100.00
50	Film Favourites	1948	£2.00	£100.00
50	Film Stars	1947	£1.40	£70.00
50	Footballers	1948	£2.00	£100.00
50	Olympics 1948	1948	£2.20	£110.00
50	Radio Celebrities	1950	55p	£27.50
50	Sports	1949	£1.50	£75.00
50	Zoo Animals	1954	20p	£10.00

CARRERAS LTD. — cont.

Qty		*Date*	*Odds*	*Sets*
"BLACK CAT" MODERN ISSUES				
50	British Birds	1976	15p	£4.00
50	Flowers all the Year Round	1977	20p	£10.00
50	Kings & Queens of England	1977	20p	£10.00
50	Military Uniforms	1976	15p	£4.50
50	Palmistry	1979	£1.00	£50.00
50	Sport Fish	1978	15p	£4.00
50	Vintage Cars (With "Filter")	1976	15p	£6.00
50	(Without "Filter")	1976	15p	£6.00
AUSTRALIAN ISSUES				
72	Film Stars Series (Smile Away)	1933	£2.40	—
72	(Standard)	1933	£1.25	£90.00
72	Football Series	1933	£1.50	£108.00
24	Personality Series	1933	£1.75	£42.00
72	Personality Series, Film Stars	1933	£1.20	£85.00
72	Personality Series, Footballers	1933	£1.50	£108.00

CARRERAS & MARCIANUS

1	Photo Miniatures Folder (3 Printings)	1909	—	*£100.00*
100	War Series	1915	£65.00	—

CARRICK

12	Military Terms	1900	£65.00	—

P. J. CARROLL & CO.

25	Birds	1939	80p	£20.00
25	British Naval Series	1915	£40.00	—
25	Derby Winners (Black Back)	1914	*£90.00*	—
25	(Green Back)	1914	*£100.00*	—
K26	Grand Slam Spelling Bee Cards	1936	*£12.50*	—
24	Jig-Saw Puzzles	1935	£17.50	—
20	Louth All-Ireland Champions	1912	£27.50	—
25	Ship Series	1934	£7.00	£175.00
M24	The Irish Open Golf Championship	Unissued	*£10.00*	—

THE CASKET TOBACCO & CIGARETTE CO. LTD.

?1	Bowling Fixture Cards	1909	*£250.00*	—
?4	Cricket Fixture Cards	1905	*£300.00*	—
?2	Cyclists Lighting Up Table	1909	*£250.00*	—
?17	Football Fixture Cards	1909	*£350.00*	—
?49	Road Maps	1909	*£250.00*	—

S. CAVANDER & CO.

?50	Beauties "PLUMS"	1898	*£225.00*	—

CAVANDERS LTD.

25	Ancient Chinese	1926	£1.40	£35.00
25	Ancient Egypt	1928	£1.30	£32.50

CAVANDERS LTD. — cont.

Qty		Date	Odds	Sets
L25	Ancient Egypt (Different)	1928	£1.40	£35.00
F36	Animal Studies	1936	30p	£11.00
F50	Beauty Spots of Great Britain	1927	30p	£15.00
MF50	Beauty Spots of Great Britain	1927	30p	£15.00
F54	Camera Studies	1926	20p	£8.50
MF56	Camera Studies	1926	20p	£11.00
30	Cinema Stars	1934	£1.25	£37.50
MS50	Coloured Stereoscopic	1931	55p	£27.50
25	Feathered Friends	1926	£2.40	£60.00
25	Foreign Birds (Same Subjects As Above)	1926	£1.30	£32.50
MS50	Glorious Britain	1930	50p	£25.00
25	Little Friends	1924	90p	£22.50
FS72	Peeps into Many Lands, A Series	1927	40p	£30.00
MFS72	Peeps into Many Lands, A Series	1927	80p	£57.50
XFS36	Peeps into Many Lands, A Series	1927	£1.80	£65.00
FS72	Peeps into Many Lands, 2nd Series	1928	75p	£54.00
MFS72	Peeps into Many Lands, 2nd Series	1928	75p	£54.00
FS48	Peeps into Many Lands, 3rd Series	1929	30p	£14.50
MFS48	Peeps into Many Lands, 3rd Series	1929	90p	£45.00
MFS48	Ditto (Reprinted)	1929	£1.50	£72.00
FS48	Peeps into Prehistoric Times, 4th Series	1930	70p	£35.00
MFS48	Peeps into Prehistoric Times, 4th Series	1930	£1.20	£60.00
F33	Photographs	1935	£1.40	£46.50
L48	Regimental Standards	1923	£11.00	—
25	Reproductions of Celebrated Oil Paintings	1925	90p	£22.50
F108	River Valleys	1926	25p	£25.00
MF108	River Valleys	1926	30p	£31.50
25	School Badges (Dark Blue Back)	1928	£1.00	£25.00
25	(Light Blue Back)	1928	£1.00	£25.00
MF30	The Colonial Series (Large Captions)	1925	40p	£12.00
MF30	(Small Captions)	1925	30p	£9.00
F54	The Homeland Series (Black Back)	1924	30p	£16.00
F50	(Blue Back)	1924	£1.00	£50.00
MF50	The Homeland Series "Hand Coloured"	1924	30p	£15.00
MF56	"Real Photos"	1924	40p	£22.50
MF56	Uncoloured	1924	40p	£22.50
MF56	"Reprinted"	1925	40p	£22.50
M25	The Nation's Treasures	1925	40p	£10.00
MF30	Wordsworth's Country	1926	60p	£18.00

R. S. CHALLIS & CO. LTD.

50	Comic Animals	1936	60p	£30.00
?44	Flickits (Fresher Cigarettes)	1936	£35.00	—
36	Wild Birds at Home (Baldric Cigarettes)	1935	65p	£23.50
36	(Baldric Deleted)	1935	£1.25	—

H. CHAPMAN & CO.

30	Army Pictures, Cartoons, etc	1916	*£175.00*	—

CHARLESWORTH & AUSTIN

50	Beauties "BOCCA"	1900	£27.50	£1375.00
16	British Royal Family	1902	£42.50	—

CHARLESWORTH & AUSTIN — cont.

Qty		*Date*	*Odds*	*Sets*
50	Colonial Troops (Black Back)	1901	£32.50	—
30	(Brown Back)	1901	£30.00	—
20	Cricketers Series	1902	£300.00	—
30	Flags & Flags with Soldiers	1903	£30.00	—

CHESTERFIELD CIGARETTES

M6	Chesterfield Cocktails	1980	50p	£3.00

A. CHEW & CO.

30	Army Pictures, Cartoons, etc	1916	*£110.00*	—

CHING & CO. (Channel Isles)

L24	Around & About in Jersey, 1st Series	1963	30p	£7.50
L24	Around & About in Jersey, 2nd Series	1964	55p	£13.50
25	Do You Know?	1962	—	£2.40
M48	Flowers	1962	85p	£41.00
L24	Jersey Past & Present, A Series	1960	—	£6.00
L24	Jersey Past & Present, Second Series	1962	75p	£18.00
L24	Jersey Past & Present, Third Series	1963	—	£6.00
25	Ships and their Workings	1961	—	£2.50
50	Veteran and Vintage Cars (Mauve)	1960	40p	£20.00
25	(Blue, 26-50)	1960	—	£15.00

W. A. & A. C. CHURCHMAN

36 Page Reference Book — £3.50

24	Actresses, Unicoloured (Blue Printing)	1897	£65.00	—
24	(Brown Printing)	1897	£65.00	—
26	Actresses, "FROGA A"	1900	£32.50	—
26	Actresses, "FROGA B"	1900	£37.50	—
M48	Air-Raid Precautions	1938	25p	£12.00
25	Army Badges of Rank	1916	£4.50	£112.50
50	Association Footballers, A Series	1938	80p	£40.00
50	Association Footballers, 2nd Series	1939	£1.20	£60.00
50	A Tour Round the World	1911	£6.50	£325.00
12	Beauties "CERF"	1899	£55.00	£660.00
25	Beauties "CHOAB"	1900	£100.00	—
M?25	Beauties "CHOAB" (Circular)	1900	*£400.00*	—
25	Beauties "FECKSA"	1903	£85.00	—
25	Beauties "GRACC"	1898	£80.00	—
50	Birds & Eggs	1906	£6.00	£300.00
20	Boer War Cartoons	1901	£95.00	—
41	Boer War Celebrities & Actresses	1901	£17.00	£700.00
20	Boer War Generals "CLAM" (Black)	1901	£35.00	—
20	(Brown)	1901	£32.50	£650.00
25	Boxing	1922	£5.00	£125.00
50	Boxing Personalities	1938	£1.60	£100.00
50	Boy Scouts, A Series	1916	£6.50	£325.00
50	Boy Scouts, 2nd Series	1916	£6.50	£325.00
50	Boy Scouts, 3rd Series (Blue Back)	1916	£10.00	—
50	(Brown Back)	1916	£6.50	£325.00

W. A. & A. C. CHURCHMAN — cont.

Qty		*Date*	*Odds*	*Sets*
25	British Film Stars	1934	£1.60	£40.00
54/55	Can You Beat Bogey at St. Andrews?	1934	£2.00	£180.00
54/55	Ditto (Red Overprint)	1934	£2.20	£200.00
25	Cathedrals & Churches	1924	£1.80	£45.00
X12	Cathedrals & Churches	1924	£9.00	£108.00
50	Celebrated Gateways	1925	£1.80	£90.00
M1	Christmas Greeting Card	1938	—	£1.60
25	Civic Insignia and Plate	1926	£1.80	£45.00
50	Contract Bridge	1935	85p	£42.50
50	Cricketers	1936	£3.20	£160.00
25	Curious Dwellings	1926	£1.80	£45.00
L12	Curious Dwellings	1926	£4.25	£51.00
25	Curious Signs	1925	£1.80	£45.00
38	Dogs and Fowls	1908	£7.25	—
25	Eastern Proverbs, A Series	1931	80p	£20.00
L12	Eastern Proverbs, A Series	1931	£3.75	£45.00
25	Eastern Proverbs, 2nd Series	1932	80p	£20.00
L12	Eastern Proverbs, 2nd Series	1932	£2.25	£27.00
L12	Eastern Proverbs, 3rd Series	1933	£2.25	£27.00
L12	Eastern Proverbs, 4th Series	1934	£1.75	£21.00
50	East Suffolk Churches (Black Front)	1912	£1.70	£85.00
50	(Sepia Front)	1917	£1.50	£75.00
50	Empire Railways	1931	£2.30	£115.00
25	Famous Cricket Colours	1928	£3.60	£90.00
50	Famous Golfers	1927	£8.50	£625.00
L12	Famous Golfers, A Series	1927	£24.00	—
L12	Famous Golfers, 2nd Series	1928	£24.00	—
25	Famous Railway Trains	1929	£2.50	£62.50
L12	Famous Railway Trains, A Series	1929	£5.50	£66.00
L12	Famous Railway Trains, 2nd Series	1929	£4.50	£54.00
50	Fish & Bait	1914	£6.00	£300.00
50	Fishes of the World	1912	—	£250.00
30/50	Fishes of the World	1924	£1.50	£45.00
50	Flags & Funnels of Leading Steamship Lines	1912	£6.00	£300.00
50	Football Club Colours	1909	£10.00	—
50	Footballers (Brown)	1914	£27.50	£1375.00
50	Footballers (Coloured)	1914	£14.00	£700.00
52	Frisky	1935	£3.50	£182.00
1	Frisky (Instructions)	1935	—	£11.50
50	History & Development of the British Empire	1934	£1.60	£80.00
M48	Holidays in Britain (Views & Maps)	1937	25p	£12.00
M48	Holidays in Britain (Views Only)	1938	25p	£12.00
40	Home & Colonial Regiments	1902	£42.50	—
40	Howlers	1937	25p	£10.00
L16	Howlers	1937	50p	£8.00
50	Interesting Buildings	1905	£6.25	£312.50
25	Interesting Door-Knockers	1928	£2.30	£57.50
25	Interesting Experiments	1929	£1.20	£30.00
50	In Town To-Night	1938	35p	£17.50
L12	Italian Art Exhibition, 1930, 1st Series	1930	£1.50	£18.00
L12	Italian Art Exhibition, 1930, 2nd Series	1931	£1.25	£15.00
50	Kings of Speed	1939	60p	£30.00
50	Landmarks in Railway Progress	1931	£2.50	£125.00
L12	Landmarks in Railway Progress, 1st Series	1932	£4.75	£57.00
L12	Landmarks in Railway Progress, 2nd Series	1932	£4.75	£57.00

Qty		Date	Odds	Sets
50	Lawn Tennis	1928	£3.50	£175.00
L12	Lawn Tennis	1928	£10.00	—
50	Legends of Britain	1936	80p	£40.00
L12	Legends of Britain	1936	£1.50	£18.00
25	Life in a Liner	1930	£1.60	£40.00
L12	Life in a Liner	1930	£3.50	£42.00
50	Medals	1910	£6.25	£312.50
50	Men of the Moment in Sport	1928	£2.35	£250.00
L12	Men of the Moment in Sport, 1st Series	1928	£7.50	£245.00
L12	Men of the Moment in Sport, 2nd Series	1928	£7.50	—
M48	Modern Wonders	1938	25p	£12.50
25	Musical Instruments	1924	£3.30	£82.50
25	Nature's Architects	1930	£1.20	£30.00
L12	Nature's Architects	1930	£2.00	£24.00
D55	Olympic Winners Through the Years	1960	£1.75	—
50	Phil May Sketches (Gold Flake)	1912	£5.50	£275.00
50	(No Brand)	1912	£7.50	—
25	Pipes of the World	1927	£2.60	£65.00
50	Prominent Golfers	1931	£8.00	£500.00
L12	Prominent Golfers	1931	£20.00	£375.00
50	Racing Greyhounds	1934	£2.60	£130.00
25	Railway Working, A Series	1926	£3.40	£85.00
L12	Railway Working, A Series	1926	£7.50	—
25	Railway Working, 2nd Series	1927	£2.40	£60.00
L13	Railway Working, 2nd Series	1926	£8.00	£104.00
L12	Railway Working, 3rd Series	1927	£8.00	£96.00
50	Regimental Colours & Cap Badges	1912	£6.00	£300.00
50	Rivers & Broads	1921	£5.50	£275.00
50	Rivers & Broads of Norfolk & Suffolk	1922	£4.00	£200.00
50	Rugby Internationals	1935	£1.70	£85.00
50	Sectional Cycling Map	1913	£5.50	£275.00
50	Silhouettes of Warships	1915	£8.00	£400.00
50	Sporting Celebrities	1931	£2.40	£150.00
25	Sporting Trophies	1927	£2.20	£55.00
L12	Sporting Trophies	1927	£5.00	£60.00
25	Sports & Games in Many Lands	1929	£3.00	£150.00
25	The Houses of Parliament & Their Story	1931	£1.80	£45.00
25	The Inns of Court	1922	£2.50	£62.50
50	The King's Coronation	1937	20p	£10.00
L15	The King's Coronation	1937	80p	£12.00
M48	The Navy at Work	1937	30p	£15.00
50	The Queen Mary	1936	£1.40	£70.00
L16	The Queen Mary	1936	£2.50	£40.00
M48	The R.A.F. at Work	1937	£1.00	£48.00
50	The Story of London	1934	£1.30	£65.00
L12	The Story of London	1934	£2.75	£33.00
50	The Story of Navigation	1937	40p	£20.00
L12	The Story of Navigation	1937	£1.25	£15.00
D40	The World of Sport	1961	£1.60	—
36	3 Jovial Golfers	1934	£3.25	£117.00
73	3 Jovial Golfers (Irish Issue)	1934	£7.00	—
50	Treasure Trove	1937	20p	£9.00
L12	Treasure Trove	1937	£1.25	£15.00
25	Types of British & Colonial Troops	1899	£42.50	—
25	Warriors of All Nations	1929	£2.50	£62.50

W. A. & A. C. CHURCHMAN — cont.

Qty		*Date*	*Odds*	*Sets*
L12	Warriors of All Nations, A Series	1929	£3.75	£45.00
L12	Warriors of All Nations, 2nd Series	1931	£3.75	£45.00
50	Well-Known Ties, A Series	1934	75p	£37.50
L12	Well-Known Ties, A Series	1934	£1.60	£19.50
50	Well-Known Ties, Second Series	1935	70p	£35.00
L12	Well-Known Ties, 2nd Series	1935	£1.60	£19.50
25	Wembley Exhibition (2 Printings)	1924	£2.20	£55.00
50	West Suffolk Churches	1919	£1.40	£70.00
50	Wild Animals of the World	1907	£6.50	£325.00
M48	Wings Over the Empire	1939	50p	£24.00
50	Wonderful Railway Travel	1937	40p	£20.00
L12	Wonderful Railway Travel	1937	£1.25	£15.00
50	World Wonders Old and New	Unissued	—	£17.50

OVERSEAS ISSUES (No I.T.C. Clause)

M48	Air-Raid Precautions	1938	£1.60	—
M48	Holidays In Britain (Views & Maps)	1937	£1.60	—
M48	Holidays In Britain (Views Only)	1938	£1.60	—
M48	Modern Wonders (Plain Base)	1938	£1.60	—
M48	(Silver Line at Base)	1938	£5.00	—
M48	The Navy at Work	1937	£2.00	—
M48	The R.A.F. at Work	1937	£1.75	—
25	Warriors of All Nations (No Name on front)	1929	£8.00	—
M48	Wings Over the Empire	1939	£1.60	—

CIGARETTE COMPANY (Channel Isles)

72	Jersey Footballers (Blue Background)	1910	£5.75	—
50	Jersey Footballers (Grey Background)	1910	£5.75	—
?53	Jersey Footballers (No Frame for Name)	1910	£12.50	—

WM. CLARKE & SON

25	Army Life	1915	£11.00	£275.00
16	Boer War Celebrities	1901	£25.00	£400.00
50	Butterflies & Moths	1912	£7.50	£375.00
30	Cricketer Series	1901	£140.00	—
66	Football Series	1902	£25.00	—
25	Marine Series	1907	£12.50	£312.50
50	Royal Mail	1914	£10.00	£500.00
50	Sporting Terms (Multi-backed)	1900	£40.00	—
20	Tobacco Leaf Girls	1898	£375.00	—
25	Well-Known Sayings	1900	£23.00	£575.00

J. H. CLURE & SON

30	Army Pictures, Cartoons, etc. (No Brands)	1916	*£95.00*	—
30	(Havana Mixture)	1916	*£95.00*	—
50	War Portraits	1916	*£75.00*	—

J. LOMAX COCKAYNE

50	War Portraits	1916	*£75.00*	—

COHEN WEENEN & CO.

Qty		Date	Odds	Sets
F40	Actresses, Footballers & Jockeys	1901	£45.00	—
26	Actresses "FROGA"	1900	*£60.00*	—
?111	Bandmaster Conundrums — was Drapkin	1907	£9.00	—
25	Beauties "BOCCA"	1899	£70.00	—
25	Beauties "GRACC"	1899	*£85.00*	—
45	Boer War Celebrities, Coloured ("100" Back)	1901	£5.00	£225.00
45	("250" Back)	1901	£8.00	—
65	Celebrities, Black & White ("250" Back)	1900	£5.00	—
25	("500" Back)	1900	£10.00	—
76	Celebrities, Coloured ("250", Different)	1901	£4.50	£330.00
30	Celebrities, Gainsborough ("400" Back)	1902	£11.00	£330.00
M39	("250" Back)	1902	£37.50	—
M40	(Metal Frame)	1902	*£55.00*	—
MF?177	Celebrities, Gainsborough (No Frame)	1901	£4.25	—
MF?177	(Metal Frame)	1901	£15.00	—
25	Cricketers	1926	£14.00	£350.00
20	Cricketers, Footballers & Jockeys	1900	£17.50	£350.00
25	Famous Boxers (Black Back)	1912	£13.50	—
25	(Green Back)	1912	£10.00	£375.00
25	(Anonymous)	1912	£16.00	—
40	Fiscal Phrases (Copyright Registered)	1902	£11.00	£440.00
40	Fiscal Phrases (No Copyright Clause)	1902	£11.00	£440.00
60	Football Captains 1907-8	1908	£12.50	£750.00
100	Heroes of Sport	1897	£75.00	—
40	Home & Colonial Regiments ("100" Back)	1901	£8.00	£320.00
40	("250" Back)	1901	£12.00	—
40	(Gold Border)	1901	*£100.00*	—
20	Interesting Buildings & Views (Plain)	1902	£10.00	£200.00
20	(Gold Surround)	1902	*£90.00*	—
K52	Miniature Playing Cards (Bandmaster)	1910	£4.00	—
20	Nations (Non Descriptive)	1902	£12.00	£240.00
20	(Descriptive)	1923	£4.50	£90.00
40	Naval & Military Phrases (Blue Back)	1904	£25.00	—
40	(Red Back)	1906	£16.00	£640.00
40	(Gold Border)	1906	*£90.00*	—
50	Owners, Jockeys, Footballers, Cricketers Series 2	1906	£12.50	£625.00
20	Owners, Jockeys, Footballers, Cricketers Series 3	1907	£13.00	£260.00
30	Proverbs	1903	£15.00	£450.00
20	Russo Japanese War Series	1904	£16.50	£330.00
25	Silhouettes of Celebrities	1903	£12.00	£325.00
50	Star Artistes	1907	£10.00	£500.00
L16	Victoria Cross Heroes (Silk)	1915	£40.00	—
50	Victoria Cross Heroes (51-100)	1916	£9.00	£450.00
25	(51-75, Anonymous)	1916	£12.00	—
50	War Series	1916	£8.50	£425.00
25	Ditto (26-50, Anonymous)	1916	£12.00	—
30	Wonders of the World (Green Back)	1908	£7.00	£210.00
30	Wonders of the World (Grey Back)	1923	£2.60	£78.00

T. H. COLLINS

25	Homes of England (Black Front)	1924	*£12.50*	—
25	(Mauve Front)	1924	£5.00	£125.00
25	Sports & Pastimes	1923	£6.20	£180.00

F. COLTON JR.

Qty		Date	Odds	Sets
30	Army Pictures, Cartoons, etc. ("Best Brands")	1916	*£100.00*	—
30	("Trade Supplied")	1916	*£100.00*	—
50	War Portraits	1916	*£75.00*	—

T. W. CONQUEST (Tobacconist)

30	Army Pictures, Cartoons, etc	1916	*£100.00*	—

CONTINENTAL CIGARETTE FACTORY

25	Charming Portraits (Firm's Name)	1920	£5.00	£125.00
25	(Club Mixture, Blue)	1920	£6.50	—
4	(Club Mixture, Brown)	1920	£9.00	—
25	(Plain Back)	1920	£3.50	—

COOPER & CO.

25	Boer War Celebrities "STEW" (Alpha)	1901	*£120.00*	—
25	(Gladys)	1901	*£120.00*	—

CO-OPERATIVE WHOLESALE SOCIETY (C.W.S.)

6	Advertisement Cards	1915	£240.00	—
24	African Types	1936	50p	£12.00
X2	Beauties	1925	*£50.00*	—
M50	Beauty Spots of Britain	1936	20p	£10.00
50	Boy Scout Badges	1939	£1.20	£60.00
25	Boy Scout Series	1912	£30.00	—
48	British and Foreign Birds	1938	70p	£35.00
50	British Sport Series (Multi-Backed)	1904	£26.50	—
25	Cooking Recipes	1923	£2.20	£55.00
28	Co-operative Buildings & Works	1916	£13.00	£365.00
24	English Roses	1924	£3.75	£90.00
50	Famous Bridges	1937	80p	£40.00
48	Famous Buildings	1935	75p	£36.00
25	How To Do It (Mixed Backs)	1924	—	£60.00
25	(Anglian Mixture)	1924	£2.50	—
25	(Equity Tobacco)	1924	£2.50	—
25	(Jaycee Brown Flake)	1924	£2.50	—
25	(Raydex Gold Leaf)	1924	£2.50	—
48	Musical Instruments	1934	£3.50	£168.00
25	Parrot Series	1910	£32.50	—
48	Poultry	1927	£7.00	£336.00
48	Railway Engines	1936	£3.25	£156.00
24	Sailing Craft	1935	£1.40	£33.50
18	War Series	1914	£25.00	—
48	Wayside Flowers (Brown Back)	1923	£2.00	£96.00
48	Wayside Flowers (Green Back, Different)	1928	£1.00	£48.00
48	Wayside Woodland Trees	1924	£2.50	£120.00
24	Western Stars	1957	75p	£18.00

COPE BROS. & CO. LTD.

KF?47	Actors & Actresses	1900	£25.00	—

Qty		Date	Odds	Sets
20	Actresses "BLARM" (Plain Back)	1902	£35.00	—
20	(Printed Back, 63mm Long)	1902	£35.00	—
20	(Printed Back, 70mm Long)	1902	£34.00	£680.00
6	Actresses "COPEIS"	1898	£150.00	—
26	Actresses "FROGA"	1900	£90.00	—
F50	Actresses & Beauties	1900	£13.00	£650.00
P6	Advertising Postcards	1924	£70.00	—
52	Beauties, Playing Card Inset	1899	£42.50	—
15	Beauties "PAC"	1898	£75.00	—
50	Boats of the World	1912	£13.00	£650.00
25	Boxers (1-25)	1915	£16.00	£400.00
25	Boxers (26-50)	1915	£14.00	£350.00
25	Boxers (51-75)	1915	£14.00	£350.00
25	Boxers (76-100)	1915	£18.00	£450.00
25	Boxers (101-125)	1915	£13.00	£325.00
1	Boxers (New World's Champion)	1915	—	£37.50
25	Boxing Lessons	1935	£4.00	£100.00
35	Boy Scouts & Girl Guides (English)	1910	£12.00	£420.00
35	(Scandinavian)	1910	£30.00	—
X25	Bridge Problems	1924	*£24.00*	—
25	British Admirals	1915	£12.00	£300.00
50	British Warriors (Black Printing)	1912	£7.00	£350.00
50	(Grey Printing)	1912	£8.50	£425.00
25	Castles	1939	£1.20	£30.00
25	Cathedrals	1939	£1.30	£32.50
50	Characters from Scott	1900	£12.00	£600.00
20	Chinese Series (1-20)	1903	£11.50	£230.00
20	Chinese Series (21-40, Bond of Union)	1903	£11.00	—
20	(21-40, Cope's Courts)	1903	£11.00	—
20	(21-40, Golden Cloud)	1903	£11.00	—
20	(21-40, Golden Magnet)	1903	£11.00	—
20	(21-40, Solace)	1903	£11.00	—
25	Chinese Series (41-65, 2 Printings)	1903	£11.00	—
50	Chinese Series (66-115, Multi-Backed)	1903	£11.50	—
X6	Comic Hunting Scenes	1885	*£200.00*	—
P?2	Comic Scenes with Dog (Folders)	1885	*£200.00*	—
50	Cope's Golfers	1900	£80.00	£4000.00
L25	Dickens Character Series	1939	£1.00	£25.00
50	Dickens Gallery (Back-Listed)	1900	£10.00	£500.00
50	(Solace Back)	1900	£85.00	—
E1	Dickens Gallery Album	1900	—	£130.00
50	Dogs of the World (English)	1912	£12.00	£600.00
50	(Scandinavian)	1912	£35.00	—
25	Eminent British Regiments Officers Uniforms			
	(English, Brown Back)	1908	£12.00	£300.00
	(English, Claret Back)	1908	£13.00	£325.00
	(Scandinavian)	1908	£27.50	—
24	Flags, Arms & Types of All Nations (Numbered)	1904	£7.00	£168.00
24	(Unnumbered)	1904	*£75.00*	—
30	Flags of Nations (Black Back)	1903	£11.00	£330.00
30	(Indian, Blue Back)	1903	£65.00	—
30	(Plain Back)	1903	£8.00	£240.00
M50	General Knowledge	1925	£3.75	—
M32	Golf Strokes	1923	£13.00	—
60	Happy Families	1937	£1.50	£90.00
M50	Household Hints	1925	£1.60	£80.00
X20	Kenilworth Phrases	1910	*£175.00*	—

COPE BROS. & CO. LTD. — cont.

Qty		Date	Odds	Sets
25	Lawn Tennis Strokes	1924	£5.40	£135.00
5	Lawn Tennis Strokes (26-30)	1925	£17.50	—
L50	Modern Dancing	1926	£13.00	—
50	Music Hall Artistes ("Series of 50")	1913	£32.50	£1625.00
50	(No Quantity)	1913	£10.00	£500.00
120	Noted Footballers (Clips, 120 Subjects)	1910	£14.00	—
162	Noted Footballers (Clips, 282 Subjects)	1910	£14.00	—
471	Noted Footballers (Clips, 500 Subjects)	1910	£14.00	—
1	Noted Footballers (Clips, Unnumbered)	1910	—	£50.00
195	Noted Footballers (Solace Cigarettes)	1910	£15.00	—
24	Occupations for Women	1897	£85.00	—
X6	Phases of the Moon	1885	*£200.00*	—
T12	Photo Albums for the Million (Buff)	1902	£14.00	£168.00
T12	Photo Albums for the Million (Green)	1902	£13.00	£156.00
25	Pigeons	1926	£7.40	£185.00
52	Playing Cards (Rounded Corners)	1902	£10.00	—
52	(Squarer Corners)	1902	£10.00	—
30	Scandinavian Actors & Actresses	1910	£40.00	£1200.00
50	Shakespeare Gallery	1900	£12.50	£625.00
G14	Smoke Room Booklets	1890	£18.00	—
25	Song Birds	1926	£7.00	£175.00
25	Sports & Pastimes	1925	£4.00	£100.00
L25	The Game of Poker	1936	50p	£12.50
X7	The Seven Ages of Man	1885	*£200.00*	—
25	The World's Police	1937	£4.40	£110.00
L25	Toy Models – The Country Fair	1925	50p	£12.50
25	Uniforms (Circular Medallion Back)	1898	£26.00	£650.00
25	(Square Medallion Back, Narrow)	1898	£21.00	£525.00
25	(Square Medallion Back, Wide)	1898	£55.00	—
50	V.C & D.S.O. Naval & Flying Heroes (Unnumbered)	1917	£7.00	£450.00
25	V.C & D.S.O. Naval & Flying Heroes (Numbered 51-75)	1917	£8.50	—
20	War Pictures	1915	£10.00	£200.00
25	War Series	1915	£12.50	—
25	Wild Animals & Birds (English)	1907	£16.00	£400.00
25	(Scandinavian)	1907	£35.00	—

E. CORONEL

25	Types of British & Colonial Troops	1900	£60.00	—

DAVID CORRE & CO.

40	Naval & Military Phrases (With Border)	1904	£70.00	—
40	(No Border)	1904	£70.00	—
1	The New Alliance Card	1903	*£300.00*	—

JOHN COTTON LTD.

L50	Bridge Hands	1934	£9.00	—
50	Golf Strokes A/B	1936	£8.00	£400.00
50	Golf Strokes C/D	1937	£9.00	—
50	Golf Strokes E/F	1938	£12.50	—
50	Golf Strokes G/H	1939	*£400.00*	—
50	Golf Strokes I/J	1939	*£400.00*	—

A. & J. COUDENS LTD.

Qty		Date	Odds	Sets
F60	British Beauty Spots (Numbered)	1923	£1.25	£75.00
F60	(Unnumbered)	1923	£2.25	—
F60	(Rubber Stamped)	1923	£4.00	—
F60	(Plain Back Anonymous)	1923	£3.80	—
F60	Holiday Resorts in East Anglia	1924	£1.10	£66.00
25	Sports Alphabet	1924	£8.00	£200.00

THE CRAIGMILLAR CREAMERY CO.

M?1	Scottish Views	1901	*£350.00*	—

W. R. DANIEL

30	Colonial Troops (Black Back)	1902	*£75.00*	—
30	(Brown Back)	1902	£75.00	—
25	National Flags & Flowers-Girls	1901	*£125.00*	—

W. F. DANIELL

X?1	Puzzle Cards	1895	*£200.00*	—

W. T. DAVIES & SONS

50	Actresses	1902	£80.00	—
30	Aristocrats of the Turf, A Series (1-30)	1924	£5.50	£165.00
12	Aristocrats of the Turf (31-42)	1924	£17.50	—
36	Aristocrats of the Turf, Second Series	1924	£4.50	£162.00
25	Army Life	1915	£10.00	£250.00
12	Beauties	1903	£42.50	—
25	Boxing	1924	£4.00	£100.00
50	Flags & Funnels of Leading Steamship Lines	1913	£10.00	—
?12	Newport Football Club	1904	£200.00	—
?5	Royal Welsh Fusiliers	1904	*£200.00*	—

S. H. DAWES (Tobacconist)

30	Army Pictures, Cartoons, etc	1916	*£125.00*	—

J. W. DEWHURST

30	Army Pictures, Cartoons, etc	1916	*£100.00*	—

R. I. DEXTER

30	Borough Arms	1900	£1.40	£42.00

DIANELLOS & VERGOPOULOS

XF?7	Views of Cyprus	1926	*£35.00*	—

GEORGE DOBIE & SON LTD.

M?28	Bridge Problems	1933	*£30.00*	—
M32	Four Square Books (1-32)	1959	£2.00	—

GEORGE DOBIE & SON LTD. — cont.

Qty		*Date*	*Odds*	*Sets*
M32	Four Square Books (33-64)	1960	£2.00	—
M32	Four Square Books (65-96)	1960	£2.00	—
25	Weapons of All Ages	1924	£6.00	£150.00

DOBSON & CO. LTD.

8	The European War Series	1917	£37.50	—

DOMINION TOBACCO CO. (1929) LTD.

25	Old Ships, 1st Series	1934	£2.20	£55.00
25	Old Ships, 2nd Series	1935	£1.00	£25.00
25	Old Ships, 3rd Series	1936	£1.00	£25.00
25	Old Ships, 4th Series	1936	£1.60	£40.00

JOSEPH W. DOYLE LTD.

F12	Beauties (Series CC.D)	1928	£26.00	—
F12	Beauties (Series CC.E)	1928	*£26.00*	—
F12	British Views (Series CC.B)	1928	£26.00	—
F12	Castles (Series CC.C)	1928	£26.00	—
XF18	Children	1928	£12.50	—
F12	Dirt Track Riders (Series CC.A)	1928	*£50.00*	—

DOYLE'S (READING)

?	Merry Miniatures (Booklets)	1924	£100.00	—

MAJOR DRAPKIN & CO.

12	Actresses	1910	£7.00	—
8	Advertisement Cards	1926	£7.00	£56.00
M1	Army Insignia	1915	*£150.00*	—
50	Around Britain	1929	£1.25	£62.50
L50	Around Britain	1929	£2.50	—
50	Around the Mediterranean	1926	£1.40	£70.00
L50	Around the Mediterranean	1926	£2.50	—
F40	Australian & English Test Cricketers	1928	£1.75	£70.00
25	British Beauties	1930	£2.60	£65.00
F36	Celebrities of the Great War (Printed Back)	1916	65p	£23.50
F34	(Plain Back)	1916	60p	£20.50
M96	Cinematograph Actors	1913	£11.00	—
15	Dogs and their Treatment	1924	£5.20	£78.00
L15	Dogs and their Treatment	1924	£6.20	£93.00
50	Girls of Many Lands	1929	£4.00	—
M50	Girls of Many Lands	1929	60p	£30.00
25	How To Keep Fit (Crayol Cigarettes)	1912	£14.00	£350.00
25	How To Keep Fit (Drapkin's Cigarettes)	1912	£14.00	£350.00
54	Life at Whipsnade Zoo	1934	50p	£27.00
50	Limericks	1929	£1.40	£70.00
F36	National Types of Beauty	1928	65p	£23.50

CODE NAMES

When cigarette cards first became popular in this country the most prolific subjects were actresses and militaria—since virtually all cigarette smokers were men! In the golden age around the turn of the century many manufacturers including many of the largest issued some of the same sets as their competitors. In order to distinguish the many similar series a coding system has been developed for series of Actresses and Boer War subjects that in general do not have a series title of their own. This is based on the first letter (or letters) of the names of some of the leading issuers of the particular set.

Thus Beauties PAC were issued by Pritchard & Burton, Adkin and Cope, and Beauties HOL by Harris, Ogden & Lambert & Butler. Actresses HAGG were issued by Hill, Anonymous, Gabriel and Glass (as well as Baker and Bell), while Boer War Celebrities CLAM, is taken from Churchman, Lambert & Butler, Anonymous and Muratti. The most popular of this set must surely have been Actresses FROGA which includes four sets all similar in appearance and was issued by more than 25 different companies, including Dunn's Hats in Britain, and tobacco issuers in Canada and India.

It is fortunate that so many of the series had an anonymous version, allowing the frequent use of the letter 'A', and hence some sort of pronounceable acronyms.

As a general rule in British issues Actress series are those in which the subject's name is printed, while the unidentified ladies are known as Beauties.

BRAND ISSUES

A brand issue is a card which bears the name of the cigarette with which it was inserted, but not the name of the issuing firm. This does not normally present a problem to compilers of catalogues and other lists, since most brand names have been registered, so that they cannot be used by a competitor—just as "Nostalgia" is a registered brand name for plastic albums!

Whenever possible we have listed brand issues under the name of the firm. This often enables us to bring together alternative printings of the same set, such as Hill Aviation and Decorations & Medals, each of which was issued either with the Hill name at the base or just advertising Gold Flake Honeydew. Similarly, under B. Morris there will be found four printings of Beauties CHOAB, 2 of which do not mention the firm's name.

One difficulty that occurs is that one Company may take over another, and inherit brand names. Hence Honest Long Cut was used by Duke and then the American Tobacco Co., which also took over brands such as Kinney's Sweet Caporal and Lorillard's Red Cross.

The most difficult problem however concerns groups of Companies which may use the same brand name under a different firm in different countries. Thus the Phillips Group used "Greys" as a U.K.T.C. brand in Britain, but as a Phillips brand in Australia. Similarly, Flag Cigarettes was used by Wills in Asia and U.T.C. in South Africa.

In the Catalogue on Pages 18-20 there appears an Index of brands with the name of the issuing firm (or firms), and the catalogue section in which they are listed. Names will only appear in the index when the firm's name does NOT appear AS WELL AS the brand on the card. When the issuer of the brand is not known, such as Field Favorite Cigarettes, the brand will not appear in the Index, and the set will be listed in the normal alphabetic order in the catalogue.

In a similar way to cigarette cards, there may also be brand issues of chocolates, periodicals etc. These have their own index at the beginning of section 3 of the Catalogue.

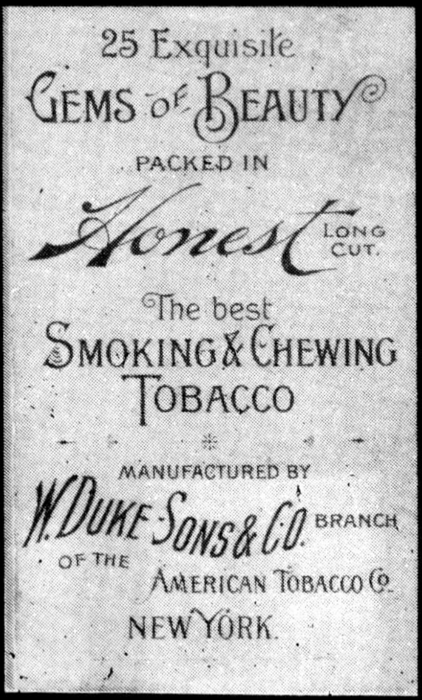

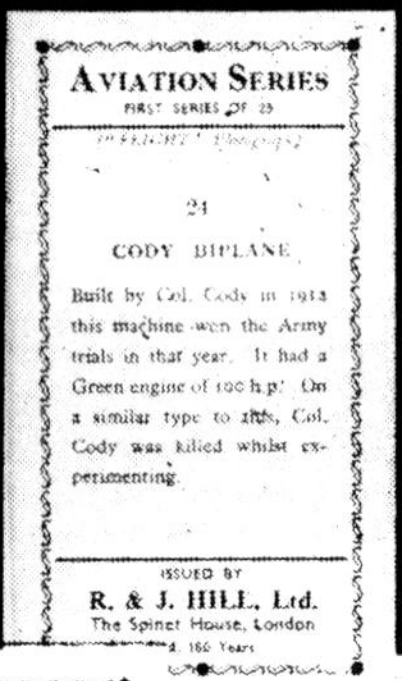

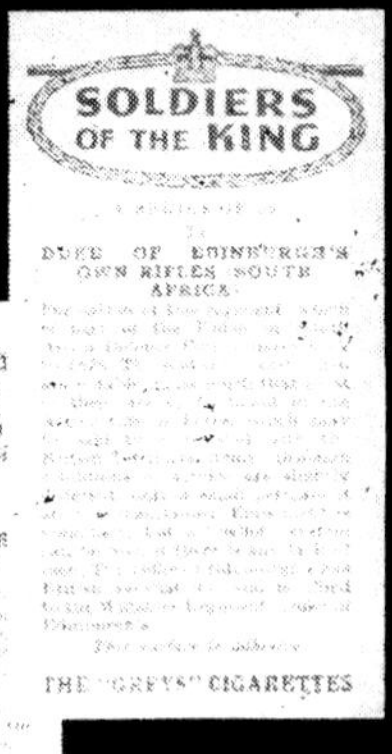

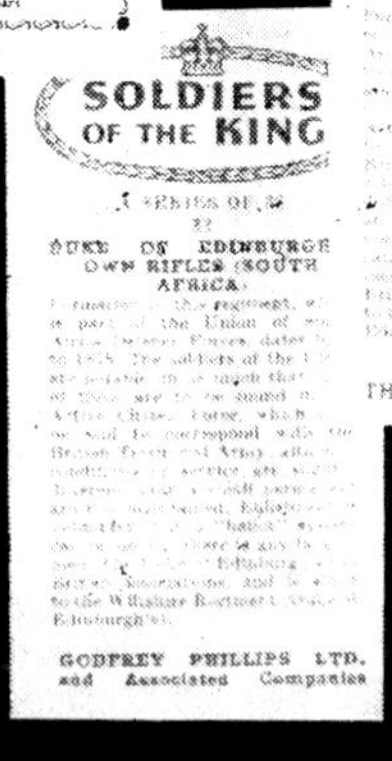

MAJOR DRAPKIN & CO. — cont.

Qty		*Date*	*Odds*	*Sets*
25	Optical Illusions (Panel 23 x 7mm)	1926	£3.20	£80.00
25	(Panel 26 x 9mm)	1926	£3.00	£75.00
L25	Optical Illusions	1926	£3.40	£85.00
25	Palmistry	1927	£3.00	£75.00
L25	Palmistry	1927	£3.00	£75.00
48	Photogravure Masterpieces	1915	£9.00	—
25	Puzzle Pictures	1926	£3.60	£90.00
L25	Puzzle Pictures	1926	£3.80	£95.00
M40	Regimental Colours & Badges of the Indian Army			
	(Silk, "Buffs")	1915	£4.00	—
	(Silk, No Brand)	1915	*£30.00*	—
?26	Shots from the Films (Package Issue)	1934	*£7.50*	—
T25	Soldiers & their Uniforms (Die-Cut)	1914	—	£74.00
T25	(Crayol)	1914	90p	—
T25	(Drapkin)	1914	90p	—
T22/25	Soldiers & their Uniforms (Die-Cut)	1914	—	£20.00
F35/36	Sporting Celebrities in Action	1930	£2.50	£200.00
40	The Game of Sporting Snap	1928	£3.75	£150.00
1	The Greys Advertisement Card	1935	—	£3.00
12	Views of the World	1910	£5.00	—
6/8	Warships	1912	£10.00	£60.00

DRAPKIN & MILLHOFF

?2	Beauties "KEWA" (Eldona Cigarettes)	1899	*£125.00*	—
?1	(Explorer Cigarettes)	1899	*£125.00*	—
25	Boer War Celebrities "PAM" (Multi-Backed)	1901	£27.50	—
25	(Plain Backs)	1901	*£45.00*	—
30	Colonial Troops (Multi-Backed)	1902	£45.00	—
X?6	Pick-Me-Up Paper Inserts	1900	*£100.00*	—
?3	Pretty Girl Series "BAGG"	1898	*£125.00*	—

DU MAURIER CIGARETTES

X?50	Advertising Inserts	1931	£6.50	—

J. DUNCAN & CO. LTD.

47/50	Evolution of the Steamship	1925	80p	£38.00
48	Flags, Arms & Types of Nations (Blue)	1911	£26.50	—
48	(Green)	1911	*£42.50*	—
20	Inventors & their Inventions	1915	*£50.00*	—
30	Scottish Clans, Arms of Chiefs (Black)	1912	*£100.00*	—
30	(Green)	1912	£16.50	£495.00
L72	Scottish Gems (Coloured)	1912	£12.50	—
L50	Scottish Gems, 2nd Series	1913	£13.50	—
L50	Scottish Gems, 3rd Series	1914	£11.00	£550.00
L50	Scottish Gems (Reissue, Black & White)	1925	50p	£25.00
25	Types of British Soldiers	1910	£42.50	—

GEO. DUNCOMBE (Tobacconist)

30	Army Pictures, Cartoons, etc	1916	*£110.00*	—

ALFRED DUNHILL LTD.

Qty		Date	Odds	Sets
M25	Dunhill King Size Ransom	1985	£1.50	—

EDWARDS, RINGER & CO.

X50	How to Count Cribbage Hands	1908	*£75.00*	—

EDWARDS, RINGER & BIGG

25	Abbeys & Castles (Exmoor Hunt Back)	1912	£7.50	£187.50
25	(New York Back)	1912	£7.50	£187.50
25	Abbeys and Castles (Type Set Back)	1912	£8.50	£212.50
25	Alpine Views (Exmoor Hunt Back)	1912	£7.00	£175.00
25	(New York Back)	1912	£7.00	£175.00
50	A Tour Round the World	1909	£9.00	£450.00
12	Beauties "CERF"	1905	£60.00	£720.00
25	Beauties "FECKSA"	1900	£36.00	—
50	Birds & Eggs	1906	£12.00	—
?25	Boer War Sketches	1901	*£110.00*	—
25	Boer War Celebrities "STEW"	1901	£40.00	—
25	British Trees & their Uses	1933	£2.40	£60.00
1	Calendar & Lighting up Table	1899	—	*£250.00*
1	Calendar	1905	—	*£225.00*
1	Calendar (Empire Back)	1910	—	*£250.00*
1	(New York Back)	1910	—	*£250.00*
50	Celebrated Bridges	1924	£2.30	£115.00
50	Cinema Stars	1923	£1.40	£70.00
L25	Cinema Stars	1923	£2.00	£50.00
25	Coast and Country (Exmoor Hunt Back)	1911	£7.50	£187.50
25	(New York Back)	1911	£7.50	£187.50
23	Dogs Series (Exmoor Hunt Back)	1908	£9.00	—
23	(Klondyke Back)	1908	£4.00	£92.00
3	Easter Manoeuvres of our Volunteers	1897	£250.00	£750.00
25	Flags of All Nations (1st Series)	1907	£6.50	£162.50
12	Flags of All Nations (2nd Series)	1907	£6.50	£78.00
37	(Exmoor Hunt)	1907	£6.50	£240.00
37	(Globe & Flags)	1907	£6.50	£240.00
37	(Stag Design)	1907	£6.50	£240.00
37	(Vertical Back)	1907	£6.50	—
25	Garden Life	1934	£3.20	£80.00
25	How to Tell Fortunes	1929	£3.60	£90.00
50	Life on Board a Man of War	1905	£10.00	£500.00
1	Miners Bound for Klondyke	1897	—	*£375.00*
50	Mining	1925	£2.40	£120.00
25	Musical Instruments	1924	£3.40	£85.00
25	Optical Illusions	1936	£2.80	£70.00
25	Our Pets, A Series	1926	£2.40	£60.00
25	Our Pets, 2nd Series	1926	£2.20	£55.00
25	Past & Present	1928	£3.20	£80.00
10	Portraits of His Majesty the King	1902	£37.50	£375.00
25	Prehistoric Animals	1924	£4.80	£120.00
25	Sports & Games in Many Lands	1935	£3.20	£150.00
56	War Map, Western Front	1916	£9.00	£500.00
54	War Map of the Western Front, Series 2			
	(Exmoor Hunt Back)	1917	£9.50	—
	(New York Back)	1917	£9.00	£485.00

S. EISISKI

Qty		Date	Odds	Sets
?26	Actresses "ANGOOD"	1900	*£150.00*	—
6	Actresses "COPEIS"	1899	*£150.00*	—
?23	Beauties "FENA" (Printed Back)	1899	*£150.00*	—
?23	(Rubber Stamped Back)	1899	*£150.00*	—
?2	Beauties "KEWA" (Birds Eye Back)	1900	*£150.00*	—
?2	(New Gold Back)	1900	*£150.00*	—
?1	(Rubber Stamped Back)	1900	*£150.00*	—

R. J. ELLIOTT & CO. LTD.

1	Bulldog Advertisement Card (2 Types)	1910	—	*£150.00*

EMPIRE TOBACCO CO.

6	Franco British Exhibition	1907	*£200.00*	—

ENCHANTERESSE EGYPTIAN CIGARETTE CO.

?23	Actresses "ANGOOD"	1898	*£150.00*	—
K52	Miniature Playing Cards	1931	*£5.00*	—

THE EXPRESS TOBACCO CO. LTD.

M50	How It Is Made (Motor Cars)	1939	£2.60	£150.00

L. & J. FABIAN

F24	The Elite Series (Numbered LLF1-24)	1932	*£32.50*	—
F?47	The Elite Series (Plain Numerals)	1932	*£32.50*	—

FAIRWEATHER & SONS

50	Historic Buildings of Scotland	1914	£40.00	£2000.00

W. & F. FAULKNER

12 Page Reference Book — £3.50

26	Actresses "FROGA"	1900	£45.00	—
25	Angling	1929	£6.50	£162.50
12	'Ation Series	1901	£22.00	£264.00
25	Beauties (Coloured)	1898	£60.00	—
49	Beauties "FECKSA"	1901	£20.00	£1000.00
16	British Royal Family	1901	£32.50	£520.00
50	Celebrated Bridges	1925	£2.30	£115.00
12	Coster Series	1900	£24.00	£288.00
20	Cricketers Series	1902	£250.00	—
12	Cricket Terms	1899	£75.00	—
12	Football Terms, 1st Series	1900	£25.00	£300.00
12	Football Terms, 2nd Series	1900	£25.00	£300.00
12	Golf Terms	1901	£90.00	—
12	Grenadier Guards	1899	£24.00	£288.00

W. & F. FAULKNER — cont.

Qty		*Date*	*Odds*	*Sets*
40	Kings & Queens	1902	£22.00	—
12	Kipling Series	1900	£22.00	£264.00
12	Military Terms, 1st Series	1899	£22.00	£264.00
12	Military Terms, 2nd Series	1899	£22.00	—
12	Nautical Terms, 1st Series (2 Printings)	1900	£20.00	£240.00
12	Nautical Terms, 2nd Series (Grenadier)	1900	£20.00	£240.00
12	(Union Jack)	1900	£22.00	£264.00
25	Old Sporting Prints	1930	£3.40	£85.00
25	Optical Illusions	1935	£2.60	£65.00
90	Our Colonial Troops (Grenadier)	1900	£12.50	£1125.00
30	(Grenadier, with "Copyright", 1-30)	1900	£26.50	—
60	(Union Jack, 31-90)	1900	£16.00	—
20	Our Gallant Grenadiers (No I.T.C. Clause)	1902	£15.00	£300.00
20	(I.T.C. Clause)	1903	£27.50	£550.00
20	Our Gallant Grenadiers (Numbered 21-40)	1902	£23.00	£460.00
25	Our Pets, A Series	1926	£3.00	£75.00
25	Our Pets, 2nd Series	1926	£2.60	£65.00
12	Policemen of the World (Grenadier)	1899	*£135.00*	—
12	(Nosegay)	1899	£30.00	£360.00
12	Police Terms	1899	£25.00	£300.00
25	Prominent Racehorses of the Present Day	1923	£3.20	£80.00
25	Prominent Racehorses of the Present Day, 2nd Series	1924	£5.00	£125.00
12	Puzzle Series (Grenadier)	1898	*£135.00*	—
12	(Nosegay)	1898	£62.50	—
25	South African War Series	1901	£15.00	£375.00
12	Sporting Terms	1900	£30.00	£360.00
12	Street Cries	1902	£22.00	£264.00
12	The Language of Flowers (Grenadier)	1900	£27.50	£330.00
12	(Nosegay)	1900	£27.50	£330.00

FIELD FAVORITES CIGARETTES

F?	Footballers	1893	*£750.00*	—

THE FIGARO CIGARETTE

X?12	Caricatures	1880	*£500.00*	—

FINLAY & CO. LTD.

?27	Our Girls	1910	£125.00	—
30	World's Aircraft	1912	£65.00	—

FLYNN

26	Beauties "HOL"	1899	*£250.00*	—

C. D. FOTHERGILL

M?	Football Shields	1900	*£125.00*	—

FRAENKEL BROS.

Qty		*Date*	*Odds*	*Sets*
?2	Beauties — Don Jorge (2 Printings)	1897	*£300.00*	—
?23	Beauties — "FENA"	1899	£90.00	—
25	Beauties — "GRACC"	1898	*£125.00*	—
24	Beauties — "HUMPS"	1899	*£110.00*	—
26	Music Hall Artistes (Pink Card)	1900	£90.00	—
26	(White Card)	1900	£90.00	—
25	Types of British & Colonial Troops	1900	£65.00	—

FRANKLYN DAVEY & CO.

12	Beauties "CERF"	1905	£60.00	£720.00
50	Birds	1896	£60.00	—
10	Boer War Generals	1901	£80.00	—
25	Boxing	1924	£3.20	£80.00
25	Ceremonial and Court Dress	1915	£9.00	£225.00
50	Children of All Nations	1934	90p	£45.00
1	Comic Dog Folder	1898	—	*£300.00*
50	Football Club Colours	1909	£13.50	—
50	Historic Events	1924	£2.50	£125.00
25	Hunting	1925	£1.00	£25.00
50	Modern Dance Steps, A Series	1930	£5.00	—
50	Modern Dance Steps, 2nd Series	1931	80p	£40.00
50	Naval Dress & Badges	1916	£11.00	—
50	Overseas Dominions (Australia)	1923	£4.50	—
25	Star Girls	1901	*£150.00*	—
10	Types of Smokers	1898	£50.00	£500.00
50	Wild Animals of the World	1902	£11.50	—

A. H. FRANKS & SONS

56	Beauties	1901	£65.00	—
24	Nautical Expressions	1902	*£75.00*	—
25	Types of British & Colonial Troops	1900	£60.00	—

J. J. FREEMAN & CO.

12	Actresses "FRAN"	1915	£40.00	—
12	Views of the World	1910	£40.00	—

J. R. FREEMAN

33	Football Challenge (3 Printings)	1969	£4.50	—
M12	Manikin Cards	1915	*£70.00*	—

C. FRYER & SONS LTD.

25	Boer War & General Interest (3 Backs)	1900	£110.00	—
X50	Clan Sketches	1930	£11.00	£550.00
40	Naval & Military Phrases	1904	£55.00	—
?13	Vita Berlin Series	1901	*£165.00*	—

FRYER & COULTMAN

Qty		*Date*	*Odds*	*Sets*
X12	Almanack	1893	*£250.00*	—
?50	Beauties "PLUMS"	1896	*£300.00*	—

J. GABRIEL

10	Actresses "HAGG"	1900	£70.00	—
25	Beauties "GRACC"	1898	*£120.00*	—
20	Cricketers Series	1902	*£350.00*	—
40	Home & Colonial Regiments	1902	*£80.00*	—
?52	Pretty Girl Series "BAGG"	1898	£65.00	—
25	Types of British & Colonial Troops	1899	£62.50	—

GALA CIGARETTES

1	Stamp Cards	1910	—	£110.00

GALLAHER LTD.

40 Page Reference Book — £3.50

F110	Actors & Actresses (2 Printings)	1901	£5.00	—
P3	Advertising Postcards	1923	£65.00	—
48	Aeroplanes	1939	90p	£45.00
25	Aesop's Fables ("Series of 25")	1931	£1.20	£30.00
25	("Series of 50")	1931	£1.40	£35.00
100	Animals & Birds of Commercial Value	1921	55p	£55.00
48	Army Badges	1939	70p	£33.50
L24	Art Treasures of the World	1930	£1.00	£24.00
100	Association Football Club Colours	1910	£7.00	£700.00
52	Beauties (Playing Card Inset)	1905	£11.00	£570.00
52	(No Inset)	1905	£11.50	£600.00
MF48	Beautiful Scotland	1939	£1.00	£48.00
50	Birds & Eggs ("Gallaher Ltd" Only Label)	1905	*£35.00*	—
50	("Manufactured By" Label)	1905	£7.50	—
100	Birds, Nests & Eggs	1919	£1.30	£130.00
100	Boy Scout Series (Green, Belfast & London)	1911	£2.20	£220.00
86	(Green, London & Belfast)	1911	£2.40	—
100	Boy Scout Series (Brown Back, Redrawn)	1922	£1.70	£170.00
48	British Birds	1937	50p	£24.00
100	British Birds by George Rankin	1923	£1.20	£120.00
100	by Rankin	1923	£12.50	—
75	British Champions of 1923	1924	£1.60	£120.00
50	British Naval Series	1914	£4.50	£225.00
48	Butterflies & Moths	1938	50p	£24.00
25	Champion Animals & Birds of 1923	1924	£1.60	£40.00
48	Champions, A Series (No Captions on Front)	1934	80p	£38.00
48	(Captions on Front)	1934	60p	£29.00
48	Champions, 2nd Series	1935	50p	£24.00
48	Champions of Screen & Stage			
	(Red Back)	1934	50p	£24.00
	(Blue Back, Gallaher's Cigarettes)	1934	£1.00	£48.00
	(Blue Back, Gallaher Ltd.)	1934	£1.75	—
100	Cinema Stars	1926	£1.40	£140.00
MF48	Coastwise	1938	£1.25	—

Qty		Date	Odds	Sets
24	Dogs (Caption in Block)	1934	£1.35	£32.50
24	(Caption in Script)	1934	£2.25	£54.00
L24	Dogs (Caption in Block)	1934	£1.60	£38.50
L24	(Caption in Script)	1934	£2.25	£54.00
48	Dogs, A Series	1936	75p	£36.00
48	Dogs, 2nd Series	1938	50p	£24.00
F100	English & Scotch Views	1910	£2.75	£275.00
100	Fables & their Morals (No. by Caption)	1912	£1.40	£140.00
100	(Thick Numerals)	1922	65p	£65.00
100	(Thin Numerals)	1922	70p	£70.00
100	Famous Cricketers	1926	£2.60	£260.00
48	Famous Film Scenes	1935	75p	£36.00
50	Famous Footballers (Brown Back)	1926	£2.00	£100.00
100	Famous Footballers (Green Back)	1925	£1.75	£175.00
48	Famous Jockeys (Blue Printing)	1936	£1.25	£60.00
48	(Mauve Printing)	1936	£2.50	—
48	Film Episodes	1936	60p	£29.00
48	Film Partners	1935	85p	£41.00
M24/25	Flags (Silk)	1915	£7.00	—
MF48	Flying	1938	£1.50	—
50	Footballers (1-50)	1928	£2.50	£125.00
50	Footballers (51-100)	1928	£2.60	£130.00
50	Footballers in Action	1927	£2.20	£110.00
48	Garden Flowers	1938	20p	£9.00
100	How to do it	1916	£3.00	£300.00
F100	Interesting Views (Black & White)	1923	£1.30	£130.00
F100	(Coloured)	1923	£2.20	£220.00
400	Irish View Scenery (Numbered on Back)	1908	£1.50	—
400	Irish View Scenery ("Ltd" in Block Letters)	1908	75p	£300.00
F400	(Chocolate Front)	1910	£2.75	—
F400	(Plain Back)	1910	£3.00	—
F400	("Ltd" in Script)	1910	75p	£300.00
F200	Irish View Scenery (401-600)	1910	£1.75	£350.00
LF48	Island Sporting Celebrities	1938	£2.25	—
100	Kute Kiddies Series	1916	£3.50	£350.00
F50	Latest Actresses (Black & White)	1909	£12.00	£600.00
F50	(Chocolate Front)	1909	£16.50	—
50	Lawn Tennis Celebrities	1928	£4.00	£200.00
24	Motor Cars	1934	£4.50	£110.00
48	My Favourite Part	1939	75p	£36.00
MF48	Our Countryside	1938	£1.25	—
100	Plants of Commercial Value	1917	65p	£65.00
48	Portraits of Famous Stars	1935	£1.00	£48.00
48	Racing Scenes	1938	75p	£36.00
50	Regimental Colours & Standards	1899	£6.00	£300.00
100	Robinson Crusoe	1928	£1.50	£150.00
50	Royalty Series	1902	£6.00	£300.00
LF48	Scenes from the Empire	1939	30p	£15.00
48	Shots from Famous Films	1935	60p	£29.00
MF24	Shots from the Films	1936	£3.25	—
48	Signed Portraits of Famous Stars	1935	£2.00	£96.00
M20	Silk Cut Advertisement Cards	1993	—	£10.00
48	Sporting Personalities	1936	40p	£20.00
100	Sports Series	1912	£5.50	£650.00
?98	Stage & Variety Celebrities (Multi-Backed)	1899	£70.00	—

Qty		Date	Odds	Sets
48	Stars of Screen & Stage (Brown Back)	1935	£1.65	£80.00
48	(Green Back)	1935	60p	£29.00
25	The Allies Flags	1914	£4.00	£100.00
100	The Great War Series	1915	£2.20	£220.00
100	The Great War Second Series	1915	£2.30	£230.00
25	The Great War V.C. Heroes, 1st Series	1915	£4.00	£100.00
25	The Great War V.C. Heroes, 2nd Series	1915	£4.00	£100.00
25	The Great War V.C. Heroes, 3rd Series	1915	£4.00	£100.00
25	The Great War V.C. Heroes, 4th Series	1916	£4.00	£100.00
25	The Great War V.C. Heroes, 5th Series	1916	£4.00	£100.00
25	The Great War V.C. Heroes, 6th Series	1917	£4.00	£100.00
25	The Great War V.C. Heroes, 7th Series	1917	£4.00	£100.00
25	The Great War V.C. Heroes, 8th Series	1918	£4.00	£100.00
48	The Navy (Gallaher)	1937	£1.25	£60.00
48	(Park Drive)	1937	75p	£36.00
100	The Reason Why	1924	55p	£55.00
111	The South African Series	1901	£5.00	£550.00
100	The Zoo Aquarium	1924	£1.00	£100.00
48	Trains of the World	1937	£1.00	£48.00
100	Tricks & Puzzles Series (Green Back)	1913	£4.50	£550.00
100	Tricks & Puzzles Series (Black Back)	1933	£1.20	£120.00
50	Types of the British Army			
	(Battle Honours Back)	1897	£9.00	£450.00
	(Green Back)	1898	£8.00	£400.00
	(1-50, "Three Pipe Tobaccos " in Brown)	1898	£7.50	£375.00
	(1-50, "Now in Three Strengths")	1898	£7.50	£375.00
50	Types of the British Army (51-100)			
	"Three Pipe Tobaccos"(2 Printings)	1898	£7.50	£375.00
	"Now In Three Strengths"	1898	£7.50	£375.00
100	Useful Hints Series	1915	£2.75	£275.00
25	Views in North of Ireland	1912	£45.00	£1125.00
50	Votaries of the Weed	1916	£6.00	£300.00
100	Why Is It? (Brown Back)	1915	£3.00	£300.00
100	(Green Back)	1915	£2.75	£275.00
48	Wild Animals	1937	30p	£15.00
48	Wild Flowers	1939	60p	£30.00
100	Woodland Trees Series	1912	£4.50	£450.00
50	Zoo Tropical Birds, 1st Series	1928	£1.30	£65.00
50	Zoo Tropical Birds, 2nd Series	1929	£1.30	£65.00

GASPA

?14	Our Great Novelists	1930	*£60.00*	—

SAMUEL GAWITH

X25	The English Lakeland	1926	£17.50	£437.50

F. GENNARI

50	War Portraits	1916	*£90.00*	—

LOUIS GERARD LTD.

Qty		Date	Odds	Sets
50	Modern Armaments (Numbered)	1938	£1.20	£60.00
50	(Unnumbered)	1938	£1.50	£75.00
24	Screen Favourites (Gerard & Co)	1937	£3.75	—
24	(Gerard Ltd)	1937	£3.25	£78.00
48	Screen Favourites & Dancers (Matt)	1937	£2.40	£115.00
48	(Varnished)	1937	£3.00	—

GLASS & CO. LTD.

20	Actresses "BLARM"	1900	£70.00	—
10	Actresses "HAGG"	1900	£70.00	—
25	Beauties "FECKSA"	1903	*£90.00*	—
20	Boer War Cartoons	1901	*£100.00*	—
25	Boer War Celebrities "STEW"	1901	£75.00	—
16	British Royal Family	1901	£65.00	—
20	Cricketers Series	1902	*£350.00*	—
40	Naval & Military Phrases	1902	*£90.00*	—
19	Russo Japanese Series	1904	£55.00	—

R. P. GLOAG & CO.

?9	Actresses "ANGLO" (The Challenge Flat)	1896	*£200.00*	—
?9	(Citamora)	1896	*£200.00*	—
?10	Beauties "PLUMS" (Black & White, Citamora)	1896	£90.00	—
?60	(Black & White, Challenge Flat)	1896	£85.00	—
?10	(Brown, Plain Back)	1896	*£150.00*	—
?10	(Brown, Printed Back)	1896	*£150.00*	—
40	Home & Colonial Regiments	1900	£40.00	—
30	Proverbs	1901	£85.00	—
25	Types of British & Colonial Troops	1900	£50.00	—

THE GLOBE CIGARETTE CO.

25	Actresses – French	1898	£200.00	—

GOLDS LTD.

1	Advertisement Card	1905	*£300.00*	—
18	Motor Cycle Series (Blue Back)	1914	£45.00	—
18	(Grey Back Numbered)	1914	£50.00	—
18	(Grey Back Unnumbered)	1914	£60.00	—
L?21	Prints from Noted Pictures (3 Brands)	1908	*£110.00*	—
L?21	(5 Brands)	1908	*£110.00*	—
L?21	(No Firm's Name)	1908	£100.00	—

T. P. & R. GOODBODY

?23	Actresses "ANGOOD"	1898	*£175.00*	—
?10	Beauties "KEWA" (Mauve Back)	1898	*£125.00*	—
?10	(Red Back)	1898	*£125.00*	—

T. P. & R. GOODBODY — cont.

Qty		Date	Odds	Sets
25	Boer War Celebrities (Multi-Backed)	1901	£32.00	—
16	Boer War Celebrities (Different)			
	(Complete Frame, Multi-Backed)	1900	£32.00	—
	(No Vertical Lines, Multi-Backed)	1900	£35.00	—
	(2 Horizontal Lines, Multi-Backed)	1900	£35.00	—
50	Colonial Forces (Black Back)	1900	£65.00	—
50	(Brown Back)	1900	*£70.00*	—
M50	Colonial Forces	1900	*£150.00*	—
67	Dogs (Multi-Backed)	1898	£80.00	—
26	Eminent Actresses (Name At Bottom)	1900	£40.00	£1000.00
26	(Name At Top)	1900	*£125.00*	—
20	Irish Scenery (Donore Castle Cigarettes)	1905	£40.00	—
20	(Furze Blossom Cigarettes)	1905	£40.00	—
20	(Primrose Cigarettes)	1905	£40.00	—
20	(Royal Wave Cigarettes)	1905	£40.00	—
20	(Straight Cut Cigarettes)	1905	£40.00	—
?14	Pretty Girl Series "BAGG" (Grey Back)	1898	*£125.00*	—
?14	"BAGG" (Mauve Back)	1898	*£125.00*	—
?14	"BAGG" (Red Back)	1898	*£125.00*	—
?14	"BAGG" (No Brands)	1898	*£125.00*	—
50	Questions & Answers in Natural History	1924	£2.20	£110.00
25	Sports & Pastimes	1925	£6.00	£175.00
25	Types of Soldiers	1914	£55.00	—
20	War Pictures	1915	£30.00	£600.00
12	With the Flag to Pretoria	1901	£100.00	—

GORDON'S

?4	Billiards	1912	*£250.00*	—

F. GOUGH

M?	Play Up Sporting Shields	1900	*£50.00*	—

GRAVESON

30	Army Pictures, Cartoons, etc. (3 Backs)	1916	*£125.00*	—

FRED GRAY

25	Types of British Soldiers	1914	*£100.00*	—

GRIFFITHS BROS.

XF18	Beauties	1928	*£75.00*	—

GUERNSEY TOBACCO CO. (Channel Isles)

49	And When Did You Last See Your Father? (Sect.)	1936	£1.75	—
K52	Miniature Playing Cards	1933	£1.00	—
48	The Laughing Cavalier (Sect.)	1935	£2.00	—
48	The Toast (Sect., Black Back)	1936	£1.60	£77.00
48	(Sect., Green Back)	1936	*£6.50*	—

HARRIS & SONS

Qty		Date	Odds	Sets
26	Beauties "HOL"	1900	£32.00	—
30	Colonial Troops	1901	*£85.00*	—
25	Star Girls (6 Backs)	1899	£200.00	—

JAS. H. HARRISON

18	Motor Cycle Series	1914	*£70.00*	—

HARVEY & DAVY

50	Birds & Eggs	1905	£4.30	£215.00
35	Chinese & South African Series	1901	*£120.00*	—
30	Colonial Troops	1902	£75.00	—
25	Types of British & Colonial Troops	1901	*£80.00*	—

HARVEY'S NAVY CUT

M?	Play Up Sporting Shields	1900	*£45.00*	—

W. HEATON

?6	Birkby Views	1912	*£200.00*	—

HENLY & WATKINS LTD.

25	Ancient Egyptian Gods (Plain Back)	1924	£6.50	£162.50
25	(Printed Back)	1924	£6.00	—

HIGNETT BROS. & CO.

50	Actors Natural & Character Studies	1938	£1.60	£80.00
26	Actresses, "FROGA"	1900	£55.00	—
25	Actresses, Photogravure	1900	£25.00	—
28	Actresses, "PILPI" I	1901	£16.50	£462.00
F50	Actresses, "PILPI" II	1901	£11.00	£550.00
P1	Advertisement Card, Calendar Back	1884	—	*£325.00*
50	A.F.C. Nicknames	1933	£5.60	£280.00
50	Air-Raid Precautions	1939	£1.20	£60.00
60	Animal Pictures	1899	£28.50	—
50	Arms & Armour	1924	£2.70	£135.00
25	Beauties "CHOAB"	1900	*£135.00*	—
50	Beauties, Gravure (Cavalier)	1898	£70.00	—
50	(Golden Butterfly)	1898	£70.00	—
MF50	Beauties (Chess Cigarettes) (Set 1)	1927	£1.30	£65.00
MF50	(No Brand) (Set 1)	1927	£1.60	—
MF50	Beauties (Chess Cigarettes) (Set 2)	1927	£1.40	£70.00
50	British Birds & Their Eggs	1938	£2.60	£130.00
50	Broadcasting	1935	£2.50	—
19	Cabinet 1900	1900	£80.00	—
25	Cathedrals & Churches	1909	£3.25	£82.50
50	Celebrated Old Inns	1925	£2.80	£140.00
50	Champions of 1936	1936	£2.75	—
25	Common Objects of the Sea-Shore	1924	£2.20	£55.00
25	Company Drill	1915	£3.40	£85.00

HIGNETT BROS. & CO. — cont.

Qty		Date	Odds	Sets
50	Coronation Procession	1937	£2.00	—
P8	Counter Display Cards – Beauties	1890	*£250.00*	—
X6	Diamond Jubilee	1897	*£250.00*	—
50	Dogs	1936	£2.10	£105.00
50	Football Caricatures	1935	£3.20	£160.00
50	Football Club Captains	1936	£3.20	£160.00
25	Greetings of the World	1907	£2.60	£65.00
25	Historical London	1926	£2.60	£65.00
50	How to Swim	1935	£1.00	£50.00
50	Interesting Buildings	1905	£5.50	£275.00
25	International Caps and Badges	1924	£3.60	£90.00
25	Life in Pond & Stream	1925	£3.00	£75.00
40	Medals	1900	£25.00	—
25	Military Portraits	1914	£4.40	£110.00
50	Modern Railways	1936	£2.60	£130.00
25	Modern Statesmen (Butterfly Cigarettes)	1906	£4.50	£112.50
25	(Pioneer Cigarettes)	1906	£4.50	£112.50
20	Music Hall Artistes	1898	£55.00	£1100.00
50	Ocean Greyhounds	1938	£1.60	£80.00
M1	Oracle Butterfly (Several Printings)	1898	—	£80.00
25	Panama Canal	1914	£6.00	£150.00
12	Pretty Girl Series "RASH"	1900	£50.00	£600.00
50	Prominent Cricketers of 1938	1938	£3.20	£160.00
50	Prominent Racehorses of 1933	1934	£2.50	£125.00
G1	Riddle Folder	1893	—	*£250.00*
50	Sea Adventure	1939	60p	£30.00
25	Ships, Flags & Cap Badges, A Series	1926	£4.20	£110.00
25	Ships, Flags & Cap Badges, 2nd Series	1927	£4.20	£110.00
50	Shots from the Films	1936	£3.50	£175.00
X6	Story of a Boy who robs a Stork's Nest	1890	*£250.00*	—
25	The Prince of Wales Empire Tour	1924	£2.00	£50.00
50	Trick Billiards	1934	£4.00	—
25	Turnpikes	1927	£2.40	£60.00
P8	Uniforms & Armies of Countries	1899	*£250.00*	—
25	V.C. Heroes	1901	£50.00	£1250.00
20	Yachts (Black Back)	1898	£60.00	—
20	(White Back)	1898	£65.00	—
50	Zoo Studies	1937	£1.00	£50.00

R. & J. HILL LTD.

28 Page Reference Book — £3.50

25	Actresses-Belle of New York (39mm Wide)	1899	£22.00	£550.00
25	Actresses-Belle of New York (41mm Wide)	1899	£24.00	£600.00
20	Actresses-Chocolate (Hill Cigarettes)	1917	£17.00	—
20	(Hill Tobaccos)	1917	£17.00	—
20	(Plain Back)	1917	£17.00	—
30	Actresses-Continental (Whisky Back)	1906	£17.50	—
30	(Seven Wonders)	1906	£16.00	£480.00
30	(Plain Back)	1906	£17.50	—
26	Actresses "FROGA"	1900	£55.00	—
16	Actresses "HAGG" (High Class Cigarettes)	1900	£32.50	—
16	(Stockrider)	1900	£32.50	—

Qty		Date	Odds	Sets
20	Animal Series (Crowfoot Cigarettes)	1909	£25.00	—
20	(Hill's)	1909	£26.00	—
20	(Anonymous, Cigarettes Back)	1909	*£27.50*	—
20	(Anonymous, Space at Base)	1909	£24.00	—
20	(Anonymous, Plain Back)	1909	£24.00	—
F25	Artistas Teatrais Portuguesos	1924	*£35.00*	—
25	Aviation Series (Hill Name)	1934	£3.20	£80.00
25	(Gold Flake Honeydew)	1934	£3.20	£80.00
?17	Battleships (Printed Back)	1914	*£150.00*	—
?17	(Plain Back)	1914	£42.50	—
25	Battleships & Crests	1901	£17.50	£437.50
12	Boer War Generals – Campaigners	1901	£32.00	£384.00
20	Breeds of Dogs (Archer's M.F.H.)	1914	£19.00	—
20	(Badminton)	1914	£19.00	—
20	(Spinet Tobacco)	1914	£19.00	—
20	(Verbena Mixture)	1914	£19.00	—
L30	Britain's Stately Homes (Silk)	1917	£3.60	£108.00
?48	British Navy Series	1902	£25.00	—
L40	Canvas Masterpieces Series 1 (Badminton)	1916	£1.25	£50.00
L40	(Spinet)	1916	£2.00	£80.00
L40	Canvas Masterpieces Series 2 (Silk)	1922	£2.50	£100.00
X10	Canvas Masterpieces Series 2 (Silk)	1916	£2.00	—
50	Caricatures of Famous Cricketers	1926	£3.00	£150.00
L50	Caricatures of Famous Cricketers	1926	£2.00	£100.00
?	Celebrated Pictures	1905	*£150.00*	—
50	Celebrities of Sport (Hill Name)	1939	£2.00	£100.00
50	(Gold Flake)	1939	£3.50	—
P4/5	Chinese Pottery & Porcelain (Silk)	1915	50p	£2.00
P5	(Complete Set).	1915	—	£30.00
X11	Chinese Pottery & Porcelain 2 (Silk)	1915	£5.00	—
10	Chinese Series	1912	£65.00	—
35	Cinema Celebrities (Spinet House)	1936	£1.00	£35.00
35	(Anonymous)	1936	£1.00	£35.00
30	Colonial Troops (Leading Lines)	1901	£22.50	£675.00
30	(Perfection Vide Dress)	1901	£22.00	£660.00
50	(Sweet American)	1901	£21.00	£1050.00
40	Crystal Palace Souvenir Cards (Matt)	1937	£2.20	£88.00
40	(Varnished)	1937	£1.60	£64.00
48	Decorations and Medals (Hill Back)	1940	£1.50	£75.00
48	(Gold Flake)	1940	£3.00	—
F48	Famous Cinema Celebrities (Spinet – 2 Printings) .	1931	£4.25	—
F48	(No Brand)	1931	£3.75	£180.00
LF48	Famous Cinema Celebrities, Series A (Kadi)	1931	*£4.00*	—
LF48	(No Brand)..	1931	£4.00	—
F50	Famous Cinema Celebrities, Series C (Devon)	1932	*£6.50*	—
F50	(Toucan)	1932	£6.50	—
F50	(No Brand)..	1932	£3.50	—
LF50	Famous Cinema Celebrities, Series D (Kadi)	1932	£3.25	—
LF50	(No Brand)..	1932	£4.25	—
28	Famous Cricketers Series (Blue Back)	1912	£60.00	—
28	(Red Back)	1912	£60.00	—
40	Famous Cricketers	1923	£4.75	£190.00
50	Famous Cricketers, including the S. African Team	1925	£4.80	£240.00
L50	Famous Cricketers, including the S. African Team	1925	£5.20	£260.00
50	Famous Dog Breeds	1952	£8.00	—

Qty		Date	Odds	Sets
L30	Famous Engravings, Series XI	1910	£4.00	£120.00
40	Famous Film Stars (English Text)	1938	£1.10	£44.00
40	(Arabic Text)	1938	£1.00	£40.00
20	Famous Footballers Series	1912	£22.00	£440.00
50	Famous Footballers (Brown)	1923	£3.40	£170.00
50	Famous Footballers (Coloured, Archer)	1939	£2.40	£120.00
50	(Coloured, With Address)	1939	£2.20	£110.00
25	Famous Footballers, Additional (51-75)	1939	£2.60	£65.00
25	Famous Pictures (Fine Art Cigarettes)	1913	£3.40	£85.00
25	(Cigarette Series)	1913	£3.50	£87.50
50	Famous Ships (Matt)	1940	£1.50	£75.00
50	(Varnished)	1940	£1.00	£50.00
48	Film Stars and Celebrity Dancers	1935	£1.40	£67.00
30	Flags & Flags with Soldiers	1901	£23.00	—
24	Flags, Arms & Types of Nations	1910	£10.00	£240.00
20	Football Captain Series (Large Print)	1906	£42.50	—
20	(Small Print)	1906	£32.50	—
20	Fragments from France (Coloured)	1916	£22.50	£450.00
10	(Buff)	1916	£25.00	£250.00
10	(Black & White)	1916	£75.00	—
L23	Great War Leaders, Series 10 (Silk)	1917	£5.00	£115.00
50	Historic Places from Dickens' Classics	1926	50p	£25.00
L50	Historic Places from Dickens' Classics (2 Printings)	1926	50p	£25.00
50	Holiday Resorts (Brown Back)	1925	£1.25	—
50	(Green Back)	1925	60p	£30.00
L50	Holiday Resorts (Brown Back)	1925	£1.25	—
L50	(Green Back)	1925	80p	£40.00
20	Inventors & Their Inventions (1-20)	1907	£4.00	£80.00
20	Inventors & Their Inventions (21-40)	1908	£7.00	£140.00
15	Japanese Series (Black & White)	1904	£42.00	£630.00
15	(Black & White, Lind Back)	1904	*£125.00*	—
15	(Coloured, Blue Panel)	1904	*£125.00*	—
15	(Coloured, Red Panel)	1904	£62.50	—
20	Lighthouse Series (No Frame Line)	1903	£34.00	£680.00
30	(With Frame Line)	1903	£32.50	£975.00
50	Magical Puzzles	1938	£2.00	£100.00
50	Modern Beauties	1939	£1.00	£50.00
30	Music Hall Celebrities – Past & Present	1930	£2.30	£69.00
L30	Music Hall Celebrities – Past & Present	1930	£2.30	£69.00
20	National Flag Series (Printed Back)	1914	£7.50	£150.00
20	(Plain Back)	1914	£6.50	£130.00
30	Nature Pictures	1930	£1.00	£30.00
30	Nautical Songs	1937	£1.20	£36.00
M25	Naval Series (Unnumbered)	1901	£45.00	—
20	Naval Series (Numbered 21-40)	1911	£12.00	£240.00
10	Naval Series (Numbered 41-50)	1911	£55.00	—
30	Our Empire Series	1929	35p	£10.50
L30	Our Empire Series	1929	50p	£15.00
M30	Popular Footballers, Series A	1935	£3.00	£90.00
M20	Popular Footballers, Series B	1935	£3.40	£68.00
20	Prince of Wales Series	1911	£11.00	£220.00
50	Public Schools and Colleges	1923	60p	£30.00
L50	Public Schools and Colleges	1923	60p	£30.00

R. & J. HILL LTD. — cont.

Qty		*Date*	*Odds*	*Sets*
75	Public Schools and Colleges	1923	80p	£60.00
L75	Public Schools and Colleges	1923	90p	£67.50
50	Puzzle Series	1937	£1.30	£65.00
42	Real Photographs Set 1 (Space at Back)	1930	£2.50	—
F42	(Space at Back)	1930	£2.50	—
42	(London Idol)	1930	£2.20	£92.50
F42	(London Idol)	1930	£2.40	—
F42	Real Photographs Set 2	1930	£3.00	—
20	Rhymes	1904	£25.00	£500.00
F50	Scenes from the Films	1934	£3.25	—
40	Scenes from the Films	1938	80p	£32.00
35	Scientific Inventions and Discoveries (Black/White)	1929	£1.00	£35.00
35	(Coloured)	1929	£1.20	£42.00
20	(Plain Back)	1934	£1.35	£27.00
L35	Scientific Inventions and Discoveries (Coloured)	1929	£1.20	£42.00
F50	Sports	1934	£4.40	£220.00
F50	Sports Series (as above)	1934	*£10.00*	—
F50	Sports Series (as above, no title)	1934	*£10.00*	—
30	Statuary Set 1 (Matt Front)	1898	*£35.00*	—
30	(Varnished)	1898	£10.00	—
30	Statuary Set 2	1899	£7.50	£225.00
26	Statuary Set 3 (Black Panel)	1898	£25.00	—
26	(Grey Panel)	1898	*£50.00*	—
26	(White Panel)	1898	£24.00	—
30	The All Blacks	1924	£6.00	£180.00
50	The Railway Centenary, A Series	1925	£1.25	£62.50
L50	The Railway Centenary, A Series (Brown Back)	1925	£1.25	£62.50
L50	(Grey Back)	1925	£3.25	—
25	The Railway Centenary, 2nd Series	1925	£1.60	£40.00
L25	The Railway Centenary, 2nd Series	1925	£1.80	£45.00
25	The River Thames (1-25)	1924	£1.60	£40.00
25	The River Thames (26-50)	1924	£1.30	£32.50
L50	The River Thames (Green Back)	1924	£1.30	£65.00
100	Transfers	1935	£6.00	—
20	Types of the British Army (Badminton)	1914	£26.50	—
20	(Verbena)	1914	£26.50	—
LF48	Views of Interest, 1st Series (Spinet)	1938	25p	£12.00
LF48	(Sunripe)	1938	25p	£12.00
LF48	Views of Interest, 2nd Series	1938	25p	£12.00
LF48	Views of Interest, 3rd Series	1939	25p	£12.00
LF48	Views of Interest, 4th Series	1939	35p	£17.00
LF48	Views of Interest, 5th Series	1939	35p	£17.00
LF48	Views of Interest – Canada	1940	25p	£12.00
LF48	Views of Interest – India	1940	£2.50	£120.00
50	Views of London	1925	75p	£37.50
L50	Views of London	1925	80p	£40.00
L50	Views of The River Thames (Green & Black)	1924	£1.40	£70.00
25	War Series	1915	£11.00	£275.00
50	Who's Who in British Films	1927	£1.60	£80.00
L50	Who's Who in British Films	1927	£1.70	£85.00
84	Wireless Telephony	1923	£1.30	£110.00
L20	Wireless Telephony – Broadcasting Series	1923	£2.50	£50.00
25	World's Masterpieces, Second Series	1914	£2.00	£50.00
50	Zoological Series	1924	80p	£40.00
L50	Zoological Series	1924	90p	£45.00

L. HIRST & SON

Qty		*Date*	*Odds*	*Sets*
T25	Soldiers & Their Uniforms (Cut-outs)	1914	*£125.00*	—

J. W. HOBSON

18	Motor Cycle Series	1914	£85.00	—

HOCKINGS BAZAAR, PORTHCAWL

30	Army Pictures, Cartoons, etc	1916	*£100.00*	—

J. & T. HODGE

?4	Britain's Naval Crests	1896	*£300.00*	—
16	British Royal Family	1901	*£140.00*	—
?11	Scottish Views (Size 74 x 39mm)	1898	*£125.00*	—
?10	(Size 80 x 45mm)	1898	*£125.00*	—

HOOK OF HOLLAND CIGARETTES

?5	Footballers	1900	*£250.00*	—

HUDDEN & CO.

26	Actresses "FROGA"	1900	£60.00	—
25	Beauties "CHOAB"	1901	£50.00	—
20	Beauties, Crown Seal	1898	£125.00	—
24	Beauties "HUMPS" (Blue Back)	1899	£65.00	—
24	(Orange Back – 2 Printings)	1899	£40.00	—
24	(Type Set Back)	1899	*£200.00*	—
12	Comic Phrases	1900	£100.00	—
25	Famous Boxers	1927	*£32.50*	—
25	Flags of all Nations	1904	£22.00	£550.00
48	Japanese Playing Cards (Dandy Dot)	1900	*£120.00*	—
48	(Hudden's Cigarettes)	1900	£80.00	—
18	Pretty Girl Series "RASH"	1900	£75.00	—
50	Public Schools and Colleges	1924	£2.00	£100.00
25	Soldiers of the Century	1903	£40.00	£1000.00
25	Sports and Pastimes	1926	£55.00	—
25	Star Girls	1900	£90.00	—
25	Types of Smokers	1903	£40.00	—

HUDSON'S

?26	Actresses "ANGOOD"	1898	*£225.00*	—
25	Beauties "BOCCA"	1900	*£225.00*	—

HUNTER

?11	Footballers	1910	*£500.00*	—

MULTI-BACKS

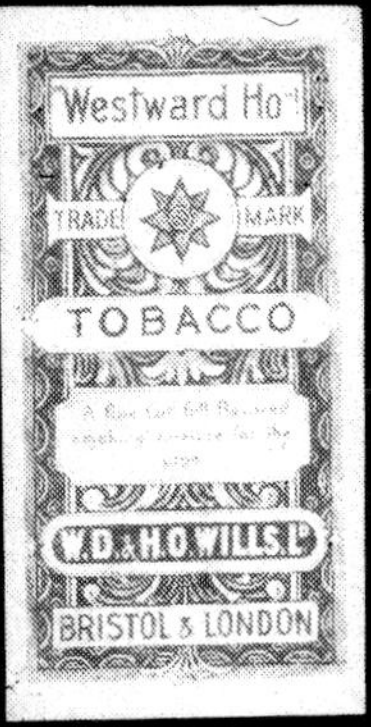

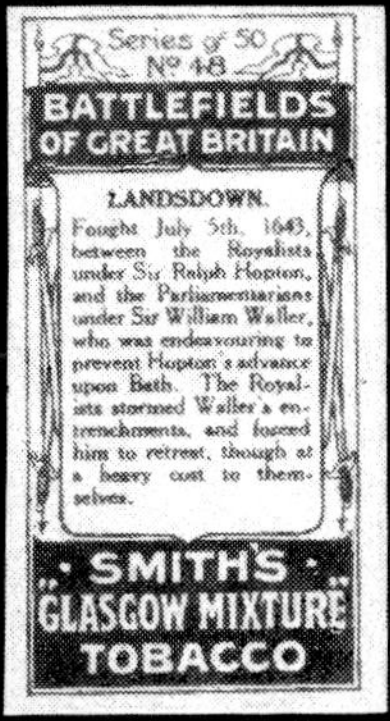

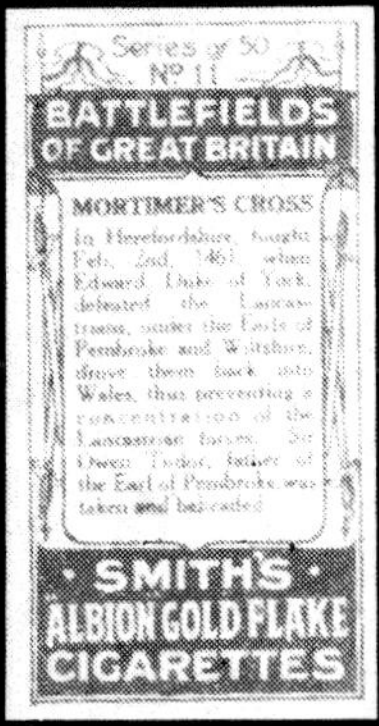

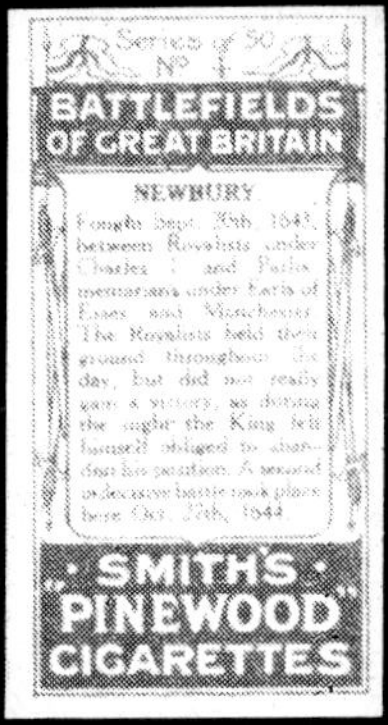

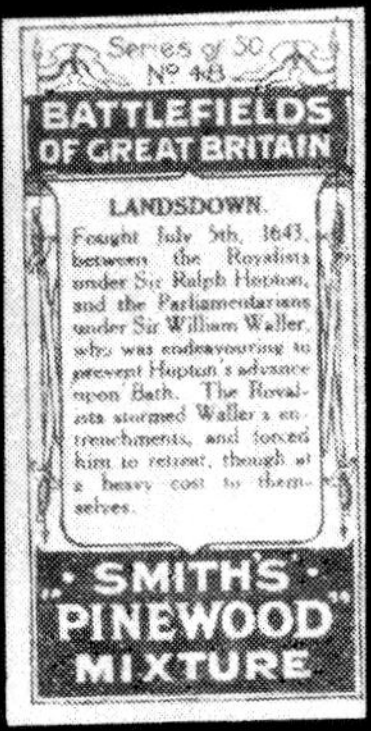

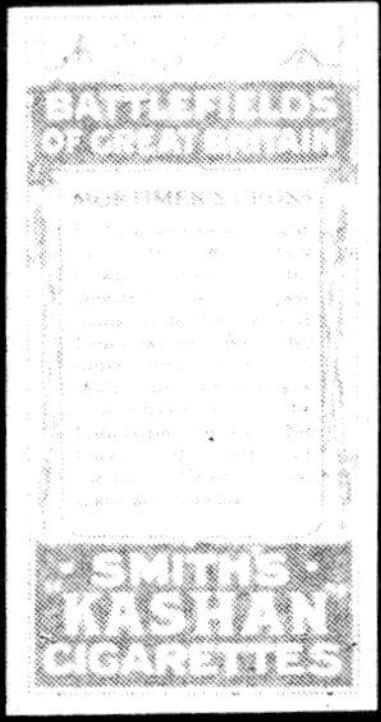

There are many instances in the enlarged catalogue when a set by one issuer is noted as occurring in more than one back. For example, each card in Wills Seaside Resorts can be found with six different brands advertised, while in the case of Smith Battlefields of Great Britain each number can have no less than 15 different advertisements!

In addition to these varieties there are also many series, particular among the earlier issues, where there are different backs, but not every front may be found with every back. These are known as multi-backs. A good example of this is the Wills set Sports of All Nations, which like Seaside Resorts also has six advertisements; however in this case each number only occurs with two different brands, and these run in distinct groups of numbers. The issues of Smith are also an excellent source of multi-backed series, with many series including Champions of Sport, Medals and Phil May Sketches featuring prominently. Indeed the Smith issues are so complicated that it has been necessary to publish a separate Reference Book detailing all the varieties known.

In the catalogue we now show when a series is multi-backed, but without indicating all the options available; this would have been too complicated, especially for a series such as Adkin Pretty Girl Series RASH, with its 50 different backs! Most type collectors would probably wish to obtain one of each of these multi-backs, and full information is normally to be found in the Cartophilic Society's Reference Books.

One additional term worth remembering is "vari-backed". This is used when there are different advertisements on the back, but where each front can be found with one back only.

DISSIMILAR SERIES

When a firm decides to issue a new set of cards it may have undertaken some market research, but it will never be certain how successful it may become. If the response is positive it may then produce an extra set, which would normally be distinguished as 2nd or continuation series. In the case of Lea's Pottery or Ogden Boy Scouts this extended to five series. Sometimes when a subject appeared popular, different aspects would be covered by sets with different titles, as in the case of Player with their aircraft sets and Ogden with its racing series.

Sometimes a popular series was extended by producing it in different sizes. Apart from the better known multi sized sets such as those of International T.C. and Jackson, there are examples where the small and large cards depict different subjects. These include Wills English Period Costumes, Baker Actresses and Carreras Old Staffordshire Figures.

Another quite complicated situation can occur when a Company decides to issue a completely new series under the same title as an earlier set. Wills were very fond of this, with two or more series titled Wild Flowers, Association Footballers, Garden Flowers and Speed. Ogden too issued a later set of Boy Scouts some years after its first five, but its newer series of Bird's Eggs and British Birds were easily distinguishable by being cut-outs!

Finally, there is a group of series which are not quite the same. There are series where the pictures have been re-drawn, and show minor differences. These include two sets by Gallaher—Boy Scouts and the first series of Champions; also half the set of Carreras Famous Footballers and Huntley & Palmer's Sports.

JAMES ILLINGWORTH LTD.

Qty		*Date*	*Odds*	*Sets*
MF48	Beautiful Scotland	1939	£2.00	£96.00
M25	Cavalry	1924	£5.00	£125.00
MF48	Coastwise	1938	£1.00	£48.00
25	'Comicartoons' of Sport	1927	£5.60	£140.00
MF48	Flying	1938	£1.75	£84.00
25	Motor Car Bonnets	1925	£7.20	£180.00
25	Old Hostels	1926	£5.50	£137.50
MF48	Our Countryside	1938	£2.00	—
MF24	Shots from the Films	1937	£4.50	—
25	Views from the English Lakes	1894	£150.00	—

IMPERIAL TOBACCO CO. LTD.

50	British Birds	1909	£4.60	£230.00
X1	Coronation Folder	1902	—	£85.00
T12	Russ Abbot Advertising Cards	1993	—	£12.00

INGRAMS (Eastleigh) (Tobacconist)

30	Army Pictures, Cartoons, etc.	1916	*£100.00*	—

INTERNATIONAL TOBACCO CO. LTD.

28	Domino Cards	1938	20p	£5.50
D50	Famous Buildings & Monuments, Series A			
	(International Tobacco Co. Ltd.)	1934	90p	£45.00
	(International Tobacco (Overseas) Ltd.)	1934	£1.30	—
D50	Famous Buildings & Monuments, Series B	1934	£1.60	—
100	Film Favourites (Black Back)	1937	£2.00	
100	(Brown Back)	1937	£1.80	£180.00
D100	Gentlemen! The King! (Black Back)	1938	20p	£20.00
D100	(Blue Back)	1938	50p	—
50	International Code of Signals	1934	90p	£45.00
48	Screen Lovers (Summit)	Unissued	£3.00	£144.00

PETER JACKSON

F28	Beautiful Scotland	1939	£1.25	£35.00
MF48	Beautiful Scotland	1939	£1.00	£48.00
F28	Coastwise	1938	£1.25	£35.00
MF48	Coastwise	1938	£1.25	£60.00
F28	Famous Film Stars	1935	£3.50	£100.00
F27	Famous Films	1934	£3.50	£95.00
F28	Film Scenes	1936	£3.50	£100.00
LF28	Film Scenes (Different)	1936	£4.50	£126.00
F28	Flying	1938	£3.00	£84.00
MF48	Flying	1938	£3.25	—
D100	Gentlemen! The King!			
	(Overprinted on Black International)	1938	£1.00	—
	(Overprinted on Blue International)	1938	£1.00	—
	(Reprinted Black with Jackson Name)	1938	£1.00	—
	(Reprinted Blue with Jackson Name)	1938	*£2.00*	—

PETER JACKSON — cont.

Qty		Date	Odds	Sets
F28	Life in the Navy	1937	£1.65	£46.50
LF28	Life in the Navy (Different)	1937	£2.40	£67.50
F28	Our Countryside	1938	£1.00	£28.00
MF48	Our Countryside	1938	£1.25	—
F28	Shots from the Films	1937	£3.00	£84.00
MF24	Shots from the Films	1937	£3.50	£84.00
D250	Speed through the Ages (Mixed Sizes)	1937	25p	£62.50
F28	Stars in Famous Films	1934	£3.50	£98.00
D150	The Pageant of Kingship (P. Jackson)	1937	50p	—
D150	(P. Jackson Overseas Ltd.)	1937	30p	£45.00

JACOBI BROS. & CO. LTD.

?32	Boer War Celebrities "JASAS"	1901	*£130.00*	—

JAMES & CO. (B'HAM) LTD.

M20	Arms of Countries	1915	£120.00	—

JAMES'S

?11	Pretty Girl Series "BAGG"	1898	*£225.00*	—

JERSEY TOBACCO CO. LTD. (Channel Isles)

K53	Miniature Playing Cards	1933	85p	—

SOCIETE JOB (J. Bardou & Co.)

25	British Lighthouses	1925	£6.50	£162.50
M48	Cinema Stars (Numbered)	1926	*£6.50*	—
M48	Cinema Stars (Unnumbered)	1926	£1.00	£75.00
48	Cinema Stars (Numbered)	1926	£3.00	—
48	Cinema Stars (Unnumbered)	1926	£3.00	—
25	Dogs	1911	£22.00	£550.00
25	Liners	1912	£30.00	—
53	Miniature Playing Cards	1926	*£6.50*	—
25	Orders of Chivalry	1924	£3.40	£85.00
25	Orders of Chivalry, 2nd Series	1927	£3.40	£85.00
3	Orders of Chivalry (Unnumbered)	1927	£8.00	£24.00
25	Racehorses	1909	£22.00	£550.00

GERMAN ISSUES

X70	Sport in Zehn Bildern	1930	*£2.50*	—

J. B. JOHNSON & CO.

25	National Flags and Flowers – Girls	1901	*£150.00*	—

JOHNSTON'S

Qty		*Date*	*Odds*	*Sets*
?1	British Views	1910	*£200.00*	—

JONES BROS.

10/13	Spurs Footballers	1911	£10.00	£100.00
4/6	Spurs Footballers	1912	£10.00	£40.00

A. I. JONES & CO. LTD.

M1	Advertisement Card	1901	—	*£350.00*
12	Nautical Terms	1905	£45.00	£540.00

ALEX JONES & CO.

?23	Actresses "ANGOOD" (Brown Front)	1898	*£140.00*	—
?23	(Green Front)	1898	*£150.00*	—
1	Diamond Jubilee 1897	1897	—	£135.00

A. S. JONES

30	Army Pictures, Cartoons, etc	1916	*£100.00*	—

T. E. JONES & CO.

?12	Conundrums	1900	*£140.00*	—
50	Flags of All Nations	1899	*£80.00*	—
16	Well-known Proverbs	1900	*£140.00*	—
50	Welsh Rugby Players	1900	*£135.00*	—

C. H. JORDEN LTD.

F12	Celebrities of the Great War	1915	£75.00	—

J. & E. KENNEDY

25	Beauties "FECKSA"	1902	£50.00	—

RICHARD KENNEDY

P?24	Army & Navy Cartoons	1906	*£150.00*	—
50	War Portraits	1916	*£85.00*	—

KINNEAR LTD.

13	Actresses	1899	£110.00	—
M1	A Gentleman in Kharki	1900	—	£67.50
15	Australian Cricket Team	1897	£200.00	—
?17	Cricketers	1898	*£350.00*	—
X1	Cricket Fixture Folder	1903	—	*£500.00*
25	Footballers & Club Colours	1898	£150.00	—
12	Jockeys, Set 1	1898	£55.00	£660.00

KINNEAR LTD. — cont.

Qty		Date	Odds	Sets
1	Jockeys, Tod Sloan	1898	—	£90.00
?4	Jockeys (Different), (Large Caption)	1898	£100.00	—
25	(Small Caption)	1898	£95.00	—
2	Prominent Personages	1902	*£300.00*	—
13	Royalty	1897	£40.00	£520.00
L1	The Four Generations	1900	—	*£225.00*
K?32	Views	1898	*£400.00*	—

KINNEAR, WHITWHAM & CO. LTD.

18	Motor Cycle Series	1914	*£100.00*	—

B. KRIEGSFELD & CO.

1	Advertisement Card	1900	—	*£500.00*
?61	Beauties "KEWA" (Matt Front)	1898	£75.00	—
?6	(Semi Glossy Front)	1898	*£140.00*	—
?10	Celebrities (Horizontal Back)	1901	*£150.00*	—
?10	(Vertical Back)	1901	£150.00	—
50	Flags of All Nations	1899	£65.00	—
50	Phrases & Advertisements	1900	£75.00	—

A. KUIT LTD.

K?12	Arms of Cambridge Colleges	1914	*£80.00*	—
K?12	Arms of Companies	1914	*£80.00*	—
F30	British Beauties (Oval)	1914	£50.00	—
F?43	Crosmedo Bijou Cards	1915	*£115.00*	—
25	Principal Streets of British Cities & Towns	1915	£100.00	—
F50	Types of Beauty	1914	£100.00	—

L. & Y. TOBACCO MFG. CO.

26	Actresses "FROGA"	1900	*£200.00*	—

LAMBERT & BUTLER

32 Page Reference Book — £3.50

10	Actresses & Their Autographs (Narrow, Tobaccos)	1898	£125.00	—
10	(Wide, Cigarettes)	1898	£140.00	—
20	Actresses "BLARM"	1900	£27.50	—
50	Admirals (Mixed Backs)	1900	—	£800.00
50	(Bird's Eye)	1900	£16.00	—
50	(Flaked Gold Leaf Honeydew)	1900	£16.00	—
50	(May Blossom)	1900	£16.00	—
50	(Viking)	1900	£16.00	—
1	Advertisement Card	1898	—	£325.00
50	Aeroplane Markings	1937	£1.80	£90.00
25	A History of Aviation (Brown Front)	1933	£2.60	£65.00
25	A History of Aviation (Green Front)	1932	£2.00	£50.00
40	Arms of Kings & Queens of England	1906	£4.50	£180.00
25	Aviation	1915	£3.60	£90.00
26	Beauties "HOL" (Mixed Backs)	1899	—	£780.00
26	(Flaked Gold Leaf)	1899	£30.00	—
26	(Log Cabin)	1899	£30.00	—
26	(May Blossom)	1899	£30.00	—
26	(Viking Navy Cut)	1899	£30.00	—

Qty		Date	Odds	Sets
50	Birds & Eggs	1906	£2.80	£140.00
25	Boer War & Boxer Rebellion – Sketches	1901	£30.00	—
20	Boer War Generals "CLAM" (Black Back)	1901	£30.00	—
20	(Brown Back)	1901	£30.00	—
10	Boer War Generals "FLAC"	1901	£35.00	—
25	British Trees & Their Uses	1927	£1.60	£40.00
1	Colonel R.S.S. Baden-Powell, The King of Scouts	1901	—	*£350.00*
25	Common Fallacies	1928	£2.00	£50.00
50	Conundrums (Blue Back)	1901	£20.00	—
50	(Green Back)	1901	£15.00	£750.00
12	Coronation Robes	1902	£17.50	£210.00
25	Dance Band Leaders	1936	£4.00	£100.00
28	Dominoes (Packets)	1955	£4.00	—
50	Empire Air Routes	1936	£1.80	£90.00
25	Famous British Airmen & Airwomen	1935	£1.60	£40.00
25	Fauna of Rhodesia	1929	90p	£22.50
50	Find Your Way! (Drury Lane In Address)	1932	£1.40	£70.00
50	(Without Drury Lane)	1932	£1.40	£70.00
50	(Red Overprint)	1932	£1.50	£75.00
1	Find Your Way Joker Card	1932	—	£12.00
50	Footballers 1930-1	1931	£3.60	£180.00
25	Garden Life	1930	80p	£20.00
25	Hints & Tips for Motorists	1929	£3.60	£90.00
50	Horsemanship	1938	£2.30	£115.00
25	How Motor Cars Work	1931	£2.40	£60.00
50	Interesting Customs & Traditions of the Navy, Army & Air Force	1939	£1.00	£50.00
25	Interesting Musical Instruments	1929	£2.60	£65.00
50	Interesting Sidelights on the Work of the G.P.O.	1939	£1.00	£50.00
20	International Yachts, American v England since 1871	1902	£55.00	£1100.00
25	Japanese Series	1904	£6.50	£162.50
4	Jockeys (No Frame)	1902	£50.00	£200.00
10	Jockeys (With Frame, Different)	1902	£50.00	—
50	Keep Fit	1937	90p	£45.00
25	London Characters	1934	£2.20	£55.00
25	Motor Car Radiators	1928	£5.50	£137.50
25	Motor Cars, A Series (Green Back)	1922	£2.50	£62.50
25	Motor Cars, 2nd Series (26-50)	1923	£2.50	£62.50
50	Motor Cars, 3rd Series	1926	£3.80	£190.00
25	Motor Cars (Grey Back)	1934	£3.50	£87.50
50	Motor Cycles	1923	£3.40	£170.00
50	Motor Index Marks	1926	£2.50	£125.00
25	Motors	1908	£26.00	£650.00
25	Naval Portraits (Series of 25)	1914	£3.40	£85.00
50	(Series of 50)	1915	£3.40	£170.00
25	Pirates & Highwaymen	1926	£1.60	£40.00
25	Rhodesian Series	1928	£1.00	£25.00
X1	The Mayblossom Calendar 1900	1899	—	*£400.00*
50	The Thames from Lechlade to London			
	(Large Numerals)	1907	£6.00	—
	(Small Numerals)	1907	£5.50	£275.00
25	Third Rhodesian Series	1930	50p	£12.50
4	Types of the British Army & Navy			
	(Black Specialities Back)	1897	£65.00	—
	(Brown Specialities Back)	1897	£60.00	£240.00
	(Viking Cigarettes)	1897	£67.50	—

LAMBERT & BUTLER — cont.

Qty		Date	Odds	Sets
PF?	Warships	1910	*£50.00*	—
25	Waverley Series	1904	£11.00	£275.00
25	Winter Sports	1914	£3.80	£95.00
25	Wireless Telegraphy	1909	£4.50	£112.50
25	Wonders of Nature	1924	50p	£12.50
25	World's Locomotives (Series of 25)	1912	£3.60	£90.00
50	(Series of 50)	1912	£4.50	£225.00
25	World's Locomotives (Additional)	1913	£4.00	£100.00

OVERSEAS ISSUES

Qty		Date	Odds	Sets
50	Actors & Actresses "WALP"	1908	£3.00	—
250	Actresses "ALWICS" (With Firm's Name)	1905	£3.00	—
250	(Scout Cigarettes)	1905	£3.40	—
250	(Black Front)	1905	£6.50	—
250	(Mauve Front, 4 Backs)	1905	*£12.50*	—
250	(Red Portrait)	1905	*£12.50*	—
50	Beauties "LAWHA" (Scout Cigarettes)	1908	£3.50	—
50	(No Brand, Black, 2 Editions)	1908	£3.25	—
50	(No Brand, Unicoloured)	1908	*£12.50*	—
83	Danske Byvaabner	1926	£15.00	—
26	Etchings (Dogs)	1928	*£25.00*	—
L26	Etchings (Dogs)	1928	*£30.00*	—
25	Flag Girls of All Nations	1910	£12.50	£312.50
F50	Homeland Events	1928	*£2.00*	—
?1	Indian Women (Blue Front)	1910	*£50.00*	—
?1	(Red Front)	1910	*£50.00*	—
25	London Characters	1934	*£12.50*	—
F50	London Zoo	1927	£1.20	£60.00
50	Merchant Ships of the World	1924	£2.25	£112.50
30	Music Hall Celebrities	1906	£4.50	—
F50	Popular Film Stars (Title in 1 Line)	1925	£1.25	£62.50
F50	(Title in 2 Lines)	1925	£1.25	£62.50
F50	(Varsity Cigarettes)	1926	£2.25	£112.50
100	Royalty Notabilities & Events 1900-2	1902	£12.50	—
100	Russo Japanese Series	1905	£5.50	£550.00
F50	The Royal Family at Home and Abroad	1927	£1.30	£65.00
F50	The World of Sport	1927	£1.80	£90.00
F50	Types of Modern Beauty	1927	£1.00	£50.00
F50	Who's Who in Sport (1926)	1926	£1.60	£180.00
50	Zoological Studies	1928	*£4.00*	—

LAMBKIN BROS.

Qty		Date	Odds	Sets
36	Country Scenes (Series 1-6)	1924	£5.50	—
L36	Country Scenes (Series 7-12)	1926	£6.50	—
L?9	Irish Views (Plain Back)	1925	£30.00	—
L?5	Lily of Killarney Views	1925	£100.00	—

LAMPORT & HOLT

Qty		Date	Odds	Sets
L1	T.S.S. Vandyke and Voltaire (2 Printings)	1930	—	£3.00

ED. LAURENS LTD.

Qty		Date	Odds	Sets
M55	British Cavalry Uniforms (P/C Inset)	1975	—	£60.00

C. & J. LAW

Qty		Date	Odds	Sets
25	Types of British Soldiers	1914	£25.00	£625.00
50	War Portraits	1915	*£90.00*	—

R. J. LEA LTD.

1	Advertisement Card	1913	*£750.00*	—
M12	Butterflies & Moths (Silk)	1924	£4.75	£57.00
L12	Butterflies & Moths (Silk, Different)	1924	£4.50	£54.00
P6	Butterflies & Moths (Silk, Different)	1924	£5.00	£30.00
12	Chairman Puzzles	1910	*£200.00*	—
70	Cigarette Transfers (Locomotives)	1916	£7.00	£490.00
25	Civilians of Countries Fighting with the Allies	1914	£11.00	£275.00
F48	Coronation Souvenir (Glossy, Lea Back)	1937	60p	£29.00
F48	(Glossy, Successors)	1937	50p	£24.00
48	(Matt, Lea Back)	1937	80p	£40.00
48	(Matt, Successors)	1937	60p	£29.00
MF48	Coronation Souvenir	1937	60p	£30.00
25	Dogs (1-25)	1923	£4.00	£100.00
25	Dogs (26-50)	1923	£6.00	—
25	English Birds (Glossy)	1922	£2.60	£65.00
25	(Matt)	1922	£5.60	£140.00
F54	Famous Film Stars	1939	£1.25	£67.50
F48	Famous Racehorses of 1926	1927	£2.50	£120.00
MF48	Famous Racehorses of 1926	1927	£4.50	—
F48	Famous Views (Glossy)	1936	25p	£12.00
48	(Matt)	1936	75p	£36.00
MF48	Famous Views	1936	50p	£24.00
F36	Film Stars, 1st Series	1934	£2.75	£99.00
F36	Film Stars, 2nd Series	1934	£2.50	£90.00
25	Fish	1926	£2.00	£50.00
50	Flowers to Grow – The Best Perennials	1913	£3.40	£170.00
F48	Girls from the Shows (Glossy)	1935	£2.25	£108.00
48	(Matt)	1935	£2.50	£120.00
50	Miniatures (No Border)	1912	£2.60	£130.00
50	Miniatures (Gold Border)	1912	£2.50	£125.00
50	Miniatures (51-100)	1912	£2.40	£120.00
46/50	Modern Miniatures	1913	£1.20	£55.00
12	More Lea's Smokers (Green Border)	1906	£75.00	—
12	(Red Frame)	1906	£100.00	—
P24	Old English Pottery & Porcelain	1908	£5.00	£120.00
50	Old English Pottery & Porcelain	1912	£1.60	£80.00
50	Old Pottery & Porcelain, 2nd (Chairman)	1912	£1.40	£70.00
50	2nd (Recorder)	1912	£5.50	—
50	Old Pottery & Porcelain, 3rd (Chairman)	1912	£1.30	£65.00
50	3rd (Recorder)	1912	£5.50	—
50	Old Pottery & Porcelain, 4th Series	1913	£1.30	£65.00
50	Old Pottery & Porcelain, 5th Series	1913	£1.30	£65.00
54	Old Pottery (Silk)	1914	85p	£67.50
72	Old Pottery (Silk, Different)	1914	85p	£70.00
F54	Radio Stars (Glossy)	1935	£2.00	£108.00
54	(Matt)	1935	£2.50	£135.00
100	Regimental Crests & Badges (Silk)	1923	£1.40	—
50	Roses	1924	£1.50	£75.00
50	Ships of the World	1925	£1.80	£90.00
25	The Evolution of the Royal Navy	1925	£2.00	£50.00

R. J. LEA LTD. — cont.

Qty		Date	Odds	Sets
25	War Pictures	1915	£3.60	£90.00
25	War Portraits	1915	£4.50	£112.50
F48	Wonders of the World (Glossy)	1938	50p	£24.00
48	(Matt)	1938	£1.25	£60.00
MF48	Wonders of the World	1938	60p	£29.00

ALFRED L. LEAVER

M12	Manikin Cards	1915	*£80.00*	—

J. LEES

21	Northampton Town Football Club	1912	£100.00	—

LEON DE CUBA CIGARS

30	Colonial Troops	1902	*£110.00*	—

A. LEWIS & CO. (WESTMINSTER) LTD.

52	Horoscopes	1938	85p	£45.00

H. C. LLOYD & SON LTD.

28	Academy Gems (Green Front, Multi-Backs)	1902	£45.00	—
28	(Mauve Front, Multi-Backs)	1902	£45.00	—
28	(Orange Front, Multi-Backs)	1902	£45.00	—
26	Actresses & Boer War Celebrities	1901	£40.00	—
M?6	Devon Footballers (With Frame Line)	1902	*£110.00*	—
M42	Devon Footballers & Boer War Celebrities (2 Printings)	1902	£42.50	—
25	Star Girls (Different Printings)	1899	*£200.00*	—
L36	War Pictures	1914	*£175.00*	—

RICHARD LLOYD & SONS

?23	Actresses, Celebrities & Yachts	1900	£90.00	—
25	Atlantic Records	1936	£2.60	£65.00
25	Boer War Celebrities	1899	£34.00	—
F27	Cinema Stars (1-27)	1935	£7.00	£190.00
F27	Cinema Stars (28-54)	1935	£3.00	£81.00
F27	Cinema Stars, 3rd Series (55-81)	1936	£6.00	£162.00
25	Cinema Stars (Matt)	1937	£1.60	£40.00
25	Famous Cricketers Puzzle Series	1930	£6.20	£155.00
96	National Types, Costumes & Flags	1900	£32.50	—
25	Old English Inns	1923	£1.60	£40.00
25	Old Inns, Series 2	1924	£2.80	£70.00
50	Old Inns	1924	£1.40	£70.00
10	Scenes from San Toy	1905	£9.00	£90.00
7	The Seven Ages of Man	1900	*£500.00*	—
25	Tricks & Puzzles	1935	£1.60	£40.00
25	Types of Horses	1926	£3.60	£90.00
25	Zoo Series	1926	90p	£22.50

A. LOWNIE (Tobacconist)

30	Army Pictures, Cartoons etc.	1916	*£110.00*	—

LUSBY LTD.

Qty		Date	Odds	Sets
25	Scenes from Circus Life	1902	£110.00	—

HUGH McCALL

1	RAF Recruiting Card	1924	*£125.00*	—

D. & J. MACDONALD

10	Actresses "MUTA"	1901	£100.00	—
L?13	Cricket & Football Teams (Tontine)	1902	*£350.00*	—
L?24	(Winning Team)	1902	*£350.00*	—
25	Cricketers	1902	£350.00	—
L1	Yorkshire County Team	1900	—	*£650.00*

MACKENZIE & CO.

F50	Music Hall Artistes	1902	£20.00	£1000.00
50	The Zoo	1910	£26.00	—
50	Victorian Art Pictures	1910	£21.00	—

WM. McKINNELL (or M'Kinnell)

12	The European War Series	1915	£55.00	—
50	War Portraits	1916	*£90.00*	—

MACNAUGHTON JENKINS & CO. LTD.

M50	Castles of Ireland – Ancient & Modern	1924	£3.00	£150.00
50	Various Uses of Rubber	1924	£2.50	£150.00

A. McTAVISH (Tobacconist)

30	Army Pictures, Cartoons, etc	1916	*£100.00*	—

McWATTIE & SONS

30	Army Pictures, Cartoons, etc	1916	*£100.00*	—

THE MANXLAND TOBACCO CO.

?6	Views of the Isle of Man (Matt)	1900	*£250.00*	—
?6	(Varnished)	1900	*£250.00*	—

MARCOVITCH & CO.

F18	Beauties (Plain Back)	1932	£1.00	£18.00
6	The Story in Red and White	1955	£2.75	—
L7	The Story in Red and White	1955	£2.40	£17.00

MARCUS'S

?17	Cricketers	1897	*£350.00*	—
25	Footballers & Club Colours	1898	£160.00	—
L1	The Four Generations	1900	—	*£225.00*

MARKHAM

Qty		Date	Odds	Sets
M?27	Views of Bridgwater	1906	£85.00	—

MARSUMA CO.

50	Famous Golfers & Their Strokes	1914	£42.00	£2100.00

C. MARTIN (Tobacconist)

30	Army Pictures, Cartoons, etc	1916	*£100.00*	—

MARTINS LTD.

1	Arf A Mo Kaiser!	1915	—	£70.00
D?14	Carlyle Series (Different Printings)	1923	*£85.00*	—
P?781	Leading Artistes	1916	£5.50	—
25	V.C. Heroes	1916	£25.00	£625.00

MASCOT SPECIAL VIRGINIA CIGARETTES

?20	British Views	1925	*£50.00*	—

R. MASON & CO.

30	Colonial Troops	1902	£50.00	—
40	Naval & Military Phrases (No Border)	1904	£45.00	—
40	(White Border)	1904	£45.00	—

JUSTUS VAN MAURIK

X12	Dutch Scenes	1915	£100.00	—

MAY QUEEN VIRGINIA CIGARETTES

M10/12	Interesting Pictures	—	50p	£5.00

MENTORS LTD.

32	Views of Ireland	1912	£10.00	£320.00

J. MILLHOFF & CO. LTD.

F54	Antique Pottery	1927	80p	£43.00
MF56	Antique Pottery	1927	75p	£42.00
30	Art Treasures	1927	90p	£27.00
L50	Art Treasures	1926	60p	£30.00
L25	Art Treasures, 2nd Series (51-75)	1928	90p	£22.50
25	British Orders of Chivalry & Valour	1939	£1.60	£40.00
M20	De Reszke Rilette Pictures	1925	£2.50	—
M25	De Reszke Rilette Pictures	1925	£2.50	—
M30	De Reszke Rilette Pictures	1925	£2.50	—
M42	De Reszke Rilette Pictures	1925	£2.25	£95.00
M43	De Reszke Rilette Pictures	1925	£3.00	—
M56	De Reszke Rilette Pictures	1925	*£3.00*	—
M74	De Reszke Rilette Pictures	1925	£2.50	—

J. MILLHOFF & CO. LTD. — cont.

Qty		Date	Odds	Sets
L25	England Historic & Picturesque (1-25)	1928	80p	£20.00
L25	England Historic & Picturesque, 2nd Series	1928	80p	£20.00
F27	Famous Golfers	1928	£12.50	£450.00
F27	Famous Test Cricketers	1928	£5.00	£135.00
MF27	Famous Test Cricketers	1928	£4.50	£121.50
P24	Film Stars	1934	*£7.50*	—
M25	Gallery Pictures	1929	£1.00	£25.00
50	Geographia Map Series (Sect.)	1931	£1.70	£85.00
F36	In the Public Eye	1930	£1.40	£50.00
1	Jigsaw Advertisement Card (4 Types)	1933	—	£11.50
25	Men of Genius	1924	£5.00	£125.00
L25	Picturesque Old England	1931	£1.00	£25.00
F27	Real Photographs, A Series (Glossy)	1931	40p	£11.00
F27	(Matt)	1931	70p	£19.00
F27	Real Photographs, 2nd Series	1931	75p	£20.00
F27	Real Photographs, 3rd Series	1932	40p	£11.00
F27	Real Photographs, 4th Series	1932	60p	£16.50
F27	Real Photographs, 5th Series	1933	£1.00	£27.00
F27	Real Photographs, 6th Series	1933	£1.00	£27.00
25	Reproductions of Celebrated Oil Paintings	1928	£1.20	£30.00
L25	Roses	1927	£2.60	£65.00
MF?9	Theatre Advertisement Cards (Multi-Backed)	1905	*£85.00*	—
XF?2	Theatre Advertisement Cards (Multi-Backed)	1905	*£110.00*	—
F54	The Homeland Series	1933	25p	£13.50
MF56	The Homeland Series	1933	25p	£14.00
50	Things to Make	1935	70p	£35.00
50	What the Stars Say	1934	80p	£40.00
F36	Zoological Studies	1929	20p	£7.25

DUTCH ISSUES

F?70	Dutch Footballers	1929	*£15.00*	—
L40	Film Series 1	1932	*£6.25*	—
L60	Film Series 1 (2 Printings)	1932	£6.25	—
L60	Film Series 2 (Coloured, 2 Addresses)	1935	£6.25	—
L25	Film Series 3 (Red-Brown)	1930	*£6.25*	—
MF105	Film Series 4	1933	£5.00	—
MF?249	Film Series 4 (Inscribed Series of 206)	1934	£5.00	—
MF105	Film Series "SERIE 6"	1936	£5.00	—

MIRANDA LTD.

20	Dogs	1925	£7.75	—
25	Sports and Pastimes	1925	£5.00	£150.00

STEPHEN MITCHELL & SON

51	Actors & Actresses "FROGA" (Coloured)	1899	£20.00	—
26	Actors & Actresses "FROGA B" (Brown)	1899	£20.00	—
25	Actors & Actresses "FROGA C" (Brown)	1899	£20.00	—
50	Actors & Actresses "FROGA D" (Brown)	1899	£20.00	£1000.00
50	A Gallery of 1934	1935	£2.30	£115.00
50	A Gallery of 1935	1936	£2.00	£100.00
50	Air-Raid Precautions	1938	£1.00	£50.00
30	A Model Army	1932	£1.20	£36.00

STEPHEN MITCHELL & SON — cont.

Qty		Date	Odds	Sets
25	Angling	1928	£5.40	£135.00
50	Arms & Armour	1916	£3.60	£180.00
25	Army Ribbons & Buttons	1916	£3.60	£90.00
50	A Road Map of Scotland (Small Numeral)	1933	£3.25	—
50	(Large Numeral)	1933	£3.25	—
50	(Red Overprint)	1933	£4.25	—
1	A Road Map of Scotland (Substitute)	1933	—	£15.00
25	Boxer Rebellion – Sketches	1901	£25.00	—
25	British Warships (1-25)	1915	£6.50	£162.50
25	British Warships, 2nd Series (26-50)	1915	£6.00	£150.00
50	Clan Tartans, A Series	1927	£1.70	£85.00
25	Clan Tartans, 2nd Series	1927	£1.00	£25.00
25	Empire Exhibition, Scotland 1938	1938	£1.00	£25.00
25	Famous Crosses	1923	60p	£15.00
50	Famous Scots	1933	£1.00	£50.00
50	First Aid	1938	£1.00	£50.00
P3	Glasgow International Exhibition 1901	1901	£70.00	—
50	Humorous Drawings	1924	£2.40	£120.00
50	Interesting Buildings	1905	£7.00	£350.00
40	London Ceremonials	1928	£1.30	£52.00
25	Medals	1916	£4.40	£110.00
25	Money	1913	£4.20	£105.00
25	Old Sporting Prints	1930	£1.50	£37.50
50	Our Empire	1937	50p	£25.00
25	Regimental Crests & Collar Badges	1900	£12.50	£312.50
70	River & Coastal Steamers	1925	£3.00	£210.00
50	Scotland's Story	1929	£2.50	£125.00
25	Scottish Clan Series	1903	£12.00	£350.00
50	Scottish Footballers	1934	£2.50	£125.00
50	Scottish Football Snaps	1935	£2.30	£115.00
25	Seals	1911	£4.40	£110.00
25	Sports	1907	£12.00	£350.00
25	Stars of Screen & History	1939	£2.60	£65.00
25	Statues & Monuments	1914	£4.00	£100.00
50	The World of Tomorrow	1936	£1.20	£60.00
25	Village Models	1925	£2.20	£55.00
L25	Village Models	1925	*£5.00*	—
25	Village Models, 2nd Series	1925	£2.20	£55.00
25	2nd (Not Inscribed 2nd)	1925	£4.00	—
L25	Village Models, 2nd Series	1925	£5.00	£125.00
50	Wonderful Century	1937	70p	£35.00

MOORGATE TOBACCO CO. LTD.

D30	The New Elizabethan Age (Matt)	1953	£3.00	—
D30	(Varnished)	1953	£1.75	£52.50

B. MORRIS & SONS LTD.

30	Actresses (Black & White)	1898	£1.60	£68.00
26	Actresses "FROGA A" (Borneo Queen)	1899	£30.00	—
26	(Gold Seals)	1899	£30.00	—
26	(Morris's Cigarettes)	1899	£30.00	—
26	(Tommy Atkins)	1899	£75.00	—

B. MORRIS & SONS LTD. — cont.

Qty		*Date*	*Odds*	*Sets*
L?4	Actresses "FROGA B"	1899	*£350.00*	—
1	Advertisement Card	1900	—	*£500.00*
6	Agriculture in the Orient	1910	£6.50	£39.00
50	Animals at the Zoo (Blue Back)	1924	65p	£32.50
50	(Grey Back)	1924	80p	£40.00
6	Architectural Monuments	1910	£6.50	£39.00
35	At the London Zoo Aquarium	1928	40p	£14.00
25	Australian Cricketers	1925	£3.20	£80.00
M24	Battleship Crests (Silk)	1915	£35.00	—
50	Beauties "CHOAB" (Gold Flake Honeydew)	1900	£42.50	—
50	(Golden Virginia)	1900	£42.50	—
50	(Levant Favorites)	1900	£40.00	—
50	(Reina Regenta)	1900	£40.00	—
?53	Beauties Collotype (Multi-Backed)	1897	*£130.00*	—
21	Beauties "MOM" (Borneo Queen)	1899	£30.00	—
21	(Gold Seals)	1899	£30.00	—
21	(Morris Cigarettes)	1899	£30.00	—
21	(Tommy Atkins)	1899	£75.00	—
20	Boer War 1900	1900	£34.00	£680.00
25	Boer War Celebrities "PAM"	1901	£30.00	—
25	Captain Blood	1937	£1.00	£25.00
L25	English & Foreign Birds (Silk)	1915	£4.60	£115.00
L25	English Flowers (Silk, Panel Cigarettes)	1915	£3.60	£90.00
L25	("Cruel" Silk)	1915	£7.00	—
L25	(Silk, No Brand)	1915	£6.25	—
L50	English Flowers (Silk)	1915	£4.00	£200.00
50	Film Star Series	1923	£3.20	£160.00
25	Golf Strokes Series	1923	£6.00	£150.00
12	Horoscopes	1936	75p	£9.00
25	How Films are Made	1934	£1.60	£40.00
50	How to Sketch	1929	£1.00	£50.00
20	London Views (American Gold)	1904	£31.50	—
20	(Borneo Queen)	1904	£31.50	—
20	(Gold Flake)	1904	£31.50	—
20	(Reina Regenta)	1904	£31.50	—
25	Marvels of the Universe Series	1912	£3.40	£85.00
25	Measurement of Time	1924	£1.80	£45.00
25	Motor Series	1922	£4.20	£105.00
50	National & Colonial Arms	1917	£5.60	£280.00
25	Racing Greyhounds	1939	£2.00	£50.00
L25	Regimental Colours (Silk)	1916	£3.50	—
G4	Regimental Colours (Silk)	1916	£55.00	—
6	Schools in Foreign Countries	1910	£6.50	£39.00
24	Shadowgraphs	1925	£2.50	£60.00
6	Strange Vessels	1910	£6.50	£39.00
6	The Ice Breaker	1910	£6.50	£39.00
25	The Queen's Dolls' House	1925	£2.80	£70.00
13	Treasure Island	1924	£1.20	£16.00
50	Victory Signs Series	1928	70p	£35.00
25	War Celebrities	1916	£5.00	£125.00
25	War Pictures	1916	£7.00	£175.00
25	Wax Art Series	1931	60p	£15.00
25	Whipsnade Zoo	1932	60p	£15.00
25	Wireless Series	1923	£4.20	£105.00

PHILIP MORRIS & CO. LTD.

Qty		*Date*	*Odds*	*Sets*
50	British Views	1924	£2.30	£115.00
L50	British Views	1924	£3.00	—
T108	Classic Collection	1985	£1.25	—
M72	Motormania	1986	£1.25	—

P. MOUAT & CO.

30	Colonial Troops	1902	*£130.00*	—

MOUSTAFA LTD.

F50	Camera Studies (Printed Back)	1923	£3.00	—
F50	(Plain Back)	1923	£2.75	£137.50
25	Cinema Stars	1924	£4.50	—
40	Leo Chambers Dogs Heads	1924	£3.20	£130.00
25	Pictures of World Interest	1923	£3.00	£75.00
F25	Real Photos	1925	50p	£12.50

MUNRO

30	Colonial Troops	1902	*£175.00*	—

B. MURATTI SONS & CO. LTD.

P?24	Actresses, Collotype	1899	£100.00	—
26	Actresses "FROGA" (Cigarette Connoisseur)	1899	£23.00	£600.00
26	(Zinnia)	1899	£27.50	—
P26	Actresses "FROGA" A (Horizontal Back)	1899	*£135.00*	—
P?18	Actresses "FROGA" C (Vertical Back)	1899	£135.00	—
P?50	Actresses & Beauties (Horizontal Back)	1899	*£135.00*	—
P?50	(Vertical Back)	1899	£135.00	—
X?35	Advertisement Cards	1900	*£275.00*	—
F24	Australian Racehorses	1931	80p	£20.00
50	Beauties "CHOAB" (Black Back)	1900	£40.00	—
50	(Green Back)	1900	*£45.00*	—
P50	Beauties "CHOAB" (Printed Back)	1900	£120.00	—
P25	(Rubber Stamped Back)	1899	*£135.00*	—
P25	(Plain Back)	1899	£130.00	—
P?3	Beauties "MOM"	1900	£150.00	—
M?66	Beautiful Women	1900	£85.00	—
20	Boer War Generals "CLAM"	1900	£31.50	—
X?	Book Postcard Series	1902	*£100.00*	—
M15	Caricatures (4 Brands)	1903	£25.00	£375.00
M15	(Vassos)	1903	*£65.00*	—
M15	(Vassos Blanked Out)	1903	£45.00	—
M15	(Zinnia, Black)	1903	£25.00	£375.00
M15	(Zinnia, Brown)	1903	£30.00	—
M35	Crowned Heads	1912	£12.50	£500.00
53	Japanese Series (Printed Back)	1904	£15.00	£800.00
53	(Plain Back)	1904	£13.50	—
XF?	Midget Post Card Series (Glossy)	1902	£7.50	—
X?	(Matt)	1902	£7.50	—
X?	Queens Postcard Series	1902	£10.00	—
19	Russo Japanese Series	1904	£13.00	£250.00
25	Star Girls	1899	*£135.00*	—
50	Views of Jersey (Printed Back)	1913	£17.50	—
50	(Plain Back)	1913	£16.00	—

B. MURATTI SONS & CO. LTD. — cont.

Qty		Date	Odds	Sets
25	War Series I	1916	£20.00	—
25	War Series II (2 Printings)	1917	£12.50	£312.50
SILK ISSUES				
L40	Canvas Masterpieces, Series M (Large Globe)	1916	£5.25	—
L40	(Small Globe)	1916	£2.40	£96.00
P16	Canvas Masterpieces, Series P	1916	£12.00	—
M24	Flags, Series A (26-49)	1914	£3.50	£84.00
P3	Flags, Series A (1-3)	1914	£9.00	—
L1	Flags, Series B (No.19)	1914	—	£12.00
M25	Flags, Series C (20-44)	1914	£3.50	£87.50
P18	Flags, Series C (1-18)	1914	£9.00	—
P3	Flags, Series D (45-47)	1914	£9.00	—
M24/25	Flags, Series E (48-72, Green Back)	1914	£3.50	£84.00
M24/25	(48-72, Grey Back)	1914	£3.50	£84.00
P6	Flags, Series F (73-78)	1914	£8.50	—
P18	Great War Leaders, Series P	1916	£13.50	—
M25	Regimental Badges, Series A	1915	£4.00	£100.00
L48	Regimental Badges, Series B	1915	£5.50	£265.00
L15	Regimental Badges, Series B (Different, 4-18)	1915	£5.50	£82.50
L16	Regimental Badges, Series G (79-94)	1915	£7.50	—
L25	Regimental Colours, Series CB	1915	£9.00	—
M72	Regimental Colours, Series RB	1915	£5.00	£360.00
CONTINENTAL ISSUES				
215/216	Brennpunkte des Deutschen Sports 1	1935	80p	£172.00
X288	Brennpunkte des Deutschen Sports 2	1936	£1.00	—
X216	Brennpunkte des Deutschen Sports 3	1936	80p	—
?30	Cinema Stars Serie No. 1	1932	*£4.00*	—
?30	Cinema Stars Serie No. 2	1932	*£4.00*	—

MURRAY, SONS & CO.

20	Actresses "BLARM" (Pineapple Cigarettes)	1902	£85.00	—
20	(Special Crown Cigarettes)	1902	*£85.00*	—
F22	Bathing Beauties	1929	£5.25	—
40	Bathing Belles	1939	50p	£20.00
15	Chess and Draughts Problems	1910	£65.00	—
F22	Cinema Scenes	1929	£6.00	—
20	Cricketers (Series H, Black Front)	1912	£70.00	—
20	(Series H, Brown Front)	1912	*£135.00*	—
25	Crossword Puzzles	1923	*£65.00*	—
F26	Dancers	1929	£5.00	£130.00
F25	Dancing Girls (Belfast, Ireland)	1929	£3.20	£80.00
F25	(London & Belfast)	1929	£3.20	£80.00
F26	("Series of 26")	1930	£3.00	£78.00
25	Famous Works of Art	1910	£22.50	—
M16	Flags (Silk)	1910	£20.00	—
X3	Flags & Arms (Silk)	1910	£65.00	—
34	Footballers, Series H	1912	£37.50	—
104	Footballers, Series J	1913	£37.50	—
?28	Football Colours (Shaped, Maple Cigarettes)	1905	*£70.00*	—
?28	(Shaped, Murray Cigarettes)	1905	*£65.00*	—
25	Football Rules	1911	£26.00	£650.00
25	High Class Works of Art	1909	£22.50	—
20	Holidays by the L.M.S.	1927	£10.00	£200.00
20	Inventors Series	1924	£4.25	£85.00

MURRAY, SONS & CO. — cont.

Qty		Date	Odds	Sets
25	Irish Scenery (Hall Mark Cigarettes)	1905	£20.00	—
25	(Pine Apple Cigarettes)	1905	£20.00	—
25	(Special Crown Cigarettes)	1905	£20.00	—
25	(Straight Cut Cigarettes)	1905	£20.00	—
25	(Yachtsman Cigarettes)	1905	£20.00	—
31	Orders of Chivalry (Silk)	1925	£17.00	—
25	Polo Pictures	1910	£24.00	£600.00
M50	Prominent Politicians (With "In two strengths")	1909	£2.50	£125.00
M50	(Without "In two strengths")	1909	£16.50	—
50	Puzzle Series	1929	£6.50	—
M25	Regimental Badges (Silk)	1910	£16.50	—
50	Stage and Film Stars	1926	£3.50	£175.00
25	Steam Ships	1939	£1.30	£32.50
50	The Story of Ships	1940	50p	£25.00
25	Types of Aeroplanes	1929	£1.60	£40.00
20	Types of Dogs	1924	£6.25	£125.00
35	War Series K	1915	£24.00	£840.00
25	War Series L	1916	£2.00	£70.00

H. J. NATHAN

40	Comical Military & Naval Pictures (No Border)	1904	£55.00	—
40	(White Border)	1904	£55.00	—

JAMES NELSON

?23	Beauties "FENA"	1899	*£250.00*	—

NETTLETON AND MITCHELL

30	Army Pictures, Cartoons, etc	1916	*£150.00*	—

EDWD. J. NEWBEGIN

F50	Actors & Actresses	1901	£45.00	—
10	Actresses "HAGG"	1900	*£135.00*	—
20	Cricketers Series	1902	*£350.00*	—
1	Mabel Love Advert Card (3 Colours)	1900	—	*£400.00*
19	Russo Japanese Series	1904	*£130.00*	—
16	Well-known Proverbs	1900	*£125.00*	—
25	Well-known-Songs	1900	£125.00	—

W. H. NEWMAN LTD.

18	Motor Cycle Series	1914	£85.00	—

THE NEW MOSLEM CIGARETTE CO. LTD.

30	Proverbs	1903	£90.00	—

THOS. NICHOLLS & CO.

50	Orders of Chivalry	1916	£6.50	£325.00

Lifeboats
Oxo

Lighthouses – Ensign

Veteran and Vintage Cars
Mobil

Modern British Warplanes – King's Laundries

Alpine Sports – Sanitarium

If you were Born in
MARCH
Your Sign of the Zodiac is Aries, the Ram.
Your Birthday Jewel is the Bloodstone, which will endow you with courage.
Your Colour is Scarlet, symbol of bravery.
Your Flower is the Anemone or Wind-flower, signifying hope.

HOROSCOPE
You were born under the sign of Aries the Ram with its strong head, and consequently you too will use that member of the body, thinking and planning constantly and successfully In art, science and philosophy the children of Aries make their way, but must beware of their inclination to waste time and strength by going from one subject to another They do not work well under subjection, being very independent both in thought and action They are often admirable painters, architects, engineers and executive musicians, being quick to learn, practical and retentive of knowledge

Horoscopes – Morris

In Prairie Und Urwald
B.A.T. – Gold Dollar

History of the Wild West
Series No. 1
Como

Tea from the Garden to the Home
Robinson Bros.

Laramie
Primrose

Roy Rogers
Colour Series
Kane

Characters from Film Cartoons
Barratt

Dan Dare
Clevedon

THE NILMA TOBACCO COY.

Qty		Date	Odds	Sets
40	Home & Colonial Regiments	1903	*£85.00*	—
30	Proverbs	1903	*£80.00*	—

M. E. NOTARAS LTD.

M24	Chinese Scenes	1925	£1.25	£30.00
F36	National Types of Beauty	1925	80p	£30.00

A. NOTON

M12	Manikin Cards	1915	*£80.00*	—

OGDENS LTD.

25	A.B.C. of Sport	1927	£3.00	£75.00
50	Actors, Natural & Character Studies	1938	£1.00	£50.00
25	Actresses ("No Glycerine", Black Front)	1895	£85.00	—
25	("No Glycerine", Brown Front)	1895	£80.00	—
?97	Actresses, Collotype (Mauve Stamped Back)	1894	£50.00	—
?97	(Red Stamped Back)	1894	*£80.00*	—
?77	Actresses, Collotype (Printed Back)	1894	£50.00	—
50	Actresses, Green Gravure	1898	£10.00	£500.00
?1	Actresses, Green, Green Border	1898	*£300.00*	—
50	Actresses, Tabs Type, Red Tint	1902	£32.50	—
?204	Actresses, Woodburytype	1894	£35.00	—
F?586	Actresses, Guinea Gold Type	1900	£2.75	—
50	A.F.C. Nicknames	1933	£4.20	£210.00
50	Air-Raid Precautions	1938	80p	£40.00
50	Applied Electricity	1928	£1.00	£50.00
192	Army Crests and Mottoes	1902	£4.50	£865.00
36	Australian Test Cricketers	1928	£3.60	£130.00
28	Beauties "BOCCA"	1899	£25.00	£700.00
50	Beauties "CHOAB"	1899	£26.00	—
26	Beauties "HOL" (Blue Printed Back)	1899	£18.00	£470.00
26	(Rubber Stamped Back)	1899	*£150.00*	—
66	Beauties,Green Net Back (Black & White)	1901	£13.00	£850.00
99	(Coloured)	1901	£24.00	—
52	Beauties, P/C Inset	1899	£26.00	£1350.00
26	Beauties (No Insets, Subjects as Above)	1899	£35.00	—
52	Beauties & Military, P/C Inset	1898	£26.00	£1350.00
F75	Beauty Series (Unnumbered)	1900	£65.00	—
F50	Beauty Series (Numbered)	1900	£2.40	£120.00
50	Billiards by Tom Newman	1928	£1.80	£90.00
50	Birds' Eggs	1908	£1.50	£75.00
50	Bird's Eggs (Cut-outs)	1923	£1.00	£50.00
F?140	Boer War & General Interest	1901	£3.00	—
LF?63	Boer War & General Interest	1901	£40.00	—
50	Boxers	1915	£6.40	£320.00
25	Boxing	1914	£5.00	£125.00
50	Boy Scouts (Blue Back)	1911	£2.80	£140.00
50	(Green Back)	1911	£4.00	£200.00
50	Boy Scouts, 2nd Series (Blue Back)	1912	£2.80	£140.00
50	(Green Back)	1912	£4.00	£200.00
50	Boy Scouts, 3rd Series (Blue Back)	1912	£2.80	£140.00
50	(Green Back)	1912	£4.00	£200.00

OGDENS LTD. — cont.

Qty		*Date*	*Odds*	*Sets*
50	Boy Scouts, 4th Series	1913	£3.00	£150.00
25	Boy Scouts, 5th Series	1914	£2.80	£70.00
50	Boy Scouts (Different)	1929	£2.20	£110.00
50	British Birds	1905	£1.50	£75.00
50	British Birds, Second Series	1909	£1.90	£95.00
50	British Birds (Cut-outs)	1923	80p	£40.00
50	British Birds & Their Eggs	1939	£2.60	£130.00
50	British Costumes from 100 B.C. to 1904	1905	£5.50	£275.00
50	Broadcasting	1935	£1.60	£80.00
50	By the Roadside	1932	£1.00	£50.00
44	Captains of Association Football Clubs & Colours.	1926	£3.00	£132.00
50	Cathedrals & Abbeys	1936	£1.00	£50.00
50	Champions of 1936	1937	£1.80	£90.00
50	Children of All Nations	1924	80p	£40.00
50	Club Badges	1915	£4.60	£230.00
50	Colour In Nature	1932	80p	£40.00
?29	Comic Pictures	1897	£275.00	—
50	Construction of Railway Trains	1930	£2.30	£115.00
50	Coronation Procession (Sect.)	1937	£1.50	£75.00
	Cricket & Football-Women			
12	(Gold Medal)	1896	*£250.00*	—
12	(Cox Back, Black or Brown)	1896	£300.00	—
12	(Otto De Rose)	1896	*£325.00*	—
50	Cricketers & Sportsmen	1898	£75.00	—
50	Cricket 1926	1926	£2.50	£125.00
25	Derby Entrants 1926	1926	£2.50	£62.50
50	Derby Entrants 1928	1928	£1.90	£95.00
50	Derby Entrants 1929	1929	£2.30	£115.00
50	Dogs	1936	£2.20	£110.00
55	Dominoes	1909	£1.30	£71.50
112	Dominoes – Actress & Beauty Backs			
28	Actresses, Corners Mitred	1900	£25.00	—
28	Actresses, Corners Not Mitred	1900	£22.50	£630.00
56	Beauties, Corners Not Mitred	1900	£25.00	—
P10	English Actresses	1890	*£350.00*	—
25	Famous Dirt-Track Riders	1929	£4.40	£110.00
50	Famous Footballers	1908	£3.60	£180.00
50	Famous Rugby Players	1926	£2.30	£115.00
50	Flags & Funnels of Leading Steamship Lines	1906	£3.80	£190.00
50	Football Caricatures	1935	£2.70	£135.00
43	Football Club Badges (Shaped)	1910	£6.25	—
50	Football Club Captains	1936	£2.00	£100.00
51	Football Club Colours	1906	£3.40	£173.00
50	Foreign Birds	1924	80p	£40.00
50	Fowls Pigeons & Dogs	1904	£2.80	£140.00
25	Greyhound Racing, 1st Series	1927	£4.00	£100.00
25	Greyhound Racing, 2nd Series	1928	£4.00	£100.00
1	History of the Union Jack (Folder)	1900	—	£180.00
50	How to Swim	1935	£1.00	£50.00
50	Infantry Training	1915	£2.20	£110.00
50	Jockeys, and Owners' Colours	1927	£2.40	£120.00
50	Jockeys, 1930	1930	£2.30	£115.00
50	Leaders Of Men	1924	£1.70	£85.00
MF3	Liners (Guinea Gold Type)	1901	£140.00	—
P6	Liners (6 Brands)	1902	£125.00	—
25	Marvels of Motion	1928	£2.00	£50.00
K52	Miniature Playing Cards (Actresses)	1900	£3.50	—

OGDENS LTD. — cont.

Qty		*Date*	*Odds*	*Sets*
K102	Miniature Playing Cards (Beauty Backs)	1900	£3.50	—
K52	Miniature Playing Cards (Coolie) (No Border)	1904	£2.40	£125.00
	(White Border)	1904	£3.75	—
K52	Miniature Playing Cards (Tabs)	1909	£2.50	£130.00
50	Modern British Pottery	1925	90p	£45.00
50	Modern Railways	1936	£2.00	£100.00
50	Modern War Weapons	1915	£2.80	£140.00
25	Modes of Conveyance	1927	£2.20	£55.00
50	Motor Races 1931	1931	£2.60	£130.00
50	Ocean Greyhounds	1938	£1.00	£50.00
25	Optical Illusions	1923	£3.00	£75.00
50	Orders of Chivalry	1907	£3.00	£150.00
25	Owners, Racing Colours & Jockeys (Green Back)	1914	£3.70	£92.50
50	Owners, Racing Colours & Jockeys (Blue Back)	1906	£2.90	£145.00
25	Picturesque People of the Empire	1927	£1.20	£30.00
50	Picturesque Villages	1936	£1.00	£50.00
25	Poultry (1-25) (Ogdens on Front)	1915	£4.50	£112.50
25	(1-25) (No Ogdens on Front)	1915	£5.20	£130.00
25	Poultry, 2nd Series (26-50)	1916	£5.00	£125.00
25	Poultry Alphabet	1924	£3.80	£95.00
25	Poultry Rearing & Management, 1st Series	1922	£2.60	£65.00
25	Poultry Rearing & Management, 2nd Series	1923	£2.60	£65.00
50	Prominent Cricketers of 1938	1938	£2.20	£110.00
50	Prominent Racehorses of 1933	1934	£1.90	£95.00
50	Pugilists & Wrestlers, A Series (1-50)	1908	£4.00	£200.00
25	Pugilists & Wrestlers, Second Series (51-75)	1909	£4.60	£115.00
50	Pugilists in Action	1928	£3.40	£170.00
50	Racehorses	1907	£3.20	£160.00
50	Racing Pigeons	1931	£3.20	£160.00
25	Records of the World	1908	£2.50	£62.50
50	Royal Mail	1909	£3.60	£180.00
50	Sea Adventure	1939	80p	£40.00
50	Sectional Cycling Map	1910	£2.50	£125.00
50	Shakespeare Series (Numbered)	1905	£10.00	£500.00
50	(Unnumbered)	1905	£11.00	£550.00
50	Shots from the Films	1936	£2.00	£100.00
25	Sights of London	1923	£1.30	£32.50
50	Smugglers and Smuggling	1932	£2.20	£110.00
50	Soldiers of the King (Grey Caption)	1909	£4.50	£225.00
25	(Brown Caption)	1909	£5.80	£145.00
P30	Sporting & Other Girls	1898	£400.00	—
50	Steeplechase Celebrities	1931	£1.80	£90.00
50	Steeplechase Trainers & Owners Colours	1927	£1.80	£90.00
50	Swimming, Diving and Life-Saving	1931	£1.20	£60.00
25	Swiss Views (1-25)	1910	£2.50	£62.50
25	Swiss Views (26-50)	1910	£4.50	£112.50
50	The Blue Riband of the Atlantic	1929	£2.40	£120.00
50	The Story of Sand	1935	90p	£45.00
25	Trainers and Owners Colours, 1st Series	1925	£2.20	£55.00
25	Trainers and Owners Colours, 2nd Series	1926	£2.80	£70.00
50	Trick Billiards	1934	£1.50	£75.00
50	Turf Personalities	1929	£2.30	£115.00
48	Victoria Cross Heroes	1901	£13.50	£650.00
25	Whaling	1927	£2.60	£65.00
50	Yachts & Motor Boats	1930	£2.40	£120.00
50	Zoo Studies	1937	50p	£25.00

Qty		Date	Odds	Sets
GUINEA GOLD PHOTOGRAPHIC ISSUES				
LF1	Actresses Base C	1899	—	£50.00
F375	Actresses Base D	1900	£1.25	—
MF54	Actresses Base D (Medium Size)	1900	£12.00	—
LF270	Actresses Base D	1900	£1.50	—
F40	Actresses Base E	1900	£3.50	£140.00
F641	Actresses Base I	1899	£1.15	—
F24	Actresses Base I (¾ White Frame)	1899	£4.00	—
LF24	Actresses and Actors Base I	1899	£40.00	—
F30	Actresses Base J	1899	£3.60	£108.00
F239	Actresses Base K	1899	£2.65	—
F216	Actresses Base L	1899	£2.20	—
F60	Actresses, Base M, (¾ White Frame)	1900	£2.20	£132.00
F113	Actresses & Miscellaneous Base I	1900	£1.00	£113.00
F2888	Actresses & Miscellaneous Base M	1900	£1.10	—
LF406	Actresses & Miscellaneous Base M	1900	£1.50	—
F58	Boer War & Actresses Base F	1901	80p	£45.00
F190	Boer War & Miscellaneous Base D	1901	65p	—
LF161	Boer War & Miscellaneous Base D	1900	£1.00	—
F?322	Continental Actresses Base B	1899	£2.75	—
LF?76	Continental Actresses Base B	1899	£16.50	—
F11	Cricketers Base I	1901	£13.00	£143.00
F50	Cricketers Base M (Set 1)	1899	£18.00	—
F27	Cricketers Base M (Set 2)	1899	£27.50	—
F57	Cyclists Base M	1899	£5.50	£310.00
F58	Denumbered Group Base D	1900	£2.50	£150.00
LF50	Denumbered Group Base D	1900	£3.50	£175.00
F176	Footballers Base M	1899	£17.50	—
F320	General Interest (White Panel) Base D/I	1900	90p	£288.00
F200	General Interest Numbered 1-200	1901	50p	£100.00
F300	General Interest Numbered 201-500	1901	£1.25	—
F396/398	General Interest Numbered 501-898	1901	£1.00	£395.00
F180/200	General Interest Numbered 899-1098	1901	£1.60	£288.00
F50	General Interest Numbered 1099-1148	1901	£1.40	£70.00
F18	Golf Base I	1901	£20.00	—
F14	London Street Scenes Base I	1901	£3.25	£45.00
F400	New Series 1	1902	£1.15	£460.00
F400	New Series B	1902	£1.40	£560.00
F300	New Series C	1902	£1.10	£330.00
F46	Pantomime & Theatre Artistes Base D	1899	£3.75	£175.00
LF45	Pantomime & Theatre Artistes Base D	1899	£5.50	£250.00
F50	Pantomime & Theatre Artistes Base M	1899	£6.00	—
F60/62	Politicians, Base D	1900	£1.00	£60.00
F3	Royalty Base M	1899	£2.75	£8.25
F32	Turner Paintings Base I	1901	£1.60	£50.00
F10	Views & Scenes Abroad Base I	1901	£1.60	£16.00
TABS TYPE ISSUES				
75	Actresses (Numbered 126-200)	1900	£12.50	—
200	Actresses (Plain Back)	1900	£2.50	—
200	Actresses & Foreign Views	1900	£2.20	—
1	General De Wet	1901	—	£4.00
1	General Interest (Unnumbered)	1901	—	£6.00
?40	General Interest (No Labour Clause)	1900	£25.00	—

Qty		*Date*	*Odds*	*Sets*
150	General Interest, A Series	1901	£1.00	—
200	General Interest, B Series	1901	80p	—
200	General Interest, C Series (1-200)	1902	80p	—
100	General Interest, C Series (201-300)	1902	£2.00	—
50	General Interest, C Series (301-350)	1902	£1.00	£50.00
200	General Interest, D Series	1902	70p	£200.00
120	General Interest, E Series	1902	£1.00	—
320	General Interest, F Series (1-320)	1902	£1.00	—
99	General Interest, F Series (321-420)	1902	£2.50	—
120	General Interest (1-120)	1902	£1.10	—
196	General Interest (Item 95)	1902	80p	£160.00
100	General Interest (Item 96)	1902	85p	£85.00
100	General Interest (Item 97-1)	1902	£1.25	£125.00
21	General Interest (Item 97-2, Cricket)	1902	£6.50	£135.00
25	General Interest (Item 97-2, Football)	1902	£3.75	£95.00
15	General Interest (Item 97-2, Golf)	1902	£17.00	£255.00
139	General Interest (Item 97-2, Various)	1902	85p	£120.00
?111	General Interest (Oblong Back)	1902	£15.00	—
17	Heroes of the Ring	1901	£6.00	—
1	H.M. The Queen	1901	—	£5.00
2	H.R.H. The Prince of Wales	1901	£3.50	£7.00
14	Imperial Interest	1901	80p	£11.50
106	Imperial or International Interest	1901	70p	£75.00
3	International Interest	1901	£1.65	£5.00
14	International Interest or a Prominent British Officer	1901	70p	£9.50
71	Leading Artistes of the Day			
	(Name in Black)	1901	£1.20	£85.00
	(Name in Black, No Labour Clause)	1901	£20.00	—
25	Leading Artistes of the Day			
	(Name in White, Printed Back)	1901	£13.50	—
	(Name in White, Plain Back)	1901	£13.50	—
	(No Name)	1901	£13.00	—
?91	Leading Artistes of the Day			
	(Non Descriptive, Printed Back)	1901	£11.00	—
	(Non Descriptive, Plain Back)	1901	£11.00	—
22	Leading Athletes	1901	£2.50	£55.00
15	Leading Favourites of the Turf	1901	£4.00	£60.00
54	Leading Generals at the War	1901	90p	—
25	Leading Generals at the War (Different)	1901	90p	—
25	(No "Tabs")	1901	£1.75	—
47	Leading Generals at the War (Non Descriptive)	1901	90p	—
25	Leading Generals at the War			
	(Lucky Star)	1901	£5.00	—
	("Guinea Gold" Rubber Stamped)	1901	£8.00	—
2	Members of Parliament	1901	£3.00	£6.00
11	Notable Coursing Dogs	1901	£7.00	—
12	Our Leading Cricketers	1901	£13.00	£156.00
17	Our Leading Footballers	1901	£7.50	—
37	Prominent British Officers	1901	80p	£30.00
50	Stage Artistes & Celebrities	1900	£2.50	£125.00
1	The Yacht "Columbia"	1901	—	£6.00
1	The Yacht "Shamrock"	1901	—	£6.00

AUSTRALIAN ISSUES TABS TYPE

1	Christian De Wet	1901	—	£10.00
1	Corporal G.E. Nurse, V.C.	1901	—	*£10.00*

Qty		Date	Odds	Sets
14	English Cricketer Series	1901	£45.00	£630.00
400	General Interest (Numbered)	1901	£2.50	—
100	General Interest (Unnumbered)	1901	£5.00	—
1	Imperial Interest	1901	—	*£10.00*
?29	Imperial or International Interest	1901	£6.50	—
?6	International Interest	1901	£6.50	—
1	Lady Sarah Wilson	1901	—	*£10.00*
?41	Leading Generals at the War	1901	£6.50	—
?13	Prominent British Officers	1901	£7.00	—

OTHER OVERSEAS ISSUES

Qty		Date	Odds	Sets
51	Actresses, Black & White (Polo)	1906	£3.00	—
?30	Actresses, Black & White (Polo, Small Pictures, Numbered)	1906	*£12.50*	—
?3	Actresses, Black & White (Polo,Small Pictures, Unnumbered)	1906	*£12.50*	—
30	Actresses, Brown (Polo, 3 Printings)	1908	£2.50	£75.00
17	Animals (Polo)	1916	£11.00	—
60	Animals (Ruler)	1912	£3.00	£180.00
60	(Tabs, With Captions)	1912	£3.00	£180.00
50	(Tabs, No Captions)	1912	£3.00	£150.00
50	Aviation Series (Tabs, Ogden at Base)	1912	£6.00	—
50	(Tabs, Ogden England)	1912	£8.00	—
45	Beauties – Picture Hats (Polo)	1911	£5.25	—
50	Best Dogs of their Breed (Polo, Blue)			
	(With Eastern Characters)	1916	£7.50	—
	(Without Eastern Characters)	1916	£7.50	—
50	(Polo, Pink)	1916	£7.50	—
52	Birds of Brilliant Plumage			
	(With Frame Line, 2 Printings)	1914	£3.00	£156.00
	(No Frame Line)	1914	£2.80	£145.00
25	British Trees & Their Uses (Guinea Gold)	1927	£1.80	£45.00
25	Burmese Women (Polo, Apple Green Border)	1919	£5.00	£125.00
25	(Polo, Emerald Green)	1919	£5.00	£125.00
25	China's Ancient Warriors (Ruler)	1913	£5.25	—
25	Famous Railway Trains (Guinea Gold)	1928	£2.50	£62.50
20	Flowers (Polo Packet 49mm Long)			
	(No Eastern Characters)	1915	£5.25	—
	(With Eastern Characters)	1915	£5.25	—
20	(Polo Packet 46 mm Long)	1915	£5.25	—
30	Music Hall Celebrities (Polo)	1911	£5.50	£165.00
50	(Tabs)	1911	£5.00	—
52	Playing Cards (Polo)	1922	£12.50	—
50	Riders of the World (Polo, Reg. No.1294)	1911	£3.50	£175.00
50	(Polo, No "Reg. No.")	1911	£3.50	£175.00
50	(Polo, Cigarettes Uneven)	1911	£3.50	£175.00
50	Russo Japanese Series	1904	£20.00	—
36	Ships & Their Pennants (Polo)	1911	£5.75	—
32	Transport of the World (Polo)	1917	£5.50	—

THE ORLANDO CIGARETTE & CIGAR CO.

Qty		Date	Odds	Sets
40	Home & Colonial Regiments	1901	*£200.00*	—

W. T. OSBORNE & CO.

Qty		*Date*	*Odds*	*Sets*
40	Naval & Military Phrases (No Border)	1904	£37.50	—
40	(White Border)	1904	£37.50	—

OSBORNE TOBACCO CO. LTD.

50	Modern Aircraft (Blue Front)	1952	60p	£30.00
50	(Brown Front)	1952	£1.20	£60.00

PALMER & CO.

M12	Manikin Cards	1915	*£80.00*	—

J. A. PATTREIOUEX LTD.

EARLY PHOTOGRAPHIC ISSUES

F96	Animals (CA1-96)	1926	£1.00	—
LF50	Animals & Scenes (Unnumbered)	1924	£1.00	—
LF50	Animals & Scenes (1-50)	1925	£1.00	—
F192	Animals & Scenes (250-441, Titled, 2 Printings)	1925	£1.00	—
F192	(250-441, Junior Member)	1925	£1.00	—
F96	(346-441, 3 Brands)	1925	£1.00	—
F96	Animals & Scenes (CC1-96)	1926	£1.00	—
LF50	Animals & Scenes (I1-50, 2 Printings)	1927	£1.00	—
F96	Animals & Scenes (JS1-96A)	1928	90p	—
LF96	Animal Studies (A42-137)	1925	90p	—
LF50	Animal Studies (A151-200)	1925	90p	—
LF30	Beauties (JM1-30)	1928	£2.75	—
LF50	British & Egyptian Scenes (CM1-50A)	1927	£1.00	—
LF50	British Empire Exhibition (JM1-50B)	1928	£1.80	£90.00
XF100	Cathedrals, Abbeys & Castles (SJ1-100)	1928	£2.50	—
LF30	Child Studies (JM No.1-30)	1928	£3.60	—
F96	Famous Cricketers (C1-96, Plain Back)	1926	£40.00	—
F96	(C1-96, Printed Back)	1926	£40.00	—
F191	Famous Footballers (F1-191)	1922	£9.00	—
LF50	Famous Statues (JCM1-50C)	1928	£1.70	£85.00
F96	Footballers (FA1-96)	1922	£6.75	—
F96	Footballers (FB1-96)	1923	£6.75	—
F96	Footballers (FC1-96)	1923	£6.75	—
LF50	Football Teams (F192-241)	1922	£37.50	—
F96	Natives & Scenes (1-96B)	1926	£1.00	£96.00
F36	(1-36B) (As Above)	1926	£1.25	—
F96	Natives & Scenes (Numbered CB1-CB96)	1926	£1.00	—
F96	(Numbered 1-96)	1926	£1.00	—
F96	(JS1-96) (As Above)	1926	£1.00	£96.00
F96	Overseas Scenes (1-96C)	1926	£1.00	£96.00
LF50	Overseas Scenes (CM1-50B)	1926	£1.00	—
LF50	(JM1-50) (As Above)	1928	£1.00	£50.00
LF50	Overseas Scenes (CM101-150S)	1927	£1.00	£50.00
LF50	(S101-150) (As Above)	1929	£1.00	£50.00
F96	Overseas Scenes (1-96D)	1927	£1.50	—
LF50	Overseas Scenes (1-50E)	1928	£1.00	£50.00
LF50	Overseas Scenes (1-50F)	1928	£1.00	£50.00
LF50	Overseas Scenes (JM1-50A)	1928	£1.00	£50.00
LF50	Scenes (201-250)	1925	£1.00	£50.00
LF50	Scenes (G1-50)	1927	£1.40	£70.00

Qty		*Date*	*Odds*	*Sets*
LF50	Scenes (1-50H, Grey Back)	1927	£1.10	£55.00
LF50	(1-50H, Brown Back)	1927	£1.20	—
LF50	Scenes (JCM1-50D, With Firm's Name)	1927	£1.00	£50.00
LF50	(JCM1-50D, Junior Member No.10, 2 Sizes)	1927	£1.00	—
LF100	Scenes (S1-100)	1928	£1.00	—
LF4	Scenes (V1-4)	1928	£4.00	—

OTHER ISSUES

F28	Beautiful Scotland	1939	£1.10	£30.00
MF48	Beautiful Scotland	1939	25p	£12.00
MF48	Britain from the Air	1939	25p	£12.00
50	British Empire Exhibition Series	1929	£2.40	£120.00
MF48	British Railways	1938	80p	£40.00
50	Builders of the British Empire	1929	£2.80	£140.00
50	Celebrities in Sport	1930	£3.20	£260.00
F28	Coastwise	1939	£1.25	£35.00
MF48	Coastwise	1939	25p	£12.00
75	Cricketers Series	1928	£9.00	£675.00
50	Dirt Track Riders	1929	£9.00	—
F54	Dirt Track Riders (Descriptive)	1930	£10.00	£540.00
F54	(Non Descriptive)	1930	*£24.00*	—
PF54	Dirt Track Riders (Premium Issue)	1930	£150.00	—
MF48	Dogs	1939	60p	£30.00
30	Drawing Made Easy	1930	£2.25	£67.50
F28	Flying	1938	£1.50	£42.00
MF48	Flying	1938	40p	£19.50
F78	Footballers in Action	1934	£3.40	£265.00
100	Footballers Series (Brown Caption)	1927	£7.00	—
50	(Blue Caption)	1927	£7.50	£375.00
MF48	Holiday Haunts by the Sea	1938	25p	£12.00
X24	Jackpot Jigsaws	1969	£1.00	—
25	King Lud Problems	1936	£15.00	—
26	Maritime Flags	1931	£9.00	£234.00
F28	Our Countryside	1938	£1.50	£42.00
MF48	Our Countryside	1938	25p	£12.00
25	Photo's of Football Stars	1929	£27.50	—
50	Railway Posters by Famous Artists	1930	£7.20	£360.00
F54	Real Photographs of London	1936	£2.00	£108.00
F28	Shots from the Films	1938	£2.50	£70.00
MF48	Sights of Britain	1936	30p	£15.00
MF48	Sights of Britain, 2nd Series (2 Printings)	1936	25p	£12.00
MF48	Sights of Britain, 3rd Series	1937	40p	£20.00
MF48	Sights of London, First Series	1935	50p	£24.00
MF12	Sights of London – Supplementary Series	1935	75p	£9.00
F54	Sporting Celebrities	1935	£3.00	£162.00
MF96	Sporting Events and Stars	1935	£1.00	£200.00
50	Sports Trophies	1931	£2.50	£125.00
MF48	The Bridges of Britain	1938	25p	£12.00
52	The English & Welsh Counties	1928	£1.75	£91.00
MF48	The Navy (2 Printings)	1937	60p	£29.00
M24	Treasure Isle	1968	*£1.25*	—
F51	Views	1933	£1.10	£56.00
F54	Views of Britain	1937	£1.50	£81.00
MF48	Winter Scenes	1937	35p	£17.00

W. PEPPERDY

Qty		Date	Odds	Sets
30	Army Pictures, Cartoons, etc.	1916	*£95.00*	—

M. PEZARO & SON

25	Armies of the World (Cake Walk)	1900	*£120.00*	—
25	(Nestor)	1900	£115.00	—
?17	Song Titles Illustrated	1900	£165.00	—

GODFREY PHILLIPS LTD.

40 Page Reference Book — £3.50

50	Actresses (Oval)	1916	£6.50	£325.00
50	(Oval, Anonymous)	1916	£5.00	£250.00
25	Actresses, C Series (Ball of Beauty)	1900	£85.00	—
25	(Carriage)	1900	£27.50	£687.50
25	(Derby)	1900	£80.00	—
25	(Horseshoe)	1900	£30.00	—
25	(Teapot)	1900	£90.00	—
25	(Volunteer)	1900	£75.00	—
2	Advertisement Cards	1934	£12.00	£24.00
50	Aircraft	1938	£1.60	£80.00
54	Aircraft Series No.1 (Matt)	1938	40p	£21.50
54	(Varnished)	1938	£2.50	£135.00
54	(Millhoff Back)	1938	£3.00	£162.00
40	Animal Series	1903	£6.25	£250.00
M30	Animal Studies	1936	25p	£7.50
50	Annuals	1939	20p	£10.00
L25	Arms of the English Sees	1924	£4.20	£105.00
48	A Selection of BDV Wonderful Gifts	1930	£1.20	£60.00
48	A Selection of BDV Wonderful Gifts	1931	£1.10	£53.00
48	A Selection of BDV Wonderful Gifts	1932	£1.10	£53.00
24	Beauties "HUMPS " (Phillips Front)	1898	£75.00	—
24	(Plums Front)	1898	*£225.00*	—
30	Beauties, Nymphs	1896	£75.00	—
?14	Beauties, Plums (Black & White Front)	1897	*£140.00*	—
50	(Green Front)	1897	£65.00	—
50	(Plum Front)	1897	£65.00	—
25	Beauties (Numbered B801-B825)	1902	£12.00	£300.00
30	Beauties, Oval (Plain Back)	1914	£2.50	£75.00
44	Beauties of To-Day	1937	£1.50	£66.00
50	Beauties of To-Day	1938	90p	£50.00
36	Beauties of To-Day, 2nd Series	1940	£1.20	£44.00
F54	Beauties of To-Day	1939	£1.30	£70.00
LF36	Beauties of To-Day	1938	£2.50	£90.00
LF36	Beauties of To-Day (Different Subjects)	1938	£5.00	—
XF36	Beauties of To-Day (Unnumbered)	1937	£1.50	£54.00
XF36	Beauties of To-Day, 2nd Series	1938	£1.25	£45.00
XF36	Beauties of To-Day, 3rd Series	1938	£1.00	£36.00
XF36	Beauties of To-Day, 4th Series	1938	90p	£32.50
XF36	Beauties of To-Day, 5th Series	1938	£1.00	£36.00
XF36	Beauties of To-Day, 6th Series	1939	£1.00	£36.00
XF36	Beauties of To-Day, 7th Series	1939	£1.00	£36.00
XF36	Ditto (B.D.V. Back)	1939	40p	£14.00
36	Beauties of the World	1931	£1.50	£54.00

Qty		*Date*	*Odds*	*Sets*
36	Beauties of the World Series No. 2	1933	£1.50	£54.00
50	Beautiful Women (I.F. Series)	1908	£9.00	£450.00
50	(W.I. Series)	1908	£10.00	£500.00
L50	Beautiful Women	1908	£18.00	£900.00
P30	Beauty Spots of the Homeland	1938	30p	£9.00
50	Bird Painting	1938	75p	£37.50
25	Boxer Rebellion	1904	£27.00	£675.00
50	British Beauties (Photogravure)	1916	£7.00	£350.00
K76	British Beauties	1916	£2.70	£205.00
F54	British Beauties, 1-54	1914	£2.40	£130.00
F54	(Plain Back, Glossy)	1914	*£3.50*	—
54	(Plain Back, Brown)	1914	£3.50	—
F54	British Beauties, 55-108 (Glossy)	1915	£2.20	£120.00
54	(Matt)	1915	£2.40	—
54	(Plain Back, Sepia)	1915	£3.20	—
50	British Birds and Their Eggs	1936	£1.00	£50.00
30	British Butterflies, No.1 Issue	1911	£4.50	£135.00
25	British Butterflies	1927	90p	£22.50
25	Ditto (Transfers)	1936	80p	£20.00
25	British Orders of Chivalry & Valour	1939	£2.60	£65.00
25	British Warships	1915	£7.00	£175.00
L25	British Warships	1915	£35.00	—
F80	British Warships	1916	£13.50	—
50	Busts of Famous People (Brown Back)	1907	*£35.00*	—
50	(Green Back)	1907	£6.50	£325.00
50	(Pale Green)	1907	*£22.50*	—
M36	Characters Come to Life	1938	£1.25	£45.00
?25	Children's Stories (Booklets)	1924	£30.00	—
25	Chinese Series (English Text)	1910	£6.00	£150.00
25	(Volunteer Cigarettes)	1910	£8.00	£200.00
G?6	Chinese Series	1910	*£75.00*	—
M25	Cinema Stars (Circular)	1924	£3.20	£80.00
F52	Cinema Stars	1923	£2.75	£143.00
30	Cinema Stars (Brown)	1924	£2.75	£82.50
30	Cinema Stars (Black & White)	1925	£1.50	£45.00
32	Cinema Stars (Black & White)	1930	£1.50	£48.00
32	Cinema Stars (Brown, Hand Coloured)	1934	£1.75	£56.00
30	Cinema Stars (Plain Back)	1935	£1.00	£30.00
50	Colonial Troops	1902	£25.00	—
50	Coronation of Their Majesties	1937	30p	£15.00
M36	Coronation of Their Majesties	1937	30p	£11.00
P24	Coronation of Their Majesties (Postcard)	1937	£1.40	£34.00
P24	(Non-Postcard)	1937	£4.25	—
KF198	Cricketers (Pinnace)	1924	£7.00	—
F192	Cricketers (Brown Back)	1924	£7.50	—
LF25	Cricketers (Brown Back)	1924	£22.00	£550.00
LF?138	(Pinnace)	1924	£37.50	—
PF?223	Cricketers (Premium Issue)	1924	£35.00	—
1	Cricket Fixture Card	1936	—	£6.00
25	Derby Winners & Jockeys	1923	£3.80	£95.00
30	Eggs, Nests & Birds (Numbered)	1912	£5.50	£165.00
30	(Unnumbered)	1912	£5.50	£165.00
25	Empire Industries	1927	£1.00	£25.00
49/50	Evolution of the British Navy	1930	£1.00	£49.00
25	Famous Boys	1924	£2.40	£60.00

Qty		Date	Odds	Sets
32	Famous Cricketers	1926	£4.75	£152.00
25	Famous Crowns	1938	30p	£7.50
50	Famous Footballers	1936	£1.80	£90.00
M36	Famous Love Scenes	1939	75p	£27.00
50	Famous Minors	1936	30p	£15.00
P26	Famous Paintings	1936	£1.30	£34.00
25	Feathered Friends	1928	£1.60	£40.00
50	Film Favourites	1934	65p	£32.50
50	Film Stars	1934	65p	£32.50
P24	Film Stars (Series of Cards, Postcard)	1934	£1.10	£26.50
P24	("Series of Cards", Non-Postcard)	1934	£2.75	£66.00
P24	Film Stars (Series of 24 Cards, Postcard)	1934	£2.75	£66.00
P24	("Series of 24 Cards", Non-Postcard)	1934	£4.00	—
P24	Film Stars, 2nd (25-48, Postcard Backs)	1934	£2.75	£66.00
P24	(25-48, Non-Postcard)	1934	£5.00	—
50	First Aid	1923	£1.40	£70.00
25	First Aid Series	1914	£6.00	£150.00
25	Fish	1924	£2.40	£60.00
M30	Flower Studies	1937	30p	£9.00
P30	Flower Studies	1937	60p	£18.00
KF112	Footballers (Brown Oval Back)	1920	£3.50	—
KF400	(Black Oval Back)	1920	£1.60	—
KF?390	(Double Frame Line Back)	1921	£1.80	—
KF834	(1-940, Address "Photo")	1921	£1.00	—
KF71	(941-1109, Address "Photo")	1922	£2.00	—
KF836	(1-940, Address "Pinnace")	1922	£1.00	—
KF1514	(941-2462, Address "Pinnace")	1923	£2.00	—
LF?400	Footballers (Oval Design Back)	1920	£3.25	—
LF?1100	(Oblong Frame "Photo" Back)	1921	£6.50	—
LF?2462	("Pinnace" Back)	1922	£3.25	—
PF2462	Footballers (Premium Issue)	1921	£9.00	—
GF?	Football Teams (Premium Issue)	1923	*£175.00*	—
P1	Franco British Exhibition	1908	—	£25.00
P30	Garden Studies	1938	30p	£9.00
13	General Interest	1896	£45.00	£585.00
90	Guinea Gold Series (Numbered, Glossy)	1902	£4.25	£380.00
90	(Numbered, Matt)	1902	£4.25	£380.00
100	Guinea Gold Series	1902	£5.50	£550.00
161	Guinea Gold Series (Different)	1902	£4.25	£680.00
100	(Brown)	1902	£8.50	—
25	Home Pets	1924	£2.00	£50.00
25	How To Build a Two Valve Set	1929	£2.60	£65.00
25	How To Do It Series	1913	£7.00	£175.00
25	How To Make a Valve Amplifier	1924	£3.20	£80.00
25	How To Make Your Own Wireless Set	1923	£2.40	£60.00
25	Indian Series	1908	£13.00	£325.00
54	In The Public Eye	1935	50p	£27.00
50	International Caps	1936	£1.80	£90.00
35/37	Kings & Queens of England	1925	£1.80	£63.00
25	Lawn Tennis	1930	£3.00	£75.00
K52	Miniature Playing Cards (Red Back)	1906	*£100.00*	—
K53	Miniature Playing Cards (Blue Design)	1934	60p	—
K53	(Buff, 3 Types)	1932	50p	£26.50
K53	(White)	1933	60p	—
K53	(Yellow)	1933	60p	—
25	Model Railways	1927	£2.80	£70.00

Qty		*Date*	*Odds*	*Sets*
30	Morse Signalling	1916	£8.75	£262.50
50	Motor Cars at a Glance	1924	£3.60	£180.00
20	Novelty Series	1924	£10.00	£200.00
25	Old Favourites	1924	£1.80	£45.00
M36	Old Masters	1939	25p	£9.00
36	Olympic Champions, Amsterdam 1928	1928	£2.50	£90.00
25	Optical Illusions	1927	£2.20	£55.00
36	Our Dogs	1939	£1.50	£54.00
M30	Our Dogs	1939	65p	£19.50
P30	Our Dogs	1939	£3.30	£100.00
M48	Our Favourites	1935	25p	£12.00
P30	Our Glorious Empire	1939	50p	£15.00
M30	Our Puppies	1936	£1.80	£54.00
P30	Our Puppies	1936	£1.80	£54.00
25	Personalities of To-Day	1932	£1.60	£40.00
25	Popular Superstitions	1930	£1.40	£35.00
25	Prizes for Needlework	1925	£2.00	£50.00
25	Railway Engines	1934	£2.80	£70.00
KF27	Real Photo Series (War Leaders)	1916	£6.50	£175.00
1	Real Stamp Card	1928	—	£2.00
25	Red Indians	1927	£3.00	£75.00
20	Russo Japanese War Series	1905	*£140.00*	—
25	School Badges	1927	£1.00	£25.00
48	Screen Stars A (Embossed)	1936	£1.00	£48.00
48	(Not Embossed)	1936	£1.60	£77.00
48	Screen Stars B (Different)	1936	£1.00	£48.00
30	Semaphore Signalling	1916	£8.75	£262.50
25	Ships and their Flags	1924	£2.80	£70.00
M36	Ships that have Made History	1938	75p	£36.00
M48	Shots from the Films	1934	80p	£39.00
50	Soccer Stars	1936	£1.80	£90.00
36	Soldiers of the King (Adhesive)	1939	£1.50	£54.00
36	(Non-Adhesive)	1939	60p	£21.50
P12	Special Jubilee Series	1935	£1.75	£21.00
M20	Special Jubilee Year Series	1935	40p	£8.00
30	Speed Champions	1930	£1.80	£54.00
36	Sporting Champions	1929	£2.40	£86.50
25	Sporting Series	1910	£17.50	—
25	Sports	1923	£3.60	£90.00
50	Sportsmen – Spot the Winner (Normal)	1937	£1.50	£75.00
50	(Back Inverted)	1937	£1.10	£55.00
35	Stage and Cinema Beauties A	1933	£1.10	£38.50
35	Stage and Cinema Beauties B (Different)	1933	£1.00	£35.00
50	Stage and Cinema Beauties (Different)	1935	£1.10	£55.00
54	Stars of the Screen	1934	£1.10	£59.50
48	Stars of the Screen (Embossed)	1936	£1.00	£48.00
48	(Not Embossed)	1936	80p	£38.50
X16	Stars of the Screen (Strips of 3)	1936	£2.00	£32.00
25	Statues & Monuments (Brown Back)	1907	*£50.00*	—
25	(Green, Patent)	1907	£8.00	£200.00
25	(Green, Provisional Patent)	1907	£8.00	£200.00
25	Territorial Series (Motors Back)	1908	£22.00	£550.00
25	The 1924 Cabinet	1924	£1.80	£45.00
48	The "Old Country"	1935	50p	£24.00
50	This Mechanized Age First Series (Adhesive)	1936	30p	£15.00
50	(Non-Adhesive).	1936	40p	£20.00
50	This Mechanized Age Second Series	1937	25p	£12.50

Qty		Date	Odds	Sets
25	Types of British & Colonial Troops	1899	£42.50	—
25	Types of British Soldiers (M651-M675)	1900	£22.00	£550.00
F63	War Photos	1916	£8.00	£500.00
X20	Wrestling Holds	1930	£30.00	—
XS30	Zoo Studies – Come to Life Series	1939	£1.20	£36.00
X1	Zoo Studies Viewer	1939	—	£7.50
BDV PACKAGE ISSUES				
17	Boxers	1932	£6.00	—
54	Cricketers	1932	£7.00	—
67	Film Stars	1932	£2.25	—
136	Footballers	1932	£5.00	—
19	Jockeys	1932	£3.50	—
21	Speedway Riders	1932	£7.50	—
38	Sportsmen	1932	£3.50	—
"SPORTS" PACKAGE ISSUES				
50	All Sports 1st	1948	£4.00	—
25	All Sports 2nd	1949	£4.00	—
25	All Sports 3rd (Card or Paper)	1953	£4.00	—
25	All Sports 4th	1954	£4.00	—
25	Cricketers 1st	1948	£8.00	—
25	Cricketers 2nd (Card or Paper)	1951	£8.00	—
25	Footballers 1st	1948	£7.00	—
50	Footballers 2nd (Card or Paper)	1950	£7.00	—
25	Footballers 3rd (Card or Paper)	1951	£7.00	—
25	Jockeys (Card or Paper)	1952	£4.00	—
25	Radio Stars	1949	£2.75	—
25	Rugby & Association Footballers	1952	£5.75	—
OVERSEAS ISSUES				
50	Animal Studies	1930	£1.30	£65.00
50	Annuals	1939	£1.20	£60.00
X32	Australian Birds (Cartons)	1968	—	*£12.50*
X24	Australian Scenes (Cartons)	1965	—	*£12.50*
50	Australian Sporting Celebrities	1932	£2.60	£130.00
X32	Australian Wild Flowers (Cartons)	1967	—	*£12.50*
50	Film Stars	1934	£1.80	£90.00
E16	Gemstones (Cartons)	1970	—	£10.00
50	Stars of British Films (B.D.V.)	1934	£1.60	£80.00
50	(De Reszke)	1934	£1.60	£80.00
50	(Greys)	1934	£1.75	—
50	(No Brand)	1934	£1.75	£87.50
38	Test Cricketers (B.D.V.)	1932	£2.75	£104.50
38	(Greys)	1932	£2.75	£104.50
38	(No Brand)	1932	£3.00	£114.00
X32	The Barrier Reef (Cartons)	1968	—	£10.00
50	Victorian Footballers (B.D.V.)	1933	£2.25	£112.50
50	(Greys)	1933	£2.25	—
50	(No Brand)	1933	£2.25	—
75	Victorian Footballers	1933	£2.50	—
50	Victorian League & Association Footballers	1934	£2.60	—
100	Who's Who in Australian Sport	1933	£3.00	£300.00
SILK ISSUES				
M1	Allies Flags	1915	—	£8.00
G2	Allies Flags (Anon.)	1915	£8.50	—
G2	(B.D.V.)	1915	£8.50	—

Qty		*Date*	*Odds*	*Sets*
M62	Arms of Countries & Territories	1912	£3.70	£230.00
M32	Beauties-Modern Paintings	1910	£11.00	£350.00
P32	Beauties-Modern Paintings	1910	£40.00	—
M100	Birds	1921	£2.50	—
M12	Birds of the Tropics	1913	£10.00	£120.00
L12	Birds of the Tropics	1913	£12.50	—
P12	Birds of the Tropics	1913	£17.50	—
X24	British Admirals	1916	£6.00	—
D50	British Butterflies & Moths	1922	£5.50	—
M108	British Naval Crests (Anon., Blue Nos.)	1915	£1.80	—
M9	(Anon., Brown Nos.)	1915	£5.00	—
M108	(B.D.V.)	1915	£1.70	—
M23	Butterflies	1911	£9.00	£207.00
M47	Ceramic Art (70 x 43mm)	1925	£1.00	£47.00
M47	(70 x 48mm)	1925	80p	£38.00
L47	Ceramic Art	1925	£1.75	—
M65	Clan Tartans (68 x 44mm)	1922	£1.10	—
M65	(71 x 48mm) (B.D.V.)	1922	£1.00	£65.00
M49	(71 x 48mm) (Anon.)	1922	£1.00	£49.00
L56	Clan Tartans	1922	£2.75	—
P12	Clan Tartans	1922	£4.75	£57.00
M108	Colonial Army Badges	1913	£2.00	—
M17	County Cricket Badges (Anon.)	1921	£15.00	—
M17	(B.D.V.)	1921	£13.50	—
M108	Crests & Badges of the British Army			
	(Anon., Numbered)	1914	£1.20	£130.00
	(Anon., Unnumbered)	1914	£1.30	£141.00
	(B.D.V.)	1914	£1.20	£130.00
L105	Crests & Badges of the British Army (Anon.)	1914	£1.40	—
L108	(B.D.V.)	1914	£1.40	—
M143	Flags, Set 4-1 (Short)	1913	80p	—
M119	Flags, Set 4-2 (Short, Renumbered)	1913	90p	£107.00
M114	Flags, Set 4-3 (Short, Renumbered)	1913	90p	£100.00
L142	Flags, Set 4 (Long)	1913	£1.60	£227.50
M24	Flags, Set 5 (With Caption)	1913	80p	£19.00
M12	Flags, Set 5 (No Caption)	1913	£1.00	£12.00
P8	Flags, Set 5	1913	£12.50	—
M18	Flags, Set 6	1913	85p	£15.00
M20	Flags, Set 7	1913	85p	—
M50	Flags, 5th Series	1914	£1.60	£80.00
M120	Flags, 7th Series	1914	80p	£96.00
L120	Flags, 10th Series	1915	90p	£108.00
M120	Flags, 12th Series	1915	80p	£96.00
L65	Flags, 15th Series	1916	£1.10	—
L64	Flags, 16th Series	1916	£1.10	—
M120/132	Flags, 20th Series (B.D.V. Brown)	1917	85p	£100.00
M?48	(B.D.V. Orange)	1917	£2.00	—
M120/126	Flags, 25th Series	1917	80p	£96.00
L62	Flags, 25th Series	1917	£2.75	—
M112	Flags, 26th Series (in Brown)	1918	80p	£90.00
M?43	(in Blue)	1918	£3.50	£90.00
M70	Flags, 28th Series	1918	85p	£60.00
P17	Flags, Set 13	1914	£2.00	£34.00
G23	Flags, Set 13 (Anon.)	1914	£2.25	£52.00
G27	(B.D.V.)	1914	£2.00	£54.00

Qty		Date	Odds	Sets
M21	Football Colours (Anon.)	1914	£6.75	—
M86	(B.D.V.)	1920	£6.00	—
P78	Football Colours	1920	£5.50	—
M126	G.P. Territorial Badges	1913	£1.75	£220.00
L25	Great War Leaders (Sepia)	1915	£4.50	£112.50
M3	Great War Leaders & Celebrities (Anon.)	1916	£6.00	£18.00
M4	(B.D.V.)	1916	£6.00	£24.00
L3	Great War Leaders & Celebrities (Anon.)	1916	£6.00	£18.00
L2	(B.D.V.)	1916	£6.00	£12.00
P4	Great War Leaders & Celebrities (Anon.)	1916	£5.50	£22.00
P18	(B.D.V.)	1916	£5.50	—
G29	Great War Leaders & Celebrities (Anon.)	1916	£5.00	—
G45	(B.D.V.)	1916	£5.00	£225.00
P1	Great War Leaders (B.D.V. in Blue)	1916	—	£9.00
M52	Great War Leaders & Warships	1914	£5.50	—
M25	Heraldic Series (69 x 43mm)	1924	£1.00	£25.00
M25	(68 x 47mm)	1924	£1.00	£25.00
L25	Heraldic Series	1924	£2.75	—
P12	Heraldic Series	1924	£4.50	£54.00
M26	House Flags	1915	£8.00	£208.00
M10	Irish Patriots	1919	£11.00	£110.00
X10	Irish Patriots	1919	£12.50	—
P10	Irish Patriots	1919	£16.50	—
M1	Irish Republican Stamp	1925	—	£1.50
M1	Let 'Em All Come	1920	—	£10.00
X?	Miniature Rugs	1924	*£5.00*	—
M54	Naval Badges of Rank & Military Headdress	1917	£5.50	£300.00
G1	Nelson's Signal at Trafalgar	1921	—	*£120.00*
G40	Old Masters, Set 1	1911	£28.00	£1120.00
P20	Old Masters, Set 2 (Anon.)	1912	£4.00	£80.00
P20	(B.D.V. at Top)	1912	£3.60	£72.00
P20	(B.D.V. at Bottom)	1912	£5.50	—
M85	Old Masters, Set 3 (Anon.)	1912	£2.40	—
M40	(B.D.V.)	1912	£2.50	£100.00
M120	Old Masters, Set 4	1913	£2.00	—
M20	Old Masters, Set 5 (Anon., Unnumbered)	1922	£2.60	£52.00
M20	(Anon.,101-120)	1922	£1.60	£32.00
M60	(B.D.V. 1-60)	1922	£1.20	£72.00
M20	(B.D.V. 101-120)	1922	£1.60	£32.00
M50	Old Masters, Set 6	1924	£1.20	£60.00
M50	Old Masters, Set 7 (301-350)	1916	£2.40	£120.00
M50	Orders of Chivalry (Anon.)	1920	£2.20	£110.00
M24	Orders of Chivalry (B.D.V., 1-24)	1914	£1.60	£37.50
M24	(GP401-424)	1914	£1.80	£44.00
M25	Pilot & Signal Flags (Anon.)	1921	£3.20	£80.00
M25	(B.D.V.)	1921	£2.00	£50.00
L72	Regimental Colours	1914	£4.00	—
M50	Regimental Colours, Series 12	1918	£1.80	£90.00
M120	Regimental Colours & Crests (B.D.V.)	1915	£1.50	—
M120	(Anon.)	1915	£1.50	—
M40	(Anon., With Vignettes)	1915	£1.20	—
G120	Regimental Colours & Crests (Anon.)	1915	£6.25	—
G120	(B.D.V.)	1915	£5.75	—

GODFREY PHILLIPS LTD. — cont.

Qty		*Date*	*Odds*	*Sets*
M10	Religious Pictures	1911	£17.50	—
X10	Religious Pictures	1911	£20.00	—
P10	Religious Pictures	1911	£25.00	—
M75	Town & City Arms	1918	£1.80	£170.00
L75	Town & City Arms	1918	£2.40	—
M25	Victoria Cross Heroes I	1915	£11.00	—
M25	Victoria Cross Heroes II (With Flags)	1915	£12.00	—
M90	War Pictures	1915	£5.00	£450.00

JOHN PLAYER & SONS

44 Page Reference Book — £3.50

25	Actors & Actresses	1898	£23.00	£575.00
50	Actresses	1897	£22.50	£1125.00
6/7	Advertisement Cards (Navy Cut Back)	1894	£275.00	—
4/5	(Testimonial Back)	1894	£275.00	—
1	Advertisement Card – Sailor	1929	—	£5.00
L1	Advertisement Card – Sailor	1929	—	£18.00
L1	Advertisement Card – Wants List	1936	—	£1.00
P6	Advertisement Postcards	1906	£80.00	—
50	Aeroplanes (Eire)	1935	£1.30	£65.00
50	Aeroplanes (Civil)	1935	£1.10	£55.00
50	Aircraft of the Royal Air Force	1938	£1.00	£50.00
X10	Allied Cavalry	1914	£9.00	£90.00
L24	A Nature Calendar	1930	£3.00	£72.00
50	Animals of the Countryside	1939	20p	£10.00
50	Ditto (Eire)	1939	85p	£42.50
L25	Aquarium Studies	1932	£1.60	£40.00
L25	Architectural Beauties	1927	£2.00	£50.00
50	Arms & Armour (Blue Back)	1909	£2.25	£112.50
50	Army Corps & Divisional Signs (1-50, 2 Printings)	1924	35p	£17.50
100	Army Corps & Divisional Signs 2nd (51-150)	1925	50p	£50.00
25	Army Life	1910	£1.80	£45.00
X12	Artillery in Action	1917	£4.50	£54.00
50	A Sectional Map of Ireland	1932	£2.30	£115.00
50	Association Cup Winners	1930	£1.80	£90.00
50	Aviary and Cage Birds	1933	80p	£40.00
50	Ditto (Transfers)	1933	30p	£15.00
L25	Aviary & Cage Birds	1935	£3.40	£85.00
50	Badges & Flags of British Regiments			
	(Green Back)	1903	£1.80	£90.00
	(Brown Back, Numbered)	1904	£1.80	£90.00
	(Brown Back, Unnumbered)	1904	£2.20	£110.00
50	Birds & Their Young	1937	20p	£9.00
50	(Eire) (Adhesive)	1937	85p	£42.50
50	(Eire) (Non-Adhesive)	1937	85p	£42.50
25	(Non-Adhesive)	Unissued	30p	£7.50
25	2nd (Non-Adhesive)	Unissued	20p	£4.00

Racing Caricatures
Player

War Pictures
Home and Colonial Stores

Australian Sporting Celebrities
Godfrey Phillips

Castles
Cope

Wild Life
Goodies

Aerial Navigation
Series B
Savoy Products

Ocean Giants
Thurmer & Symes

Types of the Stage
Lorillard

Britain's Nocturnal Wildlife
Player – Doncella, Grandee

History of Aviation
Nabisco

Stars of Football 1940's
JF Sporting Collectibles

Golfing
Wills

Qty		Date	Odds	Sets
K1	Bookmark (Calendar Back)	1902	—	*£120.00*
PF10	Bookmarks (Authors)	1902	£60.00	£600.00
25	Boxing (Eire)	1934	£6.00	£150.00
50	Boy Scout & Girl Guide	1933	35p	£17.50
50	Ditto (Transfers)	1933	25p	£12.50
L25	British Butterflies	1934	£4.20	£105.00
50	British Empire Series	1904	£1.25	£62.50
25	British Live Stock	1915	£2.50	£62.50
X25	British Live Stock (Blue Back)	1923	£3.20	£80.00
X25	(Brown Back)	1916	£3.40	£85.00
L25	British Naval Craft	1939	£1.00	£25.00
X20	British Pedigree Stock	1925	£3.40	£68.00
L25	British Regalia	1937	£1.00	£25.00
50	Butterflies	1932	£1.20	£60.00
50	Ditto (Transfers)	1932	30p	£15.00
50	Butterflies & Moths	1904	£1.70	£85.00
25	Bygone Beauties	1914	£1.20	£30.00
X10	Bygone Beauties	1916	£4.25	£42.50
G?2	Cabinet Size Pictures.(Brown Front, Printed Back)	1899	*£80.00*	—
G?10	(Brown Front, Plain Back)	1899	*£80.00*	—
G?30	(Green Front, Printed Back)	1899	£75.00	—
G?30	(Green Front, Plain Back)	1899	£75.00	—
20	Castles Abbeys etc. (No Border)	1895	£25.00	£500.00
20	(White Border)	1895	£24.00	£480.00
L24	Cats	1936	£7.00	£168.00
50	Celebrated Bridges	1903	£2.50	£125.00
50	Celebrated Gateways	1909	£1.35	£67.50
25	Ceremonial and Court Dress	1911	£1.60	£40.00
L25	Championship Golf Courses	1936	£7.50	£187.50
25	Characters from Dickens, A Series (1-25)	1912	£2.00	£50.00
25	Characters from Dickens, 2nd Series (26-50)	1912	£2.00	£50.00
50	Characters from Dickens (Re-issue)	1923	£1.30	£65.00
X10	Characters from Dickens	1914	£5.00	£50.00
L25	Characters from Fiction	1933	£3.60	£90.00
25	Characters from Thackeray	1913	£1.30	£32.50
50	Cities of the World	1900	£3.60	£180.00
L20	Clocks – Old & New	1928	£4.75	£95.00
25	Colonial & Indian Army Badges	1917	£1.20	£30.00
50	Coronation Series – Ceremonial Dress	1937	20p	£10.00
25	Counties and Their Industries (Numbered)	1915	£2.00	£50.00
25	(Unnumbered)	1914	£2.00	£50.00
50	Countries Arms & Flags (Thick Card)	1905	80p	£40.00
50	(Thin Card)	1912	£1.00	£50.00
50	Country Seats and Arms (1-50)	1909	75p	£37.50
50	Country Seats and Arms, 2nd (51-100)	1910	75p	£37.50
50	Country Seats and Arms, 3rd (101-150)	1910	75p	£37.50
L25	Country Sports	1930	£5.40	£135.00
50	Cricketers 1930	1930	£1.40	£70.00
50	Cricketers 1934	1934	£1.25	£62.50
50	Cricketers 1938	1938	£1.00	£50.00
50	Cricketers, Caricatures by "RIP"	1926	£1.80	£90.00
25	Cries of London, A Series	1913	£1.80	£45.00
X10	Cries of London, A Series	1912	£4.20	£42.00
X10	Cries of London, 2nd Series	1914	£3.25	£32.50
25	Cries of London, 2nd Series (Blue Back)	1916	80p	£20.00
25	(Black Back)	1916	£4.00	—

JOHN PLAYER & SONS — cont.

Qty		Date	Odds	Sets
50	Curious Beaks	1929	80p	£40.00
50	Cycling	1939	90p	£45.00
50	(Eire) (Adhesive)	1939	£1.50	£75.00
50	(Eire) (Non-Adhesive)	1939	£1.50	£75.00
50	Dandies	1932	30p	£15.00
L25	Dandies	1932	£1.80	£45.00
50	Decorations & Medals	Unissued	£1.90	£95.00
50	Derby and Grand National Winners	1933	£1.60	£80.00
50	(Transfers)	1933	40p	£20.00
50	Dogs (Scenic Background)	1925	90p	£45.00
X12	Dogs (Scenic Background)	1924	£3.20	£38.50
50	Dogs, by Wardle (Full Length)	1931	80p	£40.00
50	(Transfers)	1931	30p	£15.00
L25	Dogs, by Wardle (Full Length)	1933	£2.50	£62.50
50	Dogs, by Wardle (Heads)	1929	£1.00	£50.00
L20	Dogs, by Wardle, A Series (Heads)	1926	£2.60	£52.00
L20	Dogs, by Wardle, 2nd Series (Heads)	1928	£2.60	£52.00
25	Dogs, by Wardle, A Series (Eire) (Heads)	1927	£1.80	£45.00
25	Dogs, by Wardle 2nd Series (Eire) (Heads)	1929	£1.80	£45.00
50	Dogs' Heads by Biegel	Unissued	£1.20	£60.00
L25	Dogs (Heads)	Unissued	£1.60	£40.00
50	Dogs' Heads (Silver Background, Eire)	1940	£3.00	£150.00
50	Drum Banners & Cap Badges (2 Printings)	1924	80p	£40.00
25	Egyptian Kings & Queens and Classical Deities	1912	£1.80	£45.00
X10	Egyptian Sketches	1915	£3.50	£35.00
25	England's Military Heroes (Narrow)	1898	£27.50	£685.00
25	(Wide)	1898	£37.50	£935.00
25	(Narrow, Plain Back)	1898	£27.50	£685.00
25	(Wide, Plain Back)	1898	£37.50	—
25	England's Naval Heroes			
	(Non-Descriptive, Narrow)	1897	£25.00	£625.00
	(Non-Descriptive, Wide)	1897	£36.00	£900.00
25	England's Naval Heroes			
	(Descriptive, Narrow)	1898	£25.00	£625.00
	(Descriptive, Wide)	1898	£36.00	£900.00
25	Everyday Phrases (by Tom Browne)	1900	£15.00	£375.00
L25	Fables of Aesop	1927	£2.20	£55.00
20	Famous Authors & Poets (Narrow)	1900	£18.00	£360.00
20	(Wide)	1900	£26.50	£530.00
L25	Famous Beauties	1937	£1.60	£40.00
50	Famous Irish-Bred Horses	1936	£3.40	£170.00
50	Famous Irish Greyhounds	1935	£5.20	£260.00
X10	Famous Paintings	1913	£3.25	£32.50
50	Film Stars	1934	£1.10	£55.00
50	Film Stars, Second Series	1934	90p	£45.00
50	Ditto (Eire)	1934	£1.60	£80.00
50	Film Stars, Third Series	1938	80p	£40.00
L25	Film Stars	1934	£3.00	£75.00
L25	Ditto (Eire)	1934	£6.00	£150.00
50	Fire-Fighting Appliances	1930	£1.50	£75.00
50	Fishes of the World	1903	£1.80	£90.00
50	Flags of the League of Nations	1928	40p	£20.00
50	Football Caricatures by "MAC"	1927	£1.20	£60.00
50	Footballers, Caricatures by "RIP"	1926	£1.20	£60.00

Qty		Date	Odds	Sets
50	Footballers 1928	1928	£1.70	£85.00
25	Footballers 1928-9, 2nd Series	1929	£1.60	£40.00
50	Fresh-Water Fishes (Pink Back)	1933	£1.20	£60.00
50	(White Back)	1934	£1.50	£75.00
L25	Fresh-Water Fishes	1935	£2.60	£65.00
L25	Ditto (Eire, Non-Adhesive)	1935	£5.00	£125.00
25	From Plantation to Smoker	1926	25p	£6.25
50	Gallery of Beauty Series	1896	£20.00	£1000.00
5	Alternative Subjects	1896	£60.00	—
50	Game Birds and Wild Fowl	1927	£1.40	£70.00
L25	Game Birds & Wild Fowl	1928	£4.60	£115.00
25	Gems of British Scenery	1917	60p	£15.00
50	Gilbert and Sullivan, A Series	1925	£1.00	£50.00
X25	Gilbert & Sullivan, A Series	1926	£3.20	£80.00
50	Gilbert and Sullivan, 2nd Series	1927	£1.00	£50.00
L25	Gilbert & Sullivan, 2nd Series	1928	£3.50	£87.50
L25	Golf	1939	£7.50	£187.50
25	Hidden Beauties	1929	20p	£5.00
25	Highland Clans	1907	£3.60	£90.00
50	Hints on Association Football	1934	80p	£40.00
X10	Historic Ships	1910	£4.00	£40.00
50	History of Naval Dress	1930	£1.00	£50.00
L25	History of Naval Dress	1929	£2.00	£50.00
50	International Air Liners	1936	40p	£20.00
50	Ditto (Eire)	1936	90p	—
25	Irish Place Names, A Series	1927	£2.00	£50.00
25	Irish Place Names, 2nd Series	1929	£2.00	£50.00
1	Joker Card (Eire)	1935	—	£4.00
M5	Jubilee Issue	1960	£1.20	£6.00
50	Kings & Queens of England	1935	£1.50	£75.00
L50	Kings & Queens of England	1935	£2.60	£130.00
50	Life on Board a Man of War – 1805 &1905	1905	£1.80	£90.00
25	Live Stock	1925	£3.50	£87.50
50	Military Head-Dress	1931	£1.00	£50.00
50	Military Series	1900	£18.00	£900.00
50	Military Uniforms of the British Empire Overseas	1938	80p	£40.00
25	Miniatures	1923	40p	£10.00
50	Modern Naval Craft	1939	50p	£25.00
50	Ditto (Eire)	1939	90p	£45.00
50	Motor Cars, A Series	1936	£1.20	£60.00
50	Motor Cars, A Series (Eire)	1936	£2.00	£100.00
50	Motor Cars, Second Series	1937	90p	£45.00
L20	Mount Everest	1925	£3.25	£65.00
25	Napoleon	1916	£1.70	£42.50
50	National Flags and Arms	1936	40p	£20.00
50	Ditto (Eire)	1936	75p	£37.50
50	Natural History	1924	25p	£12.50
X12	Natural History	1924	£1.00	£12.00
X12	Natural History, 2nd Series	1924	£1.00	£12.00
50	Nature Series	1909	£1.20	£60.00
X10	Nature Series (Birds)	1908	£8.50	£85.00
X10	Nature Series (Mammals)	1913	£5.00	£50.00
50	Old England's Defenders	1898	£17.50	£875.00
L25	Old Hunting Prints	1938	£2.50	£75.00
L25	Old Naval Prints	1936	£2.40	£60.00
X25	Old Sporting Prints	1924	£3.20	£80.00

JOHN PLAYER & SONS — cont.

Qty		Date	Odds	Sets
L25	Picturesque Bridges	1929	£2.60	£65.00
L25	Picturesque Cottages	1929	£3.00	£75.00
L25	Picturesque London	1931	£3.80	£95.00
25	Players Past & Present	1916	90p	£22.50
25	Polar Exploration, A Series	1915	£2.20	£55.00
25	Polar Exploration, 2nd Series	1916	£1.80	£45.00
L25	Portals of the Past	1930	£2.00	£50.00
50	Poultry	1931	£1.70	£85.00
50	Ditto (Transfers)	1931	30p	£15.00
25	Products of the World	1908	60p	£15.00
50	Products of the World (Different)	1928	20p	£10.00
25	Racehorses (Eire)	1926	£5.00	£125.00
40	Racing Caricatures	1925	75p	£30.00
L25	Racing Yachts	1938	£3.60	£90.00
50	R.A.F. Badges (No Motto)	1937	60p	£30.00
50	(With Motto)	1937	60p	£30.00
50	Regimental Colours & Cap Badges (Regulars)	1907	£1.00	£50.00
50	Regimental Colours & Cap Badges (Territorials, Blue Back)	1910	£1.00	£50.00
	(Territorials, Brown Back)	1910	£1.00	£50.00
50	Regimental Standards and Cap Badges	1930	65p	£32.50
50	Regimental Uniforms (Blue Back)	1912	£2.00	£100.00
50	(Brown Back)	1914	£2.00	£100.00
X10	Regimental Uniforms (Different)	1914	£7.00	£70.00
50	Regimental Uniforms, 2nd Series (51-100)	1913	£1.00	£50.00
50	Riders of the World	1905	£1.50	£75.00
P30	Rulers & Views	1902	£80.00	—
50	Sea Fishes	1935	30p	£15.00
50	Ditto (Eire)	1935	80p	—
50	Screen Celebrities (Eire)	1938	£1.70	£85.00
25	Shakespearean Series	1917	£1.20	£30.00
L20	Ship-Models	1926	£2.40	£48.00
50	Shipping	Unissued	—	£65.00
25	Ships' Figure-Heads (2 Printings)	1912	£1.80	£45.00
L25	Ships' Figure-Heads	1931	£1.70	£42.50
L8	Snap Cards	1930	£7.00	—
50	Speedway Riders	1937	£1.70	£85.00
S?148	Stereoscopic Series	1904	£85.00	—
50	Straight Line Caricatures	1926	50p	£25.00
25	Struggle for Existence (2 Printings)	1923	20p	£5.00
50	Tennis	1936	90p	£45.00
116	The Corsair Game (Eire)	1965	£1.00	—
L25	The Nation's Shrines	1929	£2.00	£50.00
X1	The Royal Family	1937	—	£2.25
P6	The Royal Family	1901	£40.00	£240.00
25	Those Pearls of Heaven	1916	£1.20	£30.00
66	Transvaal Series	1902	£5.00	—
L25	Treasures of Britain	1931	£1.60	£40.00
25	Treasures of Ireland	1930	£1.60	£40.00
L25	Types of Horses	1939	£3.60	£90.00
50	Uniforms of the Territorial Army	1939	90p	£45.00
50	Useful Plants & Fruits	1902	£1.80	£90.00
25	Victoria Cross	1914	£2.40	£60.00
90	War Decorations & Medals	1927	65p	£60.00

Qty		*Date*	*Odds*	*Sets*
50	Wild Animals' Heads	1931	60p	£30.00
25	Ditto (Transfers)	1931	£1.40	—
50	Wild Animals' Heads (Transfers, Series of 50)	1927	40p	£20.00
L25	Wild Animals (Heads), A Series	1932	£1.60	£40.00
L25	Wild Animals (Heads), 2nd Series	1932	£1.60	£40.00
45	Wild Animals of the World (Narrow) (No Ltd)	1901	£4.75	—
45	(Narrow) (With Ltd)	1901	£4.75	—
45	(Narrow) ("Branch")	1901	£6.50	—
50	Wild Animals of the World (Wide) (No Ltd)	1901	£2.40	£120.00
50	(Wide) (With Ltd)	1901	£2.30	£115.00
50	(Wide) ("Branch")	1901	£4.25	—
50	Wild Birds	1932	50p	£25.00
50	Ditto (Transfers)	1932	30p	£15.00
L25	Wild Birds	1934	£2.60	£65.00
L25	Wildfowl	1937	£3.00	£75.00
50	Wonders of the Deep	1904	£1.75	£87.50
25	Wonders of the World (Blue Back)	1916	60p	£15.00
25	(Grey Back, Eire)	1926	£1.20	£30.00
X10	Wooden Walls	1908	£5.25	£52.50
25	Wrestling & Ju-Jitsu (Blue Back)	1913	£2.00	£50.00
25	(Grey Back, Eire)	1925	£1.50	£37.50
26	Your Initials (Transfers)	1932	50p	£13.00
L25	Zoo Babies	1938	50p	£12.50

OVERSEAS ISSUES

50	Aeroplane Series	1926	£2.00	£100.00
50	Aircraft of the Royal Air Force	1938	£1.40	£70.00
50	Animals of the Countryside	1939	50p	£25.00
50	Arms & Armour (Grey Back)	1926	£2.80	£140.00
F50	Beauties	1925	£1.50	£75.00
MF50	Beauties (Coloured)	1925	£1.70	£85.00
F50	Beauties, 2nd Series	1925	£1.60	£80.00
50	Birds & Their Young	1937	60p	£30.00
52	Birds of Brilliant Plumage	1927	£3.25	—
25	"Bonzo" Dogs	1923	£4.50	£112.50
50	Boy Scouts	1924	£2.80	£140.00
L25	British Live Stock	1924	£7.00	£175.00
50	Butterflies (Girls)	1928	£5.50	£275.00
50	Coronation Series – Ceremonial Dress	1937	80p	—
50	Cricketers 1938	1938	£1.60	£80.00
50	Cycling	1939	£1.40	£70.00
25	Dogs (Heads)	1927	£1.40	£35.00
32	Drum Horses	1911	£7.50	—
L25	Famous Beauties	1937	£2.20	£55.00
50	Film Stars, Third Series	1938	£1.40	—
25	Flag Girls of All Nations	1908	£6.50	—
L25	Golf	1939	£6.50	£162.50
50	Household Hints	1928	80p	£40.00
50	International Air Liners	1936	80p	£40.00
50	Lawn Tennis	1928	£3.40	£170.00
50	Leaders of Men	1925	£2.00	£100.00
50	Military Uniforms of the British Empire Overseas			
	(Adhesive)	1938	£1.40	£70.00
	(Non-Adhesive)	1938	£1.40	£70.00
50	Modern Naval Craft	1939	90p	£45.00

Qty		*Date*	*Odds*	*Sets*
50	Motor Cars, A Series	1936	£1.80	£90.00
50	Motor Cars, Second Series	1937	£1.70	£85.00
50	National Flags and Arms	1936	60p	£30.00
L25	Old Hunting Prints	1938	£3.60	£90.00
M15/22	Old Masters (Package Issue)	1966	£1.00	£15.00
P2	Old Masters (Package Issue)	1966	£2.50	£5.00
L25	Old Naval Prints	1936	£3.20	£80.00
48	Pictures of the East	1931	£2.25	£108.00
25	Picturesque People of the Empire	1938	£2.00	£50.00
M53	Playing Cards	1929	£1.25	—
50	Pugilists in Action	1928	£3.60	£180.00
L25	Racing Yachts	1938	£4.50	—
50	R.A.F. Badges	1937	90p	£45.00
50	Railway Working	1927	£1.60	£80.00
50	Sea Fishes	1935	60p	£30.00
50	Ships Flags & Cap Badges	1930	£1.80	£90.00
50	Signalling Series	1926	£1.40	£70.00
F50	The Royal Family at Home and Abroad	1927	£2.25	—
L25	Types of Horses	1939	£4.50	£112.50
25	Whaling	1930	£2.60	£65.00
L25	Zoo Babies	1937	£1.60	£40.00

MODERN ISSUES (DONCELLA)

T32	Britain's Endangered Wildlife	1984	30p	£9.50
T30	Britain's Nocturnal Wildlife	1987	60p	£18.00
T30	Britain's Wild Flowers	1986	50p	£15.00
T32	British Butterflies	1984	60p	£19.00
T30	British Mammals	1983	50p	£15.00
T32	Country Houses and Castles	1981	20p	£4.50
T24	Golden Age of Flying	1977	25p	£6.00
T1	Golden Age of Flying Completion Offer	1978	—	£3.50
T24	Golden Age of Motoring	1975	25p	£6.00
T24	Golden Age of Motoring Completion Offer	1976	£3.50	£84.00
T24	Golden Age of Sail	1978	25p	£6.00
T1	Golden Age of Sail Completion Offer	1979	—	£3.50
T24	Golden Age of Steam	1976	30p	£7.50
T1	Golden Age of Steam Completion Offer	1977	—	£4.00
T24	History of the V.C.	1980	75p	£18.00
T1	History of the V.C. Completion Offer	1980	—	£4.00
T24	Napoleonic Uniforms	1980	25p	£6.00
T1	Napoleonic Uniforms Completion Offer	1980	—	£4.00
T30	The Living Ocean	1985	50p	£15.00

MODERN ISSUES (GRANDEE)

T30	African Wildlife	1990	40p	£12.00
T32	Britain's Endangered Wildlife	1984	25p	£8.00
T30	Britain's Nocturnal Wildlife	1987	25p	£7.50
T30	Britain's Wayside Wildlife	1988	25p	£7.50
T30	Britain's Wild Flowers	1986	25p	£7.50
T32	British Birds	1980	40p	£13.00
T32	British Butterflies	1983	40p	£13.00
T30	British Mammals (Imperial Tobacco Ltd.)	1982	20p	£6.00
T30	(Imperial Group plc.)	1983	20p	£6.00

JOHN PLAYER & SONS — cont.

Qty		*Date*	*Odds*	*Sets*
T28	Famous M.G. Marques	1981	85p	£24.00
T7	Limericks	1977	£10.00	—
T30	The Living Ocean	1985	25p	£7.50
T25	Top Dogs	1979	£1.00	£25.00
T6	World of Gardening	1976	£10.00	£60.00

MODERN ISSUES (TOM THUMB)

L30	Britain's Maritime History	1989	40p	£12.00
L32	Exploration of Space	1982	20p	£6.25
L30	History of Britain's Railways	1987	25p	£7.50
L30	History of British Aviation	1988	70p	£21.00
L30	History of Motor Racing (Imperial Tobacco Ltd.)	1986	£1.00	£30.00
L30	(Imperial Group plc.)	1986	£1.50	£45.00
L32	Myths & Legends	1981	80p	£26.00
T4	Record Breakers	1976	*£1.50*	—
L32	Wonders of the Ancient World	1984	50p	£16.00
L30	Wonders of the Modern World	1985	30p	£9.00

MODERN ISSUES (OTHER)

44	Black Jack	1984	£1.25	—
M44	Black Jack	1984	50p	—
T44	Black Jack	1984	50p	—
T8	Panama Puzzles	1976	£6.00	—
T?	Player Clues (Headings in Blue)	1987	50p	—
T?	Player Clues (Headings in Red)	1987	50p	—
T?63	Player Games (Green)	1983	*50p*	—
T?29	Player Games (Yellow)	1983	*75p*	—
T?62	Player Games (Orange)	1984	*50p*	—
T?106	Player Games (Silver)	1984	50p	—
T?	Player Games (Yellow)	1984	*75p*	—
T?127	Player Quiz (Green)	1985	65p	—
T?	Player Quiz (Blue)	1986	65p	—
T?	Player Quiz (Red)	1986	*65p*	—
T6	Play Ladbroke Spot-Ball	1975	£6.50	—
T6	Play Panama Spot Six	1977	£6.50	—
T4	Recordbreakers	1976	*£5.00*	—
T50	Super Cars (35 x 90mm)	1987	65p	—
T50	(47 x 90mm)	1987	65p	—
60	Super Deal	1984	£1.25	—
M60	Super Deal	1984	65p	—
T60	Super Deal (35 x 90mm)	1984	£1.25	—
T60	(47 x 90mm)	1984	65p	—
T108	Super Year 88 (35 x 90mm)	1988	£1.25	—
T108	(47 x 90mm)	1988	65p	—
M4	Vanguard Limericks	1981	*£1.50*	—
156	World Tour	1986	£1.25	—
M156	World Tour	1986	65p	—
T156	World Tour (35 x 90mm)	1986	£1.25	—
T156	(47 x 90mm)	1986	65p	—

JAMES PLAYFAIR & CO.

25	How To Keep Fit	1912	£32.00	£800.00

PREMIER TOBACCO MFRS. LTD.

Qty		Date	Odds	Sets
48	Eminent Stage & Screen Personalities	1936	£1.75	£84.00
K52	Miniature Playing Cards	1935	*£7.50*	—
50	Stage & Screen Personalities (Brown)	1936	£2.20	—
100	(Grey)	1936	£1.40	£140.00

PRITCHARD & BURTON

51	Actors & Actresses "FROGA" (Blue Back)	1899	£20.00	—
51	(Grey Back)	1899	*£40.00*	—
15	Beauties "PAC"	1899	£50.00	£750.00
20	Boer War Cartoons	1900	£85.00	—
30	Flags & Flags with Soldiers (Draped)	1902	£16.00	£480.00
15	(Different Back)	1902	£20.00	—
15	Flags & Flags with Soldiers (Undraped)	1902	£20.00	—
25	Holiday Resorts & Views	1902	£17.00	£425.00
40	Home & Colonial Regiments	1901	£45.00	—
25	Royalty Series	1902	£20.00	£500.00
25	South African Series	1901	£18.00	£450.00
25	Star Girls	1900	£125.00	—

G. PRUDHOE

30	Army Pictures, Cartoons, etc	1916	*£95.00*	—

Q.V. CIGARS

M?7	Barnum & Bailey's Circus Performers	1900	*£175.00*	—

JAS. QUINTON LTD.

26	Actresses "FROGA"	1899	£135.00	—

RAY & CO. LTD.

K7	Flags of the Allies (Shaped)	1916	£60.00	—
25	War Series (1-25)	1915	£12.50	—
75	War Series (26-100)	1915	£9.00	—
24	War Series (101-124)	1916	£22.50	—

RAYMOND REVUEBAR

MF25	Striptease Artistes (2 Printings)	1960	£13.00	—

RECORD CIGARETTE & TOBACCO CO.

X34	The Talkie Cigarette Card (Record Cigarette Co.)	1934	£37.50	—
X34	(Record Tobacco Co.)	1934	£42.50	—

REDFORD & CO.

Qty		*Date*	*Odds*	*Sets*
20	Actresses "BLARM"	1900	£70.00	—
25	Armies of the World	1901	£55.00	—
25	Beauties "GRACC"	1899	*£110.00*	—
30	Colonial Troops	1902	£50.00	—
24	Nautical Expressions	1900	*£65.00*	—
40	Naval & Military Phrases	1904	£55.00	—
25	Picture Series	1906	£65.00	—
25	Sports & Pastimes	1906	*£75.00*	—
50	Stage Artistes of the Day	1908	£16.50	£825.00

RELIANCE TOBACCO MFG. CO.

24	British Birds	1934	£5.00	£120.00
35	Famous Stars	1934	£4.50	£157.50

A.S. RICHARDSON

M12	Manikin Cards (2 Printings)	1915	£80.00	—

RICHMOND CAVENDISH CO. LTD.

26	Actresses "FROGA"	1900	£30.00	£780.00
28	Actresses "PILPI I"	1902	£13.00	£360.00
F50	Actresses "PILPI II"	1903	£9.50	£475.00
?179	Actresses, Gravure (Back Top-Bottom)	1904	£6.25	—
50	Actresses, Gravure (Back Bottom-Top)	1904	£7.00	£350.00
14	Beauties "AMBS" (12 Backs)	1899	£45.00	—
52	Beauties P/C Inset	1897	£45.00	—
28	Chinese Actors & Actresses	1923	£3.60	£100.00
F50	Cinema Stars	1927	£3.40	£170.00
40	Medals	1900	£18.50	£740.00
20	Music Hall Artistes	1901	£42.50	£850.00
12	Pretty Girl Series "RASH"	1899	£37.50	£450.00
20	Yachts (Black Back)	1900	£60.00	—
20	(White Back)	1900	£62.50	—

RIDGWAY'S MANCHESTER

M?	Play Up Sporting Shields	1900	*£45.00*	—

RITMEESTER CIGARS (Cigar Bands)

24	Austrian Cavalry Serie D	1976	£1.25	—
X28	Austrian Cavalry Serie D	1976	£1.00	£28.00
24	English Cavalry Serie A	1976	80p	£20.00
X28	English Cavalry Serie A	1976	£1.50	—
24	French Cavalry Serie B	1976	£1.00	£24.00
X28	French Cavalry Serie B	1976	£1.00	—
24	German Cavalry Serie C	1976	£1.25	—
X28	German Cavalry Serie C	1976	60p	£16.00
24	Military Bandsmen Serie K	1978	—	£20.00

ROBERTS & SONS

Qty		Date	Odds	Sets
26	Actresses "FROGA"	1899	*£62.50*	—
25	Armies of the World (Plain Back)	1900	£45.00	—
25	(Printed Back)	1900	£45.00	—
M50	Beautiful Women	1898	*£175.00*	—
50	Beauties "CHOAB" (Black Back)	1900	£70.00	—
50	(Blue Back)	1900	*£75.00*	—
50	Colonial Troops	1902	£37.50	£1875.00
M28	Dominoes	1905	£60.00	—
K52	Miniature Playing Cards (Blue)	1905	*£60.00*	—
K52	(Pink)	1905	*£60.00*	—
K52	(Yellow)	1905	*£60.00*	—
24	Nautical Expressions (Navy Cut Cigarettes)	1902	£55.00	—
24	(No Brand)	1902	*£60.00*	—
70	Stories Without Words	1904	£50.00	—
25	Types of British & Colonial Troops	1900	£45.00	—

ROBINSON & BARNSDALE LTD.

24	Actresses, Colin Campbell	1898	£125.00	—
?29	Actresses, Cupola	1898	*£160.00*	—
1	Advertisement Card, Colin Campbell	1897	—	£120.00
?24	Beauties, Collotype (Black Back, "NANA")	1895	*£150.00*	—
?24	(Red Back, "NANA")	1895	*£150.00*	—
?24	(Our Golden Beauties)	1895	*£150.00*	—
M?13	Beauties, Highest Honors ("Viginia")	1895	*£225.00*	—
M?13	("Virginia" Label)	1895	*£225.00*	—
?3	Beauties - "KEWA II"	1900	*£150.00*	—

E. ROBINSON & SONS LTD.

10	Beauties (10 Brands)	1897	£55.00	—
?43	Derbyshire and the Peak	1903	*£100.00*	—
25	Egyptian Studies	1914	£24.00	—
25	King Lud Problems	1934	£20.00	—
6	Medals & Decorations of Great Britain			
	(Red Terra Cotta Back)	1902	*£160.00*	—
	(General Favourite Onyx Back)	1902	*£200.00*	—
40	Nature Studies	1914	£21.00	—
25	Regimental Mascots	1916	£65.00	—
25	Types of British Soldiers			
	(General Favourite Onyx Back)	1914	*£175.00*	—
25	Wild Flowers	1915	£18.00	—

ROMAN STAR CIGARS

26	Actresses "FROGA"	1899	*£120.00*	—
25	Beauties "BOCCA"	1899	*£120.00*	—

ROTHMANS LTD.

40	Beauties of the Cinema	1939	£1.50	£60.00
L24	Beauties of the Cinema (Circular, Matt)	1939	£4.00	£96.00
L24	(Varnished)	1939	£4.00	£96.00

ROTHMANS LTD. — cont.

Qty		Date	Odds	Sets
P25	Canterbury Bankstown District Rugby League Football Club (New Zealand)	1980	*£5.00*	—
24	Cinema Stars	1925	£1.40	£33.50
L25	Cinema Stars	1925	£1.20	£30.00
P30	Country Living Cards	1974	—	£12.00
28	Dominoes	1986	£2.25	—
L50	Football International Stars	1984	40p	£20.00
15	Know Africa	1970	£2.50	£37.50
15/16	Know Your Language	1970	£2.50	£37.50
36	Landmarks in Empire History	1936	£1.00	£36.00
?	Lucky Charms (Metal)	1930	£3.75	—
50	Modern Inventions	1935	£1.00	£50.00
LF54	New Zealand	1933	80p	£43.00
24	Prominent Screen Favourites	1934	£1.25	£30.00
F50	Punch Jokes	1935	60p	£30.00
M?	Puzzle Card Series	1930	*£25.00*	—
5	Rare and Historic Banknotes	1970	£3.60	£18.00
L8	Wiggle-Woggle Picture Cards	1933	*£20.00*	—

WM. RUDDELL LTD.

?	Couplet Cards	1924	*£15.00*	—
25	Grand Opera Series	1924	£7.20	£180.00
25	Rod & Gun	1924	£6.40	£160.00
50	Songs That Will Live For Ever	1924	£3.50	£175.00

RUTHERFORDS

?1	Footballers	1900	*£1000.00*	—

I. RUTTER & CO.

15	Actresses (Printed Back)	1900	£55.00	—
15	(Rubber Stamped Back)	1900	*£70.00*	—
15	(Plain Back)	1900	£23.50	—
1	Advertisement Card	1899	—	*£400.00*
7	Boer War Celebrities (Printed Back)	1901	£50.00	£400.00
7	(Plain Back)	1901	£23.50	—
54	Comic Phrases	1905	£17.00	£920.00
20	Cricketers Series	1902	£250.00	—
30	Flags & Flags with Soldiers	1901	£24.00	£720.00
24	Girls, Flags & Arms of Countries	1900	£35.00	£840.00
25	Proverbs (Green Seal)	1904	£40.00	—
25	(Red Seal)	1904	£40.00	—
25	Shadowgraphs	1903	£40.00	—

S.D.V. TOBACCO CO. LTD.

16	British Royal Family	1901	*£225.00*	—

SACCONE & SPEED

F55	Beauties	1912	*£8.00*	—
F55	(Red Overprint)	1912	£5.00	—
?119	Picture Competition	1912	*£10.00*	—

ST. PETERSBURG CIGARETTE CO. LTD.

Qty		Date	Odds	Sets
?	Footballers	1900	*£400.00*	—

SALMON & GLUCKSTEIN LTD.

X1	Advertisement Card (Snake Charmer, 10 Different)	1897	—	£400.00
15	Billiard Terms (Large Numerals)	1905	£65.00	—
15	(Small Numerals)	1905	£60.00	£900.00
12	British Queens	1902	£42.50	£510.00
X30	Castles, Abbeys & Houses (Brown Back)	1906	£16.00	£480.00
X30	(Red Back)	1906	£24.00	—
32	Characters from Dickens	1903	£27.50	—
25	Coronation Series,1911	1911	£11.00	£275.00
L25	Famous Pictures (Brown)	1912	£10.00	£250.00
L25	Famous Pictures (Green, Different)	1912	£7.00	£175.00
6	Her Most Gracious Majesty Queen Victoria	1897	£50.00	£300.00
40	Heroes of the Transvaal War	1901	£12.00	£700.00
25	Magical Series	1923	£6.20	£155.00
48	Methods of Conveying the Mails	1900	£24.00	£1150.00
30	Music Hall Stage Characters	1902	£50.00	£1500.00
25	Occupations	1898	£375.00	—
20	Owners & Jockeys Series	1900	£70.00	£1400.00
L50	Pottery Types (Silk, Numbered Front & Back)	1916	£3.50	£175.00
L50	(Silk, Numbered Backs Only)	1916	£3.50	£175.00
6	Pretty Girl Series "RASH"	1900	£60.00	£360.00
22	Shakespearian Series (Frame on Back)	1902	£24.00	£525.00
22	(No Frame on Back)	1902	£32.50	—
25	Star Girls (Brown Back)	1899	£110.00	—
25	(Red Back)	1899	£110.00	—
50	The Great White City	1908	£12.00	£600.00
25	Traditions of the Army & Navy (Large No.)	1917	£13.00	£325.00
25	(Small No.)	1917	£13.00	£325.00
25	Wireless Explained	1923	£5.20	£130.00

W. SANDORIDES & CO. LTD.

25	Aquarium Studies From The London Zoo			
	(Large Numerals)	1925	£3.50	£87.50
	(Small Numerals)	1925	£3.00	£75.00
L25	Aquarium Studies from The London Zoo	1925	£3.50	£87.50
25	Cinema Celebrities	1924	£2.60	£65.00
X25	Cinema Celebrities	1924	£4.00	—
25	Cinema Stars (With Firm's Name)	1924	*£5.50*	—
25	(Big Gun)	1924	*£7.00*	—
25	(Lucana)	1924	*£5.50*	—
X25	Cinema Stars (Big Gun)	1924	£2.60	£65.00
X25	(Lucana 66)	1924	*£6.50*	—
50	Famous Racecourses	1926	£3.20	£160.00
L50	Famous Racecourses	1926	£4.50	£225.00
50	Famous Racehorses (With Firm's Name)	1923	£3.00	£150.00
50	(Big Gun Label)	1923	*£10.00*	—
12	London Views (4 Types)	1936	£5.00	—
25	Sports & Pastimes	1924	*£11.00*	—

SANSOM'S CIGAR STORES

Qty		*Date*	*Odds*	*Sets*
?13	London Views	1905	*£200.00*	—

NICOLAS SARONY & CO.

25	A Day On The Airway	1928	£1.00	£25.00
L25	A Day On The Airway	1928	£1.00	£25.00
50	Around The Mediterranean	1926	£1.00	£50.00
L50	Around The Mediterranean	1926	£1.00	£50.00
?7	Boer War Scenes	1901	*£250.00*	—
M100	Celebrities and Their Autographs (2 Printings)	1923	70p	£70.00
L100	Celebrities and Their Autographs (2 Printings)	1923	75p	£75.00
50	Cinema Stars	1933	£1.25	£62.50
P38	Cinema Stars	1930	£9.00	—
P42	Cinema Stars, Second Series	1930	£5.00	£210.00
P50	Cinema Stars, Third Series	1930	£5.00	£250.00
P42	Cinema Stars, Fourth Series	1930	£5.00	£210.00
P25	Cinema Stars, Fifth Series	1930	£5.00	£125.00
25	Cinema Studies	1929	£1.00	£25.00
F54	Life at Whipsnade Zoo	1934	50p	£27.00
50	Links with the Past	1925	25p	£12.50
25	(Australia)	1926	60p	—
25	(New Zealand)	1926	60p	£15.00
L50	Links with the Past	1925	25p	£12.50
L25	(Australia)	1926	60p	—
L25	(New Zealand)	1926	50p	£12.50
L25	(Presentation Issue)	1926	£1.60	—
25	Museum Series	1927	30p	£7.50
25	(New Zealand)	1927	70p	£17.50
L25	Museum Series	1927	30p	£7.50
L25	(Australia)	1927	60p	—
L25	(New Zealand)	1927	60p	—
L25	(Presentation Issue)	1927	80p	£20.00
F36	National Types of Beauty	1928	30p	£11.00
MF36	National Types of Beauty	1928	30p	£11.00
15	Origin of Games	1923	£4.00	£60.00
L15	Origin of Games	1923	£4.50	£67.50
50	Saronicks	1929	50p	£25.00
M50	Saronicks	1929	50p	£25.00
50	Ships of All Ages	1929	90p	£45.00
M50	Ships of All Ages	1929	90p	£45.00
25	Tennis Strokes	1923	£3.20	£80.00

T. S. SAUNT

30	Army Pictures, Cartoons, etc	1916	*£100.00*	—

SCOTTISH C.W.S. LTD.

25	Burns (Large Numeral)	1924	£1.50	£37.50
25	(Small Numeral)	1924	£2.40	£60.00
25	(Plain Back)	1924	*£6.00*	—
20	Dogs	1925	£10.00	—

SCOTTISH C.W.S. LTD. — cont.

Qty		Date	Odds	Sets
25	Dwellings of All Nations (Large Numeral)	1924	£2.00	£50.00
25	(Small Numeral)	1924	£3.50	£87.50
25	(Plain Back)	1924	*£6.00*	—
L25	Famous Pictures	1924	£7.50	—
L25	Famous Pictures – Glasgow Gallery			
	(Adhesive)	1927	£1.20	£30.00
	(Non-Adhesive)	1927	£2.20	£55.00
L25	Famous Pictures – London Galleries			
	(Adhesive)	1927	£1.20	£30.00
	(Non-Adhesive)	1927	£2.20	£55.00
50	Feathered Favourites (Adhesive)	1926	£1.60	£80.00
	(Non-Adhesive, Grey Border)	1926	£2.20	£110.00
	(Non-Adhesive, White Border)	1926	£2.20	£110.00
25	Racial Types	1925	£8.00	£200.00
50	Triumphs of Engineering (Brown Border)	1926	£2.00	£100.00
50	(White Border)	1926	£2.25	—
50	Wireless	1924	£3.60	£180.00

SELBY'S TOBACCO STORES

M12	Manikin Cards	1915	*£80.00*	—

SHARPE & SNOWDEN

?1	Views of England	1905	*£150.00*	—
?23	Views of London	1905	*£135.00*	—

W. J. SHEPHERD

25	Beauties "FECKSA"	1901	£85.00	—

SHORT'S

L?13	House Views (Numbered)	1924	*£60.00*	—
L6	House Views (Unnumbered)	1924	£35.00	—

SIMONETS LTD. (Channel Isles)

MF36	Beautiful Women	1928	£5.50	£200.00
F24	Cinema Scene Series	1926	£6.50	—
F27	Famous Actors and Actresses	1929	£5.00	—
50	Local Footballers	1925	£4.60	£230.00
25	Picture Series	1925	£3.60	£90.00
F27	Sporting Celebrities	1929	£8.50	—
LF50	Views of Jersey (Plain Back)	1926	£2.00	—

JOHN SINCLAIR LTD.

M?89	Actresses	1902	£70.00	—
F48	Birds	1924	£2.50	£120.00
F?50	("Specimen Cigarette Card")	1924	£7.00	—

JOHN SINCLAIR LTD. — cont.

Qty		Date	Odds	Sets
LF50	Birds	1924	£5.50	£275.00
50	British Sea Dogs	1928	£4.75	£237.50
F54	Champion Dogs, A Series	1938	£1.20	£65.00
LF52	Champion Dogs, A Series	1938	£1.20	£62.00
F54	Champion Dogs, 2nd Series	1939	£3.25	£175.00
LF52	Champion Dogs, 2nd Series	1939	£3.50	£182.00
F50	English & Scottish Football Stars	1935	£1.60	£80.00
F54	Film Stars (Series of 54 Real Photos)	1934	£2.00	£108.00
F54	Film Stars (Series of Real Photos)	1937	£1.75	£94.50
F54	Film Stars (55-108)	1937	£1.50	£81.00
M12	Flags (Numbered, Silk, 25-36)	1914	£13.50	—
M24	Flags (Unnumbered, Silk) (Blue Caption)	1914	£8.00	—
M24	(Bright Green)	1914	£7.00	—
M24	Flags (Unnumbered, Silk) (Olive Green)	1914	£6.50	—
M24	(Red Caption)	1914	£8.00	—
M25	Flags (Unnumbered, Silk) (Grey Caption)	1914	£11.00	—
M50	Flags, Fourth Series (Silk)	1914	£6.00	—
M50	Flags, Fifth Series (Silk)	1914	£6.00	—
D50	Flags, Sixth Series (Silk)	1914	£7.00	—
G10	Flags, Seventh Series (Silk)	1914	£50.00	—
F96	Flowers & Plants	1924	£2.00	£192.00
F?100	("Specimen Cigarette Card")	1924	£6.50	—
51	Football Favourites (51-101)	1908	£125.00	—
4	North Country Celebrities	1904	£65.00	£260.00
F55	Northern Gems	1902	£60.00	—
50	Picture Puzzles & Riddles Series	1916	£24.00	—
F54	Radio Favourites	1935	£1.50	£81.00
L50	Regimental Badges (Silk)	1915	£5.50	—
D24	Regimental Colours (Silk) (38-61)	1914	£12.50	—
K53	Rubicon Cards (Miniature Playing Cards)	1933	£5.00	—
K53	(Red Overprint)	1933	£7.00	—
P1	The Allies Flags (No. 37, Silk)	1915	—	£35.00
50	Trick Series	1916	£25.00	—
50	Well Known Footballers – N.E.Counties	1938	£1.30	£65.00
50	Well Known Footballers – Scottish	1938	£1.30	£65.00
50	Worlds Coinage	1914	£17.00	£850.00

ROBERT SINCLAIR TOBACCO CO. LTD.

X4	Battleships & Crests (Silk)	1915	£50.00	—
10	Billiards, First Set	1928	£8.00	£80.00
15	Billiards, Second Set	1928	£10.00	—
3	Billiards, Third Set	1928	£16.00	—
28	Dominoes	1902	*£50.00*	—
M10	Flags (Silk)	1915	£25.00	—
?5	Footballers (Black & White on Card)	1900	*£350.00*	—
?2	Footballers (Mauve on Paper)	1900	*£400.00*	—
P6	Great War Area (Silk)	1915	£40.00	—
M10	Great War Heroes (Silk)	1915	£35.00	—
12	Policemen of the World	1899	£150.00	—
X1	Red Cross Nurse (Silk)	1915	—	£50.00
M5	Regimental Badges (Silk)	1915	£27.50	—
12	The Smiler Series	1924	£6.50	—
L12	The Smiler Series	1924	£11.50	—

J. SINFIELD

Qty		Date	Odds	Sets
24	Beauties "HUMPS"	1899	*£250.00*	—

SINGLETON & COLE LTD.

50	Atlantic Liners	1910	£18.00	£900.00
25	Bonzo Series	1928	£8.00	£200.00
50	Celebrities-Boer War Period	1901	£17.50	£875.00
110	Crests & Badges of the British Army (Silk)	1915	£4.00	—
35	Famous Boxers (Numbered)	1930	£13.50	—
35	(Unnumbered)	1930	*£32.50*	—
25	Famous Film Stars	1930	£9.00	—
35	Famous Officers	1915	£13.00	£675.00
35	(Subtitled Hero Series)	1915	*£165.00*	—
50	Footballers	1905	£120.00	—
40	Kings & Queens	1902	£18.00	£720.00
M12	Manikin Cards	1915	*£80.00*	—
25	Maxims of Success (Orange Border)	1906	£26.00	£650.00
25	(Yellow Border)	1906	*£125.00*	—
10	Orient Line (Anonymous, 5 Ports on Back)	1904	£40.00	£400.00
10	(Anonymous,11 Ports on Back)	1904	£45.00	—
8	Orient Pacific Line (Anonymous)	1904	*£60.00*	—
8	Orient Royal Mail Line (Firm's Name)	1904	£42.50	£340.00
25	The Wallace-Jones Keep Fit System	1910	£24.00	£600.00

F. & J. SMITH

36 Page Illustrated Reference Book — £3.50

24	Advertisement Cards	1897	£200.00	£4800.00
50	A Tour Round the World (Postcard Back)	1904	£40.00	£2000.00
50	(Script Back)	1904	£20.00	£1000.00
50	A Tour Round the World (Descriptive, Multi-Backed)	1906	£9.00	£450.00
50	Battlefields of Great Britain (15 Backs)	1913	£14.00	£700.00
25	Boer War Series (Black & White)	1901	£65.00	—
50	Boer War Series (Coloured)	1901	£26.00	£1300.00
50	Champions of Sport (Blue Back)	1902	£80.00	—
50	Champions of Sport (Red Multi-Backed)	1902	£75.00	—
25	Cinema Stars (8 Brands)	1920	£10.00	£250.00
50	Cricketers (1-50)	1912	£15.00	£750.00
20	Cricketers, 2nd Series (51-70)	1912	£27.50	£550.00
50	Derby Winners	1913	£13.00	£650.00
50	Famous Explorers	1911	£13.00	£650.00
50	Football Club Records	1917	£15.00	£750.00
50	Football Club Records (Different)	1922	£15.00	£750.00
120	Footballers (Brown Back)	1906	£36.00	—
100	Footballers (Blue Back, No Series Title)	1908	£12.00	£1200.00
150	Footballers (Titled, Dark Blue Backs)	1912	£12.00	£1800.00
150	(Titled, Light Blue Backs)	1912	£12.00	—
50	Fowls, Pigeons & Dogs	1908	£9.00	£450.00
25	Holiday Resorts	1925	£7.00	£175.00
50	Medals (Numbered, Smith Multi-Backed)	1902	£9.00	£450.00
50	(Numbered, Imperial Tobacco Co., Multi-Backed)	1903	£32.50	—
50	(Numbered, Imperial Tobacco Company, Multi-Backed)	1906	£9.00	£450.00
20	(Unnumbered)	1905	£13.50	£270.00

LIEBIG

The Liebig Extract of Meat Co. Ltd. was formed in 1856 and was acquired by Brooke Bond in 1971. In Britain their product was renamed Oxo, which it is known as today. In a period of 100 years from 1872 the Company issued a large number of sets of cards, including postcards, menus, calendars, place cards and other novelty issues. The first series were issued in France, but eventually cards could be obtained all over Europe, in languages such as Danish, Czech, Spanish, and even Russian. Many series were printed in English, including the Oxo insert series, and issued in Britain and the U.S.A.

In all the company issued 2,000 different sets of cards. These covered an enormous variety of subjects, including the Trans-Siberian Railway, Shadowgraphs, Gulliver, Fans, Education in Ancient Greece, and the Left Bank of the River Po. There is even a set showing the life of Justus von Liebig, founder of the firm, and another showing how the cards themselves are prepared and printed.

Because of the size of the subject a separate catalogue is available (price £4.95) listing all the issues, and a small selection of series is listed on pages 252, 253 and 254.

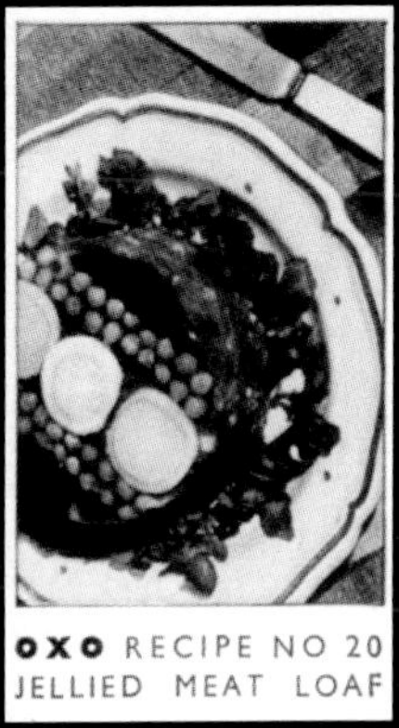

MODERN CARDS

The last few years have seen but a trickle of cigarette cards, albeit in cigar packets such as Doncella and Tom Thumb. For the most part however collectors have had to be satisfied with trade cards for their new acquisitions.

The most significant of these has been Brooke Bond, which has been issuing cards continuously since 1954 (British Birds) and has now issued over 40 different sets, usually with special albums, in Britain, North America, and Africa. One would like to think that the success of the Company, which incidentally also owns Liebig, owes as much to the quality and appeal of the cards as to the tea itself. Its rivals failed to sustain any competition in card issues, although many, such as Lyons, Horniman and Lipton, made some attempts.

Confectionery is another prolific area for card collectors, chiefly with sweet cigarettes (now discreetly called "Candy Sticks") and bubble gum. Barratt/Bassett is the premier issuer of the former, and A. & B. C./Topps of the latter, although the competition in these items is intense. Many other firms appear in these pages such as Dandy, Monty, Primrose & Somportex, and often collectors try to obtain the box or wrapper in addition to the set of cards.

Cereal products are also a fruitful source for the cartophilist. Kellogg, Nabisco and Welgar regularly include among their free incentive inserts collectable series of cards, often in novel form such as transfers or cut-outs.

The last rewarding area for cards is that of periodicals. A new feature of these has been the appearance of Panini, with free inserts in magazines and newspapers, followed by the opportunity to complete the very long sets by purchasing packets of cards. Often these sets are of footballers, and Panini invests some of its profits (with further advertising) in sponsoring family enclosures at soccer grounds.

F. & J. SMITH — cont.

Qty		Date	Odds	Sets
G1	Medal Album (Printed)	1902	—	£140.00
50	Nations of the World	1923	£6.00	£300.00
50	Naval Dress & Badges			
	(Descriptive, Multi-Backed)	1911	£9.00	£450.00
	(Non-Descriptive, Multi-Backed)	1914	£8.50	£425.00
50	Phil May Sketches (Brown, 4 Brands)	1924	£6.00	£300.00
50	(Grey, Multi-Backed)	1908	£8.50	£425.00
25	Prominent Rugby Players	1924	£11.00	£275.00
40	Races of Mankind (No Title, Multi-Backed)	1900	£60.00	—
40	(Titled, Multi-Backed)	1900	£45.00	—
25	Shadowgraphs (7 Brands)	1915	£6.00	£150.00
25	War Incidents, A Series	1914	£6.50	£162.50
25	War Incidents, 2nd Series	1915	£6.50	£162.50

F. L. SMITH LTD. (ALBANY CIGARETTES)

L?20	Advertising Inserts	1957	£5.50	—

SNELL & CO.

25	Boer War Celebrities "STEW"	1901	*£150.00*	—

SOROKO

6	Jubilee Series	1935	*£40.00*	—
L6	Jubilee Series	1935	*£40.00*	—

S. E. SOUTHGATE & SON

25	Types of British & Colonial Troops	1900	£115.00	—

SOUTH WALES TOB. MFG. CO. LTD.

30	Army Pictures, Cartoons, etc	1915	*£100.00*	—
?92	Game of Numbers	1912	*£70.00*	—
25	Views of London	1912	£24.00	£600.00

T. SPALTON

30	Army Pictures, Cartoons, etc	1916	*£95.00*	—

SPIRO VALLERI & CO.

?10	Noted Footballers	1908	*£500.00*	—

G. STANDLEY

M12	Manikin Cards	1915	*£80.00*	—

A. & A. E. STAPLETON

M12	Manikin Cards	1915	*£80.00*	—

STAR OF THE WORLD

Qty		Date	Odds	Sets
20	Boer War Cartoons	1901	£90.00	—
?32	Boer War Celebrities "JASAS"	1901	*£115.00*	—
30	Colonial Troops	1901	£70.00	—

H. STEVENS & CO.

20	Dogs	1923	£10.00	£200.00
25	Zoo Series	1926	£5.75	—

A. STEVENSON

50	War Portraits	1916	*£90.00*	—

ALBERT STOCKWELL

30	Army Pictures, Cartoons, etc	1916	*£100.00*	—

STRATHMORE TOBACCO CO. LTD.

M25	British Aircraft	1938	£3.00	£75.00

SWEET ALVA CIGARETTES

?32	Boer War Celebrities "JASAS"	1901	*£100.00*	—

T.S.S.

24	Nautical Expressions	1900	£85.00	—

TADDY & CO.

32 Page Reference Book — £3.50

72	Actresses, Collotype	1897	£95.00	—
25	Actresses with Flowers	1899	£80.00	£2000.00
37	Admirals & Generals – The War (2 Backs)	1914	£16.00	£900.00
25	Admirals & Generals – The War (S. Africa)	1914	£32.50	£812.50
25	Autographs	1912	£18.00	£450.00
20	Boer Leaders	1901	£19.00	£380.00
50	British Medals & Decorations, Series 2			
	(Steel Blue Back)	1912	£12.50	£625.00
	(Black Back)	1912	£32.50	—
50	British Medals & Ribbons	1912	£12.50	£625.00
20	Clowns & Circus Artistes	—	£650.00	—
30	Coronation Series	1902	£22.00	£660.00
238	County Cricketers	1907	£40.00	—
50	Dogs	1900	£27.00	£1350.00
5	English Royalty	1897	£625.00	—
25	Famous Actors/Famous Actresses	1903	£18.00	£450.00
50	Famous Horses and Cattle	1912	£100.00	—
25	Famous Jockeys (No Frame)	1910	£30.00	£750.00
25	(With Frame)	1910	£26.00	£650.00
50	Footballers (New Zealand)	1906	£75.00	—
25	Heraldry Series	1911	£17.00	£425.00

TADDY & CO. — cont.

Qty		Date	Odds	Sets
25	Honours & Ribbons	1915	£18.00	£450.00
10	Klondyke Series	1900	£62.50	£625.00
60	Leading M.L.A.'s (South Africa)	1900	*£625.00*	—
25	Natives of the World	1899	£60.00	£1500.00
25	Orders of Chivalry	1911	£18.00	£450.00
25	Orders of Chivalry, Second Series	1912	£24.00	£600.00
595	Prominent Footballers (No Footnote)	1907	£18.00	—
?403	Prominent Footballers (With Footnote)	1908	£18.00	—
?406	Prominent Footballers (London Mixture)	1914	£36.50	—
20	Royalty, Actresses & Soldiers	1898	£200.00	—
25	Royalty Series	1903	£18.00	£450.00
25	Russo Japanese War (1-25)	1904	£18.00	£450.00
25	Russo Japanese War (26-50)	1904	£24.00	£600.00
15	South African Cricket Team, 1907	1907	£55.00	£825.00
26	South African Football Team, 1906-7	1906	£23.00	£600.00
25	Sports & Pastimes	1912	£19.00	£500.00
25	Territorial Regiments	1908	£22.00	£550.00
25	Thames Series	1903	£34.00	£850.00
20	Victoria Cross Heroes (1-20)	1901	£60.00	£1200.00
20	Victoria Cross Heroes (21-40)	1901	£57.50	£1150.00
20	V.C. Heroes – Boer War (41-60)	1902	£19.00	£380.00
20	V.C. Heroes – Boer War (61-80)	1902	£19.00	£380.00
20	V.C. Heroes – Boer War (81-100)	1902	£20.00	£400.00
25	Victoria Cross Heroes (101-125)	1904	£55.00	—
2	Wrestlers	1908	£275.00	£550.00

TADDY & CO. (RE-REGISTERED)

(No Connection with Original Company)

8	Advertisement Cards	1980	50p	£4.00
26	Motor Cars (Clown Cigarettes)	1980	—	£8.00
26	(Myrtle Grove Cigarettes)	1980	—	£12.00
26	Railway Locomotives (Clown Cigarettes)	1980	—	£12.00
26	(Myrtle Grove Cigarettes)	1980	—	£8.00

W. & M. TAYLOR

8	The European War Series (Bendigo Cigarettes)	1915	*£40.00*	—
8	(Tipperary)	1915	*£40.00*	—
25	War Series (Bendigo Cigarettes)	1915	£20.00	£500.00
25	(Tipperary Cigarettes)	1915	£14.00	£350.00

TAYLOR WOOD

18	Motor Cycle Series	1914	£80.00	—

TEOFANI & CO. LTD.

25	Aquarium Studies From The London Zoo	1925	£11.50	—
50	Cinema Celebrities (Broadway Novelties)	1926	£4.00	—
50	(Anonymous)	1926	£3.60	—
25	Cinema Stars (Blue Band Cigarettes)	1924	*£6.75*	—
25	("Favourites" Printed)	1924	*£6.75*	—
25	("Favourites" Stamped)	1924	*£6.75*	—
25	(Three Star Cigarettes)	1924	*£6.75*	—
25	(Three Star Magnums, 2 Printings)	1924	£6.75	£169.00

TEOFANI & CO. LTD. — cont.

Qty		Date	Odds	Sets
X25	Cinema Stars	1924	*£6.75*	—
25	Famous Boxers	1925	£9.00	£225.00
F32	Famous British Ships and Officers	1934	£3.25	£104.00
L50	Famous Racecourses (Favourite Cigarettes)	1926	£16.50	—
50	Famous Racehorses	1923	£10.00	—
12	Film Actors & Actresses (Plain Back)	1936	75p	£9.00
20	Great Inventors	1924	£4.50	£90.00
20	Head-Dress of All Nations (Plain Back)	1926	£13.00	£260.00
LF50	Icelandic Girls	1929	£5.50	—
LF50	Icelandic Stage Scenes & Artistes	1929	*£12.50*	—
12	London Views (Plain Back)	1936	50p	£6.00
12	(8 Different Printed Backs)	1936	£4.00	£50.00
48	Modern Movie Stars & Cinema Celebrities	1934	£1.25	£60.00
50	Natives in Costume (Plain Back)	1926	£14.00	—
24	Past & Present "A" – The Army (No Frame)	1938	£1.75	£42.00
24	(With Frame Line on Back)	1938	£2.00	£48.00
24	Past & Present "B" – Weapons of War	1938	£1.25	£30.00
4	Past & Present "C" – Transport	1939	£5.00	£20.00
50	Public Schools & Colleges	1923	£3.20	£160.00
50	Ships and their Flags	1925	£3.20	£160.00
25	Sports & Pastimes (Plain Back)	1924	£5.00	£137.50
25	(Printed Back)	1924	£12.50	—
22	Teofani Gems	1925	£2.00	£44.00
28	Teofani Gems	1925	85p	—
36	Teofani Gems	1925	£2.00	£72.00
48	Transport Then & Now	1939	50p	£24.00
50	Views of London	1925	£2.25	—
F36	Views of the British Empire	1927	£1.00	£36.00
24	Well-Known Racehorses	1923	£8.00	—
50	World's Smokers (Plain Back)	1926	£14.00	£700.00
50	Zoological Studies	1924	£3.50	—
L50	Zoological Studies	1924	*£6.50*	—

TETLEY & SONS

1	The Allies	1915	*£350.00*	—
50	War Portraits	1916	£75.00	—
25	Worlds Coinage	1914	£60.00	—

THEMANS & CO.

?2	Anecdotes & Riddles	1913	*£250.00*	—
55	Dominoes	1913	*£80.00*	—
18	Motor Cycle Series	1914	£70.00	—
50	War Portraits	1915	£50.00	—
14	War Posters	1916	£175.00	—

SILK ISSUES (MAINLY ANONYMOUS)

M12	Crests of Warships (Series B4)	1914	£7.00	—
L4	Crests of Warships (Series C4)	1914	£10.00	—
M48	Film Stars (Series B6)	1914	£7.00	—
P14	Film Stars (Series D6)	1914	£7.00	—
M12	Flags (Series B1)	1914	*£7.00*	—

THEMANS & CO. — cont.

Qty		Date	Odds	Sets
M12	Flags (Series B2)	1914	*£7.00*	—
L12	Flags (Series C1)	1914	*£10.00*	—
L4	Flags (Series C2)	1914	*£10.00*	—
P2	Flags (Series D1)	1914	*£14.00*	—
P1	Flags (Series D2)	1914	*£14.00*	—
M12	Regimental Badges (Series B3)	1914	£7.00	—
L4	Regimental Badges (Series C3)	1914	£10.00	—
P1	Regimental Badges (Series D3)	1914	£15.00	—
M12	Views of Blackpool (Series B5)	1914	£20.00	—
P7	Views of Blackpool (Series D5)	1914	£20.00	—

THOMSON & PORTEOUS

50	Arms of British Towns	1905	£15.00	£750.00
25	Boer War Celebrities "STEW"	1901	£50.00	—
25	Shadowgraphs	1902	£40.00	—
20	The European War Series	1915	£13.00	£260.00
41	V.C. Heroes (Firm's Name at Bottom)	1916	£12.50	£550.00
41	(Firm's Name at Top)	1916	£45.00	—

TOM NODDY

P12	Children of the Year Series	1904	*£60.00*	—

TOPSY CIGARETTES

F?11	Actresses	1896	*£250.00*	—

TURKISH MONOPOLY CIGARETTE CO. LTD.

X?16	Boer War Scenes	1901	*£150.00*	—

UNITED KINGDOM TOBACCO CO. LTD.

50	Aircraft	1938	£1.40	£70.00
P48	Beautiful Britain, A Series	1929	£1.50	£72.00
P48	Beautiful Britain, Second Series	1929	£1.50	£72.00
25	British Orders of Chivalry & Valour (2 Printings)	1936	£1.60	£40.00
24	Chinese Scenes	1933	75p	£18.00
32	Cinema Stars	1933	£1.75	£56.00
50	Cinema Stars (With Firm's Name)	1934	£1.60	£80.00
50	(Anonymous)	1934	£2.20	—
36	Officers Full Dress	1936	£2.00	£72.00
52	Soldiers (Metal)	1935	£12.50	—
36	Soldiers of the King	1937	£2.00	£72.00

UNITED SERVICES MFG. CO. LTD.

50	Ancient Warriors	1938	£1.80	£90.00
25	Ancient Warriors	1957	£4.00	£100.00
50	Bathing Belles	1939	70p	£35.00
100	Interesting Personalities	1935	£2.60	£260.00
50	Popular Footballers	1936	£4.40	£220.00

UNITED SERVICES MFG. CO. LTD. — cont.

Qty		*Date*	*Odds*	*Sets*
50	Popular Screen Stars	1937	£3.60	£180.00

UNITED TOBACCONISTS ASSOCIATION LTD.

10	Actresses "MUTA"	1901	£125.00	—
12	Pretty Girl Series "RASH"	1900	*£150.00*	—

WALKERS TOBACCO CO. LTD. (W.T.C.)

60	British Beauty Spots	1924	*£17.50*	—
28	Dominoes (Old Monk)	1908	*£60.00*	—
28	Dominoes (W.T.C.)	1924	£4.50	—
F30/32	Film Stars (Tatleys)	1936	£1.60	£48.00
F48	Film Stars (Walkers)	1935	£4.50	—

WALTERS TOBACCO CO. LTD.

L6	Angling Information	1939	£1.50	—

E. T. WATERMAN

30	Army Pictures, Cartoons, etc	1916	*£100.00*	—

WEBB & RASSELL

50	War Portraits	1916	*£85.00*	—

HENRY WELFARE & CO.

22	Prominent Politicians	1912	£70.00	—

WESTMINSTER TOBACCO CO. LTD.

F36	Australia, First Series	1932	25p	£9.00
F36	Australia, 2nd Series (Plain Back)	1933	25p	£9.00
F48	British Royal and Ancient Buildings			
	(Unnumbered)	1925	75p	£36.00
	(Numbered)	1925	£1.00	£48.00
F48	British Royal and Ancient Buildings			
	Second Series	1926	25p	£12.00
F36	Canada, First Series	1926	50p	£18.00
F36	Canada, Second Series	1928	50p	£18.00
F48	Indian Empire, First Series	1925	25p	£12.00
F48	Indian Empire, Second Series	1926	25p	£12.00
F36	New Zealand, First Series	1928	25p	£9.00
F36	New Zealand, Second Series	1929	25p	£9.00
F36	South Africa, First Series	1928	50p	£18.00
F36	South Africa, Second Series	1928	50p	£18.00

OVERSEAS ISSUES

L?200	Adamson's Oplevelser	1926	£17.50	—
MF50	Beauties	1924	£2.75	—

Qty		*Date*	*Odds*	*Sets*
MF?97	Beautiful Women	1915	£2.50	—
M50	Birds, Beasts & Fishes	1923	£2.60	£130.00
?57	British Beauties (Hand Coloured)	1915	£3.00	—
102	(Uncoloured)	1915	*£3.75*	—
F48	British Royal and Ancient Buildings	1925	£1.00	£48.00
50	Butterflies & Moths	1920	£2.50	£125.00
F36	Canada, First Series	1926	90p	£32.50
F36	Canada, Second Series	1928	90p	£32.50
30	Celebrated Actresses	1921	£5.00	£150.00
X25	Champion Dogs	1934	£4.20	£105.00
100	Cinema Artistes (Green Back)	1928	*£2.75*	—
50	Cinema Artistes (Grey Back)	1931	£2.75	—
48	Cinema Celebrities (C)	1935	*£2.75*	—
F50	Cinema Stars	1927	£2.75	—
MF50	Cinema Stars (Coloured)	1926	£3.00	—
MF50	(Uncoloured)	1930	£2.75	—
M27	Dancing Girls	1917	£5.00	£135.00
50	Do You Know? (3 Printings)	1922	*£2.00*	—
24	Fairy Tales (Booklets)	1926	£6.00	—
M100	Famous Beauties (Blue Caption)	1916	£2.40	—
M100	Famous Beauties (Brown Caption)	1916	£2.00	£200.00
P35	Famous Fighting Ships of Various Nations	1910	*£25.00*	—
MF52	Film Favourites (Coloured)	1928	£3.75	—
MF52	(Uncoloured)	1928	£4.00	—
M50	Film Personalities	1931	*£3.75*	—
M50	Garden Flowers of the World	1917	£2.70	£135.00
L50	Garden Flowers of the World (Silk, 2 Printings)	1913	£5.00	£250.00
M?16	Icelandic History	1925	*£25.00*	—
F48	Indian Empire, First Series	1925	90p	£42.50
F48	Indian Empire, Second Series	1926	£1.00	—
MF50	Islenzkar Eimskipamyndir (Trawlers)	1931	£2.70	£135.00
MF50	Islenzkar Landslagsmyndir (Views)	1928	£2.00	£100.00
MF50	Islenzkar Landslagsmyndir Nr 2 (Views)	1929	£2.00	£100.00
40	Merrie England Studies	1914	£7.00	—
X24	Miniature Rugs	1924	£16.00	—
36	Modern Beauties	1938	*£3.00*	—
M?3	Monsterbeskyttet	1926	*£20.00*	—
MF52	Movie Stars	1925	£3.50	—
F36	New Zealand, First Series	1928	£1.25	—
F36	New Zealand, Second Series	1929	£1.25	—
53	Playing Cards (P.O.Box 78)	1934	£2.00	—
53	(Special Blend)	1934	£2.00	—
M55	Playing Cards (Blue Back)	1934	£1.75	—
M55	(Red Back)	1934	£1.75	—
F50	Popular Film Stars	1926	*£3.00*	—
50	Safety First	1936	£1.30	£65.00
L?200	Skjeggen's Oplevelser	1926	*£16.50*	—
F36	South Africa, First Series	1928	£1.00	—
F36	South Africa, Second Series	1928	£1.00	—
M49	South African Succulents	1937	20p	£10.00
M100	Stage & Cinema Stars (Black Caption)	1921	£2.50	—
M100	Stage & Cinema Stars (Grey Caption)	1921	£1.80	£180.00
MF50	Stars of Filmland (Firm in Brown)	1927	£3.25	—
MF50	(Firm in White)	1927	£3.50	—
50	Steamships of the World	1920	£8.00	—
40	The Great War Celebrities	1914	£7.00	£280.00
50	The World of Tomorrow	1938	£1.20	£60.00

WESTMINSTER TOBACCO CO. LTD. — cont.

Qty		*Date*	*Odds*	*Sets*
M50	Uniforms of All Ages	1917	£9.00	£450.00
F50	Views of Malaya	1930	£6.50	£325.00
25	Wireless (Several Printings)	1923	£5.00	£125.00
M50	Women of Nations	1922	£4.00	£200.00

WHALE & COMPANY

?13	Conundrums	1900	£150.00	—

M. WHITE & CO.

20	Actresses "BLARM"	1900	£140.00	—

WHITFIELD'S

30	Army Pictures, Cartoons, etc	1916	*£100.00*	—

WHITFORD & SONS

20	Inventors	1924	£42.50	—

WHOLESALE TOBACCO CO.

25	Armies of the World	1903	£65.00	—
40	Army Pictures (Home & Colonial Regiments)	1902	£85.00	—

P. WHYTE

30	Army Pictures, Cartoons, etc	1916	*£100.00*	—

W. WILLIAMS & CO.

30	Aristocrats of the Turf, A Series	1924	£7.00	—
36	Aristocrats of the Turf, Second Series	1924	£13.50	—
25	Boer War Celebrities "STEW"	1901	*£65.00*	—
25	Boxing	1923	£8.50	—
50	Interesting Buildings	1912	£12.50	—
12	Views of Chester	1912	£27.50	£330.00
12	Views of Chester (As it Was), 2nd Series	1913	£30.00	£360.00

W. D. & H. O. WILLS LTD.

418 Page Illustrated Wills and B.A.T. Book — £20.00

?13	Actresses (Typeset Back)	1895	*£750.00*	—
52	Actresses (Brown Back, P/C Inset)	1898	£15.00	£780.00
52	Actresses (Grey Back, P/C Inset)	1897	£16.00	£825.00
52	(Grey Back, No Inset)	1897	£16.50	£850.00
25	Actresses, Collotype (Wills', Brands Back)	1894	£75.00	—
25	(Wills', No Brands)	1894	£70.00	—
?43	Actresses & Celebrities, Collotype			
	(Wills's, Four Brands on Back)	1894	£85.00	—
	(Wills's, Export Manufacturers Back)	1894	£85.00	—
1	Advertisement Card (Serving Maid)	1890	—	£650.00

Qty		*Date*	*Odds*	*Sets*
4	Advertisement Cards (Cigarette Packets)	1891	*£1000.00*	—
11	Advertisement Cards (Tobacco Packings)	1891	£650.00	—
3	Advertisement Cards (Showcards, 7 brands)	1893	£275.00	—
6	Advertisement Cards (Showcards)	1893	£250.00	—
1	Advertisement Card – Three Castles	1965	—	£1.40
L1	Advertisement Card – Wants List	1935	—	60p
P4	Advertisement Postcards	1902	£100.00	—
50	Air Raid Precautions	1938	80p	£40.00
40	Ditto (Eire)	1938	£1.00	£40.00
50	Allied Army Leaders (2 Printings)	1917	£1.60	£80.00
50	Alpine Flowers	1913	80p	£40.00
49	And When Did You Last See Your Father (Sect.)	1932	£1.00	£49.00
50	Animals & Birds (Descriptive)	1900	£18.00	£900.00
50	Animals & Birds in Fancy Costume	1896	£40.00	£2000.00
48	Animalloys (Sect.)	1934	25p	£12.00
L25	Animals and Their Furs	1929	£1.80	£45.00
50	Arms of Companies	1913	60p	£30.00
50	Arms of Foreign Cities (2 Printings)	1912	60p	£30.00
L42	Arms of Oxford & Cambridge Colleges	1922	£1.00	£42.00
L25	Arms of Public Schools, 1st Series	1933	£2.00	£50.00
L25	Arms of Public Schools, 2nd Series	1934	£2.00	£50.00
50	Arms of the Bishopric	1907	90p	£45.00
50	Arms of the British Empire	1910	60p	£30.00
L25	Arms of the British Empire, 1st Series	1933	£1.60	£40.00
L25	Arms of the British Empire, 2nd Series	1933	£1.60	£40.00
L25	Arms of Universities	1923	£1.40	£35.00
50	Association Footballers (Frame on Back)	1935	£1.30	£65.00
50	Association Footballers (No Frame on Back)	1939	£1.30	£65.00
50	(No Frame, Eire)	1939	£2.40	£120.00
L25	Auction Bridge	1926	£2.20	£55.00
50	Aviation	1910	£2.20	£110.00
?20	Beauties, Collotype (Firefly)	1894	*£120.00*	—
?20	(Wills Cigarettes)	1894	*£120.00*	—
?122	Beauties, Actresses & Children	1894	*£100.00*	—
K52	Beauties, Playing Card Inset (2 Printings)	1896	£25.00	—
52	Beauties, Playing Card Inset	1897	£17.00	£885.00
10	Alternative Subjects	1897	£60.00	—
?48	Beauties (No Inset, Scroll Back)	1897	£135.00	—
?35	(No Inset, Type Set Back)	1897	£180.00	—
?10	Beauties, Girl Studies	1895	*£800.00*	—
L25	Beautiful Homes	1930	£2.50	£62.50
48	Between Two Fires (Sect.)	1930	25p	£12.00
50	Billiards	1909	£2.00	£100.00
K9	Boer War Medallions (6 Brands)	1900	£80.00	—
50	Borough Arms (Scroll Back, Numbered)	1903	£9.00	£450.00
50	(Scroll Back, Unnumbered)	1903	85p	£42.50
50	(1-50 Descriptive)	1904	90p	£45.00
50	Second Edition (1-50)	1906	80p	£40.00
50	Borough Arms, Second Series (51-100)	1904	55p	£27.50
50	Second Edition (51-100)	1906	55p	£27.50
50	Borough Arms, 3rd Series (101-150 Red)	1905	60p	£30.00
50	(101-150 Grey)	1905	75p	£37.50
50	Second Edition (101-150)	1906	55p	£27.50
50	Borough Arms, Fourth Series (151-200)	1905	55p	£27.50
24	Britain's Part in the War	1917	80p	£20.00

Qty		Date	Odds	Sets
50	British Birds	1915	£1.10	£55.00
50	British Butterflies	1927	£1.00	£50.00
L25	British Castles	1925	£2.60	£65.00
1	British Commanders in the Transvaal War (Booklet)	1900	—	£80.00
L25	British School of Painting	1927	£1.20	£30.00
M48	British Sporting Personalities	1937	£1.00	£48.00
50	Builders of the Empire	1898	£7.00	£350.00
L40	Butterflies & Moths	1938	90p	£36.00
1	Calendar for 1911	1910	—	£11.00
1	Calendar 1912	1911	—	£6.00
L25	Cathedrals	1933	£3.60	£90.00
L25	Celebrated Pictures (2 Printings)	1916	£1.80	£45.00
L25	Celebrated Pictures, 2nd Series	1916	£2.00	£50.00
50	Celebrated Ships	1911	£1.00	£50.00
25	Cinema Stars, 1st Series	1928	£1.50	£37.50
25	Cinema Stars, 2nd Series	1928	£1.40	£35.00
50	Cinema Stars, 3rd Series	1931	£1.80	£90.00
P12	Cities of Britain	1929	£8.50	£102.00
25	Conundrums (No Album Clause)	1898	£8.50	£212.50
25	(With Album Clause)	1898	£8.00	£200.00
60	Coronation Series (Narrow Arrows)	1902	£6.00	£360.00
60	(Wide Arrows)	1902	£5.00	£300.00
50	Cricketers	1896	£70.00	£3500.00
25	Cricketer Series 1901 (Plain Background)	1901	£23.00	£575.00
50	(With Vignettes)	1901	£18.00	£900.00
25	Cricketers (WILLS'S)	1908	£8.00	£200.00
50	(WILLS's)	1908	£7.00	£350.00
50	Cricketers, 1928	1928	£1.70	£85.00
50	Cricketers, 2nd Series	1929	£1.80	£90.00
50	Dogs	1937	70p	£35.00
50	Ditto (Eire)	1937	£1.30	£65.00
L25	Dogs, A Series	1914	£3.20	£80.00
L25	Dogs, 2nd Series	1915	£3.20	£80.00
50	Double Meaning	1898	£8.00	£400.00
52	Ditto (P/C Inset)	1898	£9.00	£470.00
50	Do You Know, A Series	1922	35p	£17.50
50	Do You Know, 2nd Series	1924	35p	£17.50
50	Do You Know, 3rd Series	1926	35p	£17.50
50	Do You Know, 4th Series	1933	40p	£20.00
50	Engineering Wonders	1927	80p	£40.00
50	English Period Costumes	1929	90p	£45.00
L25	English Period Costumes	1927	£2.50	£62.50
L40	Famous British Authors	1937	£1.60	£64.00
L30	Famous British Liners, A Series	1934	£4.20	£126.00
L30	Famous British Liners, 2nd Series	1935	£3.50	£105.00
L25	Famous Golfers	1930	£16.00	£450.00
50	Famous Inventions	1915	90p	£45.00
50	First Aid (No Album Clause)	1913	£1.50	£75.00
50	(With Album Clause)	1913	£1.50	£75.00
50	Fish & Bait	1910	£2.20	£110.00
25	Flags of the Empire, A Series	1926	£1.00	£25.00
25	Flags of the Empire, 2nd Series	1929	90p	£22.50
50	Flower Culture in Pots	1925	40p	£20.00
L30	Flowering Shrubs	1934	90p	£27.00
50	Flowering Trees & Shrubs	1924	50p	£25.00

Qty		Date	Odds	Sets
66	Football Series	1902	£8.00	£525.00
50	Garden Flowers	1933	70p	£35.00
50	Garden Flowers by Sudell	1939	25p	£12.50
50	Ditto (Eire)	1939	45p	£22.50
L40	Garden Flowers – New Varieties, A Series	1938	70p	£28.00
L40	Garden Flowers – New Varieties, 2nd Series	1939	60p	£24.00
50	Garden Hints	1938	20p	£8.00
50	Ditto (Eire)	1938	30p	£15.00
50	Gardening Hints	1923	20p	£10.00
50	Garden Life	1914	40p	£20.00
50	Gems of Belgian Architecture	1915	55p	£27.50
50	Gems of French Architecture	1916	£1.20	£60.00
50	Gems of Italian Architecture (Coloured)	—	£100.00	—
F50	(Reproductions)	—	—	£35.00
50	Gems of Russian Architecture	1917	60p	£30.00
L25	Golfing	1924	£8.50	£212.50
X32	Happy Families	1939	£4.75	£152.00
L25	Heraldic Signs & Their Origin	1925	£1.80	£45.00
50	Historic Events	1912	£1.00	£50.00
F54	Homeland Events	1932	35p	£30.00
50	Household Hints (Title in White)	1927	30p	£15.00
50	Household Hints, 2nd Series	1930	50p	£25.00
50	Household Hints (Different)	1936	20p	£8.00
50	Ditto (Eire)	1936	30p	£15.00
50	Hurlers (Eire)	1927	£1.60	£80.00
2	Indian Series	1900	£225.00	£450.00
P12	Industries of Britain	1930	£8.50	£100.00
25	Irish Beauty-Spots	1924	£4.00	£100.00
25	Irish Holiday Resorts	1924	£4.00	£100.00
50	Irish Industries ("Ask Your Retailer...")	1937	90p	£45.00
50	("This Surface...")	1937	£3.00	—
25	Irish Rugby Internationals	1926	£9.00	—
50	Irish Sportsmen	1936	£3.50	£175.00
50	Japanese Series	1900	£34.00	£1700.00
50	Kings & Queens (Short Card, Brown Back)	1898	£10.00	£500.00
50	(Short Card, Grey Back)	1898	£5.50	£275.00
50/51	(Long, "Wills" at Base)	1902	£5.50	£275.00
51	(Complete Set)	1902	—	£325.00
50	(Long, "Wills" at Top)	1902	£12.50	—
L25	Lawn Tennis,1931	1931	£8.50	£212.50
50	Life in the Hedgerow	Unissued	50p	£25.00
50	Life in the Royal Navy	1939	20p	£10.00
50	Life in the Tree Tops	1925	40p	£20.00
50	Locomotives & Rolling Stock (No Clause)	1901	£7.25	£362.50
7	Additional Subjects	1902	£27.50	£192.50
50	Locomotives & Rolling Stock (With ITC Clause)	1902	£7.25	£362.50
50	Lucky Charms	1923	60p	£30.00
100	Maori Series	1900	£80.00	—
?44	(Green Borders)	1900	£80.00	—
3	(Green Borders, Numbered Top Left)	1900	£150.00	—
4	(Green Borders, Unnumbered)	1900	£150.00	—
50	Medals	1906	£2.50	£125.00
50	Merchant Ships of the World	1924	£1.30	£65.00
50	Military Motors (Not Passed by Censor)	1916	£1.60	£80.00
50	(Passed by Censor)	1916	£1.60	£80.00

Qty		*Date*	*Odds*	*Sets*
53	Miniature Playing Cards			
	(Blue Back, Numbered, 5 Printings)	1931	40p	£20.00
	(Blue Back, Unnumbered)	1931	40p	£20.00
	(Blue Back, Red Overprint)	1931	40p	£20.00
	(3 Pink Backs)	1931	50p	£26.00
	(Eire, 9 Backs)	1931	£1.00	—
50	Mining	1916	£1.40	£70.00
L25	Modern Architecture	1931	£1.40	£35.00
L30	Modern British Sculpture	1928	£1.00	£30.00
48	Mother and Son (Sect.)	1931	25p	£12.00
50	Musical Celebrities	1912	£2.40	£120.00
50	Musical Celebrities, Second Series	1914	£3.30	£165.00
8	(Original Subjects)	1914	£200.00	—
25	National Costumes	1895	£175.00	—
?	National Types	1893	*£650.00*	—
50	Naval Dress & Badges	1909	£2.60	£130.00
50	Nelson Series	1905	£3.50	£175.00
50	Old English Garden Flowers	1910	£1.30	£65.00
50	Old English Garden Flowers, Second Series	1913	80p	£40.00
L25	Old Furniture, 1st Series	1923	£2.60	£65.00
L25	Old Furniture, 2nd Series	1924	£2.60	£65.00
L40	Old Inns, A Series	1936	£2.75	£110.00
L40	Old Inns, Second Series	1939	£1.60	£64.00
L25	Old London	1929	£3.40	£85.00
L30	Old Pottery & Porcelain	1934	£1.00	£30.00
L25	Old Silver	1924	£2.40	£60.00
L25	Old Sundials	1928	£2.60	£65.00
20	Our Gallant Grenadiers	1902	£30.00	£600.00
50	Our King & Queen	1937	20p	£10.00
50	Overseas Dominions (Australia)	1915	80p	£40.00
50	Overseas Dominions (Canada)	1914	50p	£25.00
50	Physical Culture	1914	90p	£45.00
25	Pond & Aquarium, 1st Series	Unissued	—	£6.00
25	Pond & Aquarium, 2nd Series	Unissued	—	*£10.00*
50	Portraits of European Royalty (1-50)	1908	£1.20	£60.00
50	Portraits of European Royalty (51-100)	1908	£1.50	£75.00
L25	Public Schools	1927	£2.40	£60.00
L25	Punch Cartoons, First Series	1916	£3.20	£80.00
L25	Punch Cartoons, Second Series	1917	£17.00	£425.00
L40	Racehorses & Jockeys, 1938	1939	£2.00	£80.00
50	Radio Celebrities, A Series	1934	70p	£35.00
50	Ditto (Eire)	1934	£1.50	—
50	Radio Celebrities, Second Series	1934	50p	£25.00
50	Ditto (Eire)	1934	£1.25	—
50	Railway Engines	1924	£1.10	£55.00
50	Railway Engines (Adhesive)	1936	90p	£45.00
50	Ditto (Eire)	1936	£1.50	—
50	Railway Equipment	1938	30p	£15.00
50	Railway Locomotives	1930	£1.50	£75.00
12	Recruiting Posters	1915	£7.50	£90.00
L25	Rigs of Ships	1929	£3.60	£90.00
50	Romance of the Heavens	1928	£1.10	£55.00
50	Roses, A Series (1-50)	1912	£1.50	£75.00

Qty		Date	Odds	Sets
50	Roses, Second Series (51-100)	1913	£1.40	£70.00
50	Roses (Different)	1926	90p	£45.00
L40	Roses (Different)	1936	£1.50	£60.00
M48	Round Europe	1936	20p	£10.00
50	Rugby Internationals	1929	£1.90	£95.00
50	Safety First	1934	£1.00	£50.00
50	Ditto (Eire)	1934	£1.65	—
50	School Arms	1906	60p	£30.00
50	Ditto (With" Series of 50")	1906	*£30.00*	—
50	Seaside Resorts (Mixed Backs)	1899	—	£450.00
	(Best Bird's Eye)	1899	£9.00	—
	(Capstan)	1899	£9.00	—
	(Gold Flake)	1899	£9.00	—
	(Three Castles)	1899	£9.00	—
	(Traveller)	1899	£9.00	—
	(Westward Ho)	1899	£9.00	—
40	Shannon Electric Power Scheme (Eire)	1931	£1.40	£56.00
25	Ships (Three Castles Back)	1895	£26.00	£650.00
25	(No "WILLS" on Front)	1895	£26.00	£650.00
50	(With "WILLS" on Front)	1896	£17.50	£875.00
100	(Brownish Card)	1897	£17.50	£1750.00
50	Ships' Badges	1925	80p	£40.00
50	Signalling Series	1911	£1.70	£85.00
50	Soldiers & Sailors (Blue Back)	1894	£37.50	£1875.00
50	(Grey Back)	1894	£40.00	£2000.00
100	Soldiers of the World (Ltd. Back)	1895	£7.00	£700.00
100/101	(No Ltd. on Back)	1895	£6.50	£650.00
52	(P/C Inset)	1896	£22.00	£1150.00
100	South African Personalities, Collotype (5 Different Printings)	1901	£100.00	—
50	Speed (Title in White)	1930	£1.40	£70.00
50	Speed (Different)	1938	30p	£15.00
50	(Eire)	1938	70p	£35.00
50	Sports of All Nations (Multi-Backed)	1901	£9.00	£500.00
50	Strange Craft	1931	£1.00	£50.00
48	The Boyhood of Raleigh (Sect.)	1931	25p	£12.00
P12	The British Empire	1929	£7.00	£84.00
50	The Coronation Series	1911	90p	£45.00
L40	The King's Art Treasures	1938	30p	£12.00
48	The Laughing Cavalier (Sect., 2 Backs)	1931	25p	£12.00
48	(Sect., Eire)	1931	£1.75	£84.00
50	The Life of H.M. King Edward VIII	Unissued	£17.50	—
50	The Reign of H.M. King George V	1935	60p	£30.00
50	The Sea-Shore	1938	20p	£10.00
50	Ditto (Eire)	1938	50p	£25.00
48	The Toast (Sect.)	1931	50p	£24.00
48	(Sect., Eire)	1931	£1.75	£84.00
25	The World's Dreadnoughts	1910	£2.60	£65.00
50	Time & Money in Different Countries (2 Printings)	1908	£1.60	£80.00
50	Transvaal Series (Black Border)	1901	£8.50	—
66	(White Border)	1901	£1.50	£100.00
66	(Non Descriptive)	1902	£5.50	£365.00
L40	Trees	1937	£1.50	£60.00
L25	University Hoods & Gowns	1926	£2.40	£60.00
50	Vanity Fair Series (Unnumbered)	1902	£5.50	£275.00
50	Vanity Fair, 1st Series	1902	£5.00	£250.00

Qty		*Date*	*Odds*	*Sets*
50	Vanity Fair, 2nd Series	1902	£5.00	£250.00
50	Waterloo	Unissued	£100.00	—
50	Wild Animals of the World (Green Scroll Back)	1900	£5.00	£250.00
15	(Grey Descriptive Back)	1902	£30.00	£450.00
52	(P/C Inset)	1900	£11.00	£570.00
50	Wild Flowers (2 Printings)	1923	70p	£35.00
50	Wild Flowers, A Series (Adhesive)	1936	40p	£20.00
50	Ditto (Eire)	1936	65p	£32.50
50	Wild Flowers, 2nd Series	1937	20p	£9.00
50	Ditto (Eire)	1937	60p	£30.00
50	Wonders of the Past	1926	60p	£30.00
50	Wonders of the Sea	1928	40p	£20.00
MODERN ISSUES (CASTELLA)				
L30	Britain's Motoring History	1991	£1.20	£36.00
P6	Britain's Motoring History	1993	—	£4.50
L30	Britain's Steam Railways	1998	£1.00	£30.00
X30	British Aviation	1994	£1.20	£36.00
P6	British Aviation (Beer Mats)	1994	40p	£2.50
L30	Classic Sports Cars	1996	£1.00	£30.00
X30	Donington Collection	1993	£1.20	£36.00
P6	Donington Collection (Beer Mats)	1993	—	£6.00
X10	Golden Era	1999	—	£12.00
X30	In Search of Steam	1992	£1.20	£36.00
X30	Soldiers of Waterloo	1995	£1.20	£36.00
L30	The Tank Story	1997	£1.20	£36.00
MODERN ISSUES (EMBASSY)				
56	Caribbean Treasure Cruise	1985	*£1.25*	—
M56	Caribbean Treasure Cruise	1985	65p	—
T48	Familiar Phrases	1986	£1.00	£48.00
L30	History of Britain's Railways	1987	£1.20	£36.00
L30	History of Motor Racing	1987	£1.50	—
T5	Pica Punchline	1984	£1.00	£5.00
L144	Punch Lines	1983	70p	—
T288	Punch Lines	1983	70p	—
T48	Ring the Changes (Anonymous)	1985	£1.00	—
T48	(Wills Name)	1985	85p	£41.00
56	Showhouse (33 x 60mm)	1988	*£1.25*	—
56	(35 x 80mm)	1988	50p	—
M56	Showhouse (47 x 68mm)	1988	*£1.25*	—
M56	(47 x 80mm)	1988	50p	£28.00
T56	Showhouse (47 x 90mm)	1988	*50p*	—
T10	Spot the Shot	1986	£2.25	£22.50
?	Wheel of Fortune	1985	£1.25	—
M?	Wheel of Fortune	1985	50p	—
56	Wonders of the World	1986	90p	—
M56	Wonders of the World	1986	65p	£36.50
T56	Wonders of the World	1986	50p	£28.00
M36	World of Firearms	1982	25p	£9.00
M36	World of Speed	1981	25p	£9.00
AUSTRALIAN ISSUES				
100	Actresses (Capstan)	1903	£2.75	£275.00
100	(Vice Regal)	1903	£2.75	—
1	Advertisement Card (Capstan)	1902	—	£160.00
60	Animals (Cut-Outs, Specialities)	1913	80p	£48.00
60	(Cut-Outs, Havelock)	1913	£1.75	—

W. D. & H. O. WILLS LTD. — cont.

Qty		*Date*	*Odds*	*Sets*
50	Arms & Armour (Capstan, "ALSO OBTAINABLE") .	1910	£1.75	—
50	(Capstan, No Extra Words)	1910	£1.60	£80.00
50	(Vice Regal)	1910	£1.60	£80.00
50	(Havelock)...................................	1910	£3.00	—
50	Arms of the British Empire (Specialities)................	1910	80p	£40.00
50	(Havelock)..................	1910	£1.75	—
M50	Arms of the British Empire (Silk)	1910	£2.50	£125.00
50	A Tour Round the World (Blue Caption)	1907	£2.60	£130.00
50	(Mauve Caption).............	1907	£2.75	—
25	Australian & English Cricketers (Numbered)..........	1903	£15.00	£375.00
25	Australian & English Cricketers			
	(Blue Border, Capstan)...................................	1909	£14.00	£350.00
	(Blue Border, Vice Regal)	1909	£14.00	£350.00
	(Red Border, Capstan).....................................	1909	£14.00	£350.00
	(Red Border, Vice Regal)	1909	£14.00	£350.00
59	Australian & English Cricketers, Titled...................	1911	—	£680.00
50	Capstan, "SERIES OF 50"...............................	1911	£12.00	—
50	Capstan, "SERIES OF ".................................	1911	£12.00	—
9	51-59, Capstan, "SERIES OF 59"	1911	£13.50	—
50	Vice Regal, "SERIES OF 50"	1911	£12.00	—
50	Vice Regal, "SERIES OF "	1911	£12.00	—
9	51-59, Vice Regal, "SERIES OF 59"................	1911	£13.50	—
50	Havelock..	1911	£36.00	—
60	Australian & South African Cricketers	1910	—	£840.00
60	Light Background, Blue Border.......................	1910	£15.00	—
60	Light Background, Red Border	1910	£15.00	—
24	Dark Background (Mixed Printing)	1910	—	£360.00
24	Dark Background, Blue Border, Capstan.........	1910	£15.00	—
24	Dark Background, Blue Border, Vice Regal.....	1910	£15.00	—
24	Dark Background, Red Border, Capstan	1910	£15.00	—
24	Dark Background, Red Border, Vice Regal......	1910	£15.00	—
60	Light Background, Havelock...........................	1910	£36.00	—
M50	Australian Butterflies (Silk)	1914	£2.60	£130.00
40/46	Australian Club Cricketers	1905	—	£700.00
40	Blue Back, With State	1905	£17.50	—
40	Blue Back, No State.......................................	1905	£17.50	—
40	Green Back	1905	£17.50	—
39/46	Blue Back, Brown Frame Line........................	1905	£22.50	—
MF100	Australian Scenic Series	1925	70p	£70.00
50	Australian Wild Flowers (Specialities)	1913	80p	£40.00
50	(Havelock)	1913	£1.60	—
1	Australia Day	1915	—	£13.50
75	Aviation (Black Back, Capstan)	1910	£1.80	£135.00
75	(Black Back, Vice Regal)..........................	1910	£1.80	£135.00
75	(Black Back, Havelock)	1910	£2.75	—
75	(Green Back, Capstan).............................	1910	£2.00	—
75	(Green Back, Vice Regal)	1910	£2.00	—
75	(Green Back, Havelock)	1910	£3.25	—
85	(Capstan)...	1910	£2.25	—
85	(Vice Regal)	1910	£2.25	—
50	Best Dogs of Their Breed (Specialities)	1914	£4.00	—
50	(Havelock)	1914	£6.50	—
M50	Birds and Animals of Australia (Silk)......................	1915	£3.00	£175.00
100	Birds of Australasia (Green, Capstan)	1912	£1.10	£110.00
100	(Green, Vice Regal).................	1912	£1.10	£110.00
100	(Green, Havelock)..................	1912	£2.00	—
100	(Yellow Back).........................	1912	£1.10	£110.00
100	(Yellow, Havelock)	1912	£2.00	—

Qty		*Date*	*Odds*	*Sets*
50	Britain's Defenders (1-50)	1915	£1.00	£50.00
50	(Havelock)	1915	£2.20	£110.00
7	Britain's Defenders (51-57)	1915	£8.50	—
50	British Empire Series (Capstan)	1912	80p	£40.00
50	(Vice Regal)	1912	80p	£40.00
50	(Havelock)	1912	£1.60	£80.00
M68	Crests and Colours of Australian Universities, Colleges and Schools	1929	65p	—
M50	Crests and Colours of Australian Universities, Colleges & Schools (Silk)	1916	£2.60	£130.00
M1	Crests and Colours of Australian Schools (Silk, Unnumbered)	1929	—	£25.00
50	Cricketer Series (Grey Scroll Back, No Frame)	1901	£100.00	—
25	Cricketer Series (Grey Scroll Back, Fancy Frame)	1902	£100.00	—
F63	Cricketers (Plain Back)	1926	£7.00	£440.00
F40/48	Cricket Season, 1928-29	1929	£3.00	£120.00
L20	Dogs, A Series (Three Castles & Vice Regal)	1927	£3.00	—
L20	(World Renowned, Album Clause)	1927	£3.00	—
L20	(World Renowned, No Album Clause)	1927	£3.00	—
L20	Dogs, 2nd Series	1928	£3.00	—
L25	English Period Costumes	1929	£1.60	£40.00
100	Famous Film Stars	1934	£1.00	—
M100	Famous Film Stars	1933	£1.80	—
MF100	Famous Film Stars	1933	£2.60	—
M20	Fiestas (Cartons)	1968	70p	—
50	Fish of Australasia (Capstan)	1912	90p	£45.00
50	(Vice Regal)	1912	90p	£45.00
50	(Havelock)	1912	£1.75	—
50	Flag Girls of All Nations	1908	—	£80.00
50	Capstan, Small Captions	1908	£1.60	—
24	Capstan, Large Captions	1908	£2.75	—
50	Vice Regal, Small Captions	1908	£1.60	—
24	Vice Regal, Large Captions	1908	£2.75	—
8	Flags (Shaped, Metal, 6 Printings)	1915	£8.00	—
M13	Flags (Lace)	1916	£4.50	£58.50
28	Flags of the Allies (Silk, Capitals)	1915	£1.75	£49.00
23	(Silk, Small Letters)	1915	£2.00	£46.00
25	Flags of the Empire	1926	*£6.00*	—
28	Football Club Colours & Flags (Capstan)	1913	£3.50	£100.00
28	(Havelock)	1913	£5.50	—
200	Footballers 1933	1933	90p	£180.00
M200	Footballers 1933	1933	£1.60	—
?5	Footballers (Shaped)	1910	£75.00	—
?27	Football Pennants (Shaped, Capstan)	1905	*£35.00*	—
?27	(Shaped, Havelock)	1905	*£40.00*	—
50	Girls of All Nations (Capstan)	1908	£2.40	£120.00
50	(Vice Regal)	1908	£2.40	£120.00
X?2	Havelock Comics	1904	*£75.00*	—
50	Historic Events (Specialities)	1913	90p	£45.00
50	(Havelock)	1913	£1.75	£87.50
L25	History of Naval Dress	1929	*£16.00*	—
50	Horses of Today (Capstan)	1906	£2.60	£130.00
50	(Vice Regal)	1906	£2.60	£130.00
50	(Havelock)	1906	£4.50	—
50	Interesting Buildings	1905	£2.00	£100.00
5	Islands of the Pacific	1917	*£150.00*	—
38	Kings & Queens of England (Silk)	1910	£4.50	£171.00

THEMATIC COLLECTING

Many people come into the hobby not because of an interest in cards themselves, but as an extension of an already existing interest. For there cannot be one subject that is not covered by at least one set of cards, in every case with an illustration and often with informative text.

One of the most popular themes to be collected is sport, and particularly cricket, golf and soccer. The value to the enthusiast can be shown by series such as Taddy County Cricketers and Prominent Footballers which depicted almost every first class player of the time, and the series of 2,462 different Footballers issued in the 1920's by Godfrey Phillips with their Pinnace Cigarettes. In the U.S.A. Baseball is the main cartophilic interest, while in Canada it is hockey. Other games sought by collectors are tennis, billiards, chess and archery.

Militaria, shipping and cinema are other themes that were issued in large numbers and have many devotees. Subjects such as aviation, opera, motoring, music hall and railways are also extensively covered, as are modern subjects such as space exploration and television. The significance of most of these is that they are contemporary records, and one can trace the development of the subject through a period of nearly a century.

Tobacco Companies occasionally felt the need to reprint their own cards; the most notable example of this was Player after the Great War not having any new series prepared, and therefore re-issuing 'Cries of London 2nd Series, Miniatures, Players Past & Present and Characters from Dickens. However a new dimension was achieved by Brooke Bond, who have reprinted many of their earlier sets (with a different coloured back) SOLELY FOR SELLING TO COLLECTORS.

Several other commercial reprints appeared before Murray Cards (International) Ltd., began their "Nostalgia" reprints; these are carefully selected old series, which are very difficult to obtain in the original form, such as Wills 1896 Cricketers, Cope Golfers and Player Military Series. More recently Victoria Gallery and Imperial Publishing have printed under license from Imperial Tobacco Co. a number of their series, including two that were never actually issued! There have also been a number of reprints in North America, mainly of Baseball and Hockey cards, but also of the modern set, Mars Attacks. All these cards are clearly marked to show that they are reprints.

Early fears about the proliferation of reprints have proved to be unfounded. Their advantages are that on the one hand they have made available to a large number of collectors, cards that they would otherwise be unable to obtain or afford. In the other case they have fulfilled a demand for cards to be sold commercially in frames, and thereby relieved some of the pressure on supply of the originals, to the benefit of general collectors. In no case has the presence of reprints adversely affected the value of the originals.

One problem that has arisen, is the attempt by some dishonest people to remove all mention of the reprint and attempt to pass the cards off as originals. This has also happened in the case of Taddy Clowns and Wills Advertisement Cards, which have been cut from book illustrations and doctored. It therefore behoves the collector to be extremely careful when offered such rarities, or better still only to buy from a reputable dealer.

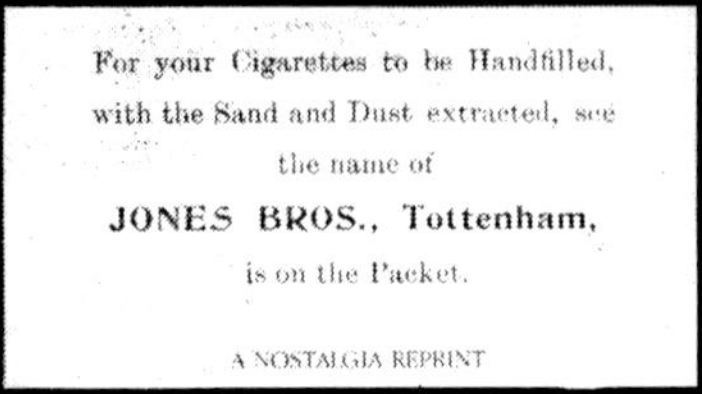

Qty		*Date*	*Odds*	*Sets*
45	Melbourne Cup Winners	1906	£7.00	—
40	Merrie England Studies	1916	£5.50	£220.00
50	Modern War Weapons (Specialities)	1915	£1.60	£80.00
50	(Havelock)	1915	£2.75	—
50	Past & Present Champions (Cigarettes)	1908	£5.50	—
50	(Tobacco)	1908	£5.00	£250.00
M50	Popular Flowers (Silk, Large Packets)	1913	£4.25	—
M50	(Silk, 1/- Packets)	1913	£3.75	£187.50
L70	Practical Wireless	1923	£6.75	—
50	Prominent Australian and English Cricketers (1-50)	1907	£12.00	£700.00
23	Prominent Australian and English Cricketers (51-73, Grey Captions)	1907	£16.00	£370.00
8	Prominent Australian and English Cricketers (66-73, Red Captions)	1907	£16.00	£128.00
10	Recruiting Posters (Anonymous Back)	1915	£6.50	£65.00
50	Riders of the World	1913	£1.50	£75.00
50	(Havelock)	1913	£3.00	—
50	Royal Mail (Capstan)	1913	£3.60	£180.00
50	(Vice Regal)	1913	£3.60	£180.00
50	(Anonymous Printed Back)	1913	£5.00	—
50	(Anonymous Plain Back)	1913	£5.50	—
50	(Havelock, 2 Printings)	1913	£5.00	—
50	Signalling Series (Capstan)	1912	£1.00	£50.00
50	(Vice Regal)	1912	£1.00	£50.00
50	(Havelock)	1912	£2.00	—
39/40	Sketches in Black & White	1905	£2.20	£85.00
?39/40	(White on Black)	1905	*£65.00*	—
50	Soldiers of the World	1902	£7.50	£375.00
25	Sporting Terms (Capstan)	1905	£12.00	£300.00
25	(Vice Regal)	1905	£12.00	£300.00
50	Sports of the World	1917	£4.00	£200.00
50	Stage & Music Hall Celebrities (Capstan)	1904	£3.00	£150.00
50	(Vice Regal)	1904	£3.00	—
50	(Havelock)	1904	£4.00	—
50	Stage & Music Hall Celebrities (Square)	1904	£3.25	—
L25	The Nation's Shrines	1928	£1.20	£30.00
25	The World's Dreadnoughts (Capstan)	1910	£2.00	£50.00
25	(Vice Regal)	1910	£2.00	£50.00
50	Time & Money in Different Countries			
	(Capstan)	1907	£1.40	—
	(Vice Regal, Album Clause)	1907	£1.30	£65.00
	(Vice Regal, No Album Clause)	1907	£1.30	£65.00
	(Havelock)	1907	£2.50	£125.00
50	Types of the British Army			
	(Capstan, 2 Printings)	1912	£2.00	£100.00
	(Vice Regal, 2 Printings)	1912	£1.80	£90.00
50	Types of the Commonwealth Forces			
	(Capstan, 2 Printings)	1910	£2.00	£100.00
	(Vice Regal, 2 Printings)	1910	£2.00	£100.00
	(Havelock)	1910	£4.00	—
P1	Union Jack (Silk)	1915	—	£25.00
25	United States Warships (Capstan)	1911	£2.60	£65.00
25	(Vice Regal)	1911	£2.50	£62.50
25	(Havelock)	1911	£4.00	—

Qty		Date	Odds	Sets
25	Victoria Cross Heroes (Specialities)	1915	£2.20	£55.00
25	(Havelock)	1915	£3.60	£90.00
29	Victorian Football Pennants			
	(Capstan, Multi-Backed)	1910	£3.00	—
	(Vice-Regal, Multi-Backed)	1910	£3.00	—
	(Havelock, Multi-Backed)	1910	£4.50	—
FS165	Views of the World (Capstan)	1908	80p	—
FS165	(Vice Regal)	1908	80p	—
50	War Incidents, A Series (Specialities)	1915	£1.80	£90.00
50	(Havelock)	1915	£2.75	—
50	War Incidents, 2nd Series (Specialities)	1915	£2.60	—
50	(Havelock)	1915	£3.00	—
L67	War Medals (Silk)	1916	£3.00	£200.00
50	War Pictures (Specialities)	1915	£1.20	£60.00
50	(Havelock)	1915	£2.00	£100.00
?1	Warships	1905	*£50.00*	—
50	Wild Animals' Heads	1934	60p	£30.00
M25	Wild Animals (Heads)	1934	£1.20	£30.00
50	Wild Animals of the World	1906	£5.00	£250.00
LF50	Zoological Series	1922	£1.75	£87.50

BRAND ISSUES

(A) Autocar Cigarettes

40	Chinese Trades	1905	£6.00	—

(B) Flag Cigarettes

67	International Footballers, 1909-1910	1911	£9.00	—
50	Jiu-Jitsu	1911	£4.75	—
50	Types of the British Army	1912	£4.50	—

(C) Four Aces Cigarettes

52	Birds of Brilliant Plumage (P/C Inset)	1924	£2.75	£143.00
75	Film Favourites	1928	£1.60	£120.00
25	Modes of Conveyance	1928	£1.80	£45.00
50	Stage & Film Stars (Numbered)	1926	£1.60	£80.00
50	(Unnumbered)	1926	£1.80	£90.00
F52	Stars of the Cinema	1926	£4.00	—

(D) Pirate Cigarettes

G?	Advertisement Cards	1910	£70.00	—
?95	Baseball Series	1912	*£150.00*	—
52	Birds of Brilliant Plumage			
	(P/C Inset, Frame Line)	1916	£3.50	£180.00
	(P/C Inset, No Frame)	1916	£2.75	£143.00
100	China's Ancient Warriors (Multi-Backed)	1911	£2.40	£240.00
28	Chinese Actors & Actresses	1907	£2.75	£77.00
50	Chinese Beauties (Multi-Backed)	1909	£1.40	£70.00
50	Chinese Costumes	1928	£3.25	—
P25	Chinese Pagodas	1911	£37.50	—
50	Chinese Proverbs (Brown, 2 Backs)	1928	£1.20	£60.00
50	(Coloured, 4 Backs)	1915	£1.20	£60.00
33	Houses of Parliament	1914	£1.20	£40.00
50	Products of the World	1913	£1.10	£55.00

(E) Purple Mountain Cigarettes

20	Chrysanthemums (Numbered)	1914	*£10.00*	—
100	Chrysanthemums (Unnumbered)	1915	*£8.50*	—

Qty		Date	Odds	Sets
25	Roses (Wills on Front)	1912	£5.50	£137.50
25	(Without Wills on Front)	1912	£5.00	£125.00
(F) Ruby Queen Cigarettes				
30	Birds & Animals (2 Backs)	1911	£2.00	£60.00
50	Birds of the East (Multi-Backs & Fronts)	1912	£1.20	£60.00
30	Chinese Children's Games (2 Backs)	1911	£1.75	—
50	Chinese Proverbs	1927	*£4.00*	—
41	Chinese Transport (3 Backs)	1914	£2.50	—
(G) Scissors Cigarettes				
50	Actresses (Black & White)	1904	£8.00	—
50	Actresses (Four Colour Surround)	1904	£6.50	—
30	Actresses (Green Surround)	1905	£3.00	£90.00
30	Actresses (Mauve Surround)	1916	£1.50	£45.00
30	(Orange Surround)	1916	£2.00	£60.00
30	Actresses (Purple Brown, Brown Back)	1908	£2.00	£60.00
30	(Purple Brown, Red Back)	1908	£1.60	£48.00
30	Actresses (Purple Brown, Long Card)	1909	£1.80	£54.00
25	Army Life	1914	£2.20	£55.00
30	Beauties (Green Surround)	1921	£4.25	£127.50
52	Beauties (P/C Inset – Lattice Back)	1911	£3.00	£156.00
52	(P/C Inset – No Lattice Back)	1911	£5.00	—
52	(P/C Inset – No Packets)	1911	*£25.00*	—
32	Beauties (Picture Hats)	1914	£3.25	£104.00
40	Beauties (Brown Tint)	1913	£1.40	£56.00
30	Beauties & Children	1910	£2.30	£85.00
36	Boxers	1911	£8.00	£288.00
50	Britain's Defenders (Green Back)	1915	£1.60	£80.00
50	(Red Back & Front)	1915	£1.50	£75.00
50	Britain's Defenders (Blue Front)	1915	£1.40	£70.00
43	British Army Boxers Series	1913	£4.60	£200.00
25	Cinema Stars	1916	£2.30	£57.50
F50	Cinema Stars	1926	*£3.50*	—
27	Dancing Girls (27 Subjects)	1915	£2.25	£61.00
27/28	(28 Subjects)	1915	£2.25	£61.00
25	Derby Day Series	1914	£6.60	£165.00
25	Series A (No Series Title)	1914	£9.00	—
32	Drum Horses (Horizontal Back)	1909	£6.50	£208.00
32	(Vertical Back)	1909	£7.50	£240.00
50	Famous Footballers	1914	£8.25	£412.50
25	Flag Girls of All Nations (Numbered)	1908	£8.00	£200.00
25	(Unnumbered)	1908	£10.00	—
50	Football Club Colours	1907	£7.50	£375.00
25	Governors-General of India	1912	£6.00	£150.00
30	Heroic Deeds	1913	£3.20	£96.00
50	Indian Regiments Series	1912	£7.00	£350.00
67	International Footballers, 1909-1910	1910	£8.25	—
50	Jiu-Jitsu	1910	£5.50	£275.00
53	Jockeys & Owners Colours (P/C Inset)	1914	£6.50	£350.00
25	Military Portraits	1917	£3.60	£90.00
50	Music Hall Celebrities	1911	£6.00	—
K52	Playing Cards	1906	£10.00	—
25	Puzzle Series (Green, United Service Backs)	1910	£6.00	£150.00
25	(Yellow, United Service Backs)	1910	£6.50	—
50	Regimental Colours & Cap Badges	1907	£1.25	£62.50

Qty		*Date*	*Odds*	*Sets*
33	Regimental Pets	1911	£5.25	£173.00
30	Sporting Girls	1913	£7.25	£217.50
50	Types of the British Army	1908	£4.50	£225.00
25	Victoria Cross Heroes	1915	£2.60	£65.00
50	War Incidents	1915	£2.20	£110.00
30	What It Means	1916	£1.00	£30.00
F50	"Zoo"	1927	£3.60	—
(H) United Service Cigarettes				
50	Arms & Armour	1910	£2.80	£140.00
32	Drum Horses	1909	£5.50	£176.00
25	Flag Girls of All Nations	1908	£2.50	£62.50
67	International Footballers, 1909-1910	1910	£8.50	—
	Puzzle Series-See Scissors Cigarettes			
50	Regimental Colours & Cap Badges (Blue Back)	1907	£1.25	£62.50
50	(Red Back)	1907	£1.40	£70.00
(I) Wild Woodbine Cigarettes				
50	British Army Uniforms	1909	£5.50	£275.00
CHANNEL ISLANDS ISSUES				
50	Air Raid Precautions	1938	90p	£45.00
50	Association Footballers	1935	£2.00	—
50	Dogs	1937	£1.00	£50.00
50	Garden Flowers by Sudell	1939	35p	£17.50
50	Garden Hints	1938	35p	£17.50
50	Household Hints	1936	35p	£17.50
50	Life in the Royal Navy	1939	35p	£17.50
50	Our King & Queen	1937	40p	£20.00
50	Railway Equipment	1938	40p	£20.00
50	Speed	1938	40p	£20.00
50	The Sea-Shore	1938	35p	£17.50
50	Wild Flowers, A Series	1936	50p	£25.00
50	Wild Flowers, 2nd Series	1937	35p	£17.50
NEW ZEALAND ISSUES				
F50	A Sporting Holiday in New Zealand	1928	65p	£32.50
LF50	A Sporting Holiday in New Zealand (Different)	1928	80p	£40.00
F50	Beautiful New Zealand	1928	25p	£12.50
50	Birds, Beasts and Fishes	1924	30p	£15.00
F48	British Royal and Ancient Buildings	1925	30p	£15.00
45	British Rugby Players	1930	£2.20	£100.00
50	Children of All Nations	1925	55p	£27.50
50	Coaches and Coaching Days	1925	£1.70	£85.00
50	Dogs	1926	80p	£40.00
P10	English Views and Buildings	1925	£11.50	—
F25	English Cricketers	1926	£2.60	£65.00
26	Etchings (Dogs)	1925	£2.40	£62.50
L26	Etchings (Dogs)	1925	£5.00	—
P10	Famous Castles	1926	£9.00	£90.00
50	Famous Inventions	1926	80p	£40.00
L25	Heraldic Signs & Their Origin	1925	£1.50	£37.50
F50	Homeland Events	1927	50p	£35.00
50	Household Hints (Wills at Top Back)	1927	30p	£15.00
50	(Scroll at Top Back)	1927	£1.50	—
50	Lighthouses	1926	£1.80	£90.00
50	Merchant Ships of the World	1925	£1.00	£50.00
48	Motor Cars	1923	£1.70	£85.00
F50	Motor Cars	1926	£1.40	£70.00

Qty		*Date*	*Odds*	*Sets*
50	Motor Cycles	1926	£3.00	£150.00
50	New Zealand Birds	1925	60p	£30.00
F50	New Zealand – Early Scenes & Maori Life	1926	25p	£12.50
F50	New Zealand Footballers	1927	£1.00	£50.00
50	New Zealand Race Horses	1928	80p	£40.00
50	N.Z. Butterflies, Moths & Beetles	1925	60p	£30.00
25	Past & Present	1929	£1.00	£25.00
25	Picturesque People of the Empire	1928	£1.00	£25.00
25	Pirates & Highwaymen	1925	£1.20	£30.00
50	Products of the World	1929	25p	£12.50
50	Railway Engines	1925	£1.00	£50.00
50	Railway Working	1927	£2.00	—
50	Regimental Standards and Cap Badges	1928	60p	£30.00
50	Riders of the World	1926	80p	£40.00
50	Romance of the Heavens	1928	£1.40	—
50	Safety First	1935	70p	£35.00
F50	Ships and Shipping	1928	80p	£40.00
50	Ships' Badges	1925	80p	£40.00
P10	Splendours of New Zealand	1927	£9.00	£90.00
F50	The Royal Family at Home and Abroad	1927	£1.00	—
F50	The Royal Navy	1929	£1.50	£75.00
F50	Units of the British Army and R.A.F.	1928	50p	£25.00
50	U.S.S. Co's. Steamers	1930	£2.50	£125.00
50	V.C.'s	1926	£1.70	£85.00
25	Village Models Series	1925	£1.00	£25.00
L25	Village Models Series	1925	*£6.00*	—
50	Warships	1926	£1.40	£70.00
25	Wonders of the World	1926	60p	£15.00
F50	"Zoo"	1926	20p	£10.00
OTHER OVERSEAS ISSUES				
50	Actors & Actresses "WALP" (Black)	1905	£3.00	—
50	(Flesh Tint)	1905	£2.25	£112.50
250	Actresses "ALWICS" (Black & Red Front)	1905	£1.40	£350.00
250	(All Red Front)	1905	£2.75	—
?2	(All Black Front)	1905	£2.50	—
?56	(No Address on Back)	1905	£3.25	—
25	Actresses, Tabs Type (101-125)	1902	£16.00	£400.00
50	Actresses, Four Colour Surround (Matt)	1904	£2.40	£120.00
50	(Varnished)	1904	£2.40	£120.00
50	Aeroplanes	1926	£3.00	£150.00
50	Animals and Birds (With Series Title)	1912	£4.25	£212.50
50	(No Series Title)	1909	£4.50	£225.00
50	Arms of the British Empire	1911	80p	£40.00
50	Art Photogravures – Set 1	1912	50p	£25.00
M50	Art Photogravures – Set 1 (2 Printings)	1912	60p	£30.00
50	Art Photogravures – Set 2	1913	50p	£25.00
50	Aviation Series (Wills on Back)	1911	£3.25	—
50	(Anonymous Back, Album Clause)	1911	£3.00	—
50	(Anonymous Back, No Clause)	1911	£3.00	£150.00
50	Beauties "LAWHA" (Red Tinted)	1905	£1.80	£90.00
40	Beauties (Brown Tint)	1913	£2.60	£104.00
52	Beauties (P/C Inset)	1911	£4.75	—
32	Beauties (Picture Hats)	1914	£5.25	£168.00
M72	Beauties	1923	£11.00	—
MF50	Beauties (Hand Coloured)	1925	£3.50	—
F25	Beauties	1925	£3.00	—

W. D. & H. O. WILLS LTD. — cont.

Qty		Date	Odds	Sets
F50	Beauties, 2nd Series	1925	£3.00	—
52	Birds of Brilliant Plumage (P/C Inset)	1914	£4.00	£208.00
36	Boxers	1911	£8.00	£288.00
50	Britain's Defenders	1915	£1.70	£85.00
101	British Beauties	1915	£1.75	£175.00
50	British Costumes from 100 BC to 1904	1905	*£50.00*	—
50	Chateaux	1925	£4.50	£225.00
50	Conundrums	1903	£11.00	£550.00
25	Derby Day Series A	1914	£8.00	—
32	Drum Horses	1909	£6.25	£200.00
26	Etchings (Gold Flake Cigarettes)	1925	£6.50	—
26	(Dutch Text, Frame on Back)	1925	£8.00	—
26	(Dutch Text, No Frame Line)	1925	£7.50	—
50	Famous Footballers	1914	£8.00	£400.00
25	Flag Girls of All Nations	1908	£2.50	£62.50
126	Flags & Ensigns	1904	£1.40	£175.00
6	Flags of the Allies (Shaped)	1915	£12.00	£72.00
50	Girls of All Nations	1908	£2.50	—
32	Houses of Parliament	1912	£2.00	£64.00
50	Indian Regiments Series	1912	£8.00	—
24	Merveilles du Monde	1927	£6.00	—
M25	Miniatures (Metal)	1914	£50.00	£1250.00
F48	Movie Stars	1927	£3.00	—
50	National Flags and Arms	1936	£1.40	—
FS50	Nature Studies	1928	£1.40	—
25	Police of the World	1910	£9.00	£225.00
25	Products of the World	1913	£1.60	£40.00
50	Races of Mankind	1911	£11.00	£550.00
100	Royalty, Notabilities & Events, 1900-2	1902	£2.25	£225.00
27	Rulers of the World	1912	£7.00	£190.00
100	Russo Japanese Series (Black Front, 2 Printings)	1905	£1.75	£175.00
50	(Red Front)	1905	£7.00	—
LF48	Scenes from the Empire	1939	£1.75	£84.00
30	Semaphore Signalling	1910	£3.00	£90.00
36	Ships & Their Pennants	1913	£5.00	£180.00
75	Soldiers of the World	1903	£9.00	—
F52	Stars of the Cinema	1926	*£4.50*	—
25	The Evolution of the British Navy	1915	£2.80	£70.00
25	The World's Dreadnoughts	1910	£2.40	£60.00
50	Wild Animals of the World (Star,Circle & Leaves)	1906	£7.50	—

WILSON & CO.

50	War Portraits	1916	*£90.00*	—

W. WILSON

30	Army Pictures, Cartoons, etc	1916	*£100.00*	—

HENRI WINTERMANS (UK) LTD.

T30	Disappearing Rain Forest	1991	30p	£9.00
T30	Wonders of Nature	1993	30p	£9.00

A. & M. WIX

Qty		Date	Odds	Sets
D250	Cinema Cavalcade	1940	£1.20	£300.00
D250	Cinema Cavalcade, Volume II	1940	£1.20	£300.00
100	Film Favourites	1937	£2.25	—
100	Film Favourites, 2nd Series	1938	£2.25	—
100	Film Favourites, 3rd Series	1939	£1.25	£125.00
L?23	Maxims of Max (Package Issue, Various Formats).	1952	*£7.50*	—
X100	Men of Destiny	1934	£1.80	£180.00
D250	Speed – Through the Ages (English Text)	1938	40p	—
D250	(2 Languages)	1938	30p	£75.00
D250	This Age of Power & Wonder	1935	30p	£75.00

J. WIX & SONS LTD.

Qty		Date	Odds	Sets
F?	Animals	1928	*£35.00*	—
P80	Bridge Favours & Place Cards	1930	£13.00	—
P50	Bridge Hands	1930	*£16.00*	—
L48	British Empire Flags (Silk)	1934	90p	£43.50
L48	(Printed in U.S.A.)	1934	80p	£38.50
50	Builders of Empire	1937	60p	£30.00
42	Card Tricks	1938	£4.50	—
M42	Card Tricks	1938	£5.00	—
50	Coronation (Kensitas)	1937	25p	£12.50
50	(Wix)	1937	25p	£12.50
L50	Henry	1935	80p	£40.00
P25	Henry	1935	£2.50	£62.50
L50	Henry, 2nd Series (No Album Price)	1936	£2.00	—
L50	(With Album Price)	1936	£1.00	£50.00
P25	Henry, 2nd Series (Last line of text "throat")	1936	£3.00	£75.00
P25	(Last line of text "your throat")	1936	£5.00	—
L50	Henry, 3rd Series	1936	80p	£40.00
L50	Henry, 4th Series	1936	70p	£35.00
L50	Henry, 5th Series	1937	70p	£35.00
L102	Jenkynisms, 1st Series (Yellow)	1932	85p	—
L50	Jenkynisms, 2nd Series(Yellow)	1932	85p	—
L25/30	Jenkynisms, 3rd Series (Yellow)	1932	85p	—
L1	Jenkynisms, 4th Series (Yellow)	1932	—	*£2.50*
?21	Jenkynisms (Red Borders, Unnumbered)	1931	£3.50	—
?44	Jenkynisms (Red Borders, Numbered)	1931	£3.50	—
?30	Jenkynisms (Red Borders, Series B)	1931	*£3.50*	—
?19	Jenkynisms (Red Borders, Series C)	1931	*£3.50*	—
?34	Jenkynisms (Red Borders, Series D)	1931	*£3.50*	—
6	Jenkynisms (Red Borders, Vertical)	1931	£4.50	—
M?21	Jenkynisms (Red Borders, Unnumbered)	1931	*£3.50*	—
M?44	Jenkynisms (Red Borders, Numbered)	1931	£3.50	—
M?30	Jenkynisms (Red Borders, Series B)	1931	*£3.50*	—
M?19	Jenkynisms (Red Borders, Series C)	1931	*£3.50*	—
M?34	Jenkynisms (Red Borders, Series D)	1931	*£3.50*	—
M6	Jenkynisms (Red Borders, Vertical)	1931	*£4.50*	—
P96	Ken-Cards	1969	25p	£24.00
60	Kensitas Flowers (Silk, Plain Back)	1933	£3.00	£180.00
60	(Silk, 3 Printed Backs)	1933	£3.00	£180.00
L60	Kensitas Flowers (Silk, Plain Back)	1933	£4.50	£270.00
L60	(Silk, 3 Printed Backs)	1933	£4.50	£270.00
P30	Kensitas Flowers (Silk, Plain Backs)	1933	£40.00	—
P30	(Silk, 3 Printed Backs)	1933	£40.00	£1200.00

J. WIX & SONS LTD. — cont.

Qty		Date	Odds	Sets
40	Kensitas Flowers, Second Series (Silk)	1934	£5.00	£350.00
L40	Kensitas Flowers, Second Series (Silk)	1934	£5.75	£450.00
25	Love Scenes from Famous Films, 1st Series	1932	£2.80	£70.00
L25	Love Scenes from Famous Films, 1st Series	1932	£2.60	£65.00
P25	Love Scenes from Famous Films, 1st Series	1932	£5.00	—
19/25	Love Scenes from Famous Films, 2nd Series	1932	£2.50	£47.50
L19/25	Love Scenes from Famous Films, 2nd Series	1932	£3.00	—
P19/25	Love Scenes from Famous Films, 2nd Series	1932	*£7.50*	—
K53	Miniature Playing Cards (Blue Scroll)	1938	20p	£8.50
K53	(Red Scroll)	1938	20p	£9.00
K53	(Revenge)	1938	25p	£13.00
K53	(Victory)	1938	25p	£13.00
L60	National Flags (Silk)	1934	£1.00	£70.00
F24	Royal Tour in New Zealand	1928	£12.00	—
25	Scenes from Famous Films, Third Series	1932	£2.50	£62.50
P25	Scenes from Famous Films, Third Series	1932	*£6.50*	—

T. WOOD & SON

30	Army Pictures, Cartoons, etc	1916	*£100.00*	—

WOOD BROS.

28	Dominoes	1910	£60.00	—

JOHN J. WOODS

?23	Views of London	1905	*£150.00*	—

W. H. & J. WOODS LTD.

25	Aesop's Fables	1932	£1.60	£40.00
F50	Modern Motor Cars	1936	£4.50	£225.00
25	Romance of the Royal Mail	1931	£1.40	£35.00
25	Types of Volunteer & Yeomanry	1902	£27.50	—

J. & E. WOOLF

?4	Beauties "KEWA"	1898	*£250.00*	—

M. H. WOOLLER

25	Beauties "BOCCA"	1899	*£275.00*	—

T.E. YEOMANS & SONS LTD.

M72	Beauties	1900	£150.00	—
50	War Portraits	1916	*£95.00*	—

JOHN YOUNG & SONS LTD.

12	Naval Skits	1904	£135.00	—
12	Russo Japanese Series	1904	£75.00	—

A. ZICALIOTTI

1	Milly-Totty Advertisement Card	1900	—	*£400.00*

Part 2

OVERSEAS TOBACCO MANUFACTURERS

AFRICAN TOBACCO MANUFACTURERS (S. Africa)

Qty		Date	Odds	Sets
L29	All Blacks South African Tour, 1928	1928	£15.00	—
60	Animals (2 Types)	1922	£3.25	£195.00
MF48	British Aircraft	1926	£4.25	—
M100	Caravaning in South Africa	1939	*£25.00*	—
50	Chinese Transport	1923	£3.75	—
MF48	Cinema Artistes	1926	£3.25	£156.00
50	Cinema Stars "OMBI"	1923	£1.80	£90.00
50	Cinema Stars "OMBI", Second Series	1923	£2.00	£100.00
M50	Famous & Beautiful Women	1938	£2.50	—
L50	Famous & Beautiful Women	1938	£2.00	—
33	Houses of Parliament	1923	£6.00	—
?58	Miniatures	1924	£6.00	—
MF48	National Costumes	1926	£3.00	£144.00
53	Playing Cards (MP)	1929	£2.50	—
53	(Scots)	1929	£1.60	—
MF48	Popular Dogs	1926	£5.00	£240.00
M100	Postage Stamps – Rarest Varieties	1930	£1.40	£140.00
M80	Prominent N.Z. & Australian Rugby Players & Springbok 1937 Touring Team (2 Types)	1937	£3.50	—
L80	Prominent N.Z. & Australian Rugby Players & Springbok 1937 Touring Team (2 Types)	1937	£2.75	—
29	S. A. Rugby Football Team, 1912-1913	1912	£25.00	—
L30	Some Beautiful Roses (Silk)	1928	£8.00	£240.00
M?125	S. A. Members of Legislative Assembly	1919	£27.50	—
25	The Arcadia Fair	1923	*£9.00*	—
25	The Race Course	1923	£10.00	—
M100	The World of Sport	1939	£3.00	—
L100	The World of Sport	1939	£2.50	£400.00
L25	Types of British Birds (Silk)	1928	£8.00	£200.00
L20	Types of British Butterflies (Silk)	1928	£10.00	—
L25	Types of Railway Engines (Silk)	1928	£24.00	—
L25	Types of Sea Shells (Silk)	1928	£12.50	—

AGUERE (Belgium) (Imitation Cigar Bands)

24	Military Head-Dress	1975	—	£5.50

M. V. ALBERT (France)

12	Film Actors & Actresses	1936	£2.50	—

ALLEN TOBACCO CO. (U.S.A.)

X250	Views & Art Studies (55 x 90mm)	1912	£2.25	—
X?117	Views & Art Studies (80 x 72mm)	1912	£4.50	—

ALLEN & GINTER (U.S.A.)

50	American Editors	1887	£26.00	£1300.00
X50	American Editors	1887	£33.00	—
50	Arms of All Nations	1887	£18.00	£900.00
50	Birds of America	1888	£12.00	£600.00
X50	Birds of America	1890	£23.00	£1150.00
50	Birds of the Tropics	1889	£13.00	£650.00
X50	Birds of the Tropics	1889	£23.00	—
50	Celebrated American Indian Chiefs	1888	£32.00	£1600.00
50	City Flags	1888	£12.00	£600.00
50	Fans of the Period	1889	£23.00	£1150.00

Qty		Date	Odds	Sets
50	Fish from American Waters	1889	£13.00	£650.00
X50	Fish from American Waters	1889	£24.00	—
48	Flags of All Nations (7 Types)	1887	£7.50	£360.00
50	Flags of All Nations, Second Series	1890	£9.00	£450.00
47	Flags of the States and Territories (2 Printings)	1888	£10.00	£470.00
50	Fruits	1891	£18.00	£900.00
50	Game Birds	1889	£11.50	£575.00
X50	Game Birds	1889	£22.00	—
50	General Government and State Capitol Buildings of the United States	1889	£11.00	£550.00
50	Great Generals	1886	£28.00	£1400.00
50	Natives in Costume	1886	£25.00	£1250.00
50	Naval Flags	1887	£12.50	£625.00
50	Parasol Drill	1888	£19.00	£950.00
F?	Photographic Cards (Many Types)	1885	£4.00	—
F66	Photographic Cards (Girl Cyclists)	1885	£22.50	—
50	Pirates of the Spanish Main	1888	£28.00	£1400.00
50	Prize & Game Chickens	1892	£19.00	£950.00
50	Quadrupeds	1890	£13.50	£675.00
X50	Quadrupeds	1890	£24.00	—
50	Racing Colors of the World (No Border)	1888	£18.00	£900.00
50	(White Border)	1888	£17.50	£875.00
50	Song Birds of the World	1890	£12.00	£600.00
X50	Song Birds of the World	1890	£25.00	—
X50	The American Indian	1888	£42.50	—
50	The World's Beauties	1888	£17.50	£875.00
50	The World's Beauties, Second Series	1888	£17.50	£875.00
50	The World's Champions	1888	£25.00	—
50	The World's Champions, Second Series	1889	£27.50	—
X50	The World's Champions, Second Series	1889	£50.00	—
50	The World's Decorations	1890	£12.50	£625.00
X50	The World's Decorations	1890	£23.00	£1150.00
50	The World's Racers	1888	£23.00	—
50	Types of All Nations	1889	£19.00	£950.00
50	Wild Animals of the World	1888	£13.00	£650.00
50	World's Dudes	1889	£17.50	£875.00
50	World's Smokers	1888	£16.00	£800.00
50	World's Sovereigns	1889	£24.00	£1200.00
"SPECIAL ISSUES" (U.S.A. & BRITAIN)				
F?137	Actresses, Celebrities & Children, Gold Border	1887	£45.00	—
25	Actresses, Collotype	1887	£65.00	—
25	Actresses (Group 3, Coloured)	1891	£9.00	—
20	Children, Gold Background, Set 1, (U.S.A.)	1887	£70.00	—
20	(Holborn Viaduct Address)	1887	£135.00	—
?49	Children, Gold Background, Set 2, Plain Back	1887	£75.00	—
30	Children, Gold Background, Set 3	1887	£70.00	—
10	Dickens Characters Burlesqued	1887	*£150.00*	—
?67	Sepia-Litho Series	1887	£55.00	—
9	Women Baseball Players (2 Types)	1887	£70.00	—
?93	Woodburytype Series	1887	£65.00	—
PRINTED ALBUMS (EXCHANGED FOR COUPONS)				
	American Editors	1887	—	*£175.00*
	Birds of America	1888	—	£100.00
	Birds of the Tropics	1889	—	£110.00
	Celebrated American Indian Chiefs	1888	—	*£400.00*

Qty		Date	Odds	Sets
	City Flags	1888	—	£100.00
	Decorations of the Principal Orders	1890	—	*£100.00*
	Fish from American Waters	1889	—	£100.00
	Flags of All Nations	1890	—	£100.00
	Game Birds	1889	—	£100.00
	General Government and State Capitol Buildings of the United States	1889	—	£90.00
	George Washington	1889	—	*£130.00*
	Napoleon	1889	—	*£120.00*
	Our Navy	1889	—	*£120.00*
	Paris Exhibition 1889	1889	—	£100.00
	Quadrupeds	1890	—	*£120.00*
	Racing Colors of the World	1888	—	*£200.00*
	Song Birds of the World	1890	—	£100.00
	With the Poets in Smokeland	1890	—	£90.00
	World's Beauties, 1st Series	1888	—	*£150.00*
	World's Beauties, 2nd Series	1888	—	*£150.00*
	World's Champions, 1st Series	1888	—	*£1500.00*
	World's Champions, 2nd Series	1889	—	*£1500.00*
	World's Inventors	1888	—	*£115.00*
	World's Racers	1888	—	£175.00

AMERICAN CIGARETTE CO. (China)

Qty		Date	Odds	Sets
10	Admirals & Generals	1900	£47.50	£475.00
25	Beauties (Black Back)	1902	£17.00	—
?15	Beauties (Green Back)	1901	£17.50	—
53	Beauties, Playing Card Inset	1901	£47.50	—
?5	Chinese Girls	1900	£75.00	—
50	Flowers	1902	£12.50	£625.00

AMERICAN EAGLE TOBACCO CO. (U.S.A.)

Qty		Date	Odds	Sets
20	Actresses, Blue Border (Double 5)	1886	£55.00	—
15	Actresses, Brown Front	1886	£60.00	—
36	Flags of All Nations	1890	£27.50	—
36	Flags of States	1890	£27.50	—
50	Occupations for Women	1892	£45.00	—
F?	Photographic Cards	1886	£8.50	—
LF?	Photographic Cards	1886	*£12.50*	—
23	Presidents of the U.S.	1890	£45.00	—

AMERICAN TOBACCO CO. (U.S.A.)

EARLY ISSUES

Qty		Date	Odds	Sets
25	Actresses (Plain Back)	1902	*£11.00*	—
F?126	Actresses (Black Back)	1901	£3.25	—
F300	Actresses (Blue Back, 2 Types)	1901	£2.25	—
F?40	Actresses (Richmond Straight Cut)	1902	£37.50	—
MF?47	Actresses (Richmond Straight Cut)	1902	£27.50	—
44	Australian Parliament	1901	£3.60	£160.00
25	Battle Scenes	1901	£10.00	£250.00
150	Beauties (Typeset Back)	1901	£2.40	—
?364	Beauties (Old Gold Back)	1901	£2.20	—
?112	Beauties (Label Back) (2 Types)	1901	£3.25	—
?564	Beauties (Green Net Back)	1901	£2.20	—
75	Beauties (Blue Net Back)	1901	£12.00	—
24	Beauties (Plain Back, Carton)	1901	£4.50	—
25	Beauties, Black Background	1900	£10.00	£250.00

AMERICAN TOBACCO CO. (U.S.A.) — cont.

Qty		*Date*	*Odds*	*Sets*
25	Beauties, Blue Frame Line	1900	£18.00	—
25	Beauties, Curtain Background	1900	£8.50	£212.50
28	Beauties, Domino Girls (Blue Net Back)	1895	£19.00	£530.00
28	(Type Set Back)	1895	£18.00	£500.00
25	Beauties, Flower Girls	1900	£7.50	£187.50
25	Beauties, Flowers Inset (Green Back)	1900	£8.50	£212.50
25	(Yellow Back)	1900	£7.00	£175.00
25	Beauties, Fruit Girls	1903	*£30.00*	—
25	Beauties, International Code of Signals			
	1st Series, Green Back	1900	£8.25	—
	1st Series, Yellow Back	1900	£6.75	—
25	Beauties, International Code of Signals			
	2nd Series, Green Back	1900	£8.50	£212.50
	2nd Series, Yellow Back	1900	£7.25	£181.00
50	Beauties, Marine & Universe Girls	1900	*£25.00*	—
25	Beauties, Numbered (Black Front)	1900	£16.50	—
25	(Mauve Front)	1900	£14.00	£350.00
25	Beauties, Orange Framelines	1900	£26.00	—
25	Beauties, Palette Girls (Plain Border)	1900	£8.50	£212.50
25	(Red Border)	1900	*£30.00*	—
F?40	Beauties, Photographic	1894	*£13.50*	—
52	Beauties, Playing Card Inset, Set 1	1900	£10.00	—
52	Beauties, Playing Card Inset, Set 2 (Green Net Back)	1900	£8.50	£440.00
52	(Type Set Back)	1900	£8.00	£415.00
	Beauties, Playing Card Superimposed			
52	("52 Subjects")	1900	£8.00	£415.00
53	("53 Subjects")	1900	£8.50	£450.00
25	Beauties, Star Girls (Green Net Back)	1900	£16.00	—
25	(Type Set Back)	1900	£14.00	—
25	Beauties, Star Series	1900	£13.00	—
25	Beauties, Stippled Background	1900	£8.50	—
100	Beauties, Thick Border	1895	£27.50	—
25	Boer War, Series A (Numbered)	1901	£4.00	£100.00
25	(Unnumbered)	1901	£5.00	£125.00
25	(No Series Letter)	1901	£6.50	—
22	Boer War, Series B	1901	£7.00	£154.00
L47	Boer War Celebrities (Kimball)	1901	£30.00	—
L10	Boer War Celebrities "RUTAN"	1901	£32.50	£325.00
50	Butterflies	1895	£18.00	—
32	Celebrities	1900	£6.00	£192.00
25	Chinese Girls	1900	£11.00	—
1	Columbian & Other Postage Stamps	1895	—	£10.00
25	Comic Scenes	1901	£8.00	£200.00
50	Congress of Beauties, World's Fair (Backlisted)	1893	£19.00	—
50	(Type Set Back)	1893	*£35.00*	—
25	Constellation Girls	1894	£25.00	—
25	Dancers	1895	£11.50	—
50	Dancing Women	1895	£17.00	—
50	Fancy Bathers	1895	£17.00	—
25	Fish from American Waters (Green Net)	1900	£7.50	£187.50
50	(Back Listed)	1895	£11.00	—
28	Flags, Dominoes Superimposed (Carton)	1900	£5.00	£140.00
50	Flags of All Nations	1895	£8.50	—
X25	French Novelties	1891	*£60.00*	—
50	Heroes of the Spanish American War (Carton)	1900	£6.50	—

Qty		*Date*	*Odds*	*Sets*
?45	Japanese Girls	1900	£50.00	—
50	Jokes	1906	*£16.00*	—
25	Military Uniforms, A	1894	£13.00	—
25	Military Uniforms, B	1896	£11.50	£287.50
27	Military Uniforms, C (Green Net Back)	1900	£6.50	£175.00
27	(Typeset Back)	1900	£7.50	£200.00
25	Military Uniforms, D	1900	£12.00	£300.00
50	Musical Instruments	1895	£13.00	—
50	National Flags & Arms (Green Net Back)	1895	£8.50	—
50	(Type Set Back)	1895	£8.50	—
25	National Flags & Flower-Girls	1900	£17.50	—
25	Old Ships, 1st Series	1900	£4.50	£112.50
25	Old Ships, 2nd Series	1900	£7.00	£175.00
50	Savage & Semi Barbarous Chiefs & Rulers	1895	£19.00	—
25	Songs A (2 Types)	1900	£12.00	£300.00
25	Songs B	1900	£11.00	£275.00
25	Songs C, 1st Group	1900	£7.00	£175.00
25	Songs C, 2nd Group	1900	£10.00	—
25	Songs D	1900	£7.00	£175.00
27	Songs E	1900	£10.00	£270.00
25	Songs F (2 Types)	1900	£9.00	£225.00
25	Songs G	1900	£8.50	£212.50
25	Songs H	1900	£17.00	£425.00
25	Songs I	1900	£21.50	—
X25	Stars of the Stage	1891	*£60.00*	—
F150	Views	1901	£2.50	—
LATER ISSUES				
L50	Actors	1911	£5.75	—
L50	Actresses "Between The Acts"	1902	£9.00	—
G25	Actresses "Turkish Trophies" (Premiums)	1902	£16.00	£400.00
M85	Actress Series	1909	£6.25	—
L80	Animals	1909	£1.75	£140.00
L25	Arctic Scenes	1910	£5.00	£125.00
?55	Art Reproductions	1910	£4.75	—
21	Art Series (Grand Duke)	1902	£14.00	—
P10	Artistic Pictures	1910	*£10.00*	—
18	Ask Dad	1916	£12.00	—
L50	Assorted Standard Bearers of Different Countries	1914	£4.80	—
M25	Auto-Drivers	1910	£12.50	—
M50	Automobile Series	1910	£12.00	£600.00
L50	Baseball Folders	1907	£22.50	—
M121	Baseball Series (T204)	1907	*£35.00*	—
208	Baseball Series (T205, Gold Border)	1907	£16.00	—
522	Baseball Series (T206, White Border)	1907	£15.00	—
200	Baseball Series (T207, Brown Background)	1911	*£20.00*	—
?642	Baseball Series (T210, Red Borders)	1907	*£20.00*	—
75	Baseball Series (T211, Southern Assocation)	1907	*£22.50*	—
?406	Baseball Series (T212, "Obak")	1907	*£22.50*	—
?184	Baseball Series (T213, "Coupon")	1907	*£22.50*	—
?51	Baseball Series (T214, Victory Tobacco)	1907	*£60.00*	—
?172	Baseball Series (T215, Red Cross)	1907	*£22.50*	—
L76	Baseball Triple Folders	1907	*£35.00*	—
50	Bird Series (Gold Border)	1910	£2.20	£110.00
50	Bird Series (White Border)	1910	£2.20	£110.00
30	Bird Series (Fancy Gold Frame)	1911	£2.50	£75.00

Qty		Date	Odds	Sets
M361	Birthday Horoscopes	1911	£2.00	—
P80	Bridge Favors & Place Cards	1930	£6.00	—
P100	Bridge Game Hands	1930	£8.50	—
M24	British Buildings	1939	£2.50	£60.00
M42	British Sovereigns	1939	£2.50	£105.00
M50	Butterfly Series	1910	£3.75	—
L153	Champion Athlete & Prizefighter Series	1910	£5.50	—
X50	Champion Athlete & Prizefighter Series (Prizefighters Only)	1910	£9.00	—
L50	Champion Pugilists	1910	£17.50	—
X100	Champion Women Swimmers	1906	£7.00	—
M150	College Series	1909	£2.50	£375.00
G25	College Series (Premiums)	1910	£30.00	—
M50	Costumes and Scenery for All Countries of the World	1911	£3.20	£160.00
X49	Cowboy Series	1911	£5.75	£282.00
M?41	Cross Stitch	1906	£8.00	—
L?17	Embarrassing/Emotional Moments	1906	*£17.50*	—
M50	Emblem Series	1911	£3.00	£150.00
L100	Fable Series	1910	£2.50	£250.00
PF?60	Famous Baseball Players, American Athletic Champions & Photoplay Stars	1910	*£35.00*	—
100	Fish Series	1910	£2.20	£220.00
200	Flags of All Nations Series	1909	£1.40	£280.00
L100	Flags of All Nations Series (Red Cross)	1909	*£10.00*	—
50	Foreign Stamp, Series A	1911	£5.50	—
L505	Fortune Series	1910	£1.80	—
G12	Hamilton King Girls (1-12, Sketches)	1902	£16.50	—
G12	Hamilton King Girls (13-24, Girls)	1902	£14.00	£168.00
G12	Hamilton King Girls (25-36, Bathing Girls)	1902	£14.00	£168.00
G25	Hamilton King Girls (37-61, Period Gowns)	1902	£14.00	£350.00
G25	Hamilton King Girls (62-86, Flag Girls)	1902	£13.00	£325.00
G25	Hamilton King Girls (1-25)	1912	£16.00	—
L?6	Helmar Girls	1902	*£40.00*	—
M79	Henry	1937	£2.25	£180.00
X50	Heroes of History	1912	£6.00	£300.00
M50	Historic Homes	1910	£3.50	£175.00
X24/25	Historical Events Series	1911	£5.75	—
M15	Home Art Gallery Pictures	1915	£4.25	£64.00
M25	Hudson-Fulton Series	1909	£5.20	£130.00
45	Imitation Cigar Bands	1909	£2.50	—
L50	Indian Life in the "60's"	1910	£6.00	£300.00
L?268	Jig Saw Puzzle Pictures	1910	£7.00	—
L50	Light House Series	1910	£4.50	£225.00
X50	Men of History, 2nd Series	1912	£5.50	£275.00
M100	Military Series (White Border)	1910	£4.25	£425.00
50	Military Series (Gold Border)	1911	£4.50	£225.00
50	Military Series (Recruit)	1908	£4.25	£212.50
50	Movie Stars	1915	£4.00	—
L100	Movie Stars	1915	£4.00	—
M25	Moving Pictures (Flip Books)	1910	*£17.50*	—
M?84	Moving Picture Stars Series	1915	*£16.00*	—
X50	Murad Post Card Series	1905	£7.00	—
?100	Mutt & Jeff Series (Black & White)	1908	£4.25	—
?183	Mutt & Jeff Series (Coloured)	1908	£4.50	—
F16	National League & American League Teams	1910	*£30.00*	—
X50	Postcard Series	1910	£11.50	—

Qty		Date	Odds	Sets
G126	Prominent Baseball Players & Athletes (Premium)	1911	*£26.50*	—
50	Puglistic Subjects	1908	*£17.00*	—
X18	Puzzle Picture Series	1904	*£13.50*	—
L200	Riddle Series	1910	£2.40	—
X?60	Royal Bengal Souvenir Cards	1906	£7.00	—
M150	Seals of the United States & Coats of Arms of All Countries of the World	1909	£1.60	£240.00
L?24	Series of Champions	1912	£22.50	—
X50	Sights & Scenes of the World	1912	£3.40	£170.00
X50	Silhouettes	1908	£7.00	—
L25	Song Bird Series	1905	*£25.00*	—
50	Sports Champions	1910	*£16.50*	—
45	Stage Stars (Transfers)	1910	*£7.50*	—
M25	State Girl Series	1910	£6.00	£150.00
L50	Theatres Old and New Series	1912	£6.25	—
L?100	The World's Best Short Stories	1910	£12.00	—
L25	The World's Greatest Explorers	1914	£4.75	—
L50	Toast Series (Sultan)	1910	*£7.50*	—
M550	Toast Series (Mogul)	1909	£1.75	—
L25	Toasts	1910	*£12.00*	—
50	Types of Nations Series	1912	£2.40	£120.00
M25	Up To Date Baseball Comics	1908	*£15.00*	—
L26	Up To Date Comics	1908	£7.50	—
250	Up To The Minute War Pictures	1916	£1.60	—
F?481	World Scenes & Portraits	1914	£2.25	—
X50	World's Champion Athletes	1909	£10.00	—

SILK ISSUES

Qty		Date	Odds	Sets
M?113	Actresses	1910	£3.60	—
X?10	Actresses	1910	*£50.00*	—
L15	Animals	1910	£6.25	—
P250	Athlete and College Seal	1910	£10.00	—
G250	Athlete and College Seal	1910	£12.50	—
M25	Automobile Pennants	1910	*£50.00*	—
M?117	Baseball – Actress Series	1910	£5.50	—
M?122	Baseball Players	1910	*£16.00*	—
G25	Baseball Players	1910	*£30.00*	—
M25	Bathing Beach Girls	1910	£8.60	£215.00
G6	Bathing Girls	1910	£13.00	£78.00
T50	Birds, Set 1	1910	£4.50	—
M26	Birds, Set 2	1910	£4.75	—
L26	Birds, Set 2	1910	£5.00	—
M30	Birds, Set 3	1910	£4.75	—
L20	Birds in Flight	1910	£5.50	£110.00
L25	Breeds of Dogs	1910	£12.00	£300.00
L10	Breeds of Fowls	1910	£12.00	£120.00
P6	Butterflies	1910	£13.00	£78.00
L25	Butterflies & Moths, Set 1	1910	£5.25	—
L50	Butterflies & Moths, Set 2	1910	£4.25	—
L25	Butterflies & Moths, Set 3	1910	£4.25	—
M77	City Seals	1910	£3.50	—
G50	College Flag, Seal, Song, Yell	1910	£9.00	—
T44	College Pennants	1910	*£6.00*	—
M144	College Seals	1910	£2.50	—
G?14	College Yells	1910	*£15.00*	—

Semaphore Signals
Tyson

Danske Byvaabner
Lambert & Butler

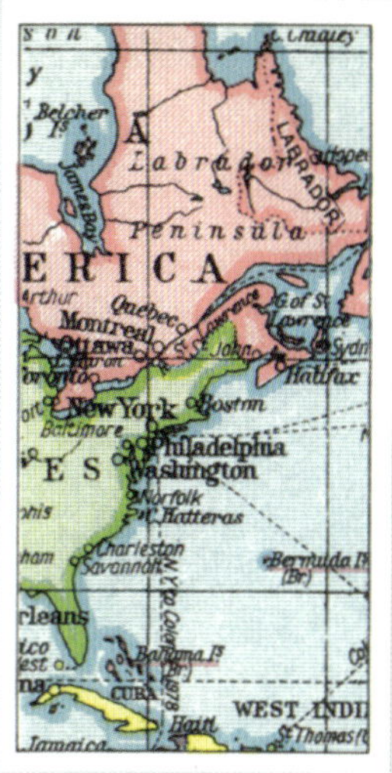

Modern School Atlas
Ardath

Sights of London
Toby

Flag Series
Cadbury

Wild Wisdom in Africa
Chivers

Wonders of the Past
Wills
Also B.A.T.

Dutch Scenes
B.A.T.

Photo's of Cricketers
Tuckett's

England's Top Goal Scorers
Philip Neill

Irish Sportsmen
Wills

Famous Voyages
Typhoo

Views Abroad
Peek Frean

Qty		*Date*	*Odds*	*Sets*
L10	Comics	1910	£9.00	—
M25	Domestic Animals' Heads	1910	£6.00	£150.00
G6	Domestic Animals' Heads	1910	£13.00	£78.00
M50	Emblem Series	1910	£4.50	—
L15	Famous Queens	1910	£9.00	£135.00
L11	Feminine Types	1910	£8.00	£88.00
D322	Flags & Arms (Woven)	1910	£2.00	—
P24	Flag Girls of All Nations	1910	£8.50	£205.00
G24	Flag Girls of All Nations	1910	£10.00	—
X50	Flowers, Set 1	1910	£5.50	—
M25	Flowers, Set 2	1910	£4.50	—
L50	Flowers, Set 2	1910	£5.50	—
L54	Flowers, Set 3	1910	£5.25	—
M?28	Foreign Postage Stamps	1910	*£25.00*	—
L10	Fruits	1910	£6.50	£65.00
G5	Generals	1910	£75.00	—
M10	Girls (Portrait in Circle)	1910	*£20.00*	—
L10	Girls (Portrait in Circle)	1910	£35.00	—
G10	Girls (Portrait in Circle)	1910	*£45.00*	—
G15	Great War Leaders	1915	*£60.00*	—
G?38	Hatbands	1910	£11.00	—
M50	Indian Portraits	1910	£8.00	£400.00
G6	Indian Portraits	1910	£22.50	—
L25	Indian Portraits & Scenes	1910	£8.50	—
P10	Indian Portraits & Scenes	1910	£14.00	—
G12	King Girls	1910	£12.00	£144.00
G20	Kink Series	1910	*£40.00*	—
M51	Military & Lodge Medals	1910	£3.50	£175.00
L?7	Miniature National Flags	1910	*£20.00*	—
L10	Mottoes & Quotations	1910	£7.00	£70.00
L25	National Arms (Silko)	1910	£3.50	£87.50
M42	National Arms (Woven)	1910	£3.20	£135.00
L154	National Flags	1910	£1.60	—
T?2	National Flags (Egyptian Banner Cigarettes)	1910	*£5.00*	—
G?157	National Flags (Many Styles)	1910	£3.00	—
L25	National Flags & Arms	1910	£2.50	—
X40	National Flags & Arms	1910	£2.50	—
P53	National Flags & Arms (Many Styles)	1910	£2.50	—
X27	National Flag, Song & Flower	1910	£4.50	—
P20	National Flag, Song & Flower	1910	£5.00	—
G17	National Flag, Song & Flower	1910	£6.00	—
E5	National Flag, Song & Flower	1910	*£7.00*	—
M?37	Orders & Military Medals	1910	£5.50	—
M24	Presidents of U.S.	1910	£7.50	—
P24	Ruler with National Arms	1910	£12.50	—
P10	Rulers of the Balkans & Italy	1910	£13.00	£130.00
L120	Silk National Flags (Paper Backs)	1910	£1.75	—
M36	State Flags	1910	£3.75	—
M?11	State Flowers (80 x 45mm)	1910	*£8.50*	—
M25	State Flowers (Different, 80 x 47mm)	1910	£6.25	—
L25	State Girl & Flower	1910	£6.75	—
M50	State Maps & Maps of Territories	1910	£6.25	—
M48	State Seals	1910	£3.75	—
X?81	Twelfth Night Miscellany	1910	£9.00	—
M25	Women of Ancient Egypt	1910	£10.00	£250.00
L10	Zira Girls	1910	£8.50	£85.00

Qty		*Date*	*Odds*	*Sets*
BLANKET ISSUES				
P?	Animal Pelts	1908	£8.00	—
G90	Baseball Players	1908	*£25.00*	—
P?50	Butterflies	1908	£5.00	—
G?50	Butterflies	1908	£5.00	—
P250	College Athlete, Pennant, Seals	1908	£7.50	—
G?11	College Pennants	1908	*£6.50*	—
G?41	College Seals	1908	£3.50	—
X?	Conventional Rug Designs	1908	£3.50	—
P?	Conventional Rug Designs	1908	£4.00	—
G?	Conventional Rug Designs	1908	£5.00	—
X?5	Domestic Pets	1908	£7.00	—
P?	Miniature Indian Blankets	1908	£8.50	—
G?	Miniature Indian Blankets	1908	£8.50	—
E6	National Arms	1908	£5.00	—
P45	National Flags	1908	£3.00	—
G71	National Flags	1908	£3.00	—
E31	National Flags	1908	£3.50	—
G?20	National Flags and Arms and Medals	1908	£4.00	—
X?10	Nursery Rhymes	1908	*£8.50*	—
X12	Soldiers	1908	£12.50	£150.00
LEATHER ISSUES				
M15	Breeds of Dogs	1908	£8.50	—
X?100	College Building, Shield, etc	1908	£5.00	—
P19	College Buildings	1908	£5.00	—
M?15	College Fraternity Seals	1908	*£7.50*	—
M166	College Pennants	1908	£2.00	—
M?30	(Shaped)	1908	£2.50	—
X23	College Pennant, Yell, Emblem	1908	£5.50	—
M148	College Seals	1908	£2.00	—
M?122	(Shaped)	1908	£2.50	—
M53	(Card Suit Shaped)	1908	£3.00	—
M20	Comic Designs	1908	£4.00	—
M25	Flowers	1908	£4.50	—
M?11	Girls	1908	£6.50	—
M26	Girls (Alphabet Background)	1908	£7.50	—
M?96	Mottoes & Quotations	1908	£3.00	—
M97	Movie Film Personalities	1908	£8.00	—
M?23	National Flags	1908	*£3.25*	—
M?51	Nursery Rhymes Illustrated	1908	£5.00	—
M56	State Seals	1908	£1.25	—
M18	(Pennant Shaped)	1908	£1.75	—
CELLULOID BUTTONS & PINS				
K?251	Actresses	1901	£2.75	—
K152	Baseball Players	1901	*£15.00*	—
K9	Boer War Leaders	1901	£75.00	—
K?370	Comic Pictures	1901	£3.25	—
K?449	Comic Sayings	1901	£3.00	—
K14	Cricketers	1901	£130.00	—
K?129	Flags	1901	£2.25	—
K?49	Girls' Heads	1901	*£6.25*	—
K?29	Jockeys	1901	*£25.00*	—
K48	State Arms	1901	£2.75	£132.00
K187	Yellow Kid Designs	1901	*£8.00*	—

A.T.C. OF NEW SOUTH WALES (Australia)

Qty		Date	Odds	Sets
25	Beauties, Group 1	1902	£11.00	£275.00
25	Beauties, Group 2	1902	£11.00	£275.00

A.T.C. OF VICTORIA LTD. (Australia)

100	Beauties	1902	£11.00	—

ANONYMOUS ISSUES (Cigar Bands)

48	Famous Buildings and Monuments	1976	—	£10.00
48	Great Inventions	1975	—	£7.00

THE ASHEVILLE TOBACCO WORKS CO. (U.S.A.)

?39	Actresses "ASVERI"	1890	£50.00	—

ATLAM CIGARETTE FACTORY (Malta)

150	Beauties	1924	*£5.00*	—
M65	Beauties	1924	£2.50	—
M519	Celebrities	1924	£1.00	£520.00
L50	Views of Malta	1924	*£5.00*	—
M128	Views of the World	1924	*£5.00*	—

BANNER TOBACCO CO. (U.S.A.)

X?41	Actors & Actresses	1890	£55.00	—
X25	Beauties	1890	£30.00	—

AUG. BECK & CO. (U.S.A.)

?52	Beauties-Burdick 488	1888	£50.00	—
25	National Dances	1889	*£55.00*	—
F?	Photographic Cards	1886	*£10.00*	—
?44	Picture Cards	1893	£55.00	—
23	Presidents of the U.S.A. (Coloured)	1890	£55.00	—
23	Presidents of the U.S.A. (Sepia, Different)	1890	*£55.00*	—
?14	State Seals	1887	*£60.00*	—

DE BEER & CO. (Australia)

20	Admirals & Warships of the U.S.A.	1908	£40.00	—
?16	Caricatures of Cyclists	1908	*£60.00*	—

A. BENITEZ (Canary Islands)

50	Swiss Views	1912	£5.00	—

BOOKER TOBACCO CO. (U.S.A.)

35	Indian Series (2 Printings)	1906	£32.50	£1150.00
?17	U.S. Battleships	1906	£32.50	—

NICOLA BOSIOS (Malta)

Qty		Date	Odds	Sets
?84	Opera Singers	1920	£35.00	—
K?23	Opera Singers	1920	*£40.00*	—

BRITISH AMERICAN TOBACCO CO. LTD. (B.A.T.)

418 Page Illustrated B.A.T. & Wills Book — £20.00

(1) SERIES WITH FIRM'S NAME

30	Actrices	1905	£6.00	—
48	A Famous Picture Series, The Toast (Sect.)	1931	*£2.75*	—
MF50	Beauties	1925	£2.00	—
MF40	Beauties	1925	£2.00	—
25	Beauties, Art Series	1903	£11.00	—
25	Beauties, Black Background	1903	£10.00	—
25	Beauties, Blossom Girls	1903	£36.00	—
25	Beauties, Flower Girls	1903	£8.00	£200.00
25	Beauties, Fruit Girls	1903	£12.00	£300.00
25	Beauties, Girls in Costumes	1903	£12.00	£300.00
20	Beauties, Group 1	1903	£8.00	£160.00
25	Beauties, Lantern Girls	1903	£8.00	£200.00
50	Beauties, Marine & Universe Girls	1903	£9.00	£450.00
25	Beauties, Numbered	1903	£16.50	—
25	Beauties, Palette Girls (Plain Border)	1903	£8.00	£200.00
25	(Red Border)	1903	£12.50	—
53	Beauties, Playing Card Superimposed	1903	£8.00	£425.00
24	Beauties, Smoke Girls	1903	£14.00	£335.00
25	Beauties, Star Girls	1903	£14.00	—
25	Beauties, Stippled Background	1903	£7.50	£187.50
25	Beauties, Water Girls	1903	£8.00	£200.00
32	Beauties of Old China	1933	£4.00	—
M50	Birds, Beasts & Fishes	1934	£1.80	—
50	Buildings	1905	£8.50	£425.00
25	Chinese Girls "A"	1904	£8.50	—
25	Chinese Girls "B" (Silver Borders)	1904	£8.50	—
25	Chinese Girls "C" (Sky Background)	1904	£8.50	£212.50
25	Chinese Girls "D" (2 Printings)	1904	£8.25	—
25	Chinese Girls "E"	1904	£8.50	—
25	Chinese Girls "F1" (2 Printings)	1904	£8.50	£212.50
25	Chinese Girls "F2" (2 Printings)	1904	£8.50	£212.50
50	Chinese Girls "F3" (2 Printings)	1904	£8.50	—
40	Chinese Trades	1904	£6.00	£240.00
50	Danish Athletes	1905	£11.00	£550.00
28	Dominoes	1905	£6.00	£170.00
48	Fairy Tales	1928	*£3.50*	—
25	New York Views	1908	£9.00	—
53	Playing Cards	1908	£10.00	—
M50	Wild Animals	1930	£1.60	—

(2) SERIES WITH BRAND NAMES

(A) Albert Cigarettes (Belgium Etc.)

L50	Aeroplanes (Civils)	1935	*£10.00*	—
50	Artistes de Cinéma (1-50)	1932	£2.75	—
50	Artistes de Cinéma (51-100)	1933	£2.75	—
50	Artistes de Cinéma (101-150)	1934	£2.75	—
MF72	Beauties	1928	£3.00	—
M75	Belles Vues de Belgique	1928	£2.50	£187.50
M50	Birds, Beasts & Fishes	1934	£3.25	—
M50	Butterflies (Girls)	1926	£5.50	—

Qty		Date	Odds	Sets
M50	Cinema Stars, Set 1 (Brown) (2 Printings)	1927	£3.00	—
M100	Cinema Stars, Set 2	1928	£3.00	—
M208	Cinema Stars, Set 3 (Unnumbered)	1928	£3.00	—
M100	Circus Scenes	1930	*£3.00*	—
M100	Famous Beauties	1916	*£3.00*	—
M100	La Faune Congolaise	1934	£1.25	—
M50	L'Afrique Equatoriale de L'Est à L'Ouest	1932	£2.50	—
M50	Les Grands Paquebots du Monde	1924	£6.00	—
M50	Merveilles du Monde	1927	*£3.25*	—
M50	Women of Nations	1922	£3.75	—
(B)	**Atlas Cigarettes (China)**			
50	Buildings	1907	*£5.00*	—
25	Chinese Beauties	1912	£2.40	—
?8	Chinese Trades, Set 3	1912	*£5.00*	—
50	Chinese Trades, Set 4	1912	£2.25	—
85	Chinese Trades, Set 6	1912	£2.50	—
(C)	**Battle Ax Cigarettes**			
M100	Famous Beauties	1916	£3.75	£375.00
M50	Women of Nations	1922	£4.50	£225.00
(D)	**Cameo Cigarettes (Australia)**			
50	Horses of To-Day	1906	*£8.50*	—
(E)	**Copain Cigarettes (Belgium)**			
52	Birds of Brilliant Plumage (P/C Inset)	1927	£5.00	—
(F)	**Domino Cigarettes (Mauritius)**			
25	Animaux et Reptiles	1961	—	£2.50
25	Coursaires et Boucaniers	1961	—	£2.50
25	Figures Historiques, Une Serie	1961	—	£2.50
25	Figures Historiques, Seconde Serie	1961	—	£12.50
25	Fleurs de Culture	1961	—	£2.50
25	Les Oiseaux et L'Art Japonais	1961	—	£17.50
25	Les Produits du Monde	1961	—	£2.50
50	Voitures Antiques	1961	—	£60.00
(G)	**Eagle Bird Cigarettes (China & Siam)**			
50	Animals & Birds	1909	£1.80	£90.00
50	Aviation Series	1912	£3.25	—
25	Birds of the East	1912	£1.80	—
25	China's Famous Warriors	1911	£2.80	£70.00
25	Chinese Beauties, 1st Series (2 Types)	1908	£2.50	—
25	Chinese Beauties, 2nd Series (2 Types)	1909	£1.75	—
50	Chinese Trades	1908	£2.00	—
25	Cock Fighting	1911	£7.50	—
60	Flags & Pennons	1926	£1.25	£75.00
50	Romance of the Heavens	1929	£1.60	£80.00
50	Siamese Alphabet (2 Types)	1922	£1.25	£62.50
50	Siamese Dreams & Their Meaning	1923	£1.00	£50.00
50	Siamese Horoscopes	1916	£1.00	£50.00
50	Siamese Play – Inao	1916	£1.30	—
50	Siamese Play – Khun Chang Khun Phaen 1	1917	£1.30	£65.00
50	Siamese Play – Khun Chang Khun Phaen 2	1917	£1.30	£65.00
36	Siamese Play – Phra Aphai, 1st	1918	£1.25	£45.00
36	Siamese Play – Phra Aphai, 2nd	1919	£1.25	£45.00
150	Siamese Play – Ramakien I	1913	£1.00	—
50	Siamese Play – Ramakien II	1914	£1.30	—
50	Siamese Uniforms	1915	£1.80	£90.00

Qty		Date	Odds	Sets
50	Views of Bangkok	1928	£3.00	—
50	Views of Siam (2 Types)	1928	£3.00	—
30	War Weapons	1914	£1.75	£52.50
(H)	**Gold Dollar Cigarettes (Germany)**			
M270	Auf Deutscher Scholle	1934	£1.50	—
M270	Der Weltkrieg (1914)	1933	£1.50	—
M270	Deutsche Kolonien	1931	£1.50	—
M270	Die Deutsche Wehrmacht	1935	£1.50	—
?50	Do You Know?	1928	£4.50	—
M100	Filmbilder	1935	£1.25	£125.00
M100	In Prarie Und Urwald	1930	£1.20	£120.00
100	Wild-West	1932	£1.35	—
(I)	**Kong Beng Cigarettes (China)**			
50	Animals	1912	£5.00	—
(J)	**Mascot Cigarettes (Germany)**			
100	Cinema Stars	1931	£2.75	—
M208	Cinema Stars	1924	£2.25	—
(K)	**Motor Cigarettes (Denmark)**			
50	Aviation Series (3 Printings)	1911	£7.50	—
50	Butterflies & Moths	1911	*£4.00*	—
50	Flag Girls of All Nations	1908	£7.00	—
50	Girls of All Nations	1908	£7.50	—
(L)	**Old Judge Cigarettes (Australia)**			
50	Horses of To Day	1906	*£8.50*	—
FS270	Views of the World	1908	*£7.00*	—
(M)	**Pedro Cigarettes (India)**			
50	Actors & Actresses	1906	*£3.00*	—
37	Nautch Girls (Red Border, 3 Types)	1905	£2.25	—
40	(Coloured)	1905	£2.25	—
52	(P/C Inset)	1905	£2.50	—
(N)	**Pinhead Cigarettes (China)**			
50	Chinese Modern Beauties	1912	£2.50	—
33	Chinese Heroes, Set 1	1912	£2.50	—
50	Chinese Heroes, Set 2	1913	£2.50	—
50	Chinese Trades, Set III (2 Types)	1908	£2.50	—
50	Chinese Trades, Set IV	1909	£2.50	—
50	Chinese Trades, Set V	1910	£2.50	—
50	Types of the British Army	1909	*£3.25*	—
(O)	**Railway Cigarettes (India)**			
37	Nautch Girl Series (2 Types)	1907	£2.25	£83.00
(P)	**Shantung Cigarettes (China)**			
50	Chinese Curios	1928	£6.00	—
(Q)	**Sunflower Cigarettes (China)**			
50	Chinese Trades	1906	£5.00	—
(R)	**Teal Cigarettes (Siam)**			
30	Chinese Beauties	1917	*£3.50*	—
50	Cinema Stars (Blue Back) (2 Printings)	1930	£1.80	£90.00
50	(Red Back) (2 Printings)	1930	£1.70	£85.00
50	Cinema Stars (51-100)	1931	*£3.00*	—
30	Fish Series	1916	£1.80	£54.00
L18	Fish Series (Double Cards)	1916	£4.00	—
50	War Incidents	1916	£2.00	£100.00

Qty		Date	Odds	Sets
(S)	**Tiger Cigarettes (India)**			
52	Nautch Girl Series (P/C Inset, 4 Types)	1911	£1.75	—
(T)	**Vanity Fair Cigarettes (Australia)**			
50	Horses of To Day	1906	*£8.50*	—

(3) SERIES WITH PRINTED BACK, NO MAKER'S NAME OR BRAND (See also Imperial Tobacco Co. (Canada), United Tobacco Co.)

Qty		Date	Odds	Sets
250	Actresses "ALWICS" (Design Back)	1906	£3.00	—
50	Aeroplanes (Gilt Border)	1926	£2.40	£120.00
50	Aeroplanes of Today	1936	90p	£45.00
25	Angling	1930	£4.20	£105.00
25	Animaux Préhistoriques	1925	*£5.00*	—
L25	Arabic Proverbs (Silk)	1913	£12.50	—
50	Arms & Armour	1910	£5.00	—
L50	Arms of the British Empire (Silk, Blue Back)	1911	£2.60	£130.00
L50	(Silk, Brown Back)	1911	£4.00	—
25	Army Life	1908	£6.00	—
50	Art Photogravures	1912	85p	—
L50	Australian Wild Flowers (Silk)	1913	£3.20	£160.00
22	Automobielen	1923	*£6.25*	—
22	Automobiles	1923	*£6.25*	—
75	Aviation	1910	£4.00	—
50	Aviation Series	1911	£3.25	—
50	Beauties, Red Tinted (Design Back)	1906	£2.50	—
52	Beauties, Tobacco Leaf Back (P/C Inset)	1908	£3.20	£165.00
52	(No Inset)	1908	£3.75	—
F50	Beauties	1925	£2.25	—
MF50	Beauties (Hand Coloured)	1925	£1.60	£80.00
F50	Beauties, 2nd Series	1926	£1.60	£80.00
F50	Beauties, 3rd Series	1926	£1.30	£65.00
F50	Beauties of Great Britain	1930	60p	£30.00
F50	Beautiful England	1928	40p	£20.00
M?28	Belgian Footballers	1913	£7.50	—
M75	Belles Vues de Belgique	1928	*£2.75*	—
50	Best Dogs of Their Breed	1913	£4.00	£200.00
L50	Best Dogs of Their Breed (Silk)	1913	£5.60	£280.00
50	Billiards	1929	£1.60	£80.00
50	Birds, Beasts and Fishes (Cut-outs)	1937	60p	£30.00
M50	Birds, Beasts & Fishes (Cut-outs)	1937	£1.20	£60.00
24	Birds of England	1924	£2.50	—
50	Boy Scouts	1930	£1.90	£95.00
50	Britain's Defenders (Blue Front)	1914	£2.00	—
50	Britain's Defenders (Mauve Front)	1914	£1.40	£70.00
50	British Butterflies	1930	£1.00	£50.00
50	British Empire Series	1913	£2.50	—
25	British Trees & Their Uses	1930	£1.80	£45.00
50	British Warships and Admirals	1915	£2.80	£140.00
50	Butterflies & Moths	1911	£1.75	£87.50
50	Butterflies (Girls)	1928	£5.00	£250.00
M50	Butterflies (Girls)	1928	£6.00	£300.00
M50	Celebrities of Film and Stage (2 Types)	1930	£1.50	—
LF48	Channel Islands, Past & Present (2 Types)	1939	25p	£12.50
40	Characters from the Works of Dickens	1919	—	£46.00
38/40	Characters from the Works of Dickens	1919	65p	£26.00
50	Cinema Artistes (Black & White 1-50)	1928	£1.60	£80.00
50	Cinema Artistes (Black & White 101-150)	1930	£1.60	—
60	Cinema Artistes, Set 1 (Brown, 2 Types)	1929	£2.00	—

Qty		*Date*	*Odds*	*Sets*
50	Cinema Artistes, Set 2 (Brown, 2 Types)	1931	£1.60	£80.00
M48	Cinema Artistes, Set 3	1932	£2.00	—
48	Cinema Celebrities (C)	1935	£1.00	£48.00
L48	Cinema Celebrities (C)	1935	£1.30	—
L56	Cinema Celebrities (D)	1937	£2.50	£137.50
50	Cinema Favourites	1929	£2.00	£100.00
50	Cinema Stars, Set 2 (1-50)	1928	£1.00	—
50	Cinema Stars, Set 3 (51-100)	1930	£1.50	—
50	Cinema Stars, Set 4 (101-150)	1932	£1.00	—
100	Cinema Stars (Coloured)	1931	£2.25	—
F50	Cinema Stars, Set 1	1924	£1.20	£60.00
F50	Cinema Stars, Set 2	1924	£1.00	£50.00
F50	Cinema Stars, Set 3	1925	£1.50	—
MF52	Cinema Stars, Set 4	1925	£1.60	—
MF52	Cinema Stars, Set 5	1926	£1.60	—
MF52	Cinema Stars, Set 6	1927	£2.00	—
LF48	Cinema Stars, Set 7	1927	£2.50	—
F50	Cinema Stars, Set 8	1928	£1.20	£60.00
F50	Cinema Stars, Set 9 (51-100)	1929	£2.00	—
F50	Cinema Stars, Set 10 (101-150)	1930	£2.00	—
F50	Cinema Stars, Set 11 (151-200)	1931	£2.00	—
110	Crests & Badges of the British Army (Silk)	1915	£2.50	—
M108	Crests & Badges of the British Army (Silk)	1915	£2.00	—
M50	Crests and Colours of Australian Universities, Colleges & Schools (Silk)	1916	£2.25	—
25	Derby Day Series A	1914	£9.00	—
50	Do You Know?	1930	30p	£15.00
50	Do You Know?, 2nd Series	1931	30p	£15.00
25	Dracones Posthistorici	1931	£7.00	—
?10	Dutch Footballers	1913	£8.00	—
25	Dutch Scenes	1928	£2.00	£50.00
50	Engineering Wonders (2 Types)	1929	50p	£25.00
40	English Costumes of Ten Centuries	1919	£1.35	£54.00
F25	English Cricketers	1926	£2.60	£65.00
26	Etchings (of Dogs)	1926	£2.40	£62.50
F50	Famous Bridges	1935	80p	—
50	Famous Footballers, Set 1	1923	£3.00	£150.00
50	Famous Footballers, Set 2	1924	£3.00	£150.00
50	Famous Footballers, Set 3	1925	£3.00	£150.00
25	Famous Racehorses	1926	£2.60	£65.00
25	Famous Railway Trains	1929	£1.80	£45.00
50	Favourite Flowers	1923	65p	£32.50
50	Film and Stage Favourites	1926	£1.60	£80.00
75	Film Favourites	1928	£1.20	£90.00
50	Flags of the Empire	1928	70p	£35.00
50	Foreign Birds	1930	65p	£32.50
50	Game Birds and Wild Fowl	1929	£1.30	£65.00
LF45	Grace and Beauty (1-45)	1938	30p	£13.50
LF45	Grace and Beauty (46-90)	1939	20p	£9.00
LF48	Guernsey, Alderney & Sark	1937	40p	£19.00
LF48	Guernsey, Alderney & Sark (Second Series)	1938	25p	£12.00
L80	Guernsey Footballers, Priaulx League	1938	45p	£36.00
F52	Here There & Everywhere	1929	25p	£12.50
25	Hints & Tips for Motorists	1929	£2.40	£60.00
48	Hints on Association Football (Chinese)	1934	20p	£7.00
F50	Homeland Events	1928	60p	£40.00

Qty		*Date*	*Odds*	*Sets*
50	Horses of To Day	1906	£5.00	—
32	Houses of Parliament (Red Back)	1912	£1.60	£50.00
32	(Brown Back with Verse)	1912	*£8.50*	—
50	Indian Chiefs	1930	£8.00	£400.00
50	Indian Regiments Series	1912	£8.00	—
50	International Air Liners	1937	70p	£35.00
25	Java Scenes	1929	*£8.00*	—
LF48	Jersey Then & Now	1935	75p	£36.00
LF48	Jersey Then & Now, Second Series	1937	75p	£36.00
50	Jiu-Jitsu Series	1911	£2.60	£130.00
?82	Joueurs de Football Belges	1923	£8.00	—
50	Keep Fit	1939	80p	£40.00
M?166	La Belgique Monumentale & Pittoresque (4 Series)	1926	£3.00	—
50	Leaders of Men	1929	£3.00	—
50	Life in the Tree Tops	1931	40p	£20.00
50	Lighthouses	1926	£1.40	£70.00
40	London Ceremonials	1929	£1.25	£50.00
F50	London Zoo	1927	60p	£30.00
50	Lucky Charms	1930	£1.40	£70.00
25	Marvels of the Universe Series	1925	£2.40	£60.00
45	Melbourne Cup Winners	1906	£5.50	£250.00
50	Merchant Ships of the World	1925	£4.00	—
25	Merchant Ships of the World	1925	£3.00	£75.00
25	Military Portraits	1917	£2.60	£65.00
LF36	Modern Beauties	1939	£1.25	£45.00
XF36	Modern Beauties	1936	£1.10	£40.00
36	Modern Beauties, First Series	1938	£1.00	£36.00
MF54	Modern Beauties	1937	85p	£45.00
36	Modern Beauties, Second Series	1938	50p	£18.00
MF54	Modern Beauties, Second Series	1938	85p	£45.00
XF36	Modern Beauties, Second Series	1936	70p	£25.00
MF36	Modern Beauties, Third Series	1938	£1.50	£54.00
XF36	Modern Beauties, Third Series	1937	75p	£27.00
MF36	Modern Beauties, Fourth Series	1939	85p	£31.00
XF36	Modern Beauties, Fourth Series	1937	£1.50	£54.00
XF36	Modern Beauties, Fifth Series	1938	£1.00	£36.00
XF36	Modern Beauties, Sixth Series	1938	75p	£27.00
XF36	Modern Beauties, Seventh Series	1938	£1.25	£45.00
LF36	Modern Beauties, Eighth Series	1939	£1.25	£45.00
LF36	Modern Beauties, Ninth Series	1939	£1.50	£54.00
50	Modern Warfare	1936	£1.00	£50.00
M48	Modern Wonders	1938	£1.75	£84.00
25	Modes of Conveyance	1928	£1.60	£40.00
48	Motor Cars (Coloured)	1926	£3.50	—
36	Motor Cars (Brown)	1929	£5.00	—
50	Motor Cycles	1927	£3.40	£170.00
FS50	Native Life in Many Lands (Stereo)	1932	£1.00	—
F50	Natural and Man Made Wonders of World	1937	50p	£25.00
FS50	Nature Studies	1928	50p	£25.00
50	Naval Portraits	1917	£2.20	£110.00
32	Nederlandsche Leger (Dutch Army)	1923	£4.25	£135.00
25	Notabilities	1917	£2.40	£60.00
25	Past & Present	1929	£1.60	£40.00
FS48	Pictures of the East	1930	£1.50	£72.00
M48	Picturesque China	1925	£1.00	£50.00
M53	Playing Cards	1940	20p	£6.50

Qty		*Date*	*Odds*	*Sets*
36	Popular Stage, Cinema & Society Celebrities	1928	£2.75	—
M50	Pottery Types (Silk)	1926	£7.00	—
25	Prehistoric Animals	1931	£2.80	£70.00
50	Prominent Australian and English Cricketers	1911	£35.00	—
25	Puzzle Series	1916	£5.00	£125.00
50	Railway Working	1927	£1.50	£75.00
33	Regimental Pets	1911	£6.00	—
50	Regimental Uniforms	1936	£1.40	£70.00
50	Romance of the Heavens (2 Types)	1929	70p	£35.00
FS50	Round the World in Pictures	1931	90p	£45.00
50	Royal Mail	1912	£3.50	—
27	Rulers of the World	1911	£6.50	—
40	Safety First	1931	£1.75	—
25	Ships Flags & Cap Badges, A Series	1930	£2.75	—
25	Ships Flags & Cap Badges, 2nd Series	1930	£2.75	—
F50	Ships and Shipping	1928	70p	£35.00
50	Signalling Series	1913	£3.00	—
100	Soldiers of the World (Tobacco Leaf Back)	1902	£10.00	£1000.00
50	Speed	1938	60p	£30.00
25	Sports & Games in Many Lands	1930	£5.00	£150.00
50	Stage & Film Stars	1926	£1.40	—
M50	Stars of Filmland	1927	£2.25	—
F50	The Royal Navy	1930	£1.60	£80.00
F50	The World of Sport	1927	£1.80	—
100	Transfers, Set 1	1930	£2.75	—
100	Transfers, Set 2	1930	£2.75	—
32	Transport of the World	1911	*£8.00*	—
20	Types of North American Indians	1930	£12.50	£250.00
F50	Types of the World	1936	65p	£32.50
F52	Ur Ollum Attum	1930	£3.50	—
FS270	Views of the World	1908	*£2.75*	—
48	Volaille, Pigeons & Chiens	1915	*£7.00*	—
50	War Incidents (Blue Black)	1915	£1.40	£70.00
50	War Incidents (Brown Back, Different)	1916	£1.50	£75.00
25	Warriors of All Nations (Gold Panel)	1937	£1.50	£37.50
50	Warships	1926	£4.00	—
25	Whaling	1930	£1.80	£45.00
F50	Who's Who in Sport (1926)	1927	£1.50	£150.00
50	Wild Animals of the World (Tobacco Leaf Back)	1903	£6.75	—
25	Wireless	1923	£3.50	—
50	Wonders of the Past	1930	75p	£37.50
50	Wonders of the Sea	1929	60p	£30.00
25	Wonders of the World	1928	60p	£15.00
40	World Famous Cinema Artistes	1933	£1.20	£48.00
L40	World Famous Cinema Artistes	1933	£1.25	£50.00
50	World's Products	1929	40p	£20.00
F50	Zoo	1935	60p	£30.00
50	Zoological Studies	1928	40p	£20.00
M50	Zulu Chiefs (2 Types)	1932	£12.50	—
(4)	**SERIES WITH PLAIN BACKS**			
50	Actors & Actresses "WALP"	1906	£1.75	£87.50
50	Actresses "ALWICS"	1907	£2.00	—
50	Actresses, Four Colours Surround	1905	£1.80	£90.00
30	Actresses, Unicoloured (Light Brown)	1910	70p	£21.00
30	(Purple Brown)	1910	85p	£25.50

BRITISH AMERICAN TOBACCO CO. LTD. (B.A.T.) — cont.

Qty		Date	Odds	Sets
50	Animals & Birds	1912	£1.90	£95.00
60	Animals (Cut-Outs)	1912	£1.00	£60.00
50	Art Photogravures	1912	£2.00	—
50	Aviation Series	1911	£3.25	—
40	Beauties (Brown Tinted)	1913	£2.00	—
50	Beauties, Coloured Backgrounds	1911	£2.20	£110.00
50	Beauties, "LAWHA"	1906	*£2.40*	—
32	Beauties, Picture Hats I	1914	£2.75	£88.00
45	Beauties, Picture Hats II	1914	£2.70	£122.00
30	Beauties & Children	1912	*£4.00*	—
52	Birds of Brilliant Plumage (P/C Inset)	1914	£2.40	£125.00
30	Boy Scouts Signalling (English Caption)	1922	£2.50	£75.00
30	(Siamese Caption)	1922	£2.60	£78.00
50	Butterflies & Moths	1914	£1.50	£75.00
50	Cinema Artistes	1930	£2.00	—
50	Cinema Stars "BAMT" (1-50)	1927	£1.00	£50.00
50	Cinema Stars (51-100)	1928	£1.50	—
50	Cinema Stars (101-150)	1930	£1.50	—
100	Cinema Stars (201-300)	1932	£1.00	£100.00
50	Cinema Stars (Coloured)	1928	£1.50	—
50	Cinema Stars "FLAG"	1929	£1.20	—
27	Dancing Girls	1913	£1.40	£38.00
32	Drum Horses	1910	£4.50	£144.00
50	English Period Costumes	1929	70p	£35.00
50	Flag Girls of All Nations	1908	£1.60	£80.00
165	Flags, Pennons & Signals	1907	75p	—
20	Flowers	1915	85p	£17.00
50	Girls of All Nations	1908	£1.80	£90.00
30	Heroic Deeds	1913	£1.80	£54.00
25	Hindoo Gods	1909	£6.75	—
32	Houses of Parliament	1914	£3.00	—
25	Indian Mogul Paintings	1909	£8.00	—
53	Jockeys & Owners Colours (P/C Inset)	1914	£2.60	£140.00
K36	Modern Beauties, 1st Series	1938	£2.50	£90.00
36	Modern Beauties, 2nd Series	1939	£2.50	£90.00
F48	Movie Stars	1928	£1.50	£72.00
F50	New Zealand, Early Scenes & Maori Life	1929	£1.60	—
50	Poultry & Pigeons	1926	£4.25	—
25	Products of the World	1914	85p	—
50	Royal Mail	1912	*£4.50*	—
36	Ships & Their Pennants	1913	£2.00	£72.00
75	Soldiers of the World	1904	£7.75	—
30	Sporting Girls	1913	£4.50	—
50	Sports of the World (Brown)	1917	£3.40	£170.00
50	(Coloured)	1917	£3.30	£165.00
M50	Stars of Filmland	1927	£1.75	—
25	The Bonzo Series	1923	£3.20	£80.00
32	Transport of the World	1917	£1.15	£37.00
50	Types of the British Army (Numbered)	1908	£3.00	—
50	(Unnumbered)	1908	£2.50	—
F50	Types of the World	1936	*£2.00*	—
F50	Units of the British Army & R.A.F.	1930	*£1.80*	—
FS50	Views of the World	1908	£1.30	—
50	War Leaders and Scenes	1916	£4.50	—
M50	Women of Nations (Flag Girls)	1922	£2.50	—

BRITISH-AUSTRALASIAN TOBACCO CO. (Australia)

Qty		*Date*	*Odds*	*Sets*
?254	Flags of All Nations (2 Types)	1910	£6.00	—

BRITISH CIGARETTE CO. (China)

25	Actresses and Beauties "FECKSA"	1900	£65.00	—
25	South African War Scenes	1900	£25.00	£625.00

BRITISH LEAF TOBACCO CO. (India)

?12	Actresses and Film Stars	1930	£8.00	—

BRITISH NEW GUINEA DEVELOPMENT CO.

?41	Papuan Series 1	1910	£45.00	—

BROWN & WILLIAMSON TOBACCO CORPORATION (U.S.A.)

M50	Modern American Airplanes, Series A	1940	£3.70	£185.00
M50	Ditto (No Series Letter)	1940	£2.80	£140.00
M50	Modern Airplanes, Series B	1941	£2.80	£140.00
M50	Modern Airplanes, Series C	1942	£2.80	£140.00
50	Movie Stars	1940	£4.50	—

D. BUCHNER & CO. (U.S.A.)

M48	Actors	1888	£25.00	—
X?97	Actresses	1888	£24.00	—
X?61	American Scenes with a Policeman	1888	£42.00	—
M?143	Baseball Players	1888	*£70.00*	—
X?30	Butterflies & Bugs (2 Types)	1888	£55.00	—
P200	Defenders & Offenders	1888	£34.00	—
M31	Jockeys	1888	£36.50	—
X51	Morning Glory Maidens	1888	£40.00	—
X30	Morning Glory Maidens & American Flowers	1888	*£60.00*	—
X?23	Musical Instruments	1888	£50.00	—
X?20	New York City Scenes	1888	£45.00	—
M103	Police Inspectors	1888	£24.00	—
X?92	Police Inspectors & Captains	1888	£24.00	—
X12	Presidential Puzzle Cards	1888	*£70.00*	—
X?21	Yacht Club Colors	1888	£50.00	—

BUKHSH ELLAHIE & CO.

53	Indian Girl, Playing Card Inset (3 Series)	1902	£20.00	—

CALCUTTA CIGARETTE CO. (India)

25	Actresses (Blue Front)	1906	£22.00	£550.00
25	(Brown Front)	1906	£27.50	—

A. G. CAMERON & CAMERON (U.S.A.)

?12	Actresses (Burdick 488)	1887	£60.00	—
24	Occupations for Women	1893	£42.50	—
F?	Photographic Cards	1893	*£10.00*	—
25	The New Discovery	1892	£30.00	£750.00

V. CAMILLERI (Malta)

MF104	Popes of Rome	1922	£1.60	£165.00

CAMLER TOBACCO COY. (Malta)

Qty		*Date*	*Odds*	*Sets*
F250	Footballers	1926	£6.25	—
M96	Maltese Families Coats of Arms	1925	£1.10	£105.00

M. C. CARATHANASSIS & CO. (Turkey)

48	The Post in Various Countries	1900	£30.00	—

CASTELANO BROS. LTD. (India)

52	Beauties, Playing Card Inset	1899	£22.00	£1150.00
?3	Indian Series	1900	*£50.00*	—

HENRY CLAY & CO. (Cuba)

M?1300	Album Universal	1925	£1.00	—
M500	Alrededor Del Mundo	1925	£1.00	—
M1670	Cuba En 1925	1925	£1.00	—
M1485	Espana Y La America Latina	1926	£1.00	—
?	Photo Series (Postcard Back, Many Groups)	1920	£1.50	—
F?998	Views of the World	1922	£1.00	—

J. CLIMENT & CO. (Algeria)

F?	Photo Series (Many Groups)	1910	£4.00	—

C. COLOMBOS (Malta)

F?206	Actresses	1902	£3.25	—
MF?60	Actresses	1902	£15.00	—
60	Actresses (Coloured)	1900	£12.00	—
MF?57	Celebrities	1900	£16.50	—
F136	Dante's Divine Comedy	1914	£2.20	£300.00
MF72	Famous Oil Paintings, Serie A	1910	85p	£61.50
MF108	Famous Oil Paintings, Serie B	1911	85p	£92.00
MF240	Famous Oil Paintings, Serie C	1912	85p	£204.00
MF100	Famous Oil Paintings, Serie D	1913	85p	£85.00
XF?91	Famous Oil Paintings	1911	£6.25	—
MF100	Life of Napoleon Bonaparte	1914	£2.40	£240.00
MF70	Life of Nelson	1914	£2.60	£182.00
MF70	Life of Wellington	1914	£2.50	£175.00
120	Masterpieces of Contemporary Art	1913	70p	£84.00
MF100	National Types and Costumes	1908	£2.40	£240.00
F?30	Opera Singers	1899	£27.50	—
M112	Royalty and Celebrities	1908	£2.70	£300.00

COLONIAL TOBACCOS (PTY.) LTD. (South Africa)

X150	World's Fairy Tales	1930	£3.60	—

CONDACHI BROTHERS & CO. (Malta)

25	The Bride Retires	1905	£25.00	—

D. CONDACHI & SON (Malta)

?15	Artistes & Beauties	1910	£18.00	—

CONGRESS CUT PLUG (U.S.A.)

X12	Actresses	1890	£37.50	—

CONSOLIDATED CIGARETTE CO. (U.S.A.)

Qty		Date	Odds	Sets
?24	Actresses (Consols)	1890	*£42.50*	—
25	Ladies of the White House	1893	£27.50	—
M14	Ladies of the White House	1898	£32.00	£450.00
M25	Turn Cards (72 x 41mm)	1894	£40.00	—
M25	(78 x 51mm)	1894	£45.00	—

A. G. COUSIS & CO. (Malta)

254	Actors & Actresses	1924	£1.00	—
KF100	Actors & Actresses (Hand Coloured)	1906	£1.75	—
F100	Actors & Actresses (Hand Coloured)	1906	£1.75	—
F?3	Actresses (Cairo Address)	1907	*£32.50*	—
KF100	Actresses Serie I	1907	£1.40	—
KF80	Actresses Serie II	1907	£1.40	—
F1900	Actresses Serie I to Serie XIX	1907	£1.60	—
KF?2281	Actresses (Unnumbered)	1905	90p	—
F?1285	Actresses (Unnumbered)	1905	£1.00	—
MF?221	Actresses (White Border)	1902	£8.00	—
KF100	Actresses, Partners & National Costumes (Cousis')	1906	£1.75	—
KF200	(Cousis's)	1906	£2.00	—
F100	Actresses, Partners & National Costumes	1906	£2.00	—
50	Beauties, Couples & Children (Red Back)	1923	£2.00	—
MF50	Beauties, Couples & Children, Collection No.1	1908	£2.75	—
MF50	Beauties, Couples & Children, Collection No.2	1908	£2.75	—
MF50	Beauties, Couples & Children, Collection No.3	1908	£2.75	—
F100	Bullfighters	1901	£6.50	—
F402	Celebrities (Numbered)	1906	£1.50	—
KF?2162	Celebrities (Unnumbered)	1905	£1.00	—
F?2162	Celebrities (Unnumbered)	1905	£1.00	—
XF?104	Celebrities & Warships (White Border)	1902	£9.00	—
MF72	Grand Masters of the Order of St. John	1909	£3.00	—
F100	National Costumes	1908	£2.20	—
MF60	Paris Exhibition, 1900	1900	£25.00	—
MF102	Paris Series	1902	£22.50	—
MF182	Popes of Rome (To A.D. 1241)	1904	£1.60	£290.00
MF81	Popes of Rome (Dubec, After A.D. 1241)	1904	£2.75	—
F100	Statues & Monuments (Numbered)	1905	£1.60	—
F100	(Unnumbered)	1905	£1.75	—
KF127	Views of Malta	1903	*£2.00*	—
F?115	Views of Malta (Numbered)	1903	£1.20	—
MF?127	Views of Malta (Numbered)	1903	£1.20	—
MF?59	(Unnumbered)	1903	£1.20	—
F?21	Views of the Mediterranean	1903	*£4.00*	—
MF?123	Views of the Mediterranean	1903	*£4.00*	—
F?559	Views of the World	1903	£1.20	—
MF?559	Views of the World	1903	£1.20	—
F99	Warships (White Border)	1910	£2.65	£265.00
KF850	Warships	1904	£1.50	—
MF850	Warships	1904	£1.60	—
MF?114	Warships & Liners (Dubec)	1904	£5.00	—
MF?22	Warships & Liners (Excelsior)	1904	£4.50	—
MF?40	Warships & Liners (Superior)	1904	£5.00	—

CRESCENT CIGAR FACTORY (U.S.A.)

T?13	Actresses	1886	*£60.00*	—

CROWN TOBACCO CO. (India)

Qty		*Date*	*Odds*	*Sets*
X?26	Actresses	1900	£45.00	—
E?29	Celebrities	1900	£45.00	—
96	National Types, Costumes & Flags	1900	£35.00	—
T96	National Types, Costumes & Flags	1900	£40.00	—
MF?77	Photo Series	1900	£40.00	—

CHARLES C. DAVIS & CO. (U.S.A.)

?15	Actresses	1890	£50.00	—

DIAMOND INDIAN CIGARETTES

?20	Indian Beauties	1924	£12.50	—

M. W. DIFFLEY (U.S.A.)

36	Flags of All Nations	1890	£32.50	—

DIXSON (Australia)

50	Australian M.P.s & Celebrities	1900	£15.00	—

DOMINION TOBACCO CO. (Canada)

50	Photos (Actresses, "ALWICS")	1905	*£25.00*	—
100	Photos (Actresses, Plum Background)	1905	£25.00	—
50	The Smokers of the World (2 Printings)	1904	£42.50	—

DOMINION TOBACCO CO. LTD. (New Zealand)

50	Coaches and Coaching Days	1927	£2.50	—
50	People and Places Famous in New Zealand History	1933	£1.60	£80.00
50	Products of the World	1929	80p	£40.00
50	U.S.S. Co's. Steamers	1928	£2.50	£125.00

DRUMMOND TOBACCO CO. (U.S.A.)

?29	Actresses	1895	£55.00	—
?47	Bathing Girls	1895	£70.00	—
50	Beauties "CHOAB"	1897	£75.00	—
X?10	Girls	1896	*£55.00*	—

DUDGEON & ARNELL (Australia)

M16	1934 Australian Test Team	1934	£6.00	£100.00
M55	Famous Ships	1933	£3.00	—

W. DUKE & SONS LTD. (U.S.A.)

50	Actors and Actresses, Series 1 (2 Printings)	1889	£13.50	£675.00
M50	Actors and Actresses, Series 1	1889	£32.50	—
50	Actors and Actresses, Series 2 (2 Printings)	1889	£13.50	£675.00
M50	Actors and Actresses, Series 2	1889	£32.50	—
X30	Actors and Actresses (As Above)	1889	£27.50	—
25	Actresses (Tobacco War – Overseas)	1900	£7.00	—
X25	Albums of American Stars	1886	£42.50	—
X25	Battle Scenes	1887	£30.00	£750.00
X25	Beauties, Black Border	1886	£25.00	£625.00
P25	Beauties, Folders	1886	£40.00	—

W. DUKE & SONS LTD. (U.S.A.) — cont.

Qty		Date	Odds	Sets
X25	Bicycle and Trick Riders	1891	£32.50	—
X25	Breeds of Horses	1892	£30.00	£750.00
X25	Bridges	1888	£24.00	£600.00
X25	Burlesque Scenes	1889	£26.50	—
50	Coins of All Nations (3 Printings)	1889	£14.00	£700.00
X25	Comic Characters	1887	£24.00	£600.00
X25	Cowboy Scenes	1888	£32.00	£800.00
X50	Fairest Flowers in the World	1887	£22.50	—
F45	Famous Ships	1884	*£11.00*	—
50	Fancy Dress Ball Costumes (2 Printings)	1887	£13.50	£675.00
M50	Fancy Dress Ball Costumes	1887	£32.50	—
X50	Fancy Dress Ball Costumes	1887	£23.00	—
50	Fishers and Fish	1888	£14.00	£700.00
X25	Fishes and Fishing	1888	£26.00	£650.00
X25	Flags and Costumes	1893	£26.00	£650.00
50	Floral Beauties & Language of Flowers	1892	£13.00	£650.00
X25	French Novelties	1891	£25.00	—
X25	Gems of Beauty (2 Types)	1884	£25.00	£625.00
50	Great Americans	1888	£19.00	£950.00
X16	Great Americans	1888	£30.00	—
25	Gymnastic Exercises (Duke in Blue)	1887	£27.50	—
25	(Duke in Brown)	1887	£25.00	£625.00
X25	Habitations of Man	1890	£24.00	£600.00
50	Histories of Generals (Booklets)	1889	£32.00	£1600.00
X50	Histories of Generals	1889	£35.00	—
50	Histories of Poor Boys & Other Famous People (Booklets)	1889	£25.00	£1350.00
50	Holidays	1890	£14.00	£700.00
X25	Honest Library (Booklets)	1896	£37.50	—
X25	Illustrated Songs	1893	£25.00	—
X25	Industries of the States	1889	£26.50	—
50	Jokes (2 Types)	1890	£15.00	£750.00
X25	Jokes	1890	£24.00	—
X25	Lighthouses (Die Cut)	1890	£26.00	£650.00
X25/26	Miniature Novelties	1891	£24.00	£600.00
50	Musical Instruments	1888	£18.00	£900.00
X25	Musical Instruments of the World	1888	£26.00	—
36	Ocean and River Steamers	1887	£23.00	£830.00
F?	Photographic Cards	1885	£2.50	—
MF?	Photographic Cards	1885	£5.00	—
XF?	Photographic Cards	1885	£4.00	—
53	Playing Cards (2 Types)	1888	£11.00	£580.00
50	Popular Songs and Dancers	1894	£18.00	—
50	Postage Stamps (3 Types)	1889	£13.50	£675.00
X25	Presidential Possibilities	1888	£25.00	£625.00
X15	Puzzles	1887	£37.50	—
51	Rulers, Coat of Arms, and Flag (Folders)	1888	£13.00	£660.00
X50	Rulers, Flags and Coats of Arms	1889	£22.50	—
50	Scenes of Perilous Occupations	1888	£20.00	£1000.00
X25	Sea Captains	1887	£30.00	—
50	Shadows	1889	£15.00	£750.00
X25	Snapshots from "Puck"	1889	£24.00	£600.00
X25	Stars of the Stage (White Border)	1891	£24.00	£600.00
X25	Stars of the Stage, Second Series	1891	£25.00	£625.00
X25	Stars of the Stage, Third Series	1892	£24.00	£600.00
X25	Stars of the Stage, 4th Series (Die Cut)	1893	£25.00	£625.00

Prominent Cricketers of 1938
Ogdens. Also Hignett

Boxers
Wills – Overseas

Irish Rugby Internationals
Wills

Olympic Challenge 1992
Brooke Bond

Boxing Greats
Sporting Profiles

Popular Footballers
Carreras

Speed Champions
Godfrey Phillips

Northampton Town
Football Club
Lees. Also reprint

Birds, Fowls, Pigeons & Rabbits
Sanders

A Tribute to the Endangered,
Series 5 – Santa Fe

Zoo Animals
Carreras - Turf

Strange Insects – Maynards

Vanishing Animals
Goodies

Trees in Britain
Brooke Bond

Puppies
Molassine

Devon Flowers
Pascall

W. DUKE & SONS LTD. (U.S.A.) — cont.

Qty		Date	Odds	Sets
48	State Governors, Arms & Maps (Folders)	1888	£13.00	£624.00
X48	State Governors, Arms & Maps	1888	£22.50	—
X25	Talk of the Diamond	1893	£45.00	—
50	The Terrors of America & Their Doings	1889	£14.00	£700.00
M50	The Terrors of America & Their Doings	1889	£32.50	—
X50	The Terrors of America & Their Doings	1889	£23.00	—
50	Tinted Photos	1887	£18.00	—
50	Tinted Photos (Die-Cut)	1887	£13.50	—
X25	Transparencies	1888	£50.00	—
X24	Tricks with Cards	1887	£40.00	—
X25	Types of Vessels (Die Cut)	1889	£25.00	£625.00
50	Vehicles of the World	1888	£20.00	—
X50	Yacht Club Colors of the World	1890	£25.00	—
50	Yacht Colors of the World	1890	£14.00	£700.00
M50	Yacht Colors of the World	1890	£32.50	—
PRINTED ALBUMS (EXCHANGED FOR COUPONS)				
	Costumes of All Nations (3 Series)	1890	—	£135.00
	Governors, Coats of Arms & Maps	1889	—	£100.00
	Postage Stamp Album	1889	—	*£125.00*
	Shadows	1889	—	*£135.00*
	Sporting Girls	1888	—	*£300.00*
	The Heroes of the Civil War	1889	—	£450.00
	The Rulers, Flags, Coats of Arms	1889	—	£100.00
	The Terrors of America	1889	—	*£125.00*
	Yacht Colors of the World (3 Series)	1890	—	*£140.00*

DUNGEY, RALPH & CO. (Australia)

50	Australian Footballers	1906	*£27.50*	—
?	Racehorses (Black Back)	1906	*£50.00*	—
?56	Racehorses and Incidents	1906	*£27.50*	—

EAGLE CIGARETTES (Australia)

F50	Actresses & Sportsmen (Photographic)	1890	£75.00	—

EASTERN VIRGINIA CIGARETTE CO. (Asia)

60	Dutch East Indies Footballers	1926	£3.50	—

EGYPTIAN CIGARETTE COY. (Malta)

F120	Actresses	1906	£7.00	—
XF30	Actresses	1906	*£35.00*	—
264	Decorations & Medals	1908	£11.00	—
F?95	Maltese Band Players	1910	£15.00	—

EGYPTIAN CIGARETTES MFG. CO. (China)

?79	Actresses ("MUREG")	1900	£40.00	—
25	Armies of the World	1900	£42.50	—
?3	Beauties In Late Qing Dynasty Dress	1900	*£50.00*	—
30	Beauties, Nymphs	1900	£42.50	—
35	Chinese & South African Series	1900	£55.00	—
25	National Flags & Flowers – Girls	1900	£45.00	—
30	Old Masters	1900	£40.00	—
?55	Russo-Japanese War Series	1904	£45.00	—
25	Types of British & Colonial Troops	1900	£42.50	—
25	Warships	1900	£37.50	—

H. ELLIS & CO. (U.S.A.)

Qty		Date	Odds	Sets
25	Breeds of Dogs (5 Types)	1890	£37.50	—
25	Costumes of Women	1890	£50.00	—
25	Generals of the Late Civil War	1890	£67.50	—
F?	Photographic Cards	1887	*£10.00*	—

D. FANCIULLI & CO. (Malta)

50	Il Paradiso Perduto	1906	£7.50	—

LA FAVORITA – E. FUENTES (Canary Islands)

M30/58	Flags & Soldiers (Silk)	1915	75p	£22.50

JOHN FINZER & BROS. (U.S.A.)

X10	Inventors & Inventions	1891	£36.00	£360.00

G.W. GAIL & AX (U.S.A.)

X25	Battle Scenes	1891	£32.00	—
X25	Bicycle and Trick Riders	1891	£35.00	—
X25	French Novelties	1891	£30.00	—
X25	Industries of the States	1891	£30.00	—
X25	Lighthouses (Die Cut)	1891	£26.50	—
X25	Navy Library	1890	£37.50	—
X25	Novelties (Die Cut)	1890	£28.00	—
XF?	Photographic Cards	1885	£4.00	—
X25	Stars of the Stage	1891	£27.50	—

GENERAL CIGAR CO. LTD. (Canada)

X36	Northern Birds	1977	£1.00	£40.00

GENESEE TOBACCO WORKS (U.S.A.)

?21	Actresses	1888	£45.00	—

ALEJANDRO GONZALEZ (Spain)

X8	Typical Portuguese Costumes	1962	—	£4.00

G. G. GOODE LTD. (Australia)

17	Prominent Cricketer Series	1924	*£75.00*	—

GOODWIN & CO. (U.S.A.)

50	Champions (2 Types)	1888	£32.00	—
50	Dogs of the World (3 Types)	1890	£19.00	£950.00
50	Flowers	1890	£20.00	£1000.00
50	Games and Sports Series	1889	£27.00	£1350.00
50	Holidays	1889	£25.00	—
50	Occupations for Women	1887	£50.00	—
10	Old Judge Cards (Actresses)	1886	£65.00	—
F?	Photographic Cards	1886	*£4.00*	—
50	Vehicles of the World	1888	£25.00	—
50	Wild Animals of the World	1895	£20.00	—

GOODWIN & CO. (U.S.A.) — cont.

Qty		Date	Odds	Sets
PRINTED ALBUMS (EXCHANGED FOR COUPONS)				
	Champions	1888	—	*£750.00*
	Floral Album	1890	—	*£150.00*
	Games & Sports	1889	—	*£300.00*
	Official League Ball	1888	—	*£2000.00*

W. R. GRESH & SONS (U.S.A.)

X25	Actresses (Coloured)	1890	£45.00	—
X?70	Actresses (Sepia)	1890	£35.00	—

L. O. GROTHE LTD. (Canada)

52	Bridge Hands (3 Types)	1927	£5.00	—

THOS. W. HALL (U.S.A)

154	Actors & Actresses (Dull Background)	1881	£7.50	—
111	Actors & Actresses (Black Background)	1882	£8.50	—
?194	Actors & Actresses (Fancy Corners)	1884	£16.00	—
?158	Actors & Actresses (Sun's Rays)	1890	£12.50	—
?52	Actresses (Tiled Wall)	1888	£16.50	—
?12	Actresses (No Borders, Hall on Front)	1892	£32.50	—
25	Actresses (No Borders, No Hall on Front)	1892	£25.00	£625.00
T?11	Actresses ("Ours")	1885	£70.00	—
12	Athletes	1881	£55.00	—
8	Presidential Candidates & Actresses	1880	£60.00	—
22	Presidents of the United States	1888	£30.00	—
25	Theatrical Types	1890	£32.00	£800.00

HARTLEY'S TOBACCO CO. (S. Africa)

53	Playing Cards (OK Cigarettes)	1929	£1.75	—
L19	South African English Cricket Tour 1929	1929	£65.00	—

HERNANDEZ (Brazil)

X24	Alphabet Cards	1960	—	£20.00

S. F. HESS & CO. (U.S.A.)

F?	Photographic Cards	1885	*£10.00*	—
55	Poker Puzzle Cards (2 Types)	1890	£40.00	—
25	Terms of Poker Illustrated	1890	£42.50	—

WM. G. HILLS (U.S.A.)

X25	Actresses	1888	£50.00	—

HILSON CO. (U.S.A.)

T25	Battleships & Signal Flags (2 Printings)	1898	£24.00	£600.00
T25	National Types	1900	£23.00	£575.00

HOUDE & GROTHE (Canada)

L24	Wildfowl (Package Issue)	1953	£3.25	£78.00

T. S. H. HYPPO (Belgium) (Imitation Cigar Bands)

Qty		*Date*	*Odds*	*Sets*
120	German Uniforms of the 19th Century	1975	—	£35.00

IMPERIAL CIGARETTE & TOBACCO CO. (Canada)

?24	Actresses	1900	£50.00	—

IMPERIAL TOBACCO CO. OF CANADA LTD. (Canada)

50	Actresses, Framed Border (Plain Back)	1910	£2.50	£125.00
L55/66	Aircraft Spotter Series (Packets)	1941	£2.20	£121.00
60	Animals (Millbank, 4 Types)	1916	£1.00	£60.00
L55	Animal with Flag (Silk)	1915	£3.00	£165.00
50	Arms of the British Empire	1911	£2.50	—
50	Around the World Series (Numbered)	1912	£3.25	—
50	(Unnumbered)	1912	£4.50	—
50	Aviation Series	1910	£3.75	—
90	Baseball Series	1912	*£24.00*	—
30	Beauties – Art Series (Plain Back)	1911	£10.00	—
30	(Bouquet Cigarettes)	1902	*£45.00*	—
50	Beauties (Coloured, Black Border)	1912	£2.50	£125.00
25	Beauties – Girls in Costume	1904	*£45.00*	—
24	Beauties – Smoke Girls	1904	£45.00	—
M50	Birds, Beasts & Fishes (2 Types) (Cut-outs)	1923	£1.50	£75.00
30	Bird Series	1910	£2.00	£60.00
X100	Birds of Canada	1924	£3.00	—
X100	Birds of Canada (Western Canada)	1925	£5.00	—
50	Boy Scouts	1911	£4.50	£225.00
50	British Birds	1923	65p	£32.50
50	British Man of War Series (Plain Back)	1910	£8.00	£400.00
50	Buildings (Plain Back)	1902	£7.50	£375.00
L55	Butterflies (Silk)	1912	£5.00	—
50	Butterflies & Moths	1911	£2.20	—
L24	Canada's Corvettes, 1st Series	1943	£12.50	—
L24	Canada's Corvettes, 2nd Series	1944	*£12.50*	—
T50	Canadian Cities (Silk)	1914	£6.50	—
50	Canadian Historical Portraits	1913	£2.65	—
48	Canadian History Series (I.T.C. Name)	1926	£1.50	£72.00
50	(Anon.).	1926	£1.50	—
P50	Canadian History Series (Silk)	1914	£10.00	—
T121	Canadian Miscellany (Silk)	1912	£3.60	—
50	Children of All Nations	1924	75p	£37.50
23	Dogs Series	1924	£1.50	£35.00
50	Dogs, 2nd Series	1925	£1.40	£70.00
50	Famous English Actresses	1924	80p	£40.00
50	Film Favourites (4 Types)	1926	£3.00	—
50	Fish & Bait	1924	£1.50	£75.00
50	Fishes of the World	1924	£1.60	—
50	Fish Series	1912	£2.20	£110.00
L143	Flags (Silk)	1913	£2.00	—
50	Flower Culture in Pots	1925	50p	£25.00
50	Fowls, Pigeons & Dogs	1911	£3.20	—
30	Game Bird Series	1925	£1.40	£42.00
L55	Garden Flowers (Silk, Black Numerals)	1913	£2.40	£132.00
L50	(Silk, Red Numerals)	1913	£3.50	—
G5	Garden Flowers (Silk)	1913	£24.00	—
50	Gardening Hints	1923	40p	£20.00

IMPERIAL TOBACCO CO. OF CANADA LTD. (Canada) — cont.

Qty		Date	Odds	Sets
L25	Heraldic Signs & Their Origin	1925	£1.00	£25.00
45	Hockey Players	1912	*£11.50*	—
36	Hockey Series (Coloured)	1911	*£11.50*	—
50	Hockey Series (Blue)	1910	*£13.00*	—
50	"How to do It" Series	1911	£2.50	—
50	How To Play Golf	1925	£7.00	£350.00
50	Infantry Training (4 Types)	1915	£2.20	£110.00
100	Lacrosse Series, Set 1	1910	£4.75	—
98	Lacrosse Series, Set 2	1911	£4.75	—
50	Lacrosse Series, Set 3	1912	£4.75	£237.50
50	L'Histoire du Canada	1914	£1.20	£60.00
M48	Mail Carriers and Stamps	1903	£25.00	—
50	Merchant Ships of the World	1924	£1.00	£50.00
25	Military Portraits (2 Types)	1914	£2.40	£60.00
50	Modern War Weapons	1915	£3.50	£175.00
56	Motor Cars	1921	£1.75	£100.00
50	Movie Stars	1925	£1.60	—
50	Music Hall Artistes (Plain Back)	1911	£2.20	£110.00
50	Naval Portraits (2 Types)	1915	£2.20	£110.00
25	Notabilities (2 Types)	1917	£2.20	£55.00
L55	Orders & Military Medals (Silk)	1915	£2.40	£132.00
E6	Perils of Early Golf	1926	£150.00	—
L50	Pictures of Canadian Life (2 Types)	1912	£5.75	—
53	Poker Hands (Many Types)	1924	£1.30	£70.00
25	Poultry Alphabet	1924	£2.40	£60.00
G6	Premium Silk – Flag Girls	1913	£32.50	—
G1	Premium Silk – George V	1915	—	£35.00
G1	Premium Silk – Motor Boat	1915	—	*£75.00*
G1	Premium Silk – Royal Arms	1914	—	£30.00
G1	Premium Silk – "Staunch and True"	1914	—	£40.00
G1	Premium Silk – Union Jack	1913	—	£22.00
G2	Premium Silk – Yachts	1915	£50.00	—
P45	Prominent Canadian Hockey Players	1912	*£60.00*	—
50	Prominent Men of Canada	1912	£3.00	—
50	Railway Engines (3 Types)	1924	80p	£40.00
L55	Regimental Uniforms of Canada (Silk)	1914	£3.25	£180.00
P25	Rulers with Flags (Silk)	1910	£12.00	£300.00
127	Smokers Golf Cards (2 Types)	1926	£4.75	—
50	The Reason Why	1924	80p	£40.00
25	The World's Dreadnoughts	1910	£3.50	—
50	Tricks & Puzzles Series	1911	£4.75	—
50	Types of Nations	1910	£2.50	—
25	Victoria Cross Heroes (Blue Back)	1915	£2.60	£65.00
L45	Views of the World	1912	£5.00	—
L25	Wild Animals of Canada	1912	£10.00	—
M144	World War I Scenes & Portraits	1916	£1.75	£250.00
X49	Yacht Pennants & Views (Silk)	1915	£6.00	£300.00

IMPERIAL TOB. CO. OF INDIA LTD. (India)

25	Indian Historical Views	1910	£1.80	£45.00
K52	Miniature Playing Cards	1933	90p	—
40	Nautch Girl Series (Pedro Cigarettes)	1908	£2.25	£90.00
40	(Railway Cigarettes)	1908	£2.25	£90.00
52	Nautch Girl Series (P/C Inset, Pedro)	1908	£2.00	£104.00
52	(P/C Inset, Railway)	1908	£2.00	£104.00

IMPERIAL TOB. CO. OF INDIA LTD. (India) — cont.

Qty		Date	Odds	Sets
53	Playing Cards (5 Types)	1919	£1.50	—
1	Present Ticket	1917	—	£3.00

IMPERIAL TOBACCO CO. (NFLD) LTD. (Canada)

M52	Playing Cards (2 Types)	1930	£7.00	—

JACK & JILL CIGARS (U.S.A.)

T?49	Actresses "JAKE"	1890	£50.00	—

JAMAICA TOBACCO CO.

F?104	Miniature Post Card Series	1915	£6.50	—

BILL JONES (U.S.A.)

D?17	Girls (Various Sizes)	1885	£60.00	—

JUBILE (Belgium) (Imitation Cigar Bands)

24	Ancient Military Uniforms	1975	—	£5.00
24	Inventions of Leonardo Da Vinci	1975	—	£6.00
24	Paintings of Manet	1975	—	£5.00
24	Riders of the World	1975	—	£7.50
24	Stained Glass Windows	1975	—	£5.00
12	U.S. War of Independence – Celebrities	1975	—	£4.50

DON JULIAN (Spain) (Imitation Cigar Bands)

X28	European Stamps – Series 7	1978	—	£25.00
X28	European Stamps – Series 8	1978	—	£20.00

KENTUCKY TOBACCOS (PTY) LTD. (S. Africa)

L120	The March of Mankind	1940	£1.75	—

KEY WEST FAVORS (U.S.A.)

T50	Actresses "JAKE"	1890	*£50.00*	—

KHEDIVIAL COMPANY (U.S.A.)

M10	Aeroplane Series No.103 (2 Types)	1912	£17.00	£170.00
M10	Prize Dog Series No.102 (2 Types)	1911	£18.00	£180.00
M25	Prize Fight Series No.101 (2 Types)	1910	£20.00	—
M25	Prize Fight Series No.102	1911	£22.50	—

WM. S. KIMBALL & CO. (U.S.A.)

?42	Actresses, Collotype	1887	£60.00	—
72	Ancient Coins (2 Types)	1888	£26.50	—
48	Arms of Dominions	1888	£17.50	£840.00
50	Ballet Queens	1889	£19.00	£950.00
X20	Beautiful Bathers (2 Types)	1889	£27.50	—
52	Beauties, Playing Card Inset	1895	£20.00	—
50	Butterflies	1888	£21.00	—
50	Champions of Games and Sports (2 Types)	1888	£32.00	—
50	Dancing Girls of the World	1889	£18.00	£900.00
50	Dancing Women	1889	£17.00	£850.00
50	Fancy Bathers	1889	£18.00	£900.00

WM. S. KIMBALL & CO. (U.S.A.) — cont.

Qty		Date	Odds	Sets
X25	French Novelties	1891	£34.00	—
X25	Gems of Beauty	1891	£34.00	—
50	Goddesses of the Greeks & Romans	1889	£22.00	£1100.00
X25	Household Pets	1891	£27.00	£675.00
X15	National Flags	1887	£25.00	—
F?	Photographic Cards	1886	*£6.00*	—
XF?	Photographic Cards	1886	*£7.50*	—
X20	Pretty Athletes	1890	£27.50	—
50	Savage & Semi Barbarous Chiefs & Rulers	1890	£26.00	—
L?21	Wellstood Etchings	1887	£65.00	—

PRINTED ALBUMS (EXCHANGED FOR COUPONS)

		Date	Odds	Sets
	Ancient Coins	1888	—	*£200.00*
	Ballet Queens	1889	—	*£150.00*
	Champions of Games & Sports	1888	—	*£500.00*
	Dancing Girls of the World	1889	—	*£140.00*
	Dancing Women	1889	—	*£140.00*
	Fancy Bathers	1889	—	*£140.00*
	Goddesses of the Greeks & Romans	1889	—	*£165.00*
	Savage & Semi Barbarous Chiefs & Rulers	1890	—	*£225.00*

N. KIMURA & CO. (Japan)

?44	Animals & Birds	1900	£16.50	—
?34	Japanese Uniforms	1900	£35.00	—
?22	Japanese Warships	1900	£26.50	—

KINNEY BROS. (U.S.A.)

25	Actresses "Set 1"	1893	£7.00	£175.00
25	Actresses "Set 2"	1895	£11.00	£275.00
50	Actresses (Group 2)	1891	£5.50	—
75	Actresses (Group 3)	1892	£5.50	—
50	Actresses (Group 4, Coloured)	1893	£5.50	£275.00
?125	Actresses (Group 4, Sepia, Plain Back)	1893	£2.25	—
25	Animals	1890	£17.00	£425.00
10	Butterflies of the World (White)	1888	£17.50	£175.00
50	Butterflies of the World (Gold)	1888	£14.00	£700.00
25	Famous Gems of the World	1889	£17.00	£425.00
25	Famous Running Horses (American)	1890	£20.00	£500.00
25	Famous Running Horses (English)	1889	£18.00	£450.00
F45	Famous Ships	1887	£11.00	—
25	Great American Trotters	1890	£22.00	£550.00
52	Harlequin Cards	1888	£18.00	£940.00
53	Harlequin Cards, Series 2	1889	£17.50	£925.00
L?4	Inaugural Types	1888	*£80.00*	—
X50	International Cards	1888	£34.00	—
K24	Jocular Oculars (2 Types)	1887	£35.00	—
25	Leaders	1889	£18.00	£450.00
50	Magic Changing Cards	1889	£20.00	—
50	Military Series A (Series 7)	1887	£5.50	£275.00
50	Military Series B (Series 8)	1887	£5.50	£275.00
30	Military Series C (Series 9)	1887	£5.50	£165.00
50	Military Series D (Coloured Background)	1887	£4.50	£225.00
50	Military Series E (1886)	1887	£4.50	£225.00
18	Military Series F (U.S. Continental)	1887	£5.50	£100.00
3	Military Series F (Vatican)	1887	£50.00	—

KINNEY BROS. (U.S.A.) — cont.

Qty		*Date*	*Odds*	*Sets*
5	Military Series F (Decorations)	1887	£40.00	£200.00
51	Military Series G (U.S. Army & Navy)	1887	£4.50	£230.00
85	Military Series H (U.S. State Types)	1887	£4.50	£380.00
60	Military Series I ("I.S.C." in 3 Lines)	1887	£8.00	—
50	Military Series J (England/N.G.S.N.Y.)	1887	£12.50	—
49/50	Military Series K (1853)	1887	£8.50	—
50	Military Series L (Foreign Types)	1887	£6.00	£300.00
15	Military Series M (French Army/Navy)	1887	£4.20	£63.00
5	Military Series M (State Seals)	1887	£30.00	—
50	National Dances (White Border)	1889	£15.00	£750.00
25	(No Border)	1889	£17.50	—
25	Naval Vessels of the World	1889	£18.00	£450.00
50	New Year 1890 Cards	1889	£18.00	£900.00
K25	Novelties (Circular, Thick Cards)	1888	£22.50	—
K50	Novelties (Circular, Thin Cards)	1888	£11.00	£550.00
75	Novelties (Die Cut)	1888	£7.50	—
14	Novelties (Oval)	1888	£26.50	—
44	Novelties (Rectangular)	1888	£10.00	£440.00
F?	Photographic Cards	1886	£2.00	—
LF?	Photographic Cards	1886	£4.00	—
50	Surf Beauties	1889	£19.00	£950.00
1	Sweet Caporal Calendar	1890	—	£62.50
52	Transparent Playing Cards (3 Types)	1890	£13.00	£675.00
25	Types of Nationalities (Folders 4 Types)	1890	£23.00	£575.00

PRINTED ALBUMS (EXCHANGED FOR COUPONS)

	Butterflies	1889	—	£135.00
	Celebrated American & English Running Horses	1890	—	*£200.00*
	Leaders	1889	—	*£140.00*
	Liberty Album	1889	—	£125.00
	National Dances	1889	—	*£150.00*
	Natural History	1890	—	£110.00
	Reigning Beauties	1889	—	*£165.00*
	Singers & Opera Houses	1889	—	*£175.00*
	Surf Beauties	1889	—	*£160.00*

KRAMERS TOB. CO. (PTY) LTD. (S. Africa)

50	Badges of South African Rugby Football Clubs (Multi-Backed)	1933	£7.00	—

CIE. LAFERME (Germany)

25	Types of Smokers	1900	£30.00	—

THE LAKE ERIE TOBACCO CO. (U.S.A.)

X?36	State Governors	1888	£62.50	—

B. LEIDERSDORF & CO. (U.S.A.)

T25	Actresses	1895	£40.00	—

I. LEWIS & CO. (U.S.A.)

X?53	Girls and Men in Costumes	1906	£25.00	—

LEWIS & ALLEN CO. (U.S.A.)

X120	Views & Art Studies	1912	£3.50	—

LIGGETT & MYERS TOBACCO CO. (U.S.A)

Qty		Date	Odds	Sets
?30	Actresses	1890	£42.50	—

LONE JACK CIGARETTE CO. (U.S.A.)

25	Inventors and Inventions	1887	£50.00	—
50	Language of Flowers (3 Types)	1888	£26.00	—
F?	Photographic Cards	1886	*£10.00*	—

P. LORILLARD CO. (U.S.A.)

25	Actresses (Coloured)	1888	£23.00	£575.00
M25	Actresses (Irregular Gold Frame)	1889	£24.00	—
M1	Advertisement Card	1890	—	£65.00
M175	Actresses (Fancy Surrounds)	1889	£23.00	—
M75	Actresses (Plain Surround)	1890	£19.00	—
X25	Actresses (Burdick 263)	1889	£24.00	£600.00
X25	Actresses (Burdick 264-1)	1890	£24.00	£600.00
X25	Actresses (Burdick 264-2)	1890	£25.00	—
X25	Actresses (Burdick 264-3, Grey Border)	1890	£26.00	—
X25	Actresses in Opera Roles	1892	£35.00	—
T25	Ancient Mythology Burlesqued	1893	£23.00	£575.00
T50	Beautiful Women	1893	£22.00	£1100.00
X25	Boxing Positions & Boxers	1892	£70.00	—
M?20	Busts of Girls (Die Cut)	1886	£75.00	—
X25	Circus Scenes	1888	£60.00	—
X?15	Everyday Annoyances	1886	*£80.00*	—
25	National Flags	1888	£23.00	—
T52	Playing Card Inset Girls	1885	£26.50	—
X50	Prizefighters	1887	*£70.00*	—
X?17	Song Album	1887	*£55.00*	—
T25	Types of Flirtation	1892	£45.00	—
T25	Types of the Stage	1893	£23.00	£575.00

W. C. MACDONALD INC. (Canada)

?350	Aeroplanes & Warships	1940	£1.00	—
53	Playing Cards (Many Printings)	1927	50p	—

B. & J. B. MACHADO (Jamaica)

25	British Naval Series	1916	£18.00	—
F50	Popular Film Stars	1926	£5.50	—
F52	Stars of the Cinema	1926	£5.00	—
50	The Great War – Victoria Cross Heroes	1916	£17.50	—
F50	The Royal Family at Home and Abroad	1927	£4.50	—
F50	The World of Sport	1928	£6.00	—

MACLIN-ZIMMER (U.S.A.)

X53	Playing Cards (Actresses)	1890	£20.00	£1000.00

MALTA CIGARETTE CO.

135	Dante's Divine Comedy	1905	£12.00	—
M40	Maltese Families Arms & Letters	1905	£6.00	—
?44	Prominent People	1905	£12.50	—

H. MANDELBAUM (U.S.A.)

Qty		*Date*	*Odds*	*Sets*
20	Comic Types of People	1890	£46.50	—
36	Flags of Nations	1890	£33.00	—

MARBURG BROS. (U.S.A.)

50	"National Costume" Cards (2 Types)	1887	£45.00	—
X100	Painting Reproductions (Several Printings)	1890	£55.00	—
?X17	Presidents and Other Celebrities	1886	£60.00	—
50	Typical Ships	1887	£50.00	—

MASPERO FRERES LTD. (Palestine)

50	Birds, Beasts & Fishes	1925	£3.50	—

S. MATTINNO & SONS (Malta)

X36	Britain Prepared Series	1940	£3.50	—

P. H. MAYO & BROTHER (U.S.A.)

M25	Actresses (Fancy Frame)	1890	£26.00	£650.00
?21	Actresses (Sepia)	1886	£55.00	—
M25	Actresses (Black Border)	1890	£25.00	—
L12	Actresses (Diagonal)	1888	£55.00	—
?50	Actresses (Burdick 488, 2 Types)	1888	£23.50	—
X25	Actresses (Burdick 532, 3 Printings)	1887	£42.50	—
28	Baseball Game (Die Cut)	1890	*£55.00*	—
40	Baseball Players	1892	£75.00	—
35	College Football Stars	1892	*£50.00*	—
20	Costumes & Flowers (2 Printings)	1892	£27.00	—
19	Costumes of Warriors & Soldiers (2 Printings)	1892	£25.00	£475.00
25	Head Dresses of Various Nations	1890	£27.00	£675.00
?47	National Dances (Die Cut)	1890	*£42.00*	—
M25	National Flowers (Girl & Scene)	1891	£28.00	£700.00
20	Naval Uniforms	1892	£27.00	—
F?	Photographic Cards	1887	*£11.50*	—
24	Presidents of the U.S.	1888	*£32.50*	—
35	Prizefighters (2 Types)	1890	£42.50	—
20	Shakespeare Characters	1891	£26.50	£530.00
X12	The Seasons	1888	*£60.00*	—
X15	Wings of Birds of Plumage	1888	*£60.00*	—

M. MELACHRINO & CO. (MALTA)

52	Peuples Exotiques "1 Série"	1925	80p	£42.00
52	Peuples Exotiques "2 Série"	1925	80p	£42.00
52	Peuples Exotiques "3 Série"	1925	80p	£42.00

MELIA FRERES (Algeria)

M?	Actresses (Many Groups)	1910	£4.00	—
M?128	Film Stars	1930	£2.50	—

MERCATOR (Belgium) (Imitation Cigar Bands)

24	British Empire Military Head-Dress	1976	—	£15.00
24	European Military Head-Dress	1976	—	£15.00

MEXICAN PUFFS (U.S.A.)

Qty		*Date*	*Odds*	*Sets*
20	Actresses, Blue Border	1890	£52.50	—

MIFSUD & AZZOPARDI (Malta)

KF59	First Maltese Parliament (2 Types)	1922	£6.50	—

MRS. G. B. MILLER & CO. (U.S.A.)

X?7	Actresses & Celebrities	1885	*£60.00*	—
X?52	Alphabet Cards	1887	£45.00	—
22	Photographs of all the Presidents	1888	£50.00	—

L. MILLER & SONS (U.S.A.)

49	Animals & Birds	1900	*£50.00*	—
X25	Battleships	1900	£25.00	£625.00
X100	Beauties "THIBS" (2 Types)	1900	£35.00	—
X25	Generals & Admirals (Spanish War)	1900	£26.50	—
X24	Presidents of the U.S.	1900	£22.50	£540.00
X50	Rulers of the World	1900	£19.00	£950.00

CHAS. J. MITCHELL (Canada)

26	Actresses "FROGA" (Brown Back)	1900	£32.50	—
26	(Green Back)	1900	£30.00	—
26	Actresses "FROGA"(Playing Card Back)	1900	*£42.50*	—

MONARCH TOBACCO WORKS (U.S.A.)

X?4	American Indian Chiefs	1890	£75.00	—

MOORE & CALVI (U.S.A.)

X10	Actresses "RAEMA"	1887	£65.00	—
X53	Beauties, Playing Card Inset, Set 1	1886	£21.00	£1100.00
X53	Beauties, Playing Card Inset, Set 2	1890	£19.00	£1000.00
X53	Beauties, Playing Card Inset, Set 3	1890	£18.00	£950.00

MURAI BROS. (Japan)

50	Actresses "ALWICS"	1910	£9.00	£450.00
?88	Actresses "MUREG"	1900	£37.50	—
50	Beauties	1902	£12.00	£600.00
24	Beauties "HUMPS"	1900	£26.50	—
100	Beauties, Thick Borders	1902	£27.50	—
50	Chinese Beauties (Stork Back)	1908	£4.50	£225.00
25	Chinese Beauties (Peacock Back)	1912	£2.80	£70.00
25	Chinese Beauties (Peacock, Different)	1912	£4.00	—
50	Chinese Children's Games (White Border)	1911	£2.50	—
20	Chinese Children's Games (Coloured Border)	1911	£2.75	—
M?	Chinese Girls (Various Series)	1905	£4.50	—
25	Chinese Pagodas	1911	£3.00	—
30	Chinese Series	1910	£3.00	—
50	Chinese Trades	1905	£25.00	£1250.00
26	Comic Phrases	1900	£27.50	—
50	Dancing Girls of the World	1900	£32.00	—

MURAI BROS. (Japan) — cont.

Qty		*Date*	*Odds*	*Sets*
32	Flowers	1900	£25.00	—
?107	Japanese Personalities	1900	£40.00	—
?52	Japanese Subjects – Symbol Inset	1900	£45.00	—
50	Wild Animals of the World	1900	£37.50	—
50	World's Distinguished Personages	1900	£24.00	—
50	World's Smokers	1900	£27.50	—

NATIONAL CIGARETTE & TOBACCO CO. (U.S.A.)

?12	Actresses	1886	£62.50	—
25	National Types (Sailor Girls)	1890	£24.00	£600.00
F?	Photographic Cards	1888	£6.00	—

NATIONAL CIGARETTE CO. (Australia)

13	English Cricket Team, 1897-8	1897	*£250.00*	—

NATIONAL TOBACCO WORKS (U.S.A.)

GF?	Actresses, etc. (Newsboy)	1900	£16.00	—
G100	Actresses (Coloured)	1900	£26.50	—

OLD FASHION FINE CUT (U.S.A.)

TF?	Photographic Cards	1890	*£10.00*	—

OMEGA CIGARETTE FACTORY (Malta)

KF96	Cinema Stars	1936	£2.50	£240.00
F?36	Maltese Footballers	1928	*£12.50*	—
M?16	Maltese Politicians, Cartoons by 'Mike	1940	*£20.00*	—
M97	Scenes From Films	1938	*£8.50*	—
M?4	World War II Leaders, Cartoons by Mike	1940	*£20.00*	—

OXFORD CIGARETTE CO. (Malta)

MF24	Egyptian Scenes (Anonymous)	1926	£7.50	—

M. S. PACHOLDER (U.S.A.)

10	Actresses (Sub Rosa Cigarettes)	1885	£55.00	—

PENINSULAR TOBACCO CO. LTD. (India)

50	Animals and Birds	1910	£1.80	—
52	Birds of Brilliant Plumage (P/C Inset)	1916	£2.65	—
25	Birds of the East, 1st Series	1912	£1.80	£45.00
25	Birds of the East, 2nd Series	1912	£1.80	£45.00
25	China's Famous Warriors (2 Types)	1912	£3.00	£75.00
25	Chinese Heroes	1913	£2.40	£60.00
50	Chinese Modern Beauties	1912	*£4.00*	—
50	Chinese Trades, Set 3	1912	*£2.50*	—
50	Chinese Trades, Set 5	1913	*£2.50*	—
30	Fish Series	1916	£2.00	£60.00
25	Hindoo Gods	1909	£2.40	—
37	Nautch Girl Series (3 Types)	1910	£4.50	—
25	Products of the World	1915	£1.50	£37.50

E. T. PILKINTON CO. (U.S.A.)

Qty		Date	Odds	Sets
X48	Fruits & Flowers	1890	£50.00	—

N. PIPERNO (Egypt)

6	Beauties (Different Colour Backs)	1900	£4.00	—
X?5	Beauties (Different Colour Backs)	1900	£4.00	—

PIZZUTO (Malta)

50	Milton's "Paradise Lost"	1910	£10.00	—

F. PLANELLES (Algeria)

M?153	Actresses	1905	£5.00	—

THE PLANTERS STORES (India)

50	Actresses "FROGA"	1900	£32.50	—
25	Beauties "FECKSA"	1900	£35.00	—

POLICANSKY BROS. (South Africa)

50	Aeroplanes of Today (P.O. Box 1006)	1936	£1.60	£80.00
M50	Birds, Beasts & Fishes (Nassa Cigarettes)	1924	£5.00	—
50	Regimental Uniforms (P.O. Box 1006)	1937	£2.00	—
50	South African Fauna (2 Types)	1925	£7.50	£375.00

RED MAN CHEWING TOBACCO (U.S.A.)

X40	American Indian Chiefs	1952	£7.50	£300.00

LA REFORMA (Canary Islands)

X8	Military Uniforms, Serie A-1 (Prussia)	1925	—	£15.00
X8	Military Uniforms, Serie A-3 (France)	1925	—	£15.00
D5	Military Uniforms, Serie A-4 (France)	1925	—	£10.00
D7	Military Uniforms, Serie A-5 (Spain)	1925	—	£15.00
X8	Military Uniforms, Serie A-6 (Prussia)	1925	—	£15.00
D6	Military Uniforms, Serie A-7 (Spain)	1925	—	£11.50
X6	Military Uniforms, Serie B-1 (Shaped)	1925	—	£11.50
X6	Military Uniforms, Serie B-2 (Shaped)	1925	—	£11.50

D. RITCHIE & CO. (Canada)

30	Actresses "RITAN" (Printed Back)	1887	£28.00	£840.00
30	(Plain Back)	1887	£25.00	—
?25	Actresses ("Our Production" Back)	1889	£40.00	—
?29	Actresses ("Derby" Front)	1889	£50.00	—
52	Beauties P/C Inset (Several Types)	1888	£25.00	—
36	Flags of All Nations	1888	£50.00	—
52	Playing Cards	1888	*£30.00*	—

D. E. ROSE & CO. (U.S.A.)

Qty		*Date*	*Odds*	*Sets*
G28	Imperial Cards	1890	£45.00	£1260.00

RUGGIER BROS. (Malta)

M50	The Great Siege of Malta	1924	£5.50	—

RUMI CIGARETTES (Germany)

M49	Beauties	1901	£32.50	—

JORGE RUSSO LTD. (Gibraltar)

24	Marvels of the World	1954	£5.00	—

SANTA FE NATURAL LEAF TOBACCO CO. (U.S.A.)

36	A Tribute to the Endangered	2001	£1.25	£45.00
36	A Tribute to the Endangered, Series 2	2001	£1.25	£45.00
36	Century of the Great American Spirit	2000	£1.00	—
36	Century of the Great American Spirit, Set 2	2001	£1.00	£36.00
36	Music of America	2003	£1.00	—
36	Spirit of the Old West, Series 1	1999	£1.50	—
36	Spirit of the Old West, Series 2	2000	*£1.50*	—

JOHN SCERRI (Malta)

147	Beauties & Children (Black & White)	1930	£1.20	—
180	Beauties & Children (Unicoloured)	1930	£16.00	—
?86	Beauties & Children (Large Numerals)	1930	£12.50	—
45	Beauties & Children (Coloured)	1930	£1.65	—
MF50	Beautiful Women	1931	£2.00	—
MF480	Cinema Artists	1931	£2.20	—
MF180	Cinema Stars	1931	£2.50	—
MF50	Famous London Buildings	1934	£3.20	£160.00
F60	Film Stars (First Serie)	1931	£2.50	—
F60	Film Stars (Second Serie)	1931	£2.50	—
52	Interesting Places of the World	1934	40p	£20.00
F25	International Footballers	1935	£25.00	—
401	Malta Views	1928	60p	—
MF51	Members of Parliament-Malta	1928	40p	£20.00
146	Prominent People	1930	£1.20	—
MF100	Scenes from Films	1932	£2.50	—
LF100	Talkie Stars	1932	£2.40	—
M100	World's Famous Buildings	1931	50p	£50.00

J. J. SCHUH TOBACCO CO. (Australia)

60	Australian Footballers A (½ Length)	1920	£5.00	£300.00
40	Australian Footballers B (Rays)	1921	£5.50	£220.00
60	Australian Footballers C (Oval Frame)	1922	£9.00	—
60	Australian Jockeys	1921	£4.50	£270.00
F72	Cinema Stars (Black & White)	1924	£1.75	£126.00
60	Cinema Stars (Coloured)	1924	£2.00	—
L12	Maxims of Success	1917	*£40.00*	—
F72	Official War Photographs (2 Types)	1918	£2.80	£200.00
F104	Portraits of our Leading Footballers	1920	£3.00	£310.00

G. SCLIVAGNOTI (Malta)

Qty		Date	Odds	Sets
50	Actresses & Cinema Stars	1923	£2.40	—
MF71	Grand Masters of the Order of Jerusalem	1898	£9.00	—
F102	Opera Singers	1898	£10.00	—
M100	Opera Singers	1898	£10.00	—
72	Scenes with Girls (Black & White)	1905	£32.50	—
M49	Scenes with Girls (Coloured)	1905	*£35.00*	—

SENATOR (Belgium) (Imitation Cigar Bands)

24	Decorations and Orders of Chivalry	1975	—	£5.00

SINSOCK & CO. (China)

?28	Chinese Beauties	1905	£14.00	—

SNIDERS & ABRAHAMS PTY. LTD. (Australia)

30	Actresses (Gold Background)	1905	£5.50	£165.00
14	(White Borders)	1905	£5.75	£80.00
20	Admirals & Warships of the U.S.A. (2 Types)	1908	£7.00	—
2	Advertisement Cards	1905	*£30.00*	—
60	Animals (Green, Descriptive Back)	1912	£3.00	—
60	Animals & Birds (2 Types)	1912	£2.50	£150.00
15	Australian Cricket Team	1905	£37.50	—
16	Australian Football – Incidents in Play	1906	£9.00	—
72	Australian Footballers – Series A (Full Length)	1904	£9.00	—
76	Australian Footballers – Series B (½ Length)	1906	£7.50	—
76	Australian Footballers – Series C (½ Length)	1907	£7.00	—
56	Australian Footballers – Series D (Head/Shoulders)	1908	£6.00	£336.00
140	Australian Footballers – Series D (Head/Shoulders)	1909	£6.00	—
60	Australian Footballers – Series E (Head in Oval)	1910	£6.000	£360.00
60	Australian Footballers – Series F (Head in Rays)	1911	£6.50	—
60	Australian Footballers – Series G (With Pennant)	1912	£6.00	—
60	Australian Footballers – Series H (Head in Star) 2 Types	1913	£6.00	—
60	Australian Footballers – Series I (Head in Shield) 2 Types	1914	£6.00	—
56	Australian Footballers – Series J (½ - ¾ Length)	1910	£9.50	—
48	Australian Jockeys (Blue Back)	1907	£3.75	£180.00
60	Australian Jockeys (Brown Back)	1908	£4.50	£270.00
56	Australian Racehorses (Horizontal Back)	1906	£4.50	£250.00
56	Australian Racehorses (Vertical Back)	1907	£4.50	—
40	Australian Racing Scenes	1911	£4.25	—
?133	Australian V.C.'s and Officers	1917	£5.75	—
?63	Belgian Views	1916	£2.50	—
12	Billiard Tricks	1908	£16.50	—
60	Butterflies & Moths (Captions in Capitals)	1914	£1.60	£96.00
60	(Captions in Mixed Letters)	1914	£1.60	£96.00
60	Cartoons & Caricatures (2 Types)	1907	£5.50	—
12	Coin Tricks	1908	£11.50	—
64	Crests of British Warships (2 Types)	1915	£4.50	£285.00
40	Cricketers in Action	1906	£45.00	—
12	Cricket Terms	1905	£27.50	£330.00
32	Dickens Series	1909	£4.75	£152.00
16	Dogs (4 Types)	1910	£8.50	£136.00
90	European War Series	1916	£3.25	—
?7	Flags (Shaped Metal)	1915	£5.00	—
?7	Flags (Shaped Card)	1915	£5.00	—
60	Great War Leaders & Warships (3 Types)	1915	£3.50	£210.00

SNIDERS & ABRAHAMS PTY. LTD. (Australia) — cont.

Qty		Date	Odds	Sets
30	How to Keep Fit	1907	£5.00	£150.00
60	Jokes (3 Types)	1906	£3.60	£216.00
12	Match Puzzles	1908	£11.50	—
48	Medals & Decorations	1915	£5.00	—
M48	Melbourne Buildings	1914	£6.50	—
25	Natives of the World	1904	£14.00	£350.00
12	Naval Terms	1905	£6.50	£78.00
29	Oscar Asche, Lily Brayton & Lady Smokers	1911	£5.00	£145.00
40	Shakespeare Characters	1909	£4.75	£190.00
30	Signalling Series	1916	£6.50	—
?14	Statuary	1905	£8.00	—
60	Street Criers in London, 1707	1914	£7.00	—
32	Views of Victoria in 1857 (2 Types)	1906	£8.00	—
FS?250	Views of the World	1908	£3.00	—

SOUTH INDIAN TOBACCO MFG. CO.

25	Actresses "ALWICS" and Moslem Personalities	1905	£8.00	—

SPAULDING & MERRICK (U.S.A.)

M24	Actresses and Prizefighters	1888	£55.00	—
M24/25	Animals	1890	£20.00	£480.00

STAR TOBACCO CO. (India)

?66	Beauties "STARA" (2 Types)	1898	£40.00	—
52	Beauties (P/C Inset) (3 Types)	1898	£24.00	—
52	Heroes of the Transvaal War (P/C Inset)	1901	*£60.00*	—
52	Indian Native Types (P/C Inset)	1898	£23.00	£1200.00

J. W. L. STUBBS (New Zealand)

M50	Barques and Sailing Boats	1926	*£25.00*	—
F?200	Photographic Cards	1926	£10.00	—

SURBRUG CO. (U.S.A.)

M10	Aeroplane Series No. 103	1912	£17.50	£175.00
M10	Prize Dog Series No. 102	1911	£18.50	£185.00
M25	Prize Fight Series No. 101 (2 Types)	1911	£20.00	£500.00

CIE. DE TABAC TERREBONNE (Canada)

30	Bingo-Puzzle	1924	*£5.00*	—
30	Bingo-Puzzle, 2nd Series	1925	*£5.00*	—
30	Bingo-Puzzle, 3rd Series	1926	*£5.00*	—
30	Bingo-Puzzle, 4th Series	1927	£4.00	—
30	Bingo-Puzzle, 5th Series	1928	£4.00	—

THOMPSON, MOORE & CO. (U.S.A.)

X10	Rope Knots	1888	£60.00	£600.00

LITERATURE

Although there have been tens of thousands of card sets issued, there are comparatively few books about the hobby. Foremost among the works of reference are those published by the Cartophilic Society. These include a number of books on individual firms, such as Ogden and Wills. Most important however are the five volumes of the "World Tobacco Index" and the four of the "British Trade Index". Each of these builds on the previous volumes, and records new issues, old series that have recently been discovered, and additional subjects to those sets that had been only partially seen. Because it is published annually, our catalogue is often more advanced in its information, and we always welcome news about additions and amendments, which will always be passed on to the Society's research Editor.

A number of dedicated collectors have made their own contributions by compiling lists of a more specialised nature, and we have indeed published many of these ourselves. Among works currently available are three volumes dealing with errors and varieties, two on cricket and one on tennis, a work on tobacco football cards, and one each on all known golf and boxing cards and a comprehensive list of British silk issues.

There are only two general works now available. These are "The Story of Cigarette Cards" and "Collecting Cigarette and Trade Cards". Both are superbly illustrated, well written and offer excellent value. Details of these and all other books that we stock are given in the first few pages of the Catalogue.

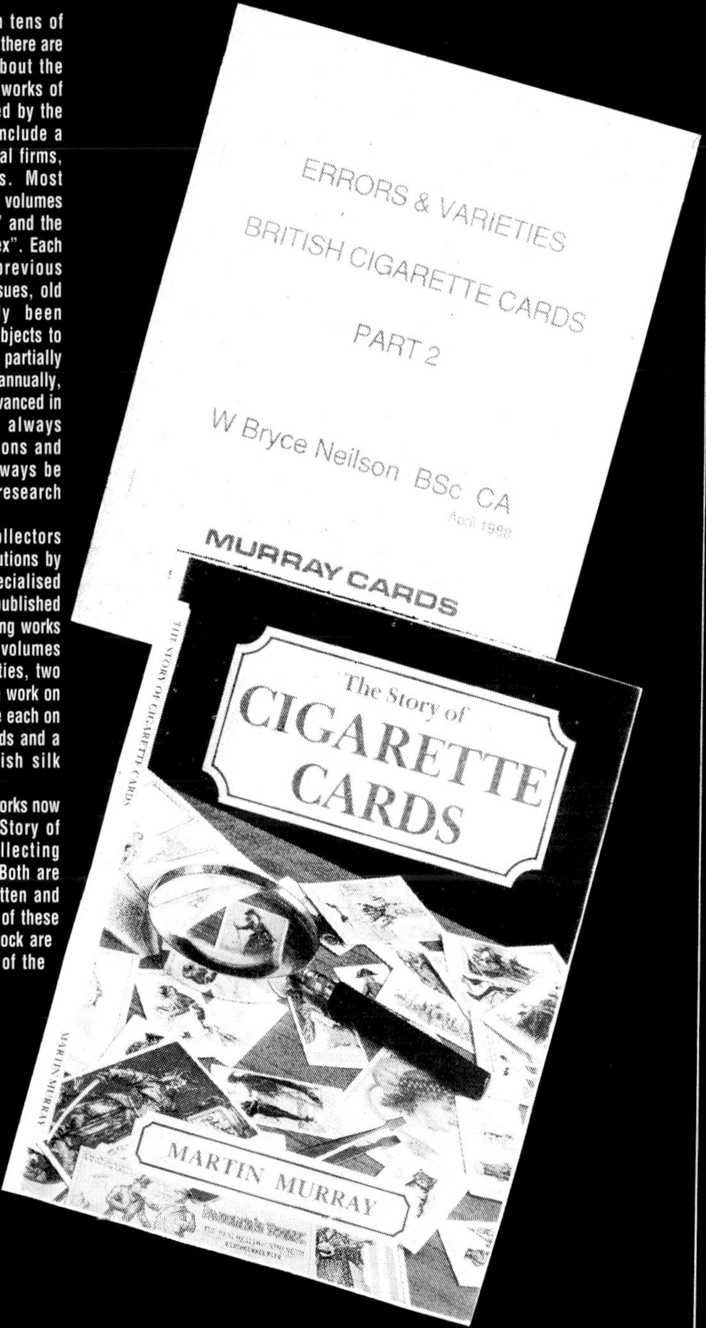

TYPE COLLECTING

There are now many collectors who concentrate on types either exclusively or in addition to their main collections. This involves keeping one or two cards from every series issued. Limitations of space and money make this a good compromise for many people, since they can have a limited goal, yet still providing a sufficient challenge to maintain their interest.

The advent of modern albums has eased one problem for type collectors, since they can now limit themselves to just one card per series, and still be able to see both front and back of that type. Further limitations may also be self-imposed by collecting the issues of just one country, or commodity. One collector 'only' collects one card from each manufacturer, while a lifetime could be spent just in trying to collect the different types issued by the tobacco firm of Wills!

The general collector can also acquire types as a method of identifying those series of which he wishes to obtain complete sets—and those that he wishes to avoid. It is also a useful idea to obtain type cards of all the varieties of one series, so that one can have a complete set of all the pictures and also a specimen of all the different backs that could be found with that front.

TOBACCO PRODUCTS CORPORATION (Canada & U.S.A.)

Qty		*Date*	*Odds*	*Sets*
48	Canadian Sports Champions	1917	*£11.50*	—
60	Do You Know?	1918	£5.00	—
60	Hockey Players	1918	*£20.00*	—
220	Movie Stars	1915	£2.25	—
120	Movie Stars (Portrait in Oval)	1915	£2.25	—
L?50	Movie Stars	1915	£3.50	—
L?100	Movie Stars, Series No.3	1916	£3.00	—
?180	Movie Stars, Series No.4	1916	*£3.00*	—
L100	Movie Stars, Series No.5	1916	£3.00	—
100	Movie Stars (Sepia)	1915	£3.00	—
18	Ship Picture Letters	1915	*£8.00*	—

TUCKETT LTD. (Canada)

M52	Aeroplane Series	1930	£4.00	—
M52	Aviation Series (as above, 3 Types)	1930	£4.00	—
25	Autograph Series (2 Types)	1913	£27.50	—
60	Badges (Regimental)	1917	£10.00	—
?114	Beauties & Scenes (2 Types)	1910	£6.50	—
25	Boy Scout Series	1914	*£20.00*	—
M8	British Gravures	1923	*£12.00*	—
L8	British Gravures	1923	*£12.50*	—
F100	British Views Plain Back	1912	£1.65	£165.00
F?224	British Views (3 Types)	1912	£2.00	—
F80	British Warships (2 Types)	1914	£8.00	—
F50	Canadian Scenes	1912	£1.80	—
?51	Card Trick Series	1928	£8.00	—
M48	Delivering Mail (Stamps)	1910	*£14.00*	—
?110	Girls and Warships	1924	*£10.00*	—
?8	Gravures	1923	*£12.50*	—
53	Playing Card Premium Certificates	1930	*£7.00*	—
M52	Tucketts Auction Bridge Series (2 Types)	1930	*£5.50*	—

TURCO-AMERICAN TOBACCO CO. (U.S.A.)

M15	Foreign Views	1908	£13.00	—

TURKISH-MACEDONIAN TOBACCO CO. (Holland)

ANONYMOUS SILKS

M?43	Animals, Birds and Butterflies	1926	£3.75	—
M18	Arms of Dutch Colonies	1926	£3.50	—
M21	Arms of Dutch & European Towns (White)	1926	£3.50	—
?32	Celebrities (White)	1926	£4.50	—
M20	Decorations and Medals	1926	£5.00	—
101	Dutch Celebrities	1934	£3.50	—
M74	Dutch Celebrities, Arms etc.	1926	£3.00	—
M12	Film Stars	1926	*£7.50*	—
M249	Flags, Arms and Standards	1926	£1.60	£400.00
D166	Flags and Arms, Series 2	1926	£2.00	—
?31	Flowers	1926	£5.00	—
M34	Flowers	1926	£3.50	—
M20	Flowers (Europa/Afrika)	1926	£4.25	—
M89	Flower Series (A-E)	1926	£3.50	—
M3	Girls of Many Lands (Black Silk)	1926	£5.00	£15.00
M50	(White Silk)	1929	£3.50	£175.00

TURKISH-MACEDONIAN TOBACCO CO. (Holland) — cont.

Qty		*Date*	*Odds*	*Sets*
M54	Illustrated Initials	1926	£3.00	—
M12	Japanese Series	1926	£6.50	—
M?46	Javanese Figures	1926	£3.50	—
M34	National Costumes	1926	£3.50	£120.00
D62	National Flags (White Silk)	1926	£2.75	—
M141	National Flags (Paper Backs)	1926	£3.00	—
M16	Nature Calendar	1926	£4.00	—
M20	Ships of All Ages	1926	*£7.50*	—
?85	Sporting Figures (Series A-E)	1926	£5.00	—
25	Sporting Figures (CA1-25)	1926	£5.00	£125.00
X18	Town Arms of Holland	1926	£4.00	—
M26	World Celebrities	1926	£5.50	—
M56	Youth Series and Miscellaneous	1926	£3.50	—

U. S. TOBACCO CO. (U.S.A.)

X25	Actresses	1890	£42.50	—

UNITED CIGAR STORES (U.S.A.)

L25	The Aviators (2 Types)	1911	£20.00	£500.00

UNITED TOBACCO COMPANIES (SOUTH) LTD. (S. Africa)

50	Aeroplanes of To-day	1936	£1.50	£75.00
50	African Fish	1937	£1.30	£65.00
48	All Sports Series	1926	*£25.00*	—
L48	All Sports Series	1926	*£25.00*	—
50	Animals & Birds (2 Types)	1923	£6.50	—
L24	Arms and Crests of Universities and Schools of South Africa	1930	£1.20	£30.00
FS50	Beauties of Great Britain	1930	£2.50	—
L52	Boy Scout, Girl Guide & Voortrekker Badges	1932	£2.00	—
M50	British Aeroplanes	1933	£1.40	£70.00
L20	British Butterflies (Silk)	1924	£9.00	—
L30	British Roses (Silk)	1924	£9.50	—
L62	British Rugby Tour of South Africa	1938	£1.70	£105.00
50	Children of All Nations	1928	80p	£40.00
50	Cinema Stars (Flag Cigarettes)	1922	£2.00	£120.00
X?10	Conundrums	1910	*£40.00*	—
40	Cricketers & Their Autographs (Plain Back)	1922	£25.00	£1000.00
28	Dominoes (Rugger Cigarettes)	1938	*£3.00*	—
60	Do You Know?	1930	50p	£30.00
50	Do You Know? 2nd Series	1930	50p	£25.00
50	Do You Know? 3rd Series	1931	50p	£25.00
30	Do You Know? (Different)	1933	60p	£18.00
50	Eminent Film Personalities	1930	£2.00	£100.00
50	English Period Costumes	1932	90p	£45.00
L50	Exercises for Men and Women	1932	£1.00	£50.00
96	Fairy Tales	1926	£1.40	£135.00
24	Fairy Tales (Folders)	1926	£8.00	—
25	Famous Figures from S. A. History	1932	£1.80	£45.00
L100	Famous Works of Art	1939	25p	£25.00
L120	Farmyards of South Africa	1934	£1.00	—
L65	Flags of All Nations (Silk)	1910	£2.50	—
25	Flowers of South Africa	1932	£1.60	£40.00

UNITED TOBACCO COMPANIES (SOUTH) LTD. (S. Africa) — cont.

Qty		*Date*	*Odds*	*Sets*
FS52	Here There and Everywhere	1930	75p	£37.50
L50	Household Hints	1926	£1.20	—
M50	Humour in Sport	1929	£3.00	—
25	Interesting Experiments	1930	£1.20	£30.00
L100	Medals and Decorations of the British Commonwealth of Nations	1941	90p	£90.00
50	Merchant Ships of the World	1925	£1.10	£55.00
30	Merrie England Studies – Female	1914	£7.00	£210.00
52	Miniature Playing Cards (Flag, 2 Sizes)	1938	£1.00	—
53	(Lifeboat)	1938	£1.75	—
53	(Lotus, 2 Colours)	1938	*£2.25*	—
53	(Needle Point)	1938	*£4.50*	—
53	(Rugger, 2 Sizes)	1938	*£2.25*	—
50	Motor Cars	1928	£3.50	£175.00
FS48	Nature Studies	1930	80p	£40.00
X28	1912-13 Springboks	1912	*£36.00*	—
X?7	Nursery Rhymes	1910	*£40.00*	—
M25	Old Masters (Silk)	1926	£8.00	—
L100	Our Land	1938	20p	£20.00
M150	Our South African Birds	1942	30p	£45.00
L150	Our South African Birds	1942	25p	£37.50
M100	Our South African Flora	1940	20p	£15.00
L100	Our South African Flora	1940	20p	£15.00
M100	Our South African National Parks	1941	20p	£15.00
L100	Our South African National Parks	1941	20p	£15.00
L200	Our South Africa – Past & Present (2 Printings)	1938	20p	£30.00
X60	Ozaka's System of Self Defence (3 Printings)	1911	*£45.00*	—
L24	Pastel Plates	1930	£1.10	£26.50
L88	Philosophical Sayings	1938	£1.00	£88.00
L50	Pictures of South Africa's War Effort	1940	20p	£10.00
FS48	Pictures of the East	1930	75p	£36.00
25	Picturesque People of the Empire	1929	£1.30	£32.50
L50	Pottery Types (Silk)	1926	£5.00	£250.00
L50	Race Horses – South Africa (Set 1)	1929	£1.70	£85.00
L52	Race Horses – South Africa (Set 2), (2 Types)	1930	£1.70	£88.00
50	Regimental Uniforms	1937	£1.75	£80.00
50	Riders of the World (Firm's Name)	1931	£1.10	£55.00
50	(C.T. Ltd.)	1931	£1.20	£60.00
L52	S. A. Flora (2 Types)	1935	30p	£16.00
M40	Ships of All Times	1931	£1.50	£60.00
10	Silhouettes of M.L.A.'s	1914	£26.00	—
25	South African Birds, A Series	1927	£1.30	£32.50
25	South African Birds, Second Series	1927	£1.30	£32.50
L52	South African Butterflies	1937	60p	£30.00
L52	South African Coats of Arms	1931	45p	£23.50
L17	South African Cricket Touring Team	1929	£20.00	—
L17	Ditto (Autographed)	1929	£16.00	£270.00
M100	South African Defence	1941	20p	£20.00
L50	South African Flowers (Silk)	1913	£3.50	£175.00
L50	South African Flowers (Second Series)	1913	£3.75	—
L50	South African Places of Interest	1934	20p	£10.00
L65	South African Rugby Football Clubs	1933	£1.70	
L52	Sports & Pastimes in South Africa	1936	£1.75	£90.00
L47	Springbok Rugby & Cricket Teams	1931	£2.80	£130.00
FS50	Stereoscopic Photographs	1928	80p	£40.00
FS50	Stereoscopic Photographs of South Africa	1929	80p	£40.00

UNITED TOBACCO COMPANIES (SOUTH) LTD. (S. Africa) — cont.

Qty		*Date*	*Odds*	*Sets*
25	"Studdy" Dogs (Bonzo)	1925	£4.50	—
M50	Tavern of the Seas	1939	40p	£20.00
50	The Story of Sand	1934	90p	£45.00
50	The World of Tomorrow	1938	90p	£45.00
?98	Transfers (2 Printings)	1925	£5.00	—
X?70	Triangular Test Cricketers 1912	1912	*£100.00*	—
L40	Views of South African Scenery	1918	£4.00	£160.00
L36	Views of South African Scenery, Second Series	1920	£4.00	£144.00
25	Warriors of All Nations (Swords at Base)	1937	£1.60	£40.00
25	What's This?	1929	£1.60	£40.00
50	Wild Animals of the World	1932	£1.25	£62.50
25	Wild Flowers of South Africa, A Series	1925	£1.00	£25.00
25	Wild Flowers of South Africa, Second Series	1926	£1.00	£25.00
M40	Wonders of the World	1931	85p	£34.00
M100	World-Famous Boxers	1939	£5.50	—

UNIVERSAL TOBACCO CO. (India)

F50	Actresses (Plain Back)	1900	£22.00	—
F50	(Printed Back)	1900	£25.00	—

UNIVERSAL TOBACCO CO. (PTY.) LTD. (S. Africa)

835	Flags of All Nations	1935	£1.00	—
M?368	Park Lane Fashions	1934	*£7.50*	—

S. W. VENABLE TOBACCO CO. (U.S.A.)

X?56	Actresses (Multi-Backed)	1888	£27.50	—
X12	Baseball & Seashore Scenes (7 Backs)	1888	£65.00	—

R. WHALEN & CO. (U.S.A.)

L25	Actresses	1890	£45.00	—
M25	Actresses (Names Only)	1890	£25.00	—

WYNEN ZIGARETTEN (Germany)

?46	Tanzerinnen Aller Welt	1900	£35.00	—

GEO. F. YOUNG (U.S.A.)

X?76	Actresses	1889	£26.00	—
X12	Baseball & Seashore Scenes	1888	*£65.00*	—
X10	National Sports – Girls	1887	£65.00	—
X?	Photographic Cards	1886	£7.50	—

Part 3

NON-TOBACCO ISSUES

INDEX OF BRANDS (Non-Tobacco)

These may appear on cards without the manufacturer's name (see also Information opposite Page 49)

A-1 DAIRIES LTD. (Tea)

Qty		Date	Odds	Sets
25	Birds and their Eggs	1965	£1.25	—
25	Butterflies and Moths	1964	—	£3.00
25	The Story of Milk	1967	—	£5.00

A-1 DOLLISDALE TEA

25	Do you know about Shipping & Trees?	1963	—	£2.50

A.B.C. (Cinemas)

10	Animals	1952	£1.75	£17.50
10	An Adventure in Space	1950	£2.50	£25.00
10	Birds	1958	—	£5.50
10	Birds & Bird-Watching	1953	£2.50	—
10	British Athletes	1955	—	£10.00
20	British Soldiers (Black Back)	1949	40p	£8.00
20	(Brown Back)	1949	30p	£6.00
10	Colorstars	1962	—	£6.00
10	Colorstars (2nd Series)	1962	£3.50	£35.00
10	Colorstars (3rd Series)	1962	£1.75	£17.50
10	Dogs	1957	£2.00	£20.00
L16	Film Stars	1935	£4.50	—
10	Film Stars	1948	£2.75	£27.50
10	Horses	1958	70p	£7.00
10	Interesting Buildings	1956	50p	£5.00
10	Journey by Land	1954	£2.50	£25.00
10	Journey by Water	1954	£2.50	£25.00
10	Journey to the Moon	1955	—	£12.50
10	Parliament Buildings	1957	60p	£6.00
10	Railway Engines	1951	£4.00	£40.00
10	Scenes from the Films	1953	£4.00	£40.00
10	Sea Exploration	1957	75p	£7.50
10	Sea Scenes	1958	50p	£5.00
10	Sports on Land	1956	—	£6.50
12	Star Series	1936	£4.50	—
10	Travel of the Future	1956	60p	£6.00
10	Water Sports	1956	—	£6.00

A. & B. C. GUM

40 Page Illustrated Reference Book — £3.50

M120	All Sport Series	1954	£3.50	£500.00
P17	Banknotes	1971	£3.00	£51.00
X55	Batman (Pink Back, Fan Club Panel)	1966	£2.00	£110.00
X55	(Pink Back, No Panel)	1966	£1.40	£77.00
X55	Batman (Numbered on Front)	1966	£2.00	£110.00
X44	Batman (1A-44A)	1966	£2.75	£121.00
X44	Batman (1B-44B)	1966	£3.50	£154.00
X38	Batman (Black Back)	1966	£3.75	£142.00
X38	(Black Back, Dutch)	1966	£5.50	—
M1	Batman Secret Decoder	1966	—	£12.50

Qty		Date	Odds	Sets
X73	Battle Cards	1966	£1.50	£110.00
X66	Battle of Britain	1970	£1.50	£99.00
X60	Bazooka Joe and his Gang	1968	£4.00	—
X60	Beatles (Black & White)	1964	£3.75	£225.00
X45	Beatles, 2nd Series	1965	£6.00	£270.00
X40	Beatles (Coloured)	1965	£10.00	—
K120	Car Stamps	1971	£2.50	—
X21	Car Stamps Albums	1971	£5.00	£105.00
L?56	Christian Name Stickers	1967	£2.75	—
X15	Civil War Banknotes	1965	£3.00	£45.00
X88	Civil War News	1965	£2.50	£250.00
X43	Comic Book Foldees	1968	£1.60	—
P24	Crazy Disguises	1970	£8.00	—
X48	Cricketers	1959	£1.75	£84.00
X48	Cricketers, 1961 Test Series 94 x 68mm	1961	£2.50	£120.00
X48	90 x 64mm	1961	£2.25	£108.00
X66	Elvis Presley Series	1956	£9.00	—
X36	Exploits of William Tell	1960	£1.75	£63.00
M22	Famous Indian Chiefs	1968	£4.00	—
X54	Fantastic Twisters	1972	£4.50	—
M48	Film & TV Stars	1953	£2.75	£132.00
M48	Film & TV Stars, No.2 Series (49-96)	1953	£3.00	£144.00
M48	Film & TV Stars, No.3 Series (97-144)	1953	£2.75	£132.00
X48	Film Stars (Plain Back)	1954	£2.50	£155.00
X73	Flags (Cut-Outs)	1971	60p	£45.00
L80	Flags of the World	1960	£1.00	£80.00
X80	Flags of the World	1959	£1.20	£96.00
40	Flag Stickers	1966	£4.00	—
X46	Footballers (Planet, 1-46)	1958	£2.25	£104.00
X46	(Without "Planet", 1-46)	1958	£2.00	£92.00
X46	Footballers (Planet, 47-92)	1958	£4.50	—
X46	(Without "Planet", 47-92)	1958	*£6.00*	—
X49	Footballers (Football Quiz, 1-49)	1959	£2.75	£135.00
X49	Footballers (Football Quiz, 50-98)	1959	£5.00	—
X42	Footballers (Black Back, 1-42)	1960	£2.50	£105.00
X42	Footballers (Black Back, 43-84)	1960	£4.00	—
XF64	Footballers (Plain Back)	1961	£3.00	—
XF44	Footballers (Plain Back, Scottish)	1962	£8.00	—
X82	Footballers (Bazooka)	1962	£4.50	—
X55	Footballers (Make-a-Photo, 1-55)	1963	£2.75	£152.00
X55	Footballers (Make-a-Photo, 56-110)	1963	£2.75	£152.00
X81	Footballers (Make-a-Photo, Scottish)	1963	£7.00	—
X58	Footballers (Quiz, 1-58)	1964	£2.50	£145.00
X45	Footballers (Quiz, 59-103)	1964	£5.50	—
X46	Footballers (Quiz, 104-149)	1964	£7.50	—
X81	Footballers (Quiz, Scottish)	1964	£7.50	—
X55	Footballers (In Pairs, 1-110)	1966	£3.00	—
X55	Footballers (In Pairs, 111-220)	1966	£5.00	—
X55	Footballers (In Pairs, Scottish)	1966	£6.00	—
X55	Footballers (Star Players)	1967	£2.75	£152.00
P12	Footballers	1967	£6.00	—
X45	Footballers (Football Quiz, Scottish)	1968	£7.00	—
X54	Footballers (Yellow, 1-54)	1968	£3.00	£162.00

Qty		*Date*	*Odds*	*Sets*
X47	Footballers (Yellow, 55-101)	1968	£2.50	£117.50
M20	Football Team Emblems	1968	£5.00	—
E26	Football Team Pennants	1968	£6.00	—
X65	Footballers (Football Facts, 1-64)	1969	£1.50	£97.50
X54	Footballers (Football Facts, 65-117)	1969	£1.50	£81.00
X55	Footballers (Football Facts, 117-170)	1969	£1.60	£88.00
MF36	Footballers	1969	£1.75	£63.00
X42	Footballers (Football Facts, Scottish, 1-41)	1969	£5.00	—
X35	Footballers (Football Facts, Scottish, 42-75)	1969	£6.00	—
MF15	Footballers (Scottish)	1969	£5.00	£75.00
X85	Footballers (Orange Back, 1-85)	1970	£1.50	£127.50
X85	Footballers (Orange Back, 86-170)	1970	£1.00	£85.00
X85	Footballers (Orange Back, 171-255)	1970	£2.50	—
72	Football Colour Transparencies	1970	£4.50	—
P14	Footballers, Pin-Ups	1970	£4.00	£56.00
X85	Footballers (Green Back, Scottish, 1-85)	1970	£2.00	£170.00
X86	Footballers (Green Back, Scottish, 86-171)	1970	£2.00	£170.00
P28	Footballers, Pin-Ups (Scottish)	1970	£5.50	—
X109	Footballers (Did You Know, 1-109)	1971	£1.50	£164.00
X110	Footballers (Did You Know, 110-219)	1971	£1.50	£165.00
X71	Footballers (Did You Know, 220-290)	1971	£3.00	—
X73	Footballers (Did You Know, Scottish, 1-73)	1971	£1.00	£73.00
X71	Footballers (Did You Know, Scottish, 74-144)	1971	£4.00	—
16/23	Football Club Crests	1971	75p	£12.00
16	Football Club Crests (Scottish)	1971	£2.50	£40.00
X109	Footballers (Orange/Red, 1-109)	1972	£1.50	£164.00
X110	Footballers (Orange/Red, 110-219)	1972	£1.75	£192.50
M22	Football Card Game	1972	75p	£16.50
M23	Footballers, Superstars	1972	£4.50	—
X89	Footballers (Rub Coin, Scottish, 1-89)	1972	£3.25	£290.00
X89	Footballers (Orange/Red, Scottish, 90-179)	1972	£3.50	—
M32	Footballers (Autographed Photos)	1973	£2.00	£64.00
X131	Footballers (Blue Back, 1-131)	1973	£2.00	—
X130	Footballers (Blue Back, 132-263)	1973	£2.50	—
X90	Footballers (Red Back, Scottish, 1-90)	1973	£3.25	—
X88	Footballers (Red Back, Scottish, 91-178)	1973	£3.50	—
E16	Football Giant Team Posters	1973	£6.00	—
X132	Footballers (Red Back, Rub Coin)	1974	£1.25	£165.00
X132	Footballers (Green Back, Scottish, Rub Coin)	1974	£2.00	—
X40	Fotostars	1961	£2.00	—
X66	Funny Greetings	1961	80p	£52.50
X66	Funny Valentines	1961	£1.75	—
X36	Golden Boys (Matt)	1958	£2.50	£90.00
XF40	(Glossy)	1958	£3.50	£140.00
L27	Grand Prix	1970	35p	£9.50
D200	Hip Patches	1968	*£1.60*	—
X55	Huck Finn	1968	£1.75	—
X60	Kung Fu	1974	£1.50	£90.00
X55	Land of the Giants	1969	£3.40	£187.00
X55	Lotsa Laffs	1970	£1.25	—
X84	Love Initials	1970	75p	£63.00
X36	Magic	1967	£2.50	—
L1	Magic Circle Club Application	1969	—	*£10.00*
X74	Man on the Moon	1969	£2.25	—

A. & B. C. GUM — cont.

Qty		Date	Odds	Sets
X55	Mars Attacks	1965	£11.00	£600.00
X52	Mickey Takers	1970	£3.00	—
M24	Military Emblem Stickers	1966	£3.00	—
X55	Monkees (Black & White)	1967	£1.00	£55.00
X55	Monkees (Coloured)	1967	£1.80	£99.00
X30	Monkees Hit Songs	1967	£2.50	£75.00
E16	Monster Tattoos	1970	£4.50	—
X49	Nutty Initial Stickers	1968	£3.25	—
E16	Olympic Posters	1972	£3.00	£48.00
X36	Olympics	1972	£3.00	£108.00
X50	Outer Limits	1966	£3.50	£175.00
X55	Partridge Family	1972	£1.20	£66.00
X120	Planes (88 x 64 mm)	1960	£1.00	£120.00
X120	Planes (94 x 67 mm)	1960	85p	£102.00
X44	Planet of the Apes	1968	£3.00	£132.00
M96	Pop Stars Fab. Photo Stamps	1965	£3.25	—
X33	Put-on Stickers	1969	£2.50	—
X48	Railway Quiz	1958	80p	£40.00
X72	Railway Quiz	1959	£1.25	£90.00
M24	Royal Portraits	1953	£2.00	£48.00
M34	Silly Stickers	1966	£2.25	—
X25	Sir Francis Drake	1961	£2.50	—
X88	Space Cards	1958	£3.00	—
X44	Stacks of Stickers	1971	£3.00	—
X55	Star Trek	1969	£6.00	—
X66	Superman in the Jungle	1968	£1.60	£105.00
X16	Superman in the Jungle (Jig-Saw)	1968	£2.75	£44.00
X45	The Champions	1969	£2.80	£126.00
M1	The Champions Secret Decoder	1969	—	£16.00
X25	The Girl from U.N.C.L.E.	1965	£3.00	—
X36	The High Chaparral	1969	£2.00	£72.00
X54	The Legend of Custer	1968	£1.50	£81.00
L55	The Man from U.N.C.L.E.	1965	£1.00	£55.00
X40	The Rolling Stones	1965	£7.50	—
X50	Top Stars	1964	£2.60	£130.00
X40	Top Stars (Different)	1964	£3.00	£120.00
E16	T.V. Cartoon Tattoos	1972	£7.00	—
X56	TV Westerns	1959	£2.00	£112.00
X44	Ugly Stickers	1967	£2.00	—
P88	Wacky Plaks	1962	£2.00	—
E16	Walt Disney Characters Tattoos	1973	£8.00	—
E16	Wanted Posters	1968	£4.50	—
X70	Who-Z-At Star?	1958	£2.25	£157.50
X55	Winston Churchill Cards	1965	80p	£44.00
X37	World Cup Footballers	1970	£3.00	—
50	World Cup Football Stickers	1966	£6.00	—
E16	World Cup Posters	1970	£4.00	—
X66	You'll Die Laughing (Creature Feature)	1974	£1.50	£99.00
X48	You'll Die Laughing (Purple Back)	1967	£1.00	£48.00

A.H.C. (Confectionery)

25	Tropical Birds (Anon.)	1955	—	£10.00
25	Wonders of the Universe	1955	—	£4.00

A & P PUBLICATIONS

Qty		Date	Odds	Sets
24	British Classic Cars	1992	—	£4.00

ABBEY GRANGE HOTEL

15	Fighting Vessels	1986	—	£2.50

ACE (Commercial)

X33	Sporting Greats - Motor Racing	1988	—	£5.00
X33	Sporting Greats - Tennis	1988	—	£8.00

ACTIVE MARKETING INTERNATIONAL INC. (U.S.A.)

X50	The James Dean Gallery	1992	—	£20.00

ADIDAS (Sportswear)

X30	World's Leading Soccer Stars	2002	—	£12.50

P. A. ADOLPH ("Subbuteo")

F50	Famous Footballers	1954	£10.00	—
24	Famous Footballers, A Series	1954	£1.25	£30.00
24	Famous Footballers, Second Series	1954	£1.25	£30.00

A. W. ALLEN (Confectionery, Australia)

32	Bradman's Records	1931	£32.00	—
72	Butterflies & Moths	1920	£1.65	—
36	Cricketers (Brown Front)	1932	£11.00	£400.00
36	Cricketers (Brown Front, Different)	1933	£11.50	—
36	Cricketers (Flesh Tinted, Frame Back)	1934	£8.00	£288.00
36	Cricketers (Flesh Tinted, No Frame)	1936	£8.00	£288.00
36	Cricketers (Coloured)	1938	£7.50	£270.00
M24	Fliers	1926	£6.00	—
48	Footballers (Action)	1939	£3.00	—
144	Footballers (Striped Colours)	1933	£2.25	—
72	Footballers (Pennants)	1934	£2.25	—
49	Kings & Queens of England	1937	£1.40	£70.00
36	Medals	1938	£1.75	—
36	Soldiers of the Empire	1938	£1.75	—
36	Sports & Flags of Nations	1936	£2.50	£90.00
M24	Wrestlers	1926	£5.50	—

ALMA CONFECTIONERY

48	James Bond 007 Moonraker	1980	£3.75	£180.00

JAMES ALMOND & SONS (Confectionery)

25	Sports and Pastimes	1925	£7.00	£200.00

AMABALINO PHOTOGRAPHIC (Commercial)

L30	Display Fireworks	1988	—	£6.50

AMALGAMATED PRESS LTD.

Qty		Date	Odds	Sets
24	Aeroplanes (Plain Back)	1933	£3.25	£78.00
32	Aeroplanes & Carriers	1932	£2.50	£80.00
M32	Australian & English Cricket Stars	1932	£9.00	£288.00
M12	Catchy Tricks and Teasers	1933	£4.00	£48.00
M16	England's Test Match Cricketers	1928	£8.75	£140.00
M22	English League (Div.1) Footer Captains	1926	£2.75	£60.00
M16	Exploits of the Great War	1929	£2.50	£40.00
16	Famous Aircraft	1927	£3.25	£52.00
M16	Famous Australian Cricketers	1928	£9.00	£144.00
16	Famous Film Stars	1927	£6.00	—
M24	Famous Footer Internationals	1926	£3.50	£84.00
F8	Famous Screen Stars (Anon., Film Fun)	1930	£5.00	—
M22	Famous Shipping Lines	1926	£5.50	—
M32	Famous Test Match Cricketers	1926	£5.25	£168.00
24	Famous Trains & Engines	1932	£2.50	£60.00
16	Fighting Planes of the World	1934	£4.00	—
32	Football Fame Series	1936	£3.25	£104.00
M16	Great War Deeds	1927	£3.00	£48.00
M32	Great War Deeds (Different)	1928	£2.75	£88.00
M16	Heroic Deeds of the Great War	1927	£3.00	£48.00
32	Makes of Motor Cars and Index Marks	1923	£2.50	£80.00
32	Mechanical Wonders of 1935	1935	£2.25	£72.00
32	Modern Motor Cars	1926	£6.00	—
24	Motors (Plain Back)	1933	£4.00	£96.00
X15	Prominent Football Teams	1938	£5.00	£75.00
24	Ships of the World (Champion)	1924	£2.25	£54.00
33	Ships of the World (Different, Anon.)	1935	£3.00	—
MF66	Sportsmen	1922	£1.25	£90.00
32	Sportsmen of the World	1934	£2.75	£88.00
M12	Sports “Queeriosities”	1933	£3.00	£36.00
X40	Test Match Favourites	1934	£7.50	£300.00
M24	The Great War 1914-1918	1928	£2.75	£66.00
M16	The Great War 1914-1918, New Series	1929	£2.25	£36.00
M16	The R.A.F. at War (Plain Back)	1940	£5.00	—
M32	Thrilling Scenes from the Great War	1927	£2.75	£88.00
M16	Thrills of the Dirt Track	1929	£9.00	—
M16	Tip-Top Tricks & Teasers	1927	£3.00	£48.00
M14	V.C.'s & Their Deeds of Valour (Plain Back)	1939	£4.00	£56.00
M24	Wonderful London	1926	£4.00	£96.00

AMANDA'S FLOWERS

L12	Flower Children	1990	—	£4.00

AMARAN TEA

25	Coins of the World	1964	—	£7.50
25	Dogs Heads	1965	—	£10.00
25	Do You Know	1969	—	£7.50
25	Flags and Emblems	1964	—	£5.00
25	Naval Battles	1971	—	£12.50
25	Old England	1969	—	£2.00
25	Science in the 20th Century	1966	—	£2.00
25	The Circus	1966	—	£10.00
25	Veteran Racing Cars	1965	—	£17.50

AMATEUR PHOTOGRAPHER (Periodical)

Qty		*Date*	*Odds*	*Sets*
P4	Advertising Postcards	1990	—	£2.00

THE ANGLERS MAIL (Periodical)

E3	Terminal Tackle Tips	1976	—	£3.00

ANGLING TIMES (Magazine)

X15	Baits	1980	—	£4.00
X24	Collect-A-Card (Floats)	1986	—	£4.50
M24	Collect-A-Card (Fish)	1988	—	£4.50
X15	Floats	1980	—	£4.00
X15	Sea Fish	1980	—	£4.00
X15	Species	1980	—	£4.00

ANGLO-AMERICAN CHEWING GUM LTD.

L36	Kidnapped (Thriller Chewing Gum)	1935	£4.50	—
X66	The Horse	1966	40p	£26.50
40	Underwater Adventure	1966	—	£4.00
50	Zoo Stamps of the World	1966	80p	£40.00

ANGLO CONFECTIONERY LTD.

X66	Captain Scarlet and The Mysterons	1968	£2.25	£148.50
L12	Football Hints (Folders)	1970	£1.00	£12.00
L84	Football Quiz	1969	£1.00	£84.00
X66	Joe 90	1968	£3.00	£198.00
L56	National Team Colours	1970	£2.75	£154.00
X84	Railway Trains & Crests	1974	75p	£63.00
X66	Space	1967	£1.50	£99.00
X66	Tarzan	1967	£1.30	£87.00
X66	The Beatles — Yellow Submarine	1968	£8.00	—
X66	The Horse	1966	£2.00	—
L56	The New James Bond 007	1970	£7.00	—
L64	U F O	1971	£3.25	£208.00
M24	Vintage Cars Series	1970	£3.00	£72.00
L78	Walt Disney Characters	1971	£4.00	£312.00
L66	Wild West	1970	£1.00	£66.00
L48	World Cup 1970	1970	£1.75	£84.00

ANONYMOUS — TRADE ISSUES

50	Animals of the World	1954	—	£3.00
29	Boy Scouts Signalling	1910	£6.00	—
25	Bridges of the World	1958	—	£2.00
25	British Uniforms of the 19th Century			
	(Black Back)	1957	—	£4.00
	(Blue Back)	1957	—	£4.00
20	Budgerigars	1950	60p	£12.00

Qty		*Date*	*Odds*	*Sets*
25	Cacti	1961	—	£2.00
25	Careless Moments	1922	80p	£20.00
M56	Caricatures of Cricketers by Durling	1959	—	£18.00
M50	Caricatures of Cricketers by Mac	1959	—	£16.00
M164	Caricatures of Cricketers	1959	—	£50.00
25	Children of All Nations	1958	—	£2.50
25	Cinema and Television Stars (Barbers Tea Reprint)	1993	—	£12.50
MF12	Cinema Stars	1929	£5.00	—
F6	Cinema Stars (Name in Black)	1930	£5.50	—
F6	Cinema Stars (Name in White)	1930	£5.50	—
25	Dogs	1958	—	£15.00
25	Do You Know?	1963	—	£2.00
25	Evolution of the Royal Navy	1957	—	£12.50
25	Family Pets	1964	—	£4.00
25	Flags & Emblems	1961	—	£4.00
25	Flowers	1971	—	£3.00
25	Football Clubs & Badges	1962	—	£5.00
40	Greats from the States (Golf)	1994	—	£17.50
25	Jockeys and Owners Colours	1963	—	£5.00
25	Medals of the World	1960	—	£7.50
100	Miscellaneous Subjects (Gum)	1965	—	£12.50
25	Modern Aircraft	1958	—	£2.00
X12	Motor Cycles (Collectors Series)	1987	—	£2.50
25	Musical Instruments	1971	—	£2.50
25	Pigeons	1971	—	£5.00
25	Pond Life	1963	—	£2.00
50	Prize & Game Chickens (Allen & Ginter Reprint)	2000	—	£10.00
M24	R.A.F. Badges	1985	—	£12.00
1	Soldier-Bugler	1965	—	£2.50
25	Sports of the Countries	1967	—	£12.50
25	The Circus	1966	—	£10.00
25	The Wild West	1960	—	£10.00
25	Train Spotters	1962	—	£5.00
1	Venice in London	1965	—	£1.00

SILK ISSUES

M1	Field-Marshal Earl Kitchener	1915	—	£3.00
P1	Field-Marshal Earl Kitchener	1915	—	£6.00
M4	Great War Incidents	1916	£12.00	£48.00
M1	King of Belgium	1915	—	£2.00
P1	King of Belgium	1915	—	£2.50
P1	Nurse Cavell with Dogs	1915	—	£6.00
M10	Revue Titles Travestied	1915	£12.50	£125.00
M4	Warships	1915	£13.00	£52.00

BELGIAN ISSUES

X90	Belgian Military Uniforms	1970	—	£22.50
X26	Cartouche (Film)	1960	—	£10.00
X100	Famous Men	1938	—	£26.50
X38	Sindbad The Sailor (Film)	1960	—	£15.00

U.S. ISSUES ("Strip Cards")

10	Film Stars "A"	1926	—	£15.00
10	Film Stars "B"	1926	—	£15.00
10	Film Stars "C"	1926	—	£15.00
10	Film Stars "D"	1926	—	£17.50
T60	Pinocchio (Bread Issue)	1939	—	£50.00

ANONYMOUS — TRADE ISSUES — cont.

Qty		Date	Odds	Sets
10	Presidents "A"	1926	—	£25.00
10	Presidents "B"	1926	—	£25.00
10	Western Pioneers	1926	—	£25.00

SPANISH ISSUES

X40	Footballers (P/C Backs)	1930	£1.40	£56.00

APLIN & BARRETT (Cheese)

X25	Whipsnade	1937	£1.20	£30.00

ARBUCKLE COFFEE CO. (U.S.A.)

P50	Animals	1890	£6.00	£300.00
P50	Cooking Subjects	1889	£5.00	—
P100	General Subjects (Unnumbered)	1890	£7.00	—
P50	General Subjects (51-100)	1890	£6.50	—
P50	History of Sports & Pastimes of the World	1893	£8.00	£400.00
P50	History of United States & Territories	1892	£8.00	£400.00
P50	Illustrated Atlas of U.S.	1889	£8.00	£400.00
P100	Illustrated Jokes	1890	£7.00	—
P50	Principal Nations of the World	1889	£6.50	£325.00
P50	Views from a Trip Around the World	1891	£6.25	£312.50

ARDMONA (Tinned Fruit, Australia)

X50	International Cricket Series III	1980	—	£10.00

ARMITAGE BROS. LTD. (Pet Foods)

25	Animals of the Countryside	1964	—	£2.50
25	Country Life	1968	—	£2.50

ARMY CAREERS INFORMATION OFFICE

M24	British Regiments	1991	—	£7.50
M24	British Regiments, 2nd Series	1992	—	£7.50

ARROW CONFECTIONERY CO.

13	Conundrums	1904	£30.00	—
12	Shadowgraphs	1904	£32.50	—

ASKEY'S (Biscuits)

25	People & Places	1971	—	£2.50
25	Then and Now	1971	—	£3.00

AUSTIN MOTOR CO. LTD.

L13	Famous Austin Cars	1953	£10.00	—

AUSTRALIAN DAIRY CORPORATION

Qty		*Date*	*Odds*	*Sets*
X63	Kanga Cards (Cricket)	1985	—	£15.00
X54	Super Cricket Card Series 1982-3	1983	—	£15.00
X50	Super Cricket Card Series 1983-4	1984	—	£15.00

AUSTRALIAN LICORICE PTY. LTD.

?27	Australian Cricketers	1930	£12.00	—
24	Australian Cricketers	1931	£11.50	£276.00
24	English Cricketers (Blue Back)	1928	£11.50	£276.00
24	English Cricketers (Black Back)	1930	£12.00	—
18	English Cricketers ("18 in Set")	1932	£11.50	£210.00
12	South African Cricketers	1931	£12.00	£144.00

AUTOBRITE (Car Polish)

25	Vintage Cars	1965	70p	£17.50

AUTOMATIC MACHINE CO.

25	Modern Aircraft	1958	—	£7.50

AUTOMATIC MERCHANDISING CO.

X25	Adventure Twins and The Treasure Ship	1958	—	£21.50

AVON RUBBER CO. LTD.

30	Leading Riders of 1963	1963	£2.20	£66.00

B.B.B. PIPES

25	Pipe History	1926	£9.00	£225.00

B.J.B. CARDS (Commercial, Canada)

L25	Famous Golfers of the 40's and 50's 1st Series	1992	—	£12.50

BP OIL UK

25	England '98 (Soccer)	1998	—	£6.50
1	Album for above	1998	—	£1.25

B.T. LTD. (Tea)

25	Aircraft	1961	60p	£15.00
25	British Locomotives	1961	70p	£17.50
25	Do You Know?	1967	40p	£10.00
25	Holiday Resorts	1963	—	£3.00
25	Modern Motor Cars	1962	£1.00	£25.00
25	Occupations	1962	—	£5.00
25	Pirates and Buccaneers	1961	£1.00	£25.00
25	The West	1964	—	£6.00

STORAGE

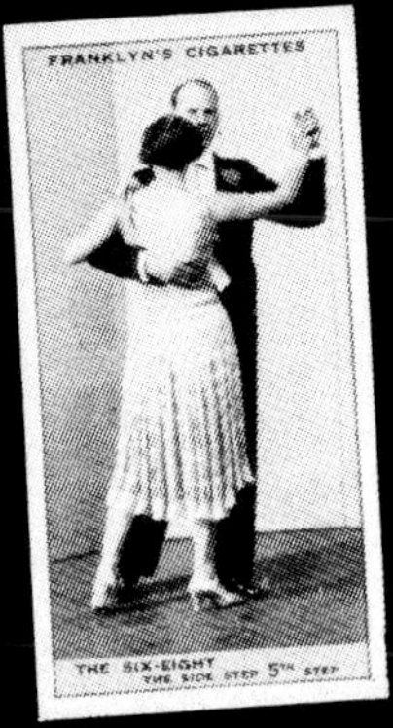

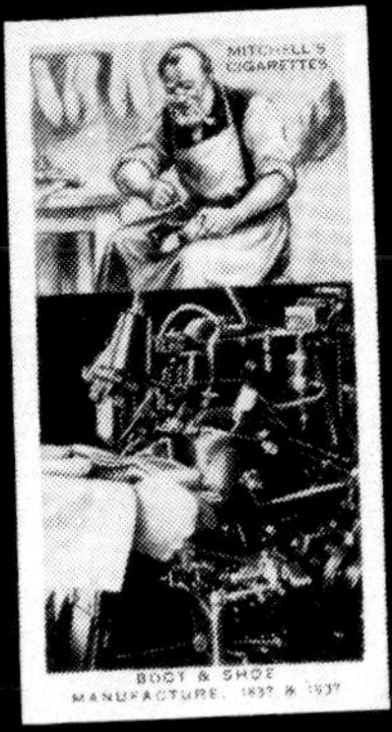

The main problem regarding the storage of cigarette cards lies in the effort to strike a balance between being able to maintain them in as good condition as possible and yet being able to examine them. If the reader is simply an investor there is no problem—he can wrap each set carefully in paper, put it into a box, and thence into a bank vault. But the only way to enjoy cigarette cards is to look at them. The modern method is to house cards in transparent pages, which can accommodate most sizes of cards and can be stored in loose leaf binders. The entire card may be viewed, both back and front, yet will not deteriorate through sticky fingers or spilt coffee. Care should be taken to use a page made from a suitable material—there are on the market now many apparently cheap pages which contain large amounts of plasticiser, a substance which could adversely affect certain cards. Full details of our own Nostalgia and Hendon albums are given on pages 16 and 17 of this book.

Another method of storage which is becoming more popular is to mount cards in frames, which can then be hung on a suitable wall. Several framing systems are now available which hold the cards in position without harming them, and enable the backs to be examined, as well as accommodating complete sets of 50 cards.

IMPERIAL TOBACCO COMPANY

This huge Company was founded on 2nd November 1901 in order to combat the spreading influence in Britain of the American Tobacco Co. The founder members were headed by Wills, and included such well known card issuers as Player, Smith, Hignett and Lambert & Butler. During the next few years they were to acquire a number of other well known companies such as Churchman and Faulkner. However their most important acquisitions were probably those of Ogden at the conclusion of the Tobacco war, and Mardon Son & Hall, the printers who became responsible for the production of most of their cigarette cards.

The formation date is most important to cartophilists, because from that time onward the card issues of the constituent firms bore the message "Branch of the Imperial Tobacco Co. (of Great Britain and Northern Ireland) Ltd." in addition to the individual firm's name. Because, for example, there are two printings of Wills Locomotives and Faulkner Our Gallant Grenadiers, one with and one without the "I.T.C. clause" as it is popularly known, it is safe to say that each of these was issued around 1901-2; or that Vanity Fair came a little earlier and Borough Arms a little later.

Cards issued abroad (including the Channel Islands) which mentioned the I.T.C. member's names did NOT include the I.T.C. clause, since they were always issued by the British American Tobacco Co. which was partly owned by I.T.C.

A cartophilic consequence of the formation of the I.T.C. was the practice of issuing identical card series under several of the firm's, or indeed by B.A.T. Hence Garden Life was issued by Edwards Ringer & Bigg, Lambert & Butler and Wills; Angling by Faulkner, Mitchell and B.A.T.; Boy Scouts by Churchman, Ogden and I.T.C. (Canada). It is always likely that series issued by I.T.C. firms with the same series title will be the same basic set, such as Air Raid Precautions by Churchman, Hignett, Mitchell, Ogden and Wills.

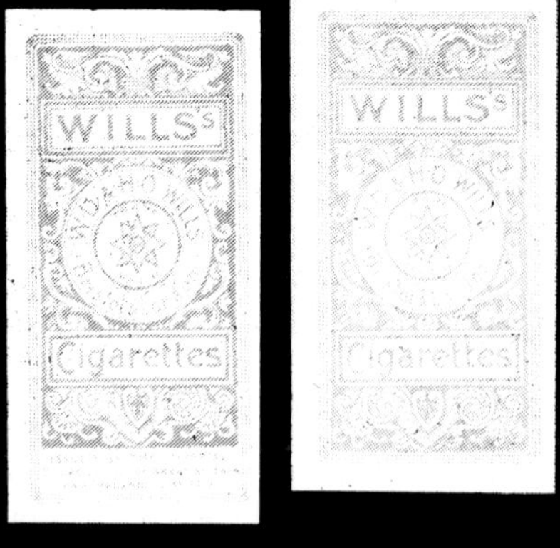

BADSHAH TEA CO.

Qty		*Date*	*Odds*	*Sets*
25	British Cavalry Uniforms of the 19th Century	1963	—	£7.50
25	Butterflies and Moths	1971	—	£2.00
25	Fish and Bait	1971	—	£4.00
25	Fruits of Trees and Shrubs	1965	—	£7.50
25	Garden Flowers	1963	—	£7.50
25	Naval Battles	1971	—	£7.50
25	People & Places	1970	—	£2.00
25	Regimental Uniforms of the Past	1971	—	£2.50
25	Romance of the Heavens	1968	£1.20	£30.00
24	The Island of Ceylon	1955	£3.25	—
25	Wonders of the World (Series of 50)	1970	40p	£10.00

BAILEY'S (Toffee)

25	War Series (Ships)	1916	£16.00	—

BAKE-A-CAKE LTD.

56	Motor Cars	1952	£3.50	£196.00

BAKER, WARDELL & CO. (Tea)

25	Animals in the Service of Man	1964	£2.20	£55.00
36	Capital Tea Circus Act	1964	£3.50	£126.00
25	Do You Know? 1st Series	1962	£3.00	—
25	Do You Know? 2nd Series	1962	£3.00	—
25	Irish Patriots	1962	*£7.50*	—
25	The History of Flight 1st Series	1963	£7.50	—
25	The History of Flight 2nd Series	1963	£6.50	—
25	They Gave Their Names	1963	£2.20	£55.00
25	Transport Present and Future	1962	£5.00	—
25	World Butterflies	1964	£6.00	—

BARBERS TEA LTD.

1	Advertising Card — Cinema & T.V. Stars	1955	—	£5.00
1	Advertising Card — Dogs	1956	—	60p
1	Advertising Card — Railway Equipment	1958	—	£4.50
25	Aeroplanes	1956	—	£7.50
24	Cinema and Television Stars	1955	£1.75	£80.00
24	Dogs	1961	—	£4.00
5	Ferry to Hong Kong	1957	*£10.00*	—
25	Locomotives	1956	£1.20	£30.00
24	Railway Equipment	1958	—	£12.00

BARCLAYS BANK

X21	Sunderland A.F.C.	1990	—	£10.00

JOHN O. BARKER (IRELAND) LTD. (Gum)

Qty		*Date*	*Odds*	*Sets*
X24	Circus Scenes	1970	£2.00	£48.00
X24	Famous People	1970	£1.50	£36.00
25	The Wild West	1970	£3.25	—

BARRATT & CO. LTD. (Confectionery)

M30	Aircraft (Varnished)	1941	£4.00	£120.00
M30	Aircraft (Unvarnished, Different)	1943	£4.50	—
25	Animals in the Service of Man	1964	—	£2.00
16	Australian Cricketers, Action Series	1926	£13.50	£215.00
15	Australian Test Players	1930	£25.00	—
45	Beauties — Picture Hats	1911	£16.50	—
25	Birds	1960	—	£6.00
50	Botany Quest	1966	£1.70	£85.00
25	British Butterflies	1965	£2.50	£62.50
25	Butterflies and Moths	1969	—	£2.50
25	Cage & Aviary Birds	1960	—	£6.50
50	Captain Scarlet and The Mysterons	1967	£2.50	£125.00
50	Cars of the World	1965	£1.50	£75.00
M122	Characters from Film Cartoons	1940	£8.00	—
K4	Coronation & Jubilee Medallions	1902	£22.50	—
25	Coronation, 1911	1911	£17.50	—
20	Cricket Team Folders	1933	£17.50	—
?260	Cricketers, Footballers & Football Teams	1925	£12.50	—
L60	Disneyland "True Life"	1956	£1.50	£90.00
L50	F.A. Cup Winners	1935	£17.50	—
P6	Europe's Best (Soccer)	1992	—	£6.00
25	Fairy Stories	1926	£3.00	£75.00
12	Famous British Constructions, Aircraft	1925	£16.50	—
25	Famous Cricketers (Numbered)	1931	£10.00	—
50	Famous Cricketers (Unnumbered)	1932	£10.00	—
X9	Famous Cricketers (Folders)	1932	£17.50	—
X34	Famous Cricketers (Folders)	1934	£13.50	—
M7	Famous Cricketers (Unnumbered)	1936	£12.50	—
M60	Famous Cricketers (Unnumbered)	1937	£10.00	—
M40	Famous Cricketers (Numbered)	1938	£10.00	—
35	Famous Film Stars	1961	£2.40	£84.00
M100	Famous Footballers (Unnumbered, Black)	1935	£8.00	—
M98	Famous Footballers (Unnumbered, Sepia)	1936	£8.00	—
M110	Famous Footballers (Numbered)	1937	£8.00	—
M20	Famous Footballers (Numbered)	1938	£8.00	—
M10	Famous Footballers (Numbered)	1939	£8.00	—
M79	Famous Footballers (Non-Descriptive)	1947	£8.00	—
M50	Famous Footballers, New Series	1950	£6.00	—
M50	Famous Footballers, New Series (Different)	1952	£5.00	—
M50	Famous Footballers Series, A.1	1953	£4.00	£200.00
M50	Famous Footballers Series, A.2	1954	£4.00	£200.00
M50	Famous Footballers Series, A.3	1955	£4.00	£200.00
60	Famous Footballers Series, A.4	1956	£3.00	£180.00
60	Famous Footballers Series, A.5	1957	£4.00	—
60	Famous Footballers Series, A.6	1958	£3.50	—
60	Famous Footballers Series, A.7	1959	£4.00	—
50	Famous Footballers Series, A.8	1960	£3.00	£150.00
50	Famous Footballers Series, A.9	1961	£3.00	£150.00
50	Famous Footballers Series, A.10	1962	£1.50	£75.00
50	Famous Footballers Series, A.11	1963	£3.00	£150.00

Qty		*Date*	*Odds*	*Sets*
50	Famous Footballers Series, A.12	1964	£3.00	£150.00
50	Famous Footballers Series, A.13	1965	£3.00	£150.00
50	Famous Footballers Series, A.14	1966	£4.00	—
50	Famous Footballers Series, A.15	1967	£1.00	£50.00
50	Famous Sportsmen	1971	£1.50	—
M45	Fastest on Earth	1953	£1.35	£60.00
32	Felix Pictures	1930	£20.00	—
50	Film Stars (No Company Name)	1934	£7.50	—
48	Film Stars (With Company Name)	1936	£7.50	—
25	Fish and Bait	1962	—	£12.50
P6	Football Action	1991	—	£6.00
12	Football Action Caricatures	1928	£20.00	—
100	Football Stars	1930	*£22.50*	—
50	Football Stars	1974	£4.00	—
X156	Football Team Folders	1933	£20.00	—
M66	Football Teams — 1st Division	1930	£12.00	—
48	Giants in Sport	1959	£3.75	—
P12	Gold Rush (Packets)	1960	£6.00	—
P6	Great Defenders (Soccer)	1992	—	£6.00
P6	Great Goalkeepers	1991	—	£6.00
P6	Great Grounds (Soccer)	1991	—	£6.00
P6	Great Managers (Soccer)	1991	—	£6.00
P6	Great Managers, Series 2	1992	—	£6.00
25	Head-Dresses of the World	1962	—	£5.00
25	Historical Buildings	1960	—	£2.50
48	History of the Air (English Text)	1959	£1.00	£50.00
32	History of the Air (Bi-Lingual)	1959	£4.00	—
25	History of the Air (Different)	1960	—	£5.00
25	Interpol	1964	£2.60	£65.00
40	Knight Rider	1987	50p	£20.00
50	Leaders of Sport	1927	£12.50	—
30	Looney Tunes Cartoons	1997	—	£7.50
45	Looney Tunes (Dominoes)	1995	—	*£5.00*
35	Magic Roundabout	1968	£1.20	—
25	Merchant Ships of the World (Black Back)	1962	—	£10.00
25	(Blue Back)	1962	—	£5.00
P6	Midfield Dynamos (Soccer)	1992	—	£6.00
L40	Modern Aircraft	1957	£1.75	£70.00
M45	Modern British Aircraft	1959	£3.00	—
13	National Flags	1914	£17.00	—
64	Natural History (Plain Back)	1940	£5.50	—
M24	Naval Ships (Plain Back)	1939	£7.00	—
M6	Our King & Queen (Plain Back)	1940	£8.50	£50.00
25	People & Places	1965	—	£2.00
25	Pirates and Buccaneers	1960	—	£7.50
12	Prominent London Buildings	1912	£16.50	£200.00
30	Robin Hood	1961	£2.50	£75.00
36	Sailing into Space	1959	£2.50	£90.00
50	Soccer Stars	1973	£2.50	£125.00
50	Soldiers of the World	1966	60p	£30.00
16	South African Cricketers	1929	£18.00	—
25	Space Mysteries	1965	—	£7.50
L20	Speed Series	1930	£7.25	—
50	Tarzan	1967	—	£20.00
35	Test Cricketers, Series A	1956	£5.00	£175.00

BARRATT & CO. LTD. (Confectionery) — cont.

Qty		Date	Odds	Sets
48	Test Cricketers, Series B	1957	£6.50	£312.00
12	The Magic Sword Quest for Camelot	1998	—	£1.00
50	The Secret Service	1970	£1.50	£75.00
24	The Wild West	1961	—	£6.00
25	The Wild West (Different)	1963	—	£7.50
50	The Wild Wild West	1969	£1.50	£75.00
P6	The World's Greatest Teams (Soccer)	1991	—	£6.00
25	The Young Adventurer	1965	£2.00	£50.00
50	Thunderbirds	1967	£3.40	£170.00
50	Thunderbirds, Second Series	1968	£1.00	£50.00
50	Tom & Jerry	1971	60p	£30.00
P6	Top Strikers (Soccer)	1991	—	£6.00
P6	Top Strikers 2	1992	—	£6.00
50	Trains	1970	—	£10.00
50	Trains of the World	1964	—	£12.50
35	T.V.'s Huckleberry Hound & Friends	1961	£1.40	£50.00
35	T.V.'s Sea Hunt	1961	£2.20	£77.00
35	T.V.'s Yogi Bear	1969	£3.75	—
35	T.V.'s Yogi Bear & Friends	1971	60p	£21.00
70	U F O	1971	£1.20	—
1	Victory V Sign	1940	—	£9.00
M35	Walt Disney Characters	1956	£4.00	£140.00
50	Walt Disney Characters, 2nd Series	1957	£4.00	£200.00
36	Walt Disney's Robin Hood	1957	£1.75	£63.00
35	Walt Disney's True Life	1962	£1.20	£42.00
25	Warriors Through the Ages	1962	40p	£10.00
25	WHAT Do You Know?	1964	—	£2.25
X72	Wild Life	1972	75p	£54.00
M50	Wild Animals by George Cansdale	1954	£1.40	£70.00
36	Wild West Series No.1	1959	£1.75	£63.00
25	Willum	1961	£5.00	—
50	Wisecracks	1970	—	£4.00
50	Wisecracks, 2nd Series	1970	40p	£20.00
50	Wisecracks, 3rd Series	1971	40p	£20.00
50	Wonders of the World	1962	—	£5.00
P6	World Beaters (World Cup Action)	1994	—	£6.00
P6	World Beaters (Worlds Greatest Players)	1994	—	£6.00
25	World Locomotives	1961	—	£7.50
50	Wunders Der Welt	1968	—	£5.00
50	Zoo Pets	1964	£1.20	£60.00

GEO. BASSETT & CO. LTD. (Confectionery)

Qty		Date	Odds	Sets
30	Adventure Game Cards	2001	—	£5.00
25	Looney Tunes Cartoons	1999	—	£6.00
25	Motor Cars — Vintage & Modern	1968	£1.20	£30.00
25	Nursery Rhymes	1966	80p	£20.00
25	Popular Dogs	1967	—	£10.00
70	U F O	1974	—	£25.00
25	Victoria Cross Heroes in Action	1970	—	£10.00

BARRATT DIVISION

Qty		Date	Odds	Sets
50	Age of the Dinosaurs	1979	£1.20	£60.00
40	Ali Cat Magicards	1978	£1.75	—
50	Asterix in Europe	1977	60p	£30.00
50	Athletes of the World	1980	20p	£10.00
48	Bananaman	1986	—	£4.00

GEO. BASSETT & CO. LTD. (Confectionery) — cont.

Qty		Date	Odds	Sets
M20	Battle (Packets)	1985	£1.75	£35.00
50	Cricket, First Series	1978	£6.00	—
50	Cricket, Second Series	1979	£3.00	£150.00
48	Dandy — Beano Collection (Black Back)	1989	—	£8.00
48	Dandy — Beano Collection (Blue Back, different)	1990	—	£8.00
50	Disney — Health & Safety	1977	—	£25.00
50	Football Action	1977	£2.75	—
50	Football Action	1978	£3.00	—
50	Football 1978-79	1979	£1.50	£75.00
50	Football 1979-80	1980	40p	£20.00
50	Football 1980-81	1981	40p	£20.00
50	Football 1981-82	1982	£1.75	—
50	Football 1982-83	1983	£1.50	£75.00
50	Football 1983-84	1984	20p	£10.00
50	Football 1984-85	1985	80p	£40.00
48	Football 1985-86	1986	20p	£10.00
48	Football 1986-87	1987	50p	£24.00
48	Football 1987-88	1988	50p	£24.00
48	Football 1988-89	1989	—	£10.00
48	Football 1989-90	1990	—	£10.00
48	Football 1990-91	1991	—	£10.00
50	Football Stars	1974	£1.50	—
50	Football Stars 1975-6	1975	£2.50	—
M50	Guinness Book of Records	1990	—	£10.00
48	Hanna Barbera's Cartoon Capers	1984	£1.25	—
24	Hologrems (Plain Backs)	1986	30p	£7.50
24	(Red Backs)	1986	—	£6.00
50	House of Horror	1982	£1.00	£50.00
50	Living Creatures of our World	1979	20p	£10.00
50	Play Cricket 1980	1980	30p	£15.00
25	Pop Stars	1974	—	£5.00
L5	Scratch and Match	1990	—	£5.00
35	Secret Island	1976	£1.20	—
40	Secret Island, Second Series	1976	—	£3.50
M20	Sky Fighters (Packets)	1986	£1.25	£25.00
49/50	Space 1999	1976	£1.00	£49.00
50	Super Heroes	1984	80p	£40.00
50	Survival on Star Colony 9	1979	50p	£25.00
40	Swim & Survive	1983	40p	£16.00
M20	The A Team	1986	—	£10.00
50	The Conquest of Space	1980	50p	£25.00
50	Tom & Jerry	1974	£2.00	—
50	World Cup Stars	1974	—	£7.50
40	World of the Vorgans	1978	£1.50	—
50	World Record Breakers	1983	£1.00	£50.00
49/50	Yogi's Gang	1976	£1.00	—

BATTLEAXE TOFFEE

24	British and Empire Uniforms	1915	£24.00	—

BAYTCH BROS. (Commercial)

64	Fighting Favourites	1951	£10.00	—

BEANO LTD. (Gum)

Qty		Date	Odds	Sets
1	Bang-O Spacesuit Coupon	1950	—	50p
25	Fascinating Hobbies	1950	£3.50	—
50	Modern Aircraft (Beano)	1951	£1.20	£60.00
50	(British Educational)	1951	—	£7.00
50	Ships of the Royal Navy	1955	60p	£30.00
50	The Conquest of Space	1956	—	£6.00
50	This Age of Speed No.1 (Aeroplanes)	1954	40p	£20.00
50	This Age of Speed No.2 (Buses & Trams)	1954	£1.00	£50.00
50	Wonders of Modern Transport (Aircraft)	1955	—	£25.00
25	Wonders of the Universe (Foto Gum)	1960	—	£2.50

BEANSTALK (Commercial)

15	Saturday Afternoon Heroes	2003	—	£5.50
15	Vintage Football Stars	2003	—	£5.50

BEATALL'S (Rubber Goods)

F?24	Beauties	1924	£25.00	—

S. N. BEATTIE & CO. (Commercial)

24	Safety Signs	1955	£3.25	—

J. J. BEAULAH (Canned Goods)

1	Boston Stump	1953	—	60p
25	Coronation Series	1953	—	£32.50
24	Marvels of the World	1954	—	£2.00
24	Modern British Aircraft	1953	—	£6.00

THE BEAUTIFUL GAME LIMITED (Commercial)

X50	Football Greats	1999	—	£15.00

T. W. BECKETT & CO. LTD. (South Africa)

M50	Animals of South Africa, Series 3	1966	20p	£8.00
M50	Birds of South Africa, Series 1	1965	20p	£8.00
M50	Birds of South Africa, Series 2	1966	—	£8.00

THE BEEHIVE STORES

25	British Uniforms of the 19th Century	1959	—	£15.00

BELLS SCOTCH WHISKY

42	Other Famous Bells (Shaped)	1975	—	£24.00
40/42	Ditto	1975	50p	£20.00

J. BELLAMY & SONS LTD. (Confectionery)

25	Vintage & Modern Trains of the World	1975	—	£6.00

BILLY BEMBO (Commercial)

Qty		Date	Odds	Sets
X54	Vanity Fair 1st Edition (Playing Cards)	1995	—	£10.00
X54	Vanity Fair 2nd Edition (Playing Cards)	1995	—	£10.00

BENSEL WORK FORCE LTD.

20	Occupations	1991	—	£3.50

VAN DEN BERGHS LTD. (Margarine Etc.)

P8	Birds	1974	—	£4.00
70	Countryside Cards	1975	60p	£42.00
X24	Pirates	1965	£2.50	£60.00
M12	Recipes from Round the World	1958	£2.25	£27.00
M12	Regional Recipes	1958	£2.25	£27.00
X24	This Modern World	1965	£1.60	£40.00

DE BEUKELAER (Biscuits)

KF100	All Sports	1932	75p	£75.00
M125	Dumbo	1940	£1.20	£150.00
KF900	Film Stars (101-1000)	1932	£1.00	—
KF100	Film Stars (1001-1100)	1937	£1.00	£100.00
KF100	Film Stars (B1-100)	1935	£1.20	£120.00
K160	Film Stars (Gold Background)	1936	£1.20	£160.00
132	Film Stars (Gold Background)	1938	£1.20	—
M125	Gulliver's Travels	1940	£1.20	£150.00
M125	Pinocchio Series	1940	£1.25	£156.00
M60	Sixty Glorious Years	1940	£1.40	—
M100	Snow White Series	1940	£1.50	£150.00

J. BIBBY & SONS LTD. (Cooking Fat)

L25	Don't You Believe It	1955	£1.00	£25.00
L25	Good Dogs	1955	£2.60	£65.00
L25	How What and Why	1955	£1.00	£25.00
L25	Isn't It Strange	1955	£1.00	£25.00
L25	They Gave It a Name	1955	£2.00	£50.00
L25	This Wonderful World	1955	£1.00	£25.00

BIRCHGREY LTD. (Sporting Promotions)

L25	Panasonic European Open	1989	—	£15.00
L15	The Ryder Cup	1988	—	£15.00

ALFRED BIRD & SONS (Custard)

K48	Happy Families	1938	£1.50	£72.00

BIRDS EYE FOODS LTD.

X6	Birds Eye Book of Record Breakers	1970	£3.00	£18.00
T12	England's Football Team	1980	—	£40.00
30	Wonders of the Seven Seas	1978	—	£15.00

BIRKUM (Cheese, Denmark)

Qty		Date	Odds	Sets
25	Motor Cars	1956	£1.00	£25.00

BISHOPS STORTFORD DAIRY FARMERS (Tea)

25	Dogs Heads	1967	—	£25.00
25	Freshwater Fish	1964	£1.00	£25.00
25	Historical Buildings	1964	—	£6.00
25	History of Aviation	1964	—	£15.00
25	Passenger Liners	1965	—	£2.50
25	Pond Life	1966	—	£3.00
25	Science in the 20th Century	1966	—	£2.00
25	The Story of Milk	1966	—	£3.00

BLACKCAT (Commercial)

15	Sunderland – Cup Kings of '73	2003	—	£5.50

BLAKEY'S BOOT PROTECTORS LTD.

72	War Series	1916	£5.50	—

BLUE BAND SERIES (Stamps)

24	History of London's Transport, 1st Series			
	Black Front	1954	—	£12.00
	Blue Front	1954	—	£18.00
	Orange Front	1954	—	£10.00
24	History of London's Transport, 2nd Series	1955	£2.25	£54.00
16	See Britain by Coach	1954	—	£6.00

BLUE BIRD STOCKINGS

P12	Exciting Film Stars	1963	£2.50	£30.00
M24	Star Cards	1963	£6.50	—

BLUE CAP LTD. (Cheese)

K144	Flixies	1952	75p	£108.00

PACKAGE SERIES

12	Animal Series D	1953	£1.25	£27.00
8	Animal Series E	1953	£1.50	—
12	Farm Series A	1953	£1.50	£18.00
12	Farm Series B	1953	£1.50	£18.00
12	Farm Series C	1953	£1.50	£18.00
12	Sports Series D	1953	£2.25	£27.00
8	Sports Series E	1953	£2.50	—

E. H. BOOTH & CO. LTD. (Tea)

25	Badges & Uniforms of Famous British Regiments and Corps	1967	—	£2.50
25	Ships and Their Workings	1971	£1.00	—
24	The Island of Ceylon	1955	£3.25	£78.00

BOW BELLS (Periodical)

Qty		*Date*	*Odds*	*Sets*
MF6	Handsome Men on the British Screen	1922	£7.50	£45.00

BOYS CINEMA (Periodical)

MF6	Cinema Stars (Anon.)	1931	£4.00	£24.00
MF6	Famous Film Heroes	1922	£4.00	£24.00
M24	Famous Heroes	1922	£3.50	—
F7	Film Stars (Anon.)	1932	£3.50	£24.50
MF8	Film Stars (Brown Front)	1930	£4.25	£34.00
MF8	Film Stars (Black Front, Different)	1931	£4.00	£32.00

BOYS COMIC LIBRARY

4	Heroes of the Wild West	1910	£15.00	—

BOYS FRIEND (Periodical)

3	Famous Boxers Series	1911	£13.00	£39.00
3	Famous Flags Series	1911	£7.00	£21.00
3	Famous Footballers Series	1911	£16.00	£48.00
3	Famous Regiments Series	1911	£8.50	£25.00
MF4	Footballers (½ Length)	1923	£5.00	£20.00
MF5	Footballers (2 per Card)	1922	£5.50	£27.50
MF15	Rising Boxing Stars	1922	£3.60	£54.00

BOYS MAGAZINE (Periodical)

M8	Boxers	1922	£8.00	£64.00
M8	Coloured Studies — Famous Internationals	1922	£5.50	£44.00
M10	Cricketers	1922	£9.00	£90.00
F10	Famous Cricketers Series	1929	£6.00	£75.00
F12	Famous Footballers Series	1929	£4.50	£54.00
MF10	Football Series	1922	£3.25	£32.50
X9	Football Teams	1925	£11.50	—
M30	Footballers (Picture 49 x 39mm)	1922	£4.50	£135.00
M64	Footballers & Sportsmen (Picture 56 x 35mm)	1922	£4.50	£288.00
12	Zat Cards (Cricketers)	1930	£8.00	£96.00
M11	Zat Cards (Cricketers)	1930	£9.00	£100.00

BOYS REALM (Periodical)

MF15	Famous Cricketers	1922	£3.20	£48.00
MF9	Famous Footballers	1922	£3.75	£34.00

C. & T. BRIDGEWATER LTD. (Biscuits)

KF48	Coronation Series	1937	20p	£7.50
KF96	Film Stars, 1st (CE Over No.)	1932	20p	£20.00
KF96	Film Stars, 2nd (E Below No.)	1933	90p	—
KF96	Film Stars, 3rd (Black & White)	1934	90p	—
KF48	Film Stars, 4th	1935	50p	£24.00
KF48	Film Stars, 5th	1937	£1.50	£72.00
KF48	Film Stars, 6th (F Before No.)	1938	£1.50	£72.00

C. & T. BRIDGEWATER LTD. (Biscuits) — cont.

Qty		Date	Odds	Sets
F48	Film Stars, 7th	1939	£1.60	£77.00
KF48	Film Stars, 8th	1940	75p	£36.00
KF48	Radio Stars 1st (Black & White)	1935	£1.50	£72.00
KF48	Radio Stars 2nd (Coloured)	1936	40p	£20.00

JOHN M. BRINDLEY (Printers)

30	Australian Cricketers	1986	—	£12.00
12	Bob Hoare Cricket Characatures	1992	—	£4.00
20	Car Badges and Emblems	1987	—	£5.00
30	Cricketers, A Series	1985	—	£12.50
30	Cricketers, 2nd Series	1985	—	£15.00
X16	Cricketers, Howzat, 3rd Series	1985	—	£10.00
30	Cricketers, 4th Series	1986	—	£10.00
X20	Cricketers, 5th Series (Sketches)	1986	—	£10.00
30	Cricket, The Old School	1987	—	£10.00
18	Famous Operatic Roles	1992	—	£5.00
20	Golf	1987	—	£8.00
20	Horse Racing	1987	—	£4.50
30	London, Brighton & South Coast Railway	1986	—	£6.50
20	Military	1987	—	£4.00
25	Old Golfing Greats	1988	—	£15.00
L6	World Boxers	1992	—	£3.00
L6	World Boxers Part 2 (7-12)	1993	—	£3.00

BRISTOL-MYERS CO. LTD. (Toothpaste)

50	Speed	1964	£3.50	£175.00

BRITISH AUTOMATIC CO. (Weight)

24	British Aircraft	1950	£1.25	£30.00
24	British Birds	1950	£1.50	£36.00
24	British Locomotives	1948	£1.20	£29.00
36	British Motor Cars	1950	£3.00	—
44	Coronation Information	1953	£1.00	—
32	Dogs, A Series	1953	60p	£20.00
32	Dogs (A Series, No "Weigh Daily", As 2nd)	1953	85p	£27.00
32	Dogs, Second Series	1953	85p	£27.00
24	Famous Trains of the World, A Series	1952	£1.50	£36.00
24	Famous Trains of the World, Second Series	1952	£1.50	£36.00
37	Fortunes, 1st Series	1950	£1.00	—
32	Fortunes, 2nd Series	1953	50p	£16.00
32	Fortunes, 3rd Series	1954	75p	£24.00
24	Fresh Water Fish	1950	£1.50	£36.00
24	History of Transport	1948	25p	£6.00
44	Jokes	1951	40p	£18.00
24	Olympic Games	1952	£4.00	—
37	Quotations	1951	75p	—
24	Racing & Sports Cars	1957	£2.50	£60.00
24	Space Travel	1955	£1.75	£42.00
24	Speed	1949	30p	£7.00

BRITISH AUTOMATIC CO. (Weight) — cont.

Qty		*Date*	*Odds*	*Sets*
24	Sportsmen	1955	£2.50	£60.00
20	Twenty Questions	1952	£2.00	£40.00
24	Warships of the World	1954	£1.25	£30.00
1	Watch Your Weight	1950	—	75p

BRITISH GAS

X20	Leeds RLFC Season 1988-89	1988	20p	—
X20	Leeds RLFC Season 1989-90	1989	20p	—
X20	Leeds RLFC Season 1990-91	1990	30p	£6.00
X20	Leeds RLFC	1991	20p	—
X20	Leeds RLFC Season 1992-93	1992	20p	£4.00

BRITISH HERITAGE LIMITED (Commercial)

X54	Victorian Advertising Poster Playing Cards	2000	—	£6.00

C. BRITTON PUBLISHING (Commercial)

L24	Golf Courses of the British Isles, 1st Series	1993	—	£7.50

BROOKE BOND & CO. LTD. (Tea)

72 Page Illustrated Reference Book — £7.25

(Special albums available for most series — ask for quote)

50	Adventurers & Explorers	1973	20p	£4.00
50	African Wild Life	1962	25p	£12.50
25	A Journey Downstream	1990	20p	£2.50
L25	A Journey Downstream (Double Cards)	1990	60p	£15.00
50	Asian Wild Life	1962	20p	£10.00
50	Bird Portraits (No Address)	1957	£1.60	£80.00
50	(With Address)	1957	70p	£35.00
20	British Birds	1954	£3.25	£65.00
50	British Butterflies	1963	40p	£20.00
50	British Costume	1967	20p	£5.00
50	British Wild Life (Brooke Bond Great Britain Ltd.)	1958	90p	£45.00
	(Brooke Bond Tea Ltd.)	1958	50p	£25.00
	(Brooke Bond & Co. Ltd.)	1958	£1.20	£60.00
50	Butterflies of the World	1964	20p	£7.50
12	Chimp Stickers	1986	75p	£9.00
12	Chimp Stickers (Tak Tik Backs)	1986	£3.50	£42.00
M24	Creatures of Legend	1994	20p	£5.00
X12	Creatures of Legend (Double Cards)	1994	80p	£10.00
50	Discovering our Coast	1989	20p	£4.00
L25	Discovering our Coast (Double Cards)	1989	40p	£10.00
50	Famous People	1969	20p	£4.50
50	Features of the World	1984	20p	£4.00
L25	Features of the World (Double Cards)	1984	40p	£10.00
50	Flags and Emblems of the World	1967	20p	£5.00
X40	40 years of the chimps television advertising	1996	30p	£12.00
50	Freshwater Fish	1960	80p	£40.00
M40	Going Wild	1994	20p	£5.00
X20	Going Wild	1994	—	£7.50

Qty		*Date*	*Odds*	*Sets*
50	History of Aviation	1972	20p	£6.00
50	History of the Motor Car	1968	30p	£15.00
40	Incredible Creatures (Last Line Sheen Lane)	1985	20p	£8.00
	(Last Line Walton...)	1986	20p	£8.00
	(Last Line P.O. Box...)	1986	20p	£4.00
	(Thick Cards, Stickers)	1987	£3.50	—
	(Green Back, Irish)	1986	£1.75	£70.00
L20	Incredible Creatures (Double, Sheen)	1986	£1.20	£24.00
L20	(Double, Walton)	1986	£2.20	—
L20	(Double, P.O. Box)	1986	80p	£16.00
X20	International Soccer Stars	1998	60p	£12.00
50	Inventors & Inventions	1975	20p	£4.00
40	Natural Neighbours	1992	30p	£12.00
L20	Natural Neighbours (Double Cards)	1992	50p	£10.00
40	Olympic Challenge 1992	1992	30p	£12.00
L20	Olympic Challenge 1992 (Double Cards)	1992	60p	£12.00
40	Olympic Greats	1979	30p	£12.00
50	Out Into Space ("Issued with...")	1956	£6.25	—
50	("Issued in...")	1958	80p	£40.00
40	Play Better Soccer	1976	20p	£3.50
40	Police File	1977	20p	£3.50
P10	Poly Filla Modelling Cards	1974	*£2.50*	—
50	Prehistoric Animals	1972	20p	£7.50
X45	Pyramid Power	1996	50p	£22.50
50	Queen Elizabeth I — Queen Elizabeth II	1982	20p	£4.00
L25	Queen Elizabeth I — II (Double Cards)	1982	£1.20	—
40	Small Wonders	1981	20p	£3.50
12	Teenage Mutant Hero Turtles	1990	20p	£2.00
L6	Teenage Mutant Hero Turtles (Doubles)	1990	85p	£5.00
20	The Dinosaur Trail (Postcode BB11PG)	1993	50p	£10.00
20	(Postcode BB111PG)	1993	20p	£3.00
L10	The Dinosaur Trail (Doubles) (Postcode BB11PG)	1993	£1.00	£10.00
L10	(Doubles) (Postcode BB111PG)	1993	40p	£4.00
12	The Language of Tea	1988	20p	£2.50
25	The Magical World of Disney	1989	20p	£5.00
L25	The Magical World of Disney (Doubles)	1989	60p	£15.00
50	The Race Into Space	1971	20p	£8.00
50	The Saga of Ships	1970	20p	£4.00
50	The Sea — Our Other World	1974	20p	£4.00
X50	The Secret Diary of Kevin Tipps	1995	20p	£10.00
X30	The Wonderful World of Kevin Tipps	1997	60p	—
50	Transport through the Ages	1966	20p	£5.00
50	Trees in Britain	1966	20p	£4.50
50	Tropical Birds	1961	20p	£8.00
40	Unexplained Mysteries of the World	1987	20p	£3.50
L20	Unexplained Mysteries (Double Cards)	1988	40p	£8.00
40	Vanishing Wildlife	1978	20p	£3.50
50	Wild Birds in Britain	1965	20p	£4.00
50	Wild Flowers, A Series	1955	£1.60	£80.00
50	Wild Flowers, Series 2 (With "issued by")	1959	25p	£12.50
50	(No "issued by")	1959	£1.75	£87.50
50	Wild Flowers, Series 3	1964	20p	£6.00
50	Wildlife in Danger	1963	20p	£4.50
50	Wonders of Wildlife	1976	20p	£4.00
40	Woodland Wildlife	1980	20p	£3.50
X50	Zena Skinner International Cookery	1974	*£4.00*	—

BROOKE BOND & CO. LTD. (Tea) — cont.

Qty		*Date*	*Odds*	*Sets*
BLACK BACK REPRINTS				
50	African Wild Life	1973	—	£4.00
50	British Butterflies	1973	—	£4.00
50	British Costume	1973	—	£4.00
50	Discovering our Coast	1994	—	£7.50
50	Famous People	1973	—	£5.00
50	Flags and Emblems of the World	1973	—	£12.50
50	Freshwater Fish	1973	—	£17.50
50	History of the Motor Car	1974	—	£10.00
40	Olympic Greats	1988	—	*£12.00*
50	Queen Elizabeth I — Queen Elizabeth II	1987	—	*£10.00*
40	Small Wonders	1988	—	£3.50
50	The Race Into Space	1974	—	£5.00
50	The Saga of Ships	1973	—	£4.00
50	Transport through the Ages	1973	—	*£12.50*
50	Trees in Britain	1973	—	£4.00
50	Tropical Birds	1974	—	£4.00
40	Vanishing Wildlife	1988	—	£4.00
50	Wild Birds in Britain	1973	—	£4.50
50	Wild Flowers, Series 2	1973	—	£4.00
50	Wildlife in Danger	1973	—	£4.00
40	Woodland Wildlife	1988	—	*£7.50*
CARD GAMES BASED ON REGULAR SERIES				
L36	British Costume Snap Game	1974	—	£15.00
L36	Flags & Emblems Snap Game	1974	—	*£15.00*
L36	Motor History Snap Game	1974	—	£15.00
CANADIAN ISSUES				
48	African Animals	1964	—	£5.00
48	Animals and Their Young ("Products")	1972	—	£8.00
48	(Tea/Coffee)	1972	£6.50	—
48	Animals of North America			
	("Roland" Back) (2 Printings)	1960	£1.25	£60.00
	("Rolland" Back)	1960	£1.25	£60.00
48	Birds of North America	1962	60p	£29.00
48	Butterflies of North America	1965	80p	£40.00
48	Canadian/American Songbirds	1966	£2.25	£108.00
48	Dinosaurs	1963	£2.25	£108.00
48	Exploring the Oceans	1971	—	£5.00
48	Indians of Canada	1974	50p	£24.00
48	North American Wildlife in Danger	1970	—	£6.00
48	Songbirds of North America			
	(Red Rose/Blue Ribbon)	1959	£1.25	£60.00
	(Red Rose Only, "Albums Available")	1959	£3.00	£144.00
	(Red Rose Only, "Mount Your Collection")	1959	£4.00	—
48	The Arctic	1973	25p	£12.00
48	The Space Age	1969	40p	£20.00
48	Transportation Through the Ages (Top Line Black)	1967	50p	£24.00
48	(Top Line Red)	1967	£4.00	—
48	Trees of North America	1968	50p	£24.00
48	Tropical Birds (Top Line Black)	1964	75p	£36.00
48	(Top Line Red)	1964	£4.00	—
48	Wild Flowers of North America	1961	60p	£30.00
RHODESIAN ISSUES				
50	African Birds	1965	£2.25	£112.50
50	African Wild Life	1963	£3.50	£175.00

BROOKE BOND & CO. LTD. (Tea) — cont.

Qty		Date	Odds	Sets
50	Asian Wild Life	1963	£3.00	£150.00
50	Butterflies of the World	1966	£2.50	£125.00
50	Tropical Birds	1962	£2.50	£125.00
50	Wildlife in Danger	1964	£3.25	£162.50
SOUTH AFRICAN ISSUES				
50	Our Pets	1967	£3.50	£175.00
50	Out Into Space	1966	£4.00	£200.00
50	Wild Van Afrika (Bilingual)	1965	£4.00	£200.00
50	(One Language)	1965	£6.50	£325.00
U.S.A. ISSUES				
48	Animals of North America (Black Back)	1960	£10.00	—
48	(Blue Back)	1960	£8.00	—
48	Birds of North America	1962	£5.50	—
48	Butterflies of North America	1964	£3.50	£170.00
48	Canadian/American Songbirds	1966	£2.50	£120.00
48	Dinosaurs	1963	£6.50	—
48	Tropical Birds	1964	£3.00	£150.00
48	Wild Flowers of North America (Dark Blue)	1961	£3.50	£175.00
48	(Light Blue)	1961	£7.50	—

BROOK MOTORS

G12	Motor Cycles (Cut from Calendars)	1975	—	£8.00
P12	Steam Engines	1973	—	£15.00
P12	Steam Engines (Different)	1970	—	£36.00
P12	The Traction Engine	1967	—	£30.00
P12	Veteran Cars	1961	—	£24.00

BROOKFIELD SWEETS (Ireland)

50	Animals of the World	1956	£3.50	—
25	Aquarium Fish, 1st Series	1957	£3.00	—
25	Aquarium Fish, 2nd Series	1957	£3.00	—
25	Motor Cars	1954	£4.00	—
50	The Conquest of Space	1956	£3.00	—

BROOKS DYE WORKS LTD.

P4	Interesting Shots of Old Bristol	1950	—	£4.00

DAVID BROWN (Tractors)

XF3	Is Your Slip Showing?	1954	£3.00	£9.00

BROWN & POLSON (Custard)

X25	Recipe Cards	1925	£4.00	—

BROWNE BROS. LTD. (Tea)

Qty		Date	Odds	Sets
25	Birds	1964	—	£15.00
25	British Cavalry Uniforms of the 19th Century	1964	—	£12.00
25	Garden Flowers	1965	£1.50	—
25	History of the Railways, 1st Series	1964	—	£12.50
25	History of the Railways, 2nd Series	1964	—	£10.00
25	Passenger Liners	1966	£1.50	—
25	People & Places	1965	—	£2.00
24	The Island of Ceylon	1961	£3.50	—
25	Tropical Birds	1966	—	£2.50
25	Wonders of the Deep	1965	—	£3.00
25	Wonders of the World	1970	—	£5.00

BRYANT & MAY LTD. (Matches)

50	Kings & Queens of England (Player Reprint)	1991	—	£9.00
50	Life in the Hedgerow (Wills Reprint)	1991	—	£10.00
L12	The Thirties	1992	—	£9.00

BUCHANAN'S (Jam)

24	Birds and their Eggs	1924	£8.00	—

JOHNNY BUNNY (Medicines)

25	Football Clubs and Badges	1958	£2.00	—

BUNSEN CONFECTIONERY CO.

?100	Famous Figures Series	1925	£16.00	—

BURDALL & BURDALL (Gravy Salt)

30	Wild Animals	1924	£6.25	—

BURTON'S WAGON WHEELS (Biscuits)

25	Indian Chiefs	1972	50p	£12.50
L7	Pictures of the Wild West	1983	£5.50	—
25	The West	1972	—	£4.00
25	Wild West Action	1972	—	£5.00

BUTTAPAT DAIRIES

25	People of the World	1915	£16.50	—

BUTTERCUP BREAD CO. (Australia)

L24	Alan Border Tribute	1994	—	£10.00
L24	Border's Ashes Heroes	1993	—	£10.00
L24	1993-94 World Series All Stars	1993	—	£10.00

C. & G. CONFECTIONERY CO.

Qty		Date	Odds	Sets
25	Box of Tricks, 1st Series	1965	£3.50	£87.50
25	Box of Tricks, 2nd Series	1965	£3.50	£87.50

CBS IRONMONGERY LTD.

30	Glamorgan Cricketers	1984	—	£15.00

CMK PUBLICATIONS INC. (U.S.A.)

X26	Cars of the World	1992	—	£3.50

CADBURY BROS. LTD. (Chocolate)

12	Age of the Dinosaur	1971	£1.00	£12.00
T12	Antarctic Series	1913	£30.00	—
X6	Bay City Rollers	1975	*£1.50*	—
L12	Birds in Springtime	1983	—	£3.00
6	Bournville Series B	1906	£17.50	£105.00
P3	Bournville Views (Script at Side)	1906	£3.00	£9.00
P6	Bournville Views (Block at Side)	1906	£3.50	£21.00
P6	Bournville Views (White Borders)	1906	£3.25	£19.50
P8	Bournville Views (Gravure)	1906	£3.50	—
6	Bournville Village Series	1906	£18.00	—
P25	British Birds (Reward Cards)	1910	£8.00	—
12	British Birds & Eggs	1910	£10.00	—
P12	British Birds & Their Eggs (Reward Cards)	1910	£8.00	—
P32	British Butterflies & Moths (Reward Cards)	1910	£5.00	£160.00
6	British Colonies, Maps & Industries	1908	£16.50	£100.00
120	British Marvels	1932	£1.20	—
120	British Marvels, Album No. 2	1933	£1.25	—
12	British Trees Series (2 Printings)	1911	£6.00	£72.00
80	Cadbury's Picture Making	1936	£1.25	—
12	Cathedral Series	1913	£6.25	£75.00
6	Colonial Premiers Series	1908	£16.50	£100.00
12	Constellations Series	1912	£7.00	£84.00
24	Copyright (Inventors) Series	1914	£12.50	—
1	Coronation	1911	—	£27.50
48	Dangerous Animals	1970	50p	£24.00
6	Dog Series	1908	£35.00	—
P12	English Industries	1908	£30.00	—
25	Fairy Tales	1924	£3.00	£75.00
27	Famous Steamships	1923	£3.00	£81.00
12	Fish	1910	£11.50	—
P6	Fish & Bait Series	1909	£35.00	—
12	Flag Series	1912	£3.00	£36.00
P6	Flag Series (Joined Pairs)	1912	£6.50	£39.00
P12	Flag Series (Different)	1910	£22.50	—
X12	Flight (Birds)	1982	50p	£6.00
32	Happy Families	1950	£2.50	—
?X5	Knotty Problems	1910	£20.00	—
1	Largest Steamers in the World	1912	—	*£40.00*
6	Locomotive Series	1906	£30.00	—
12	Match Puzzles	1906	£32.00	—
6	Old Ballad Series	1906	£20.00	—

British Empire
Kings & Queens
Hoadley's

Why?
Thomson

Advertisement Card
Major Drapkin

General Government and State Capitol Buildings
Allen & Ginter

People & Places
Askeys, Badshah, Barratt, Browne Bros., Gowers and Burgons, Hitchman's, Lamberts, Ringtons, Wilcocks & Wilcocks

Portals of the Past
Player

Wings Over the Empire – Churchman

Spadgers Monster
Collection of Spoofs
Thomson

British Medals & Ribbons
Taddy

Costumes of Warriors & Soldiers
Mayo

Reproductions of Celebrated Oil Paintings
Cavanders, Milhoff

Coronation Series
Wills

Army Corps & Divisional Signs – Player

Adventure Pictures
Thomson

CADBURY BROS. LTD. (Chocolate) – cont.

Qty		Date	Odds	Sets
X6	Panama Series	1910	£27.50	—
X5	Pop Stars	1975	£1.00	£5.00
1	Poster Series	1910	—	£27.50
X8	Prehistoric Monsters	1975	—	£6.00
P1	Puzzle Card	1910	—	£17.50
P6	Rivers of the British Isles (Reward Cards)	1910	£14.00	£84.00
24	Shadow Series	1914	£13.00	—
6	Shipping Series (4 Sizes)	1910	£10.00	—
T6	Sports Series	1906	*£37.50*	—
24	Strange But True	1970	—	£2.00
25	Transport	1925	50p	£12.50
G1	The Magic Bournville Cocoa Tins	1910	—	£17.50
L6	Wildlife Stickers	1986	—	£3.00

CADET SWEETS

25	Arms and Armour	1961	—	£2.00
50	Buccaneers	1957	—	£12.00
50	Buccaneers (Different)	1959	—	£15.00
25	Daktari	1969	—	£8.00
50	Doctor Who and The Daleks	1965	£2.40	£120.00
25	Dogs, 1st Series	1958	—	£20.00
25	Dogs, 2nd Series	1958	—	£20.00
25	Evolution of the Royal Navy	1959	—	£3.00
M22	Famous Explorers (Packets)	1960	£5.50	—
50	Fifty Years of Flying	1953	80p	£40.00
50	Footballers	1956	—	£16.50
50	Footballers (Different) Large Wording	1959	—	£20.00
50	Small Wording	1959	—	£20.00
25	How?	1969	—	£10.00
50	Motor Cars	1954	50p	£25.00
25	Prehistoric Animals	1961	—	£20.00
50	Railways of the World (Cadet)	1956	—	£7.50
50	(Paramount Laboratories)	1956	80p	£40.00
50	(Paramount Sweets)	1956	40p	£20.00
50	Record Holders of the World	1956	—	£8.50
50	Stingray	1965	—	£30.00
48	The Adventures of Rin Tin Tin	1960	50p	£24.00
50	The Conquest of Space	1957	—	£7.50
25	Treasure Hunt	1964	—	£2.50
50	U.N.C.L.E. (Line Drawings)	1966	£2.00	£100.00
50	U.N.C.L.E. (Photos)	1966	—	£60.00
25	WHAT Do You Know?	1965	—	£12.50

A. J. CALEY & SON (Confectionery)

K24	Film Stars	1930	£7.50	£180.00
10	Passenger Liners	1939	£10.00	—
48	Wisequacks (Mickey Mouse Weekly)	1932	£8.50	—

CALTEX OIL (Australia)

P6	Stargazer (Haley's Comet)	1986	—	£1.50

F. C. CALVERT & CO. LTD. (Toothpaste)

Qty		*Date*	*Odds*	*Sets*
25	Dan Dare Series	1954	£5.00	£125.00

CANDY GUM (Italy)

50	Autosprint I Serie (Printed Back)	1975	—	£6.00
50	(Plain Back)	1975	—	£7.50
30	Autosprint II Serie (Printed Back)	1975	—	£6.00
30	(Plain Back)	1975	—	£7.50

CANDY NOVELTY CO.

25	Animals of the Countryside	1964	£4.50	—
50	Animals of the World	1964	£3.50	—
M25/50	Dog Series — A1 Set	1953	—	£3.50
32	Motor Car Series	1953	£4.50	—
25	Ships Through the Ages, 2nd Series	1957	£5.00	—
32	Western Series	1953	£5.00	—

CANNINGS (Jam)

25	Types of British Soldiers	1914	£13.00	—

F. CAPERN (Bird Seed)

?10	British Birds	1925	£11.00	—
12	Cage Birds	1924	£11.50	—
P54	Cage Birds	1926	£3.00	£160.00
24	Picture Aviary	1964	—	£20.00
1	Picture Aviary Introductory Card	1964	—	25p

CAPEZIO (Ballet Shoes, U.S.A.)

XF12	Famous Dancers Gallery	1950	—	£32.50

CARD INSERT LTD.

1	Famous Footballers	1953	—	£5.00

CARD PROMOTIONS (Commercial)

50	Aeroplanes (B.A.T. Reprint)	2000	—	£8.50
48	Army Badges (Gallaher Reprint)	2001	—	£8.50
25	Battleships & Crests (Hill Reprint)	1995	—	£6.25
50	British Sea Dogs (John Sinclair Reprint)	1997	—	£8.50
50	British Warriors (Cope Reprint)	1996	—	£8.50
25	Conan Doyle Characters (Boguslavsky Reprint)	1996	—	£6.25
75	Cricketers Series (Pattrieouex Reprint)	1997	—	£13.50
25	Days of Nelson (Fry Reprint)	2003	—	£6.25
25	Days of Wellington (Fry Reprint)	2003	—	£6.25
32	Drum Horses (B.A.T. Reprint)	2000	—	£6.25
50	Famous Airmen & Airwomen (Carreras Reprint)	1996	—	£8.50

CARD PROMOTIONS (Commercial) — cont.

Qty		*Date*	*Odds*	*Sets*
25	Famous Jockeys (Taddy Reprint)	1996	—	£6.25
25	Famous Running Horses (English) (Kinney Reprint)	1996	—	£6.25
50	Flowers to Grow (Lea Reprint)	1997	—	£8.50
60	Football Captains 1907-8 (Cohen Weenen Reprint)	1998	—	£10.00
75	Footballers (Carreras Reprint)	1997	—	£13.50
30	Generals of the American Civil War (Duke Reprint)	1995	—	£6.25
40	Home & Colonial Regiments (Cohen Weenen Reprint)	1998	—	£8.50
50	Indian Regiment Series (B.A.T. Reprint)	2000	—	£8.50
50	Lawn Tennis Celebrities (Gallaher Reprint)	1997	—	£8.50
25	Military Uniforms, C (American Tobacco Co.)	2003	—	£6.25
25/24	Motor Cars (Gallaher Reprint)	1995	—	£6.25
24	Past & Present – The Army (Teofani Reprint)	2001	—	£6.25
24	Past & Present – Weapons of War (Teofani Reprint)	2001	—	£6.25
50	Pirates of the Spanish Main (Allen & Ginter Reprint)	1996	—	£8.50
48	Poultry (C.W.S. Reprint)	1996	—	£8.50
25	Railway Engines (Godfrey Phillips Reprint)	1997	—	£6.25
50	Regimental Colours & Standards (Gallaher Reprint)	1995	—	£8.50
30	Regimental Nicknames (Hustler Reprint)	1997	—	£6.25
33	Regimental Pets (B.A.T. Reprint)	1998	—	£6.25
25	Royalty Series (Taddy Reprint)	1998	—	£6.25
50/48	Signed Portraits of Famous Stars (Gallaher Reprint)	1997	—	£8.50
50	Star Artistes (Cohen Weenen Reprint)	1998	—	£8.50
25	Territorial Regiments (Taddy Reprint)	1995	—	£6.25
25	Territorial Series (Godfrey Phillips Reprint)	2000	—	£6.25
25	Thames Series (Taddy Reprint)	1996	—	£6.25
50	The Great War Series (1-50) (Gallaher Reprint)	2001	—	£8.50
50	The Great War Series (51-100) (Gallaher Reprint)	2003	—	£8.50
25	The Great War V.C. Heroes, 1st Series (Gallaher Reprint)	2001	—	£6.25
25	The Great War V.C. Heroes, 2nd Series (Gallaher Reprint)	2001	—	£6.25
25	The Great War V.C. Heroes, 3rd Series (Gallaher Reprint)	2001	—	£6.25
25	The Great War V.C. Heroes, 4th Series (Gallaher Reprint)	2001	—	£6.25
25	The Great War V.C. Heroes, 5th Series (Gallaher Reprint)	2003	—	£6.25
25	The Great War V.C. Heroes, 7th Series (Gallaher Reprint)	2003	—	£6.25
25	The Great War V.C. Heroes, 8th Series (Gallaher Reprint)	2003	—	£6.25
50	The South African Series (101-150) (Gallaher Reprint)	2000	—	£8.50
50	The South African Series (151-200) (Gallaher Reprint)	2000	—	£8.50
25	Types of British Soldiers (Godfrey Phillips Reprint)	1997	—	£6.25
50	Types of the British Army (Gallaher Reprint)	1995	—	£8.50
50	Types of the British Army 51-100 (Gallaher Reprint)	1996	—	£8.50
20	Types of the British Army (Hill Reprint)	2000	—	£6.25
25	Types of Volunteer & Yeomanry (Woods Reprint)	1996	—	£6.25
25	Uniforms (Cope Reprint)	1996	—	£6.25
50	Victoria Cross Heroes (Cohen Weenen Reprint)	1998	—	£8.50
20	Victoria Cross Heroes (1-20) (Taddy Reprint)	1996	—	£6.25
20	Victoria Cross Heroes (21-40) (Taddy Reprint)	1996	—	£6.25
20	Victoria Cross Heroes (41-60) (Taddy Reprint)	1997	—	£6.25
20	Victoria Cross Heroes (61-80) (Taddy Reprint)	1997	—	£6.25
20	Victoria Cross Heroes (81-100) (Taddy Reprint)	1997	—	£6.25
25	Victoria Cross Heroes (101-125) Taddy (Reprint)	1996	—	£6.25
15	War Series K (Murray Reprint) (Leaders)	1999	—	£5.00
20	War Series K (Murray Reprint) (Uniforms)	1999	—	£6.00
25	Winners on the Turf (Boguslavsky Reprint)	1995	—	£6.25

CARDS TO COLLECT (Commercial)

50	Deep Sea Diving	1996	—	£10.50

CARR'S BISCUITS

Qty		*Date*	*Odds*	*Sets*
M30	Animals of the World	1930	£8.00	—
G20	Cricketers	1967	£5.50	—

CARSON'S CHOCOLATE

72	Celebrities	1902	£14.00	—

CARTER'S LITTLE LIVER PILLS

28	Dominoes	1911	£1.00	£28.00

F. C. CARTLEDGE (Razor Blades)

X48	Epigrams "A"	1939	25p	£12.00
X64	Epigrams "B"	1939	25p	£16.00
X96	Epigrams "C"	1941	25p	£24.00
50	Famous Prize Fighters	1938	£2.70	£150.00

CARTOPHILIC SOCIETY

16	London Branch Personalities	1980	—	£5.00
20	London Branch Personalities, 2nd Series	1995	—	£4.00

CASH & CO. (Shoes)

20	War Series	1916	£14.00	—

CASSELLS (Periodical)

M6	British Engines	1923	£10.00	£60.00
M12	Butterflies & Moths Series	1923	£6.50	£78.00

CASTROL OIL

X18	Famous Riders	1955	£4.00	£72.00
X24	Racing Cars	1956	£3.00	£72.00

CAVE AUSTIN & CO. LTD. (Tea)

20	Inventors Series	1923	£10.00	—

CCC LTD.

L15	Arsenal Cup Winners 1992-1993	1993	—	£6.00
L20	Doctor Who	1993	—	£9.00
L1	Doctor Who Promotional Card	1993	—	50p
L6	Wild Cats	1994	—	£3.00

CECIL COURT COLLECTORS CENTRE

Qty		*Date*	*Odds*	*Sets*
L25	Ashes Winning Captains	1993	—	£8.50
L20	Christopher Columbus	1992	—	£6.50
L1	Promotional Card	1992	—	50p
L12	Class of '66 (Soccer)	2002	—	£7.50
L20	Famous Film Directors	1992	—	£6.50
L1	Promotional Card (Hitchcock)	1992	—	50p

CEDE LTD.

25	Coins of the World	1956	—	£3.50

CENTRAL ELECTRICITY AUTHORITY

M10	Interesting Careers	1961	—	£2.00

CEREBOS (SALT)

100	Sea Shells	1925	£1.75	£175.00

CEYLON TEA CENTRE

24	The Island of Ceylon	1955	—	£2.00

CHANNEL 4/CHEERLEADER PRODUCTIONS (TV)

L20	All Time Great Quarterbacks	1989	—	£27.50

H. CHAPPEL & CO. (Confectionery)

10	British Celebrities	1905	£27.50	—

CHARTER TEA & COFFEE CO. LTD.

25	Prehistoric Animals, First Series	1962	—	*£17.50*
25	Prehistoric Animals, Second Series	1962	—	*£17.50*
25	Strange But True First, Series	1961	£1.00	£25.00
25	Strange But True, Second Series	1961	—	£12.50
25	Transport Through the Ages, First Series	1961	£1.00	£25.00
25	Transport Through the Ages, Second Series	1961	60p	£15.00

CHEF & BREWER

L20	Historic Pub Signs	1984	—	£7.50

CHIVERS & SONS LTD. (Preserves)

L125	Firm Favourites	1932	£2.00	—
K53	Miniature Playing Cards	1965	£1.20	—
P6	Studies of English Fruits, Series 1	1924	£5.50	£33.00
P6	Studies of English Fruits, Series 2	1924	£5.50	£33.00

CHIVERS & SONS LTD. (Preserves) – cont.

Qty		*Date*	*Odds*	*Sets*
24	Wild Wisdom	1964	£3.00	£72.00
48	Wild Wisdom in Africa	1964	£2.50	£120.00
48	Wild Wisdom, River and Marsh	1964	£2.50	£120.00

PACKAGE ISSUES

L15	Children of Other Lands	1952	80p	£12.00
L15	Chivers British Birds	1951	£1.00	£15.00
L20	On Chivers Farms	1951	75p	£15.00

CHIX CONFECTIONERY CO. LTD.

M12	Batman (Packets)	1990	—	£6.00
X50	Famous Footballers	1960	£5.00	—
X48	Famous Footballers, No.1 Series	1953	£3.50	£168.00
X48	Famous Footballers, No.2 Series	1956	£4.00	£192.00
X48	Famous Footballers, No.3 Series	1958	£5.25	—
X50	Famous Last Words	1970	£1.00	—
X24	Footballers (Portrait & Action) 1-24	1960	—	£24.00
X24	Footballers (Portrait & Action) 25-48	1960	—	£48.00
L50	Funny Old Folk	1970	—	£12.00
L50	Happy Howlers	1970	80p	£40.00
L50	Krazy Kreatures from Outer Space	1970	£1.50	£75.00
T36	Looney Tunes (Packets)	1990	—	£8.00
L6	Looney Tunes (Packets)	1990	—	£2.50
L50	Military Uniforms	1970	—	£17.50
L50	Moon Shot	1966	£2.00	£100.00
X50	Popeye	1960	£3.00	£150.00
X24	Scottish Footballers	1960	£7.00	£168.00
X50	Ships of the Seven Seas	1968	£1.60	£80.00
X50	Soldiers of the World	1962	£1.00	£50.00
X50	Sport through the Ages	1968	£3.00	£150.00
L6	The Joker (Batman Packets)	1989	—	£8.00
P52	The Real Ghostbusters (Package Slides)	1990	—	£25.00
96	T.V. and Radio Stars	1954	£3.00	—
X50	Wild Animals	1960	£1.30	£65.00

CHUMS (Periodical)

MF23	Cricketers	1923	£5.00	£115.00
MF20	Football Teams	1922	£3.00	£60.00
F8	Football Teams New Series	1923	£3.50	£28.00
X10	Real Colour Photos (Footballers)	1922	£7.00	£70.00

CHURCH & DWIGHT (Baking Soda, U.S.A.)

M60	Beautiful Birds, New Series	1896	£3.75	£225.00
60	Beautiful Birds, New Series (Miniature)	1896	£4.25	—
60	Beautiful Birds, New Series (Standard)	1896	£5.50	—
M60	Beautiful Birds of America	1894	£5.00	£300.00
60	Beautiful Birds of America	1894	£6.00	—
M60	Beautiful Flowers	1895	£3.25	£195.00
60	Beautiful Flowers	1895	£4.00	—
X10	Birds of Prey	1976	—	£20.00
M30	Champion Dog Series	1902	£8.00	—

CHURCH & DWIGHT (Baking Soda, U.S.A.) - cont.

Qty		Date	Odds	Sets
30	Champion Dog Series	1902	£8.50	—
M30	Dairy Animals	1895	£8.75	—
30	Dairy Animals	1895	£9.00	—
M30	Fish Series	1900	£3.25	£97.50
30	Fish Series	1900	£4.50	—
M30	Game Bird Series	1904	£3.50	£105.00
30	Game Bird Series	1904	£4.50	—
M60	Interesting Animals	1897	£4.00	£240.00
60	Interesting Animals (Miniature)	1897	£5.50	—
60	Interesting Animals (Standard)	1897	£6.50	—
M30	Interesting Animals (Re-Issue)	1915	£5.00	—
30	Interesting Animals (Re-Issue)	1915	£7.75	—
M30	Mother Goose Series	1900	£5.75	£172.50
30	Mother Goose Series	1900	£7.00	—
M30	New Series of Birds	1908	£2.50	£75.00
30	New Series of Birds	1908	£3.75	—
M30	New Series of Dogs	1910	£8.00	—
30	New Series of Dogs	1910	£8.50	—
M30	Useful Birds of America	1915	£2.50	£75.00
30	Useful Birds of America	1915	£3.50	—
M30	Useful Birds of America, 2nd Series	1918	£2.25	£67.50
30	Useful Birds of America, 2nd Series	1918	£3.00	—
M30	Useful Birds of America, 3rd Series	1922	£2.25	£67.50
30	Useful Birds of America, 3rd Series	1922	£2.25	£67.50
M30	Useful Birds of America, Series 4	1924	£2.50	£75.00
30	Useful Birds of America, Series 4	1924	£2.25	£67.50
M15	Useful Birds of America, Series 5	1924	£2.50	£37.50
M15	Useful Birds of America, Series 6	1924	£2.50	£37.50
M15	Useful Birds of America, Series 7	1924	£2.50	£37.50
M15	Useful Birds of America, Series 8	1924	£2.50	£37.50
M15	Useful Birds of America, Series 9	1926	50p	£7.50
M15	Useful Birds of America, Series 10	1926	80p	£12.00

CIBA PHARMACEUTICAL PRODUCTS (U.S.A.)

P12	Medicine Men	1960	—	£20.00

CLARNICO (Confectionery)

30	Colonial Troops (Many Backs)	1900	£25.00	—
25	Great War Leaders	1915	£16.50	—
29	Wolf Cubs Signalling	1910	£35.00	—

CLASSIC GAMES INC. (U.S.A.)

X100	Deathwatch 2,000	1993	—	£13.00

CLEVEDON CONFECTIONERY LTD.

50	British Aircraft	1958	£2.75	—
25	British Orders of Chivalry & Valour	1960	£4.00	—
50	British Ships	1959	£3.00	—
M50	British Trains and Engines	1958	£6.00	—
25	Dan Dare	1961	£6.50	—

CLEVEDON CONFECTIONERY LTD. – cont.

Qty		*Date*	*Odds*	*Sets*
40	Did You Know?	1963	£3.00	—
40	Famous Cricketers	1959	£9.00	—
25	Famous Cricketers (Different)	1962	£9.00	—
50	Famous Football Clubs	1964	£2.40	£120.00
50	Famous Footballers	1961	£4.50	—
50	Famous International Aircraft	1963	£1.60	£80.00
M50	Famous Screen Stars	1959	£3.50	£175.00
40	Film Stars	1958	£3.25	—
50	Football Club Managers	1959	£10.00	—
50	Hints on Association Football	1961	£2.75	—
50	Hints on Road Safety	1962	£2.25	—
50	International Sporting Stars	1960	£2.75	—
M50	Regimental Badges	1959	£3.00	—
X25	Sporting Memories	1962	£8.00	—
50	The Story of the Olympics	1961	£2.20	£110.00
50	Trains of the World	1962	£1.80	—
M60	Wagon Train	1963	£4.25	—

CLEVELAND (Petrol)

P20	Golden Goals	1970	£1.00	£20.00

CLIFFORD (Commercial)

50	Footballers	1950	£20.00	—

CLOVER DAIRIES LTD.

25	Animals and Reptiles	1970	—	£2.00
25	British Rail	1973	—	£2.50
25	People & Places	1972	—	£2.00
25	Prehistoric Animals	1965	—	£3.00
25	Science in the 20th Century	1971	—	£2.00
25	Ships and Their Workings	1971	—	£2.00
25	The Story of Milk	1970	—	£2.50
25	Transport through the Ages	1971	—	£2.00

COCA COLA (Drinks)

X49	2002 FIFA World Cup	2002	—	£15.00
M100	Our Flower Paradise (S. Africa)	1960	—	£40.00
X96	The World of Nature (U.S.A.)	1960	—	£60.00

COFTON COLLECTIONS (Shop)

L7	Alice in Wonderland	2002	—	£3.00
25	Dogs, 1st Series	1988	—	£4.50
25	Dogs, 2nd Series	1988	—	£4.50
25	Dogs, 3rd Series	1988	—	£4.50
L25	Nursery Rhymes	1992	—	£7.50
L20	Worcestershire County Cricket Club	1989	—	£6.50

CECIL COLEMAN LTD. (Confectionery)

24	Film Stars	1935	£7.25	—

COLGATE-PALMOLIVE (Toiletries)

Qty		*Date*	*Odds*	*Sets*
M24	Famous Sporting Trophies	1979	—	£8.00
P4	Royal Britain	1951	£2.00	£8.00

COLINVILLE LTD. (Gum)

M56	Look'n See	1958	£5.00	—
X25	Prairie Pioneers	1959	£3.40	£85.00
M28	Space Fantasy, 1st Series (1-28)	1959	£5.00	—
M28	Space Fantasy, 2nd Series (29-56)	1959	£6.00	—

COLLECT-A-CARD CORPORATION (U.S.A.)

X100	Harley-Davidson Series 2	1992	—	£20.00
X100	Harley-Davidson Series 3	1993	—	£20.00
X109	Vette Set (Corvette Cars, including Hologram)	1991	—	£22.00

COLLECTABLES OF SPALDING (Shop)

25	British Cavalry Uniforms	1987	—	£5.00
25	Military Maids	1987	—	£5.00
25	Warriors through the Ages	1987	—	£5.00

COLLECTOR & HOBBYIST (Periodical)

25	Fascinating Hobbies	1950	—	£2.00

COLLECTORS' CORNER

L20	Halifax As It Was	1989	—	£4.50

COLLECTORS FARE

16	Reading F.C. Simod Cup Winners	1990	—	£2.25
X16	Reading F.C. Simod Cup Winners	1990	—	£3.00

COLLECTORS SHOP

25	Bandsmen of the British Army	1960	—	£11.50
3	Bonus Cards	1961	*£1.50*	—
2	Bonus Cards 1961-62	1961	—	£2.50

COLMAN'S MUSTARD

X8	Boer War Celebrities	1900	£23.50	—

COLT 45 (Drink)

X5/6	Advertising Slogans (Silk)	1976	*£4.00*	—
P4	American Scenes (Beer Mats)	1975	—	£4.00

COMET SWEETS ("C.S.")

Qty		*Date*	*Odds*	*Sets*
25	A. & M. Denis on Safari, 1st Series	1961	—	£2.50
25	A. & M. Denis on Safari, 2nd Series	1961	—	£2.50
50	Footballers and Club Colours	1963	70p	£35.00
25	Modern Wonders (Black Back)	1961	—	£2.50
25	(Blue Back)	1961	—	*£15.00*
25	Olympic Achievements, 1st Series	1960	—	£20.00
25	Olympic Achievements, 2nd Series	1960	—	£20.00
M22	Olympic Achievements (Package)	1960	£7.50	—
25	Record Holders of the World	1962	—	£10.00
25	Ships through the Ages, 1st Series	1963	80p	£20.00
25	Ships through the Ages, 2nd Series	1963	80p	£20.00

COMIC LIFE (Periodical)

MF4	Sports Champions	1922	£5.50	£22.00

COMMODEX (Gum)

L88	Operation Moon	1969	£2.00	£176.00
L120	Super Cars	1970	£1.75	£210.00

COMMONWEALTH SHOE & LEATHER CO. (U.S.A.)

M12	Makes of Planes	1930	£3.75	£45.00

COMO CONFECTIONERY PRODUCTS LTD.

M52	Adventures of Fireball XL5	1965	£10.00	—
L25	History of the Wild West, Series No.1	1963	£3.40	£85.00
L25	History of the Wild West, Series No.2	1963	—	£12.50
50	Lenny's Adventures	1961	£1.30	£65.00
50	Noddy and His Playmates	1962	£1.25	—
M25	Noddy's Adventures	1958	£6.00	—
L25	Noddy's Adventures, 1st Series	1958	£2.20	£55.00
L25	Noddy's Adventures, 2nd Series	1958	£2.50	—
25	Noddy's Budgie & Feathered Friends, 1st Series	1964	£1.75	—
25	Noddy's Budgie & Feathered Friends, 2nd Series	1964	£1.75	—
M25	Noddy's Friends Abroad	1959	£6.00	—
L50	Noddy's Friends Abroad	1959	£1.60	£80.00
M25	Noddy's Nursery Rhyme Friends	1959	£6.00	—
L50	Noddy's Nursery Rhyme Friends	1959	£1.50	£75.00
L50	Sooty's Adventures	1960	£1.75	—
L50	Sooty's New Adventures, Second Series	1961	£1.75	—
50	Sooty's Latest Adventures, 3rd Series	1963	£1.75	—
25	Speed, 1st Series	1962	£1.60	£40.00
25	Speed, 2nd Series	1962	—	£10.00
25	Supercar, 1st Series	1962	£5.00	—
25	Supercar, 2nd Series	1962	£3.60	£90.00
25	Top Secret, 1st Series	1965	£2.00	£50.00
25	Top Secret, 2nd Series	1965	£1.80	£45.00
L26	XL5, 1st Series	1965	£15.00	—
L26	XL5, 2nd Series	1966	£15.00	—

COMPTON'S GRAVY SALT

Qty		Date	Odds	Sets
22	Footballers, Series A (Black)	1924	*£22.50*	—
22	Footballers, Series A (Coloured)	1924	*£25.00*	—
22	Footballers, Series B (Black)	1924	*£22.50*	—
22	Footballers, Series B (Coloured)	1924	*£25.00*	—
22	Footballers, Series C	1924	*£25.00*	—
22	Footballers, Series D	1924	*£25.00*	—

COOPER & CO. LTD. (Tea)

50	Do You Know?	1962	—	£5.00
25	Inventions & Discoveries, 1st Series	1962	—	£30.00
25	Inventions & Discoveries, 2nd Series	1962	—	£30.00
25	Mysteries & Wonders of the World, 1st Series	1961	£1.00	—
25	Mysteries & Wonders of the World, 2nd Series	1961	50p	£12.50
25	Prehistoric Animals, First Series	1962	—	£30.00
25	Prehistoric Animals, Second Series	1962	—	£30.00
25	Strange But True, First Series	1961	—	£3.00
25	Strange But True, Second Series	1961	—	£4.00
24	The Island of Ceylon	1955	£3.00	—
25	Transport through the Ages, 1st Series	1961	—	£7.50
25	Transport through the Ages, 2nd Series	1961	40p	£10.00

CO-OPERATIVE SOCIETIES (Shops)

D306	Espana '82. Complete with Album	1982	—	£22.00
	Special Poster for above (only if ordered at the same time)	1982	—	£1.00
M48	World Cup Teams & Players, Complete with Poster	1982	—	£7.50

CORNERSTONE COMMUNICATIONS INC. (Commercial U.S.A.)

X110	Doctor Who	1994	—	£20.00
X110	Doctor Who Series 3	1996	—	£20.00
X90	Doctor Who Series 4	1996	—	£20.00
X82	Hammer Horror, Series 2	1996	—	£20.00
X81	The Avengers	1992	—	£30.00
X99	The Avengers in Colour Series 2	1993	—	£30.00
X86	The Avengers Return Series 3	1995	—	£30.00

COUNTY PRINT SERVICES (Commercial)

M25	Australian Test Cricketers	1993	—	£10.00
X48	County Cricket Teams 1900-1914	1992	—	£9.00
20	Cricket Pavilions	1991	—	£10.00
X24	Cricket Teams 1884-1900	1990	—	£7.00
50	Cricketers 1890	1989		£8.00
50	Cricketers 1896	1989	—	£8.00
50	Cricketers 1900	1990	—	£8.00
50	Cricketers 1906	1992	—	£8.00
20	Cricketers (Murray Reprint)	1991	—	£7.50

COUNTY PRINT SERVICES (Commercial) — cont.

Qty		Date	Odds	Sets
25	Cricketers (Reeves Ltd. Reprint)	1993	—	£8.00
M25	Cricket's Golden-Age	1991	—	£9.00
X12	Cricket's Pace Partners	1995	—	£8.00
X12	Cricket's Spin Twins	1995	—	£8.00
L25	Derbyshire Test Cricketers	1994	—	£10.00
M27	Famous Cricket Crests	1992	—	£12.50
M25	Famous Cricket Ties	1992	—	£9.00
X12	First Knock (Cricket's Opening Pairs)	1994	—	£9.00
L25	Glamorgan Test Cricketers	1993	—	£10.00
L25	Gloucestershire Test Cricketers	1994	—	£10.00
L25	Hampshire Test Cricketers	1995	—	£10.00
L25	Kent Test Cricketers	1993	—	£10.00
L25	Lancashire Test Cricketers	1993	—	£10.00
L25	Leicestershire Test Cricketers	1995	—	£10.00
L25	Middlesex Test Cricketers	1994	—	£10.00
50	1912 Triangular Tournament	1992	—	£8.00
M24	1920's Test Cricketers	1994	—	£10.00
M24	1920's Test Cricketers, 2nd Series	1995	—	£10.00
25	1995 England Cricket Characters	1995	—	£10.00
L25	Northamptonshire Test Cricketers	1993	—	£10.00
L25	Nottinghamshire Test Cricketers	1994	—	£10.00
L25	Somerset Test Cricketers	1994	—	£10.00
15	South African Cricket Team 1907 (Taddy Reprint)	1993	—	£7.50
M15	South African Cricket Team 1965	1994	—	£6.00
L25	Surrey Test Cricketers	1994	—	£10.00
L25	Sussex Test Cricketers	1994	—	£10.00
14	The England Cricket Team 1903-1904	1991	—	£4.00
15	The England Cricket Team 1907-1908	1992	—	£10.00
17	The England Cricket Team 1932-33	1995	—	£6.00
16	The England Cricket Team 1990-91	1990	—	£6.00
16	The South African Cricket Team 1894	1990	—	£8.00
M15	The South African Cricket Team 1965	1994	—	£6.00
M30	Vic Lewis Cricket Club 1952-1992	1992	—	£6.00
L25	Warwickshire Test Cricketers	1994	—	£10.00
L25	Worcestershire Test Cricketers	1995	—	£10.00

COW & GATE (Baby Food)

X24	Advertisement Cards	1928	£1.75	£42.00
X48	Happy Families	1928	£1.00	£48.00

COWANS (Confectionery, Canada)

24	Dog Pictures	1930	£6.00	£144.00
24	Horse Pictures	1930	£5.50	£132.00
24	Learn to Swim	1929	£6.50	—
24	Noted Cats	1930	£6.00	£144.00

CRESCENT CONFECTIONERY CO.

100	Sportsmen	1928	£35.00	—

CRICKET MEMORABILIA SOCIETY

X50	Memorabilia through the Ages	2000	—	£9.00

CROMWELL STORES

Qty		Date	Odds	Sets
25	Do You Know?	1963	—	£6.00
25	Racing Colours	1963	—	£10.00

CROSBIE (Preserves)

K54	Miniature Playing Cards	1938	90p	—

JOSEPH CROSFIELD & SONS LTD. (Soap)

36	Film Stars	1924	£8.00	—

THE CROXLEY CARD COMPANY LIMITED (Commercial)

L20	British Lions	1999	—	£12.00
X20	Leicester Tigers (Rugby)	2000	—	£10.00
X20	Saracens (Rugby)	2000	—	£10.00

CRYSELCO ELECTRIC LAMPS

X25	Beautiful Waterways	1939	£1.00	£25.00
X25	Buildings of Beauty	1938	£1.00	£25.00
X12	Interesting Events of Sixty Years Ago	1955	—	*£25.00*

D. CUMMINGS & SON (Commercial)

64	Famous Fighters	1949	£3.50	£224.00

D & V (Commercial)

25	Famous Boxers (Hudden Reprint)	1992	—	£6.00
35	Famous Boxers (Singleton & Cole Reprint)	1992	—	£6.00

DAILY HERALD (Newspaper)

32	Cricketers	1954	£3.50	£112.00
32	Footballers	1954	£3.25	£104.00
32	Turf Personalities	1955	£1.25	£40.00

DAILY ICE CREAM CO.

24	Modern British Locomotives	1954	£2.25	£54.00

DAILY MAIL (Newspaper)

P176	War Photographs	1916	£2.25	—

DAILY MIRROR (Newspaper)

M72	Chart Toppers	1989	—	£6.00
M100	Star Soccer Sides	1972	45p	£45.00

DAILY SKETCH (Newspaper)

40	World Cup Souvenir	1970	£2.25	£90.00

DAILY STAR (Newspaper)

Qty		Date	Odds	Sets
D412	Football	1981	—	£30.00

THE DAILY TELEGRAPH (Newspaper)

26	England Rugby World Cup 1995	1995	—	£5.00
26	Ireland Rugby World Cup 1995	1995	—	£5.00
26	Scotland Rugby World Cup 1995	1995	—	£5.00
26	Wales Rugby World Cup 1995	1995	—	£5.00

DAINTY NOVELS

10	World's Famous Liners	1922	£12.50	—

DANDY GUM

M200	Animal Fables (Black Back)	1971	35p	—
M200	(Red Back)	1971	45p	—
M200	Birds (F1-200)	1968	—	£60.00
K50	Bird Series (Transfers)	1950	£1.50	—
M160	Cars and Bikes	1977	75p	£120.00
M97	Film & Entertainment Stars (Serie G)	1968	£1.00	£97.00
M116	Flag Parade	1965	—	£25.00
M160	Flag Parade	1978	—	£36.00
M55	Football World Cup (Playing Card Inset)	1986	—	£22.50
M72	Motor Cars	1966	£1.00	£72.00
M53	Our Modern Army (Playing Card Inset)	1958	—	£50.00
M43/53	Ditto	1958	25p	£10.00
M53	Pin Ups (Playing Card Inset)	1956	£1.75	£92.50
M70	Pop Stars (Serie P)	1977	60p	£42.00
M100	Soldier Parade	1970	30p	£30.00
M200	Struggle for the Universe	1970	*25p*	*£50.00*
M72	Veteran & Vintage Cars (V1-72)	1966	£1.25	£90.00
K48	Wiggle Waggle Pictures	1969	£2.50	£120.00
M100	Wild Animals (H1-100)	1969	—	£20.00
M200	Wonderful World (Y1-200)	1978	—	£35.00

DART FLIPCARDS INC. (Canada)

X90	Pepsi Cola Premium Trading Cards	1996	—	£15.00
X100	Pepsi Cola Trading Cards	1994	—	£13.00
X72	The Frighteners	1996	—	£15.00
X90	The Munsters Collection	1996	—	£15.00

LIAM DEVLIN & SONS (Confectionery)

L36	Coaching Gaelic Football	1960	*£10.00*	—
48	Corgi Toys	1971	—	£70.00
50	Do You Know?	1964	—	£5.00
M50	Famous Footballers (New Series)	1952	£12.00	—
M50	Famous Footballers, Series A.1	1953	£12.00	—
M50	Famous Footballers, Series A.2	1954	£12.00	—
50	Famous Footballers, Series A.3	1955	£12.00	—
M54	Famous Speedway Stars	1960	£15.00	—
M45	Fastest on Earth	1953	£3.75	—
36	Flags of the Nations	1960	£3.50	—

LIAM DEVLIN & SONS (Confectionery) — cont.

Qty		*Date*	*Odds*	*Sets*
48	Gaelic Sportstars	1960	£8.00	—
48	Irish Fishing	1962	£1.50	£72.00
L36	Irish Theatre and Showland Stars	1965	£6.00	—
50	Modern Transport	1966	—	£7.50
48	Our Dogs	1963	£6.00	—
48	Right or Wrong?	1963	£4.00	—
M35	Walt Disney Characters	1956	*£5.50*	—
M48	Wild Animals by George Cansdale	1954	£4.00	—
48	Wild Wisdom	1970	£2.75	—
50	Wonders of the World	1972	—	£5.00
100	World Flag Series	1970	£5.00	—

DIAMOND COLLECTION (Commercial)

L20	Rock N Roll	1997	—	£7.50

DICKSON ORDE & CO. (Confectionery)

50	Footballers	1960	—	£15.00
25	Ships through the Ages	1961	£3.00	—
25	Sports of the Countries	1962	—	£25.00

DINKIE PRODUCTS LTD. (Hair Grips)

L24	Films (Plain Backs)	1952	£2.75	—
L20	Gone with the Wind, Fifth Series	1948	£6.00	£120.00
X20	M.G.M. Films, Third Series	1948	—	£45.00
L24	M.G.M. Films, Ninth Series	1950	£4.25	—
L24	M.G.M. Films, Tenth Series	1951	£5.00	£120.00
L24	M.G.M. Stars, Seventh Series	1949	£3.25	£78.00
L24	Paramount Pictures, Eighth Series	1950	£3.25	—
X24	Stars & Starlets, First Series	1947	£2.00	£48.00
X20	Stars & Starlets, Second Series	1947	—	£45.00
L24	United Artists Releases, Eleventh Series	1951	£5.00	£120.00
L24	Warner Bros. Artists, Fourth Series	1948	£4.00	—
L24	Warner Bros. Films, Sixth Series	1949	£3.25	£78.00

DIRECT ACCESS (Commercial)

L8	British Sporting Stars	1992	—	£6.50

DIRECT TEA SUPPLY CO.

25	British Uniforms of the 19th Century	1958	—	£16.50

F. M. DOBSON (Confectionery)

X144	Flags of the World	1980	20p	—
100	Newcastle & Sunderland's 100 Greatest Footballers	1982	—	£10.00
2	Error Cards	1982	—	£1.00

PETER DOMINIC (Vintner)

P17	Cricket Badges	1990	—	£17.00

A. & J. DONALDSON (Commercial)

Qty		*Date*	*Odds*	*Sets*
64	Golden Series (Soccer)	1955	£20.00	—
?500	Sports Favourites	1953	£8.00	—

DONRUSS (Gum, U.S.A.)

X59	B.M.X. Card Series	1984	—	£15.00
X66	1980 P.G.A. Tour	1981	—	£50.00
X66	1981 P.G.A. Tour	1982	—	£60.00
X66	Sgt. Pepper's Lonely Hearts Club Band	1978	—	£20.00
X74	Tron	1983	—	£7.50

DORMY COLLECTION (Commercial)

25	Golf — The Modern Era	1994	—	£9.00

DOUBLE DIAMOND (Beer)

P5	Puzzle Pictures (Beer Mats)	1976	—	£2.50

DRYFOOD LTD. (Confectionery)

50	Animals of the World	1956	—	£4.00
K50	Zoo Animals	1955	—	£4.00

DUCHESS OF DEVONSHIRE DAIRY CO. LTD.

L25	Devon Beauty-Spots	1936	£4.00	£100.00

DUNHILLS (Confectionery)

25	Ships and Their Workings	1962	—	£6.00

DUNKIN (Confectionery, Spain)

X88	Martial Arts	1976	80p	£70.00
M50	Motor Cycles of the World	1976	£1.90	£95.00

DUNNS (Chocolate)

60	Animals	1924	£7.00	—
48	British Birds & Their Eggs	1924	£5.00	—

DUOCARDS (U.S.A.)

X90	Gone With The Wind	1996	—	£10.00
X72	The Beatles Yellow Submarine	1999	—	£17.50

Characters Come to Life
Godfrey Phillips

Disc Stars
Kane

Hand Shadows
Ardath. Also reprint

James Bond 007 Moonraker
Alma

Beauties, Nymphs
Godfrey Phillips. Also reprint

Cinema Stars
Gallaher

Music Hall Stage Characters
Salmon & Gluckstein
Also reprint

Funny Valentines
A. & B. C. Gum

Dr Who – Weetabix

Wonderful World of Disney
Typhoo

Sherlock Holmes – Premier Collection
Riverwye

DUTTON'S BEER

Qty		Date	Odds	Sets
12	Team of Sporting Heroes	1981	—	£2.40

THE EAGLE (Periodical)

16	Wallet of Soccer Stars	1965	£2.00	£32.00

EAST KENT NATIONAL BUS CO.

X8	British Airways Holidays	1984	—	£1.50

J. EDMONDSON & CO. (Confectionery)

26	Actresses "FROGA"	1901	£50.00	—
4	Aeroplane Models	1939	£14.00	—
50	Art Picture Series	1914	£13.50	—
15	Birds & Their Eggs	1924	£10.00	—
?20	Boy Scout Proficiency Badges	1924	£35.00	—
25	British Army Series	1914	£18.50	—
20	British Ships	1925	£2.40	£48.00
20	Dogs	1924	£7.00	£140.00
20	Famous Castles	1925	£5.50	£110.00
30	Flags & Flags With Soldiers	1905	£15.00	—
40	Flags of All Nations	1923	£7.50	—
24	Pictures from the Fairy Stories	1930	£5.00	£120.00
24	Popular Sports	1930	£10.00	—
25	Sports & Pastimes Series	1916	£13.50	—
12	Throwing Shadows on the Wall	1937	£3.50	£42.00
25	War Series	1916	£13.00	—
12	Woodbine Village	1936	£3.50	£42.00
26	Zoo Alphabet	1935	£6.00	—

EDWARDS & SONS (Confectionery)

27	Popular Dogs	1954	£3.75	—
12	Products of the World	1957	—	£1.50
25	Transport Present and Future (Descriptive)	1956	—	£2.00
25	(Non-Descriptive)	1955	—	£2.50
25	Wonders of the Universe	1956	—	£2.00

ELECTROLUX (Leisure Appliances)

P16	Weekend Tours	1990	—	£5.75

ELKES BISCUITS LTD.

25	Do You Know?	1964	—	£2.50

ELY BREWERY CO. LTD.

M24	Royal Portraits	1953	£1.80	£45.00

EMAP LTD. (Magazines)

Qty		*Date*	*Odds*	*Sets*
X14/15	World Class Winners (Sport)	1997	—	£11.00

EMERALD COLLECTABLES (Commercial)

M72	Birds and Their Eggs	1996	—	£12.75

EMPIRE MARKETING BOARD

12	Empire Shopping	1926	£3.00	£36.00

H.E. EMPSON & SONS LTD. (Tea)

25	Birds	1962	—	£10.00
25	British Cavalry Uniforms of the 19th Century	1963	—	£10.00
25	Garden Flowers	1966	£1.00	£25.00
25	History of the Railways, 1st Series	1966	£1.40	£32.50
25	History of the Railways, 2nd Series	1966	£1.40	£32.50
25	Passenger Liners	1964	£1.20	£30.00
24	The Island of Ceylon	1955	£3.50	—
25	Tropical Birds	1966	50p	£12.50
25	Wonders of the Deep	1965	—	£2.50

ENGLISH & SCOTTISH C.W.S. (Shops)

50	British Sport Series	1904	£30.00	—
25	Humorous Peeps into History (1-25)	1927	£3.00	£75.00
25	Humorous Peeps into History (26-50)	1928	£4.25	—
25	In Victoria's Days	1930	£2.60	£65.00
X12	The Rose of the Orient, Film Series	1925	50p	£6.00
X12	The Rose of the Orient, 2nd Film Series	1925	50p	£6.00
X12	The Story of Tea (Blue Back)	1925	£1.00	£12.00
X12	The Story of Tea (Brown Back, Different)	1925	75p	£9.00

ENSIGN FISHING TACKLE

L6	Birds of Prey	1996	—	£3.00
L6	"Fisherman's Lore"	2002	—	£3.00
L20	Freshwater Fish	1995	—	£7.50
L6	Game Birds	1995	—	£3.00
L6	Garden Birds	1996	—	£3.00
L6	"It's a Dog's Life"	2002	—	£3.00
L6	Lifeboats	2002	—	£3.00
L6	Lighthouses	2002	—	£3.00
L6	Norman Neasom's Rural Studies, Series 1	2002	—	£3.00
L6	Norman Neasom's Rural Studies, Series 2	2002	—	£3.00
L6	Owls	1996	—	£3.00
L25	Salmon Flies	1994	—	£7.50
L6	Sea Fish	2002	—	£3.00
L6	Sharks	2002	—	£3.00
L6	The Art of Angling, A Series	1996	—	£3.00
L6	The Art of Angling, 2nd Series	1996	—	£3.00
L6	The Art of Angling, 3rd Series	2002	—	£3.00
L6	Water Loving Birds	2002	—	£3.00

EPOL (South Africa)

Qty		Date	Odds	Sets
M30	Dogs	1974	£1.00	£30.00

JOHN E. ESSLEMONT LTD. (Tea)

25	Before our Time	1966	—	£7.50
25	Into Space	1966	60p	£15.00
24	The Island of Ceylon	1961	£4.00	—

ESSO PETROLEUM CO.

P20	Olympics	1972	£2.00	£40.00
M16	Squelchers (Football)	1970	£1.50	£24.00

ESTA MEDICAL LABORATORIES INC. (U.S.A.)

E6	Curiosa of Conception	1960	—	£12.00

EVERSHED & SON LTD. (Soap)

25	Sports and Pastimes	1914	£13.50	—

EVERY GIRL'S PAPER

MF17	Film Stars	1924	£3.50	£60.00

EWBANKS LTD. (Confectionery)

25	Animals of the Farmyard	1960	—	£5.00
25	British Uniforms	1956	—	£4.00
25	Miniature Cars & Scooters	1960	—	£7.50
50	Ports and Resorts of the World	1960	—	£4.00
25	Ships Around Britain	1961	—	£2.00
25	Sports and Games	1958	—	£5.00
25	Transport through the Ages (Black Back)	1957	—	£2.00
25	(Blue Back)	1957	—	£12.50

EXPRESS WEEKLY (Periodical)

25	The Wild West (No Overprint)	1958	—	£6.00
25	(Red Overprint)	1958	—	£5.00
L25	(Doubles)	1958	—	£10.00

EXTRAS

24	Prehistoric Monsters and the Present	1979	£2.25	—

F1 SPORTSCARD MARKETING INC. (Canada)

X200	Formula 1 Racing Cards	1992	—	£20.00

F.A.I. INSURANCE GROUP (Australia)

Qty		Date	Odds	Sets
X24	Australian Cricket Team 1989/90	1989	—	£7.50

FACCHINO'S CHOCOLATE WAFERS

100	Cinema Stars	1936	70p	£70.00
50	How or Why!	1937	65p	£32.50
50	People of All Lands	1937	£2.00	—
50	Pioneers	1937	£1.60	£80.00

FAITH PRESS (Commercial)

10	Boy Scouts (LCC)	1928	£6.50	£65.00

FAMILY STAR (Periodical)

MF4	Film Stars (Pairs)	1956	£5.00	£20.00
K52	Fortune Telling Cards	1952	75p	—

FARM-TO-DOOR SUPPLIES (LUTON) LTD.

25	Castles of Great Britain	1965	£3.75	—
25	Cathedrals of Great Britain	1964	£3.50	—

FARROWS (Sauces)

50	Animals in the Zoo	1925	£6.50	£325.00

FASHODA (Commercial)

50	Motor Races 1931 (Ogdens Reprint)	1993	—	£7.50

FAULDER'S CHOCOLATES

10	Ancient v. Modern Sports	1924	£5.50	—
10	Birds and Nests	1924	£5.00	—
10	Fruits	1924	£5.00	—
10	Game	1924	£5.00	—

FAX-PAX (Commercial)

X36	ABC and Numbers	1987	—	£3.50
X36	Animal Spelling	1988	—	£3.50
X40	Cathedrals & Minsters	1989	—	£3.50
X36	Fables	1987	—	£3.50
X40	Famous Golfers	1993	—	£8.00

FAX-PAX (Commercial) — cont.

Qty		Date	Odds	Sets
X36	Football Greats	1989	—	£6.50
X36	Football Stars	1989	—	£5.00
X40	Historic Houses	1990	—	£3.50
X36	Kings & Queens	1988	—	£3.50
X36	London	1987	—	£3.50
X40	Ringlords	1991	—	£5.00
X40	Scotland's Heritage	1990	—	£3.50
X38	Tennis	1987	—	£10.00
X40	World of Sport	1993	—	£7.50

ALEX FERGUSON (Confectionery)

41	V.C. Heroes	1916	£16.50	—

THE FESTIVAL OF 1000 BIKES COMMITTEE

L24	The Vintage Motor Cycle Club	1993	—	£6.00

FIELD GALLERIES

L7	Racehorses & Jockeys, A Series	1997	—	£3.00
L7	Racehorses & Jockeys, 2nd Series	1997	—	£3.00

FILM PICTORIAL (Periodical)

P2	Film Stars (Silk)	1923	£27.50	£55.00

JOHN FILSHILL LTD. (Confectionery)

24	Birds & Their Eggs	1924	£6.50	£156.00
25	Footballers	1924	£16.00	£400.00
25	Types of British Soldiers	1914	£20.00	—

FINDUS (Frozen Foods)

20	All About Pirates	1967	—	£6.50

FINE FARE TEA

25	Inventions & Discoveries, 1st Series	1965	60p	£15.00
25	Inventions & Discoveries, 2nd Series	1965	60p	£15.00
12	Your Fortune in a Tea-Cup	1966	—	£3.00

FISH MARKETING BOARD

18	Eat More Fish	1930	£3.00	—

FITCHETT'S LTD. (Soap)

Qty		*Date*	*Odds*	*Sets*
27	Advertisement Series	1910	£20.00	—

FIZZY FRUIT (Confectionery)

25	Buses and Trams	1959	—	£20.00

FLEER GUM INC. (U.S.A.)

X72	Here's Bo!	1980	—	£6.00
E12	Here's Bo! Posters	1980	—	£3.00

FLEETWAY PUBLICATIONS LTD.

P1	Billy Fury (June)	1960	—	£1.00
P28	Football Teams 58/59	1959	£3.00	£84.00
P28	Football Teams 59/60	1960	£3.00	£84.00
P2	Pop Stars (Roxy)	1961	—	£2.50
50	Star Footballers of 1963	1963	£1.30	£65.00

FLORENCE CARDS (Commercial)

24	Luton Corporation Tramways	1983	—	£2.00
T20	Tramway Scenes	1985	—	£2.00

FORD MOTOR CO. LTD.

L50	Major Farming	1955	£6.25	—

FOSTER CLARK PRODUCTS (Malta)

50	The Sea — Our Other World	1974	—	£12.00

FOSTER'S LAGER

P4	How To Order Your Foster's (Beermats)	1988	—	£1.50

FRAMEABILITY (Commercial)

L17	British Police Vehicles	2002	—	£6.00
L17	British Steam Locomotives	2002	—	£6.00
L10	England World Cup Winners 1966	2002	—	£4.00
L17	Fire Engines	1996	—	£5.00
L17	Fire Engines 2nd Series	1998	—	£6.00
L10	Highwaymen	2003	—	£4.00
L6	Traction Engines	1999	—	£2.50

A. C. W. FRANCIS (Confectionery, Grenada)

25	Football Clubs and Badges	1967	—	£17.50
25	Pond Life	1967	—	£7.50
25	Sports of the Countries	1967	—	£20.00

LES FRERES (Shop)

25	Aircraft of World War II	1964	—	£25.00

J. S. FRY & SONS LTD. (Confectionery)

Qty		*Date*	*Odds*	*Sets*
3	Advertisement Cards	1910	£25.00	—
50	Ancient Sundials	1924	£2.70	£135.00
50	Birds & Poultry	1912	£2.40	£120.00
24	Birds and Their Eggs	1912	£3.50	£84.00
15	China & Porcelain	1907	£13.00	£195.00
P2	Coronation Postcards	1911	£9.00	—
25	Days of Nelson	1906	£11.00	£275.00
25	Days of Wellington	1906	£11.00	£275.00
25	Empire Industries	1924	£6.50	—
50	Exercises for Men & Women	1926	£4.40	£220.00
48	Film Stars	1934	£2.75	—
50	Fowls, Pigeons & Dogs	1908	£3.80	£190.00
P12	Fun Cards	1972	—	£2.00
25	Match Tricks	1921	*£26.50*	—
15	National Flags	1908	£6.50	£97.50
50	Nursery Rhymes	1917	£3.60	£180.00
50	Phil May Sketches	1905	£3.40	£170.00
25	Red Indians	1927	£6.50	£162.50
25	Rule Britannia!	1915	£5.00	£125.00
50	Scout Series	1912	£6.00	£300.00
48	Screen Stars	1928	£2.75	£132.00
120	This Wonderful World	1935	£1.50	—
50	Time & Money in Different Countries	1908	£2.80	£140.00
50	Tricks and Puzzles (Black Back)	1924	£3.40	£170.00
50	Tricks & Puzzles (Blue Back)	1918	£3.40	£170.00
L1	Vinello Advertisement Card	1922	—	£26.50
6	War Leaders (Campaign Packets)	1915	£25.00	—
25	With Captain Scott at the South Pole	1913	£11.00	£275.00

CANADIAN ISSUES

50	Children's Nursery Rhymes	1912	*£11.00*	—
25	Hunting Series	1912	*£17.50*	—
25	Radio Series	1912	£9.00	—
50	Scout Series — Second Series	1913	£10.00	—
50	Treasure Island Map	1912	£5.75	—

FUTERA (Commercial)

X90	Arsenal – Fans Selection	1997	—	£17.00
X108	Arsenal – Fans Selection (inc. Embossed Cards)	1998	—	£20.00
X108	Arsenal – Fans Selection (inc. Embossed Cards)	1999	—	£15.00
X108	Aston Villa – Fans Selection (inc. Embossed Cards)	1998	—	£20.00
X108	Aston Villa – Fans Selection (inc. Embossed Cards)	1999	—	£15.00
X108	Celtic – Fans Selection (inc. Embossed Cards)	1998	—	£20.00
X108	Celtic – Fans Selection (inc. Embossed Cards)	1999	—	£15.00
X108	Chelsea – Fans Selection (inc. Embossed Cards)	1998	—	£20.00
X108	Chelsea – Fans Selection (inc. Embossed Cards)	1999	—	£15.00
X108	Leeds United – Fans Selection (inc. Embossed Cards)	1998	—	£20.00
X108	Leeds United – Fans Selection (inc. Embossed Cards)	1999	—	£15.00
X99	Liverpool	1998	—	£25.00
X90	Liverpool – Fans Selection	1998	—	£15.00
X108	Liverpool – Fans Selection (inc. Embossed Cards)	1999	—	£15.00
X100	Man. United	1997	—	£22.50
X90	Man. United – Fans Selection	1997	—	£17.00
X99	Man. United	1998	—	£25.00

FUTERA (Commercial) — cont.

Qty		*Date*	*Odds*	*Sets*
X108	Man. United – Fans Selection (inc. Embossed Cards).	1998	—	£20.00
X108	Newcastle Utd. – Fans Selection (inc. Embossed Cards)	1999	—	£15.00
X24	World Stars 3D Football Cards	2002	—	£7.50

G. B. & T. W. (Commercial)

L20	Golfing Greats	1989	—	£10.00

GALBRAITH'S STORES LTD.

25	Animals in the Service of Man	1960	£4.00	—

GALLERY OF LEGENDS (Commercial)

71	The British Open Golf Collection	1998	—	£9.00

GAMEPLAN LEISURE LTD. (Commercial)

L25	Open Champions (Golf)	1995	—	£8.00

GARDEN NEWS

T6	Flowers	1988	—	£6.00
T6	Vegetables	1988	—	£6.00

GATEAUX (Ireland)

22	Irish World Cup Squad (Soccer)	1990	£4.50	£100.00

GAUMONT CHOCOLATE BAR

KF50	Film Stars	1936	£3.00	—

GAYCON PRODUCTS LTD. (Confectionery)

25	Adventures of Pinky & Perky, 1st Series	1961	£2.20	—
25	Adventures of Pinky & Perky, 2nd Series	1961	£2.20	—
50	British Birds and Their Eggs	1961	—	£7.50
25	British Butterflies	1962	—	£16.50
25	Do You Know?, 1st Series	1964	£1.40	£35.00
25	Do You Know?, 2nd Series	1964	£1.40	£35.00
50	Flags of All Nations	1963	£1.75	—
25	History of the Blue Lamp, 1st Series	1962	—	£12.00
25	History of the Blue Lamp, 2nd Series	1962	—	£12.00
30	Kings and Queens	1961	—	£3.00
25	Modern Motor Cars	1959	£3.75	—
25	Modern Motor Cars of the World, 1st Series	1962	£3.75	£94.00
25	Modern Motor Cars of the World, 2nd Series	1962	£4.00	—
25	Red Indians, 1st Series	1960	60p	£15.00
25	Red Indians, 2nd Series	1960	—	£10.00
25	Top Secret, 1st Series	1963	£2.25	—
25	Top Secret, 2nd Series	1963	£2.25	—

GDS CARDS (Commercial)

Qty		Date	Odds	Sets
L20	Champion Hurdle	2000	—	£12.00
L20	Cheltenham Gold Cup	2000	—	£12.00
L16	Derby Winners 1953-1968	2000	—	£10.00
L20	Famous Jockeys – Series 1	2001	—	£9.50
L20	Famous Trainers – Series 1	2001	—	£9.50
L20	Grand National	2000	—	£9.50
L16	Great Racehorses of Our Time	2000	—	£14.00
L20	Heads of Famous Winners	2001	—	£9.50
L16	Lester Piggott's Classic Winners	2000	—	£10.00

GEES FOOD PRODUCTS

30	Kings and Queens	1961	—	£12.50
16	See Britain by Coach	1959	—	£3.00

GEM LIBRARY (Periodical)

MF4	Footballers — Autographed Action Series	1923	£4.50	£18.00
MF6	Footballers — Autographed Real Action Photo Series	1922	£4.00	£24.00
MF15	Footballers — Special Action Photo	1922	£3.50	£52.50
L16	Marvels of the Future	1929	£2.75	£44.00

GENERAL FOODS (S.A.) (PTY) LTD. (South Africa)

X50	Animals and Birds	1973	20p	£10.00

ALFRED GERBER (Cheese)

M143	Glorious Switzerland	1952	£1.20	—

GIRLS CINEMA (Periodical)

F6	Film Stars (Autographed)	1929	£5.50	£33.00

GIRLS FRIEND (Periodical)

M6	Actresses (Silk)	1913	£9.00	£54.00

GIRLS MIRROR (Periodical)

MF10	Actors & Actresses	1922	£3.50	£35.00

GIRLS WEEKLY

12	Flower Fortune Cards	1912	£12.50	—

GLENGETTIE TEA

25	Animals of the World	1964	—	£3.00
25	Birds and Their Eggs	1970	—	£6.00
25	British Locomotives	1959	—	£3.00

GLENGETTIE TEA — cont.

Qty		Date	Odds	Sets
25	Do You Know?	1970	—	£2.00
25	Historical Scenes	1968	—	£2.00
25	History of the Railways, 1st Series	1974	—	£2.50
25	History of the Railways, 2nd Series	1974	—	£2.50
25	International Air-Liners	1963	—	£2.50
25	Medals of the World (Black Back)	1959	—	£2.50
25	(Blue Back)	1959	—	£10.00
25	Modern Transport (Black Back)	1963	—	£12.50
25	(Blue Back)	1963	—	£14.00
25	Naval Battles	1971	—	£2.50
25	Rare British Birds	1967	—	£5.00
25	Sovereigns, Consorts & Rulers of G.B., 1st	1970	80p	£20.00
25	Sovereigns, Consorts & Rulers of G.B., 2nd	1970	80p	£20.00
25	The British Army 1815 (Black Back)	1976	—	£3.00
25	(Blue Back)	1976	—	£2.50
25	Trains of the World	1966	—	£4.00
25	Veteran and Vintage Cars	1966	—	£15.00
25	Wild Flowers	1961	—	£8.00

GLENTONS LTD. (Shop)

24	World's Most Beautiful Butterflies	1910	£6.50	—

J. GODDARD & SONS LTD. (Metal Polish)

L4	Cleaning a Silver Teapot	1928	£3.50	—
L3	Four Generations	1923	£1.65	£5.00
L12	London Views	1925	£1.75	£21.00
L12	Old Silver	1924	£1.25	£15.00
L9	Old Silver at the Victoria & Albert Museum	1933	£2.00	£18.00
L12	Ports of the World	1928	£2.25	£27.00
L12	Present Day Silverware	1937	£1.50	£18.00
L4	Silverware with Flowers I	1928	£2.00	£8.00
L8	Silverware with Flowers II	1933	£2.00	£16.00
L2	Use & Cleaning of Silverware I	1926	75p	£1.50
L6	Use & Cleaning of Silverware II	1937	£3.50	£21.00
L8	Views of Leicester	1934	£4.25	£34.00
L12	Views of Old Leicester	1928	£4.50	£54.00

GOLD ENTERTAINMENT INC. (U.S.A.)

X5	Babe Ruth Series (Holograms)	1992	—	£10.00

GOLDEN ERA (Commercial)

T25	Aircraft of the First World War	1993	—	£7.50
L7	A.J.S.	1995	—	£3.00
L7	Alfa Romeo	1998	—	£3.00
L7	Antique Dolls	1996	—	£3.00
L7	Ariel	1995	—	£3.00
L10	Austin	1996	—	£3.75
L7	Aston Martin	1993	—	£3.00
L7	Aston Martin – The Post-War Competition Cars	2001	—	£3.00
L7	Austin Healey: The Big Healeys 1953-68	1995	—	£3.00

GOLDEN ERA (Commercial) — cont.

Qty		*Date*	*Odds*	*Sets*
L10	British Buses of the 1950s	1999	—	£3.75
L10	British Buses of the 1960s	1999	—	£3.75
L10	British Lorries 1950s & 1960s	1999	—	£3.75
L10	British Military Vehicles of WWII	2000	—	£3.75
T25	British Motor Cycles of the Fifties	1993	—	£7.50
L7	British Tanks of WWII	2000	—	£3.00
L7	British Vans of the 1950s	2002	—	£3.00
L7	British Vans of the 1960s	2002	—	£3.00
L7	BSA Motor Cycles	1993	—	£3.00
L7	BSA Motor Cycles, 2nd Series	1999	—	£3.00
L26	Cat Portraits	1995	—	£7.50
L25	Cats	1993	—	£7.50
L7	Citroen 2CV Models	2001	—	£3.00
L10	Classic American Motor Cycles	1998	—	£3.75
L9	Classic BMW	1999	—	£3.75
L26	Classic British Motor Cars	1992	—	£7.50
T25	Classic British Motor Cycles of the 1950s & 1960s	1993	—	£7.50
L7	Classic Citroen Models	2001	—	£3.00
L7	Classic Ducati	1999	—	£3.00
L7	Classic Ferrari F1 1961-2000	2002	—	£3.00
L7	Classic Fiat Models	2002	—	£3.00
L7	Classic Honda	1999	—	£3.00
L10	Classic 'Jeep'	2002	—	£3.75
L7	Classic Kawasaki	1999	—	£3.00
L10	Classic Lorries of the 1950s	2000	—	£3.75
L10	Classic Lorries of the 1960s	2000	—	£3.75
L7	Classic Lotus	1995	—	£3.00
L7	Classic Lotus — 2nd Series	1997	—	£3.00
L10	Classic Mercedes	2000	—	£3.75
L7	Classic MG	1992	—	£3.00
L7	Classic MG —2nd Series	1993	—	£3.00
L7	Classic MG Sports Cars	1996	—	£3.00
L7	Classic Morgan Sports Cars	1997	—	£3.00
L13	Classic Porsche	1996	—	£4.50
L7	Classic Rally Cars of the 70s	2001	—	£3.00
L7	Classic Rally Cars of the 80s	2001	—	£3.00
L7	Classic Rolls Royce Models	1997	—	£3.00
L7	Classic Rover	1995	—	£3.00
L10	Classic Scooters	2000	—	£3.75
L7	Classic Suzuki	1999	—	£3.00
L10	Classic Tractors	1998	—	£3.75
L7	Classic TVR	1997	—	£3.00
L13	Classic V.W.	1993	—	£4.50
L7	Classic Volkswagen Golf Gti 1975-1992	2002	—	£3.00
L7	Classic Volkswagen Karmann Ghia 1955-1974	2002	—	£3.00
L7	Classic Yamaha	1999	—	£3.00
L7	Cobra	1996	—	£3.00
X10	Corvette	1994	—	£4.50
L7	Dolls	1996	—	£3.00
L7	Escort (Twin-Cam, RS and Mexico)	1999	—	£3.00
L7	Escort (Works Rally)	1999	—	£3.00
L10	F1 Champions 1991-2000	2001	—	£3.75
X10	Famous Bombers	1997	—	£4.50
X10	Famous Fighters	1997	—	£4.50
L10	Famous TT Riders	1998	—	£3.75
L7	Ferrari 1950s and 1960s	2003	—	£3.00
L7	Ferrari 1970s and 1980s	2003	—	£3.00

Qty		Date	Odds	Sets
L6	Ford Executive	1994	—	£3.00
L10	Ford in the Sixties	1996	—	£3.75
L7	Ford RS Performance Models 1983-92	2001	—	£3.00
L7	Ford XR Models 1980-89	2001	—	£3.00
L10	Formula 1	1996	—	£3.75
L7	German Military Vehicles of WWII	2001	—	£3.00
L7	Graham & Damon Hill	2000	—	£3.00
L10	Grand Prix Greats	1996	—	£3.75
L26	Grand Prix: The Early Years	1992	—	£7.50
L10	Heavy Haulage	2000	—	£3.75
L7	Jaguar Classics	1992	—	£3.00
L7	Jaguar Classics, 2nd Series	1993	—	£3.00
L7	Jaguar Classics, 3rd Series	1997	—	£3.00
L7	Jim Clark	2000	—	£3.00
L7	Lambretta	2000	—	£3.00
L7	Lancia	1998	—	£3.00
L7	Land Rover Discovery 1989-98	2001	—	£3.00
L7	Land Rover Legends Series I	2000	—	£3.00
L7	Land Rover Legends Series II	2000	—	£3.00
L7	Land Rover Legends Series III	2000	—	£3.00
L7	Land Rover Ninety, One Ten and Defender	2000	—	£3.00
L7	Land Rover Series I	1996	—	£3.00
L7	Land Rover Series II	1996	—	£3.00
L7	Land Rover Series III	1996	—	£3.00
L10	London's Buses of the Post-War Years	1997	—	£3.75
L10	London's Buses of the Pre-War Years	1997	—	£3.75
L10	London's Country Buses of the Post-War Years	2000	—	£3.75
L7	Matchless	1995	—	£3.00
L7	Mercedes SL	1994	—	£3.00
L10	Micro & Bubble Cars	2000	—	£3.75
L10	Mini – Special Editions	1999	—	£3.75
L9	Morris Minor	1993	—	£3.75
P4	Morris Minor Van	1994	—	£2.25
L9	Morris Minor – Fifty Years	1998	—	£3.75
L10	Motorcycling Greats	1997	—	£3.75
X10	Mustang	1994	—	£4.50
L7	Norton Motor Cycles	1993	—	£3.00
L7	Norton Motor Cycles, 2nd Series	1998	—	£3.00
L7	Old Teddy Bears	1995	—	£3.00
P4	Police Vehicles	1994	—	£2.25
L7	Porsche 356 1950-65	2003	—	£3.00
L7	Porsche 911 1963-77	2003	—	£3.00
L7	Porsche 911 1978-98	2003	—	£3.00
L7	Racing & Rallying Coopers of the 60s	2000	—	£3.00
L7	Range Rover	1996	—	£3.00
L7	Senna – The Legend Lives On	2000	—	£3.00
L7	Spitfire (Triumph)	1994	—	£3.00
L7	Sporting Ford	1992	—	£3.00
L7	Spridget – Austin-Healey Sprint & MG Midget	2002	—	£3.00
L13	Superbikes of the 70s	2000	—	£4.50
L7	Tanks of WWII	2000	—	£3.00
L7	Teddies	1997	—	£3.00
L7	Teddy Bears (Antique)	1994	—	£3.00
L7	The Classic Bentley	1997	—	£3.00

GOLDEN ERA (Commercial) — cont.

Qty		*Date*	*Odds*	*Sets*
L7	The E - Type Collection	1993	—	£3.00
L10	The Ford Capri	1995	—	£3.75
L7	The Ford Cortina Story 1962-1982	2002	—	£3.00
L7	The London Taxi	2001	—	£3.00
L10	The Mini Legend	1995	—	£3.75
L7	The Ringmaster (Michael Schumacher)	2002	—	£3.00
L7	The World Famous Mini Cooper	1994	—	£3.00
L10	Thirty Five Years of the Mini	1993	—	£3.75
L10	Traction Engines	1999	—	£3.75
L7	Tractors of the Fifties	1999	—	£3.00
L7	Tractors of the Sixties	1999	—	£3.00
L7	TR Collection	1992	—	£3.00
L7	Triumph Motor Cycles	1993	—	£3.00
L7	Triumph Motor Cycles, 2nd Series	1998	—	£3.00
L7	Triumph Saloon Cars – Sixties and Seventies	2002	—	£3.00
L7	Triumph Stag 1970–1977	1995	—	£3.00
L7	U.S. Military Vehicles of WWII	2001	—	£3.00
L7	Vauxhall – Classic Vauxhalls of the 1950s & 1960s	2002	—	£3.00
L7	Velocette Motor Cycles	1993	—	£3.00
L7	Vespa	2000	—	£3.00
L7	Vincent	1995	—	£3.00
L7	VW Beetle 1949-66	1999	—	£3.00
L7	VW Beetle 1967-80	1999	—	£3.00
L7	VW Transporter 1950-79	1999	—	£3.00
SPORTS SERIES				
M20	Famous Footballers by Stubbs – Arsenal	2001	—	£5.00
M21	Famous Footballers by Stubbs – Aston Villa	2002	—	£5.00
M21	Famous Footballers by Stubbs – Chelsea	2001	—	£5.00
M21	Famous Footballers by Stubbs – Leeds United	2001	—	£5.00
M20	Famous Footballers by Stubbs – Liverpool	2001	—	£5.00
M20	Famous Footballers by Stubbs – Manchester United	2001	—	£5.00
M21	Famous Footballers by Stubbs – Newcastle United	2002	—	£5.00
M21	Famous Footballers by Stubbs – Spurs	2001	—	£5.00
M21	Famous Footballers by Stubbs – West Ham United	2002	—	£5.00

GOLDEN FLEECE (Australia)

X36	Pedigree Dogs	1972	—	£25.00

GOLDEN GRAIN TEA

25	Birds	1970	80p	£20.00
25	British Cavalry Uniforms of the 19th Century	1964	—	£5.00
25	Garden Flowers	1971	—	£2.50
25	Passenger Liners	1970	—	£5.00

GOLDEN WONDER (Potato Crisps)

24	Soccer All Stars	1978	75p	£18.00
14	Space Cards (Round Corners)	1979	—	£2.00
14	(Square Corners)	1979	—	£3.00
24	Sporting All Stars	1979	—	£3.50
24	TV All Stars	1979	—	£2.50
36	World Cup Soccer All Stars	1978	75p	—

GOLF GIFTS LTD. (Commercial)

Qty		*Date*	*Odds*	*Sets*
M24	Ryder Cup '89	1991	—	£12.50

GOODIES LTD. (Confectionery)

50	Doctor Who and The Daleks	1965	£9.00	—
25	Flags and Emblems	1961	—	£3.50
25	Indian Tribes	1975	£2.75	—
25	Mini Monsters	1975	£1.40	£35.00
24	Olympics	1972	£2.25	£54.00
25	Pirates	1976	£1.80	£45.00
25	Prehistoric Animals	1969	£2.75	—
25	Robbers & Thieves	1976	£1.60	£40.00
25	The Monkees, First Series	1967	£1.20	£30.00
25	The Monkees, Second Series	1968	£3.50	—
25	Vanishing Animals	1977	£1.60	£40.00
25	Weapons through the Ages	1974	£1.40	£35.00
25	Wicked Monarchs	1973	£1.30	£32.50
25	Wide World/People of Other Lands	1968	£1.30	£32.50
25	Wild Life	1977	£1.40	£35.00
25	World Cup	1974	£2.40	£60.00

D. W. GOODWIN & CO. (Flour)

36	Careers for Boys & Girls	1930	£7.50	—
24	Extra Rhymes, Second Series	1930	£12.00	—
36	Flags of All Nations	1930	£5.00	£180.00
36	Jokes Series	1930	£10.00	—
36	Optical Illusions	1930	£11.50	—
X60	Recipe Cards (Vertical Back, 1-60)	1930	£2.00	—
X60	Recipe Cards (Horizontal Back, 301-360)	1930	£2.00	—
36	Ships Series	1930	£10.00	—
25	Wireless	1930	£12.50	—
36	World Interest Series	1930	£6.50	—
24	World's Most Beautiful Birds	1930	*£8.25*	—
24	World's Most Beautiful Fishes	1930	£9.00	—

WILLIAM GOSSAGE & SONS LTD. (Soap)

48	British Birds & Their Eggs	1924	£2.50	£120.00
48	Butterflies & Moths	1924	£1.50	£72.00

GOWERS & BURGONS (Tea)

25	British Birds and Their Nests	1970	—	£7.00
25	Family Pets	1964	—	£2.00
25	People & Places	1970	—	£2.00
25	Prehistoric Animals	1969	£1.00	£25.00
25	Sailing Ships through the Ages	1971	£1.00	£25.00
25	The Circus	1964	*£1.40*	—
25	Veteran and Vintage Cars	1965	£1.20	£30.00
25	Veteran Racing Cars	1964	£1.20	£30.00

GRAFFITI INC. (U.S.A.)

X90	Goldeneye	1995	—	£20.00

GRAIN PRODUCTS (New Zealand)

Qty		*Date*	*Odds*	*Sets*
L20	Fire Engines	1988	—	£15.00
P10	Vintage & Veteran Cars	1985	—	£10.00

GRANGER'S

12	Dr. Mabuse Series	1926	£8.50	£100.00

GRANOSE FOODS LTD.

M48	Adventures of Billy the Buck	1956	—	£4.00
L16	Air Transport	1957	—	£2.50
L16	Animal Life	1957	—	£2.50
25	Animals in the Service of Man	1965	*£2.50*	—
L16	Aquatic & Reptile Life	1957	—	£2.50
M48	King of the Air	1956	40p	—
M48	Life Story of Blower the Whale	1956	60p	£30.00
M48	Lone Leo the Cougar	1955	50p	£25.00
L20	150 Years of British Locomotives	1981	—	£16.00
L16	Our Winged Friends	1957	35p	—
L16	Plant Life	1957	*75p*	—
M48	Silver Mane the Timber Wolf	1955	—	£4.00
L16	Space Travel	1957	—	*£6.00*
M48	Tippytail the Grizzly Bear	1956	—	£4.00
L16	Water Transport	1957	—	£2.00
L16	World Wide Visits	1957	—	£2.00

WILLIAM GRANT & SONS LTD. (Distillers)

25	Clan Tartans	1993	—	£12.50

GREGG (Jelly, New Zealand)

M48	Aquatic Birds	1974	30p	—
M40	Introduced and Other Birds	1967	30p	£12.00
M40	Land Birds of New Zealand	1974	30p	£12.00
M40	Native Birds of New Zealand	1971	30p	£12.00
M35	Rare and Endangered Birds	1974	—	£12.50
M40	Remarkable Birds of the World	1974	50p	—
M35	Unusual Birds of the World	1974	—	£11.00

ARTHUR GUINNESS SON & CO. (GREAT BRITAIN) LTD.

P18	The Pint Size Guinness Book of Records (Booklets)	1984	£1.20	£22.00

H.B. ICE CREAM LTD. (Ireland)

24	Do You Know	1968	£3.00	—

H.P. REPRINT (Commercial)

L11	Famous Golfers of the 1920s (The Liverpool & London & Globe Ins. Co. Ltd.)	1996	—	£6.00
M18	Golf Girl Series (Dah Tung Nan Tob. Co. China)	1996	—	£6.00

NICHOLAS HALL & SONS (Tea)

Qty		*Date*	*Odds*	*Sets*
25	War Series	1917	£17.50	—

HALPINS (Tea)

25	Aircraft of the World	1958	—	£2.50
L20	Aircraft of the World (Double Cards)	1958	£1.20	£25.00
25	Nature Studies	1958	—	£4.00

HAMPSHIRE CRICKET CLUB

24	Sunday League Era	1987	—	£6.00

HAPPY HOME (Periodical)

M32	Child Studies (Silk)	1912	£13.50	—
M9	Flags (Silk)	1914	£7.00	£63.00
M9	Our Lucky Flowers (Silk)	1912	£12.50	—
K14	The Happy Home Silk Button (Silk)	1914	£6.50	£91.00
M12	Women on War Work (Silk)	1914	£8.00	£96.00

HARBOUR REPROGRAPHICS

30	Cricket, Surrey v Yorkshire	1988	—	£9.00

HARDEN BROS. & LINDSAY LTD. (Tea)

50	Animals of the World	1960	40p	£20.00
50	British Birds and Their Eggs	1960	50p	£25.00
50	National Pets	1961	—	£5.00

HARRISON (Pomade)

25	Beauties	1902	£24.00	£600.00

JOHN HAWKINS & SONS LTD. (Cotton)

LF30	The Story of Cotton	1925	£5.00	£150.00

HEINEKEN (Beer)

P12	The Heineken Story (Beer Mats)	1976	—	£6.00

HEINZ (Foods)

E1	Australian Cricket Team	1964	—	£6.00

S. HENDERSON & SONS LTD. (Biscuits)

T132	General Interest Series	1908	£10.00	£1300.00

COUNTRIES OF ISSUE

Nowadays one is accustomed to reading of multi-national corporations. Surprisingly many of the larger cigarette card issuers were such almost a century ago. Duke issued cards in South Africa, Goodwin in Australia, Allen & Ginter in Britain and the Canadian firm Ritchie in Germany, Australia, India and England. The American Tobacco Co. issued many cards in Britain with its Old Gold brand, and eventually through its purchase of Ogden, which precipitated the Tobacco War. British firms flourished in their expected spheres of influence, the British Empire, with many issues in Malta, India and Australia. In some cases a series was prepared specifically for one country, but often a set would be issued in several areas.

Sometimes the series had to be adapted to suit the requirements of the country in which it was to be issued. The text of the New Zealand version of Godfrey Phillips Annuals was amended to show different dates for "planting out", while Ardath changed just one card of the Mitchell Our Empire set to include the current New Zealand Prime Minister. In the case of the Player Hints on Association Football the fronts were re-drawn to show Oriental features for the B.A.T. Chinese set.

The criterion in this catalogue for determining whether series should be shown in Part 1 or Part 2 is generally based on the main location of the issuer rather than the area of issue. So all American based Companies will be found in Part 2. Ritchie, which issued cards in Britain, is essentially a Canadian firm, so is also in Part 2. Firms such as International Tobacco Co. and A. & M. Wix, which were based in England, but most of whose issues were abroad, are nevertheless shown in Part 1. One major exception is British American Tobacco Co., which was incorporated in Britain, but all of whose cigarettes were sold abroad, and is therefore shown in Part 2. The decision has in several cases been marginal, and entirely subjective, so when in doubt consult BOTH sections!

B.A.T. ISSUES

In 1902 at the conclusion of the "Tobacco War", the British American Tobacco Co. was incorporated in Britain for the purpose of marketing all I.T.C. and A.T.C. tobacco products in countries other than the U.S.A., Cuba, Great Britain and Ireland.

In many British Empire countries B.A.T. began to market under the name of a subsidiary Company. In Canada it was the Imperial Tobacco Co. of Canada, while in India the Imperial Tobacco Co. of India shared the stage with the Peninsular Tobacco Co. In South Africa the dominant name was United Tobacco Co. and in South America Cia Chilena and Cia Nobleza. In Australia the majority of issues bore the Wills name, either with Capstan or Vice-Regal, except that some also appeared as Havelock Cigarettes, with no issuer's name. Brands in New Zealand appeared under the names of Lambert & Butler, Player and Wills, as well as the local Dominion Tobacco Co; local arrangements were made with companies such as Ardath, as may be deduced from their issue in New Zealand of their versions of sets such as Churchman Eastern Proverbs, Player Tennis and Ogden Swimming Diving & Life Saving.

Card issues appeared with all the above firms' names, as well as some, particularly earlier issues such as the tobacco war Beauties, which have the B.A.T. name. There were also many in foreign languages such as Motor Cigarettes (Portugal), Albert (Belgium) and Gold Dollar (Germany), as well as a number in Chinese and Siamese characters. A large section of B.A.T.'s card output however appears with no clues as to the issuer, both with printed backs (often mentioning cigarettes) and with plain backs.

When the B.A.T. issue utilises the name of a British firm, such as Ogden or Wills, then in the Catalogue the cards will be found listed under that firm, often in a separate group. Anonymous series that were issued exclusively in Canada or South Africa are included in Part 2 under Imperial Tobacco Co. of Canada or United Tobacco Co. respectively. All other Anonymous sets known to have been produced by B.A.T. are listed under that firm in Part 2.

A more detailed explanation of the foundation and ramifications of B.A.T. may be found in the B.A.T. Book which is combined with the Cigarette Card Issues of Wills and is priced at £20.

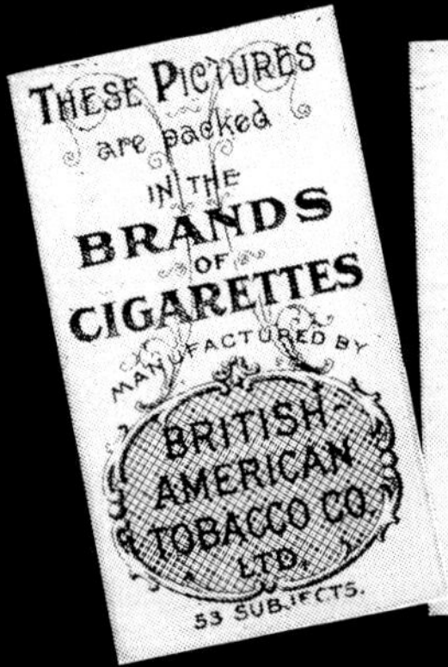

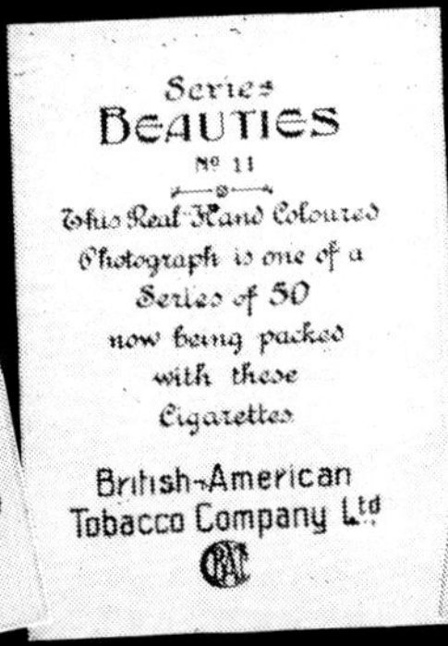

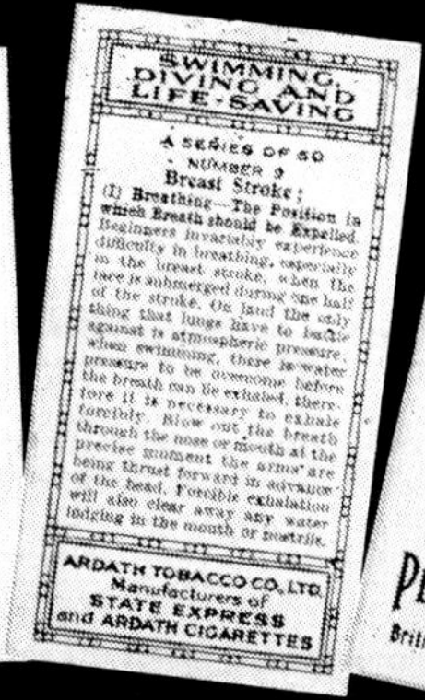

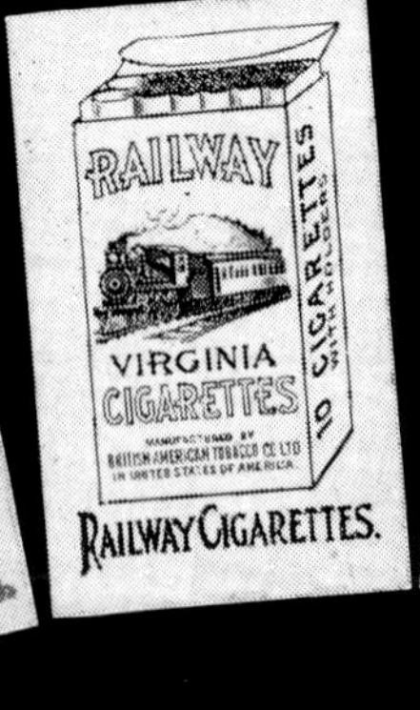

HERALD ALARMS

Qty		Date	Odds	Sets
10	Feudal Lords	1986	—	£20.00
X10	Feudal Lords	1986	—	£10.00

HERON PETROL

K16	Holidays	1960	£1.25	—

HERTFORDSHIRE POLICE FORCE

X12	Postage Stamps	1985	—	£6.00

HIGSONS (Brewery)

X26	Famous Old Higsonians	1987	£1.25	—

JOHN HINDHAUGH & CO. (Bread)

25	Railway Engines	1913	£30.00	—

HITCHMAN'S DAIRIES LTD.

25	Aircraft of World War II (Black Back)	1966	—	£10.00
25	(Blue Back)	1966	—	£17.50
25	Animals of the World	1964	—	£12.50
25	British Birds and their Nests	1970	—	£20.00
25	British Railways	1971	—	£3.50
25	Buses and Trams	1966	—	£3.00
25	Merchant Ships of the World	1970	—	£12.50
25	Modern Wonders	1962	—	£7.50
25	Naval Battles	1971	—	£5.00
25	People & Places	1971	—	£4.00
25	Regimental Uniforms of the Past	1973	—	£2.50
25	Science in the 20th Century	1966	—	£6.00
25	The Story of Milk	1965	—	£12.50
25	Trains of the World	1970	—	£25.00

HOADLEY'S CHOCOLATES (Australia)

50	British Empire Kings & Queens	1940	£1.50	£75.00
?33	Cricketers (Black Front)	1928	£12.50	—
36	Cricketers (Brown Front)	1933	£8.25	£300.00
50	Early Australian Series	1938	£1.60	£80.00
50	Empire Games and Test Teams	1932	£7.20	£360.00
40	Test Cricketers	1936	£10.00	£400.00
M36	Test Cricketers (Different)	1938	£12.50	—
50	The Birth of a Nation	1938	£1.60	£80.00
50	Victorian Footballers (Heads,1-50)	1938	£2.40	£120.00
50	Victorian Footballers (51-100)	1938	£2.40	£120.00
50	Victorian Footballers (Action)	1938	£2.60	£130.00
50	Wild West Series	1938	£1.70	£85.00

HOBBYPRESS GUIDES (Books)

Qty		Date	Odds	Sets
20	Preserved Railway Locomotives	1983	—	£3.00
20	Preserved Steam Railways, 1st Series	1983	—	£3.00
20	Preserved Steam Railways, 2nd Series	1984	—	£3.00
20	The World's Great Cricketers	1984	—	£7.50

THOMAS HOLLOWAY LTD. (Pharmaceutics)

X39	Natural History Series (Animals' Heads)	1900	£6.50	£260.00
X39	Natural History Series (Birds)	1900	£6.50	£260.00
X60	Natural History Series (Full Length)	1900	£6.50	£390.00
X50	Pictorial History of the Sports and Pastimes of All Nations	1900	£10.00	£500.00

HOME & COLONIAL STORES LTD.

26	Advertising Alphabet	1914	£6.00	£156.00
M100	Flag Pictures	1916	£3.60	—
M40	War Heroes	1916	£5.50	£220.00
M40	War Pictures	1916	£5.00	£200.00
100	War Pictures (Different)	1916	£3.50	£350.00

HOME COUNTIES DAIRIES TEA

25	Country Life	1964	—	£4.00
25	International Air-Liners	1965	—	£3.00
25	The Story of Milk	1965	—	£5.00

HOME MIRROR (Periodical)

M4	Cinema Star Pictures (Silk)	1919	£12.50	£50.00

HOME WEEKLY (Periodical)

12	Little Charlie Cards	1920	£17.50	—

GEORGE W. HORNER & CO. (Confectionery)

P24	Wireless Cards	1926	£12.50	—

HORNIMAN (Tea)

P10	Boating Ways	1910	£18.00	—
P12	British Birds & Eggs	1910	£16.00	—
48	Dogs	1961	—	£6.00
P10	Naval Heroes	1910	£17.50	£175.00
48	Pets	1960	—	£6.00
48	Wild Animals	1958	—	£6.00

HORSLEY'S STORES

Qty		*Date*	*Odds*	*Sets*
25	British Uniforms of the 19th Century	1968	—	£10.00
25	Castles of Britain	1968	£1.25	—
25	Family Pets	1968	—	£8.00

VAN HOUTEN (Chocolate)

P12	How Nature Protects the Weak	1908	£10.00	£120.00

HUGHES BISCUITS

20	War Series	1915	£13.50	—

HULL CITY FOOTBALL CLUB

X20	Footballers	1950	£10.00	£200.00

HUNT CROPP & SONS (Vedast)

15	Characters from Dickens	1912	£10.00	£150.00

HUNTLEY & PALMER (Biscuits)

63 Page Illustrated Reference Book — £10.00

P12	Animals	1900	£6.50	£78.00
P12	Aviation	1908	£50.00	£600.00
P12	Biscuits in Various Countries	1900	£5.50	£66.00
P6	Biscuits with Travellers	1900	£6.50	£39.00
P12	Children of Nations I (Gold Border)	1900	£6.00	£72.00
P12	Children of Nations II (White Border)	1900	£5.50	£60.00
P12	Children at Leisure & Play	1900	£6.50	£78.00
P12	Harvests of the World	1900	£15.00	£180.00
P12	Hunting	1900	£7.50	£90.00
P8	Inventors	1900	£16.50	£132.00
X11	Rhondes Enfantines	1900	£17.50	—
P12	Scenes with Biscuits	1900	£5.00	£60.00
X8	Shakespearian Series	1900	£6.00	£48.00
P12	Soldiers of Various Countries	1900	£11.50	£138.00
P12	Sports (Semi-Circular Background)	1900	£12.50	£175.00
P12	Sports (Plain Background)	1900	£12.50	£200.00
P12	The Seasons	1900	£11.00	£132.00
P12	Travelling During the 19th Century	1900	£17.00	—
P12	Views of Italy & The French Riviera	1900	£8.50	£100.00
P12	Warships of Nations	1900	£11.00	£132.00
P8	Watteau	1900	£6.50	£52.00
P8	Wonders of the World	1900	£17.00	£136.00

HUSTLER SOAP

Qty		Date	Odds	Sets
20	Animals, First Series	1925	£1.00	£20.00
20	Animals, Second Series	1925	£1.00	£20.00
20	Animals, Third Series	1925	£1.00	£20.00
30	Regimental Nicknames	1924	£2.00	£60.00

R. HYDE & CO. LTD. (Bird Seed)

80	British Birds	1928	£1.50	£120.00
80	Cage Birds	1930	£1.10	£88.00
80	Canary Culture	1930	£1.00	£100.00
M10	Cartoons	1924	£12.00	—
M24	Modern Wonders	1924	£12.00	£288.00

I.P.C. MAGAZINES LTD.

M25	Lindy's Cards of Fortune	1975	—	£5.00
M160	My Favourite Soccer Stars (Blue Back)	1970	75p	£120.00
M160	My Favourite Soccer Stars (Red Back)	1971	75p	£120.00

IDEAL ALBUMS LTD.

L25	Boxing Greats	1991	—	£8.50
L2	Promotional Cards	1991	—	60p

IMPERIAL PUBLISHING LTD. (Commercial)

Officially authorised reprints of Imperial Tobacco Co. series

50	A.F.C. Nicknames (Ogdens)	1996	—	£8.50
50	Aircraft of the R.A.F. (Player)	1990	—	£8.50
25	Angling (Mitchell)	1993	—	£6.00
25	Aviation (Lambert & Butler)	1997	—	£6.00
15	Billiard Terms (Salmon & Gluckstein)	1997	—	£5.00
25	Boxing (Franklyn Davey)	2002	—	£6.00
L7	Cathedrals (Wills)	2000	—	£2.50
L24	Cats (Player)	1997	—	£8.50
25	Characters from Dickens, 2nd Series (Player)	1990	—	£6.00
L25	Country Sports (Player)	2000	—	£8.50
50	Cricket Caricatures by "RIP" (Player)	1993	—	£8.50
50	Cricketers 1930 (Player)	2000	—	£8.50
50	Cricketers 1934 (Player)	1993	—	£8.50
25	Dance Band Leaders (Lambert & Butler)	1992	—	£6.00
50	Dog's Heads (Player, Eire)	1994	—	£8.50
50	Firefighting Appliances (Player)	1991	—	£8.50
50	Flags & Funnels of Leading Steamship Lines (Ogdens)	1997	—	£8.50
54	Frisky (with 2 instructions) (Churchman)	1994	—	£8.50
50	Gilbert & Sullivan, 2nd Series (Player)	1990	—	£8.50
25	Highland Clans (Player)	1997	—	£6.00
25	Hints & Tips for Motorists (Lambert & Butler)	1994	—	£6.00
50	Horsemanship (Lambert & Butler)	1994	—	£8.50
50	Kings & Queens of England (Player)	1990	—	£8.50
50	Landmarks in Railway Progress (Churchman)	1994	—	£8.50
25	London Characters (Lambert & Butler)	1992	—	£6.00
50	Military Aircraft (Wills)	1991	—	£8.50

Qty		Date	Odds	Sets
50	Military Motors(Wills)	1994	—	£8.50
50	Motor Cars, A Series (Player)	1990	—	£8.50
50	Motor Cycles (Lambert & Butler)	1990	—	£8.50
50	Naval Dress & Badges (Wills)	1997	—	£8.50
50	Old English Garden Flowers, Second Series (Wills)	1994	—	£8.50
L25	Old Hunting Prints (Player)	1997	—	£8.50
L6	Old Inns (Wills)	1990	—	£2.50
L25	Old Naval Prints (Player)	1997	—	£8.50
L25	Picturesque London (Player)	1997	—	£8.50
50	Pioneers (Churchman)	2000	—	£9.50
25	Poultry (1-25, with Ogdens on Front)	1998	—	£6.00
25	Poultry, 2nd Series (26-50) (Ogdens)	2000	—	£6.00
50	Poultry (Player)	2002	—	£8.50
50	Prominent Golfers (Churchman)	1993	—	£8.50
25	Prominent Racehorses (Faulkner)	1993	—	£6.00
25	Prominent Rugby Players (Smith)	1992	—	£8.00
L40	Puppies (Wills)	1990	—	£12.50
50	Railway Engines, 1924 (Wills)	1996	—	£8.50
50	Railway Engines, 1936 (Wills)	1993	—	£8.50
50	Railway Equipment (Wills)	1993	—	£8.50
50	Railway Locomotives (Wills)	1993	—	£8.50
25	Regimental Crests & Collar Badges (Mitchell)	1993	—	£6.00
50	Regimental Standards and Cap Badges (Player)	1993	—	£8.50
50	Regimental Uniforms, 2nd Series (51-100) (Player)	1995	—	£8.50
50	Roses, A Series (Wills)	1994	—	£8.50
50	Rugby Internationals (Wills)	1996	—	£8.50
50	Ships, Flags & Cap Badges (Player)	1997	—	£8.50
50	Soldiers of the King (Ogdens)	1993	—	£8.50
M48	The R.A.F. at Work (Churchman)	1995	—	£14.00
25	The World's Dreadnoughts (Wills)	1994	—	£6.00
L24	Treasures of Britain (Player)	1995	—	£8.50
L25	Types of Horses (Player)	1998	—	£8.50
50	Uniforms of the Territorial Army (Player)	1990	—	£8.50
50	War Incidents, 2nd Series (Wills)	1995	—	£8.50
50	Waterloo (Wills)	1990	—	£10.00
L25	Wild Birds (Player)	1997	—	£8.50
25	Winter Sports (Lambert & Butler)	1998	—	£6.00
50	World's Locomotives (Lambert & Butler)	1989	—	£8.50

ORIGINAL ISSUES

Qty		Date	Odds	Sets
L20	American Golfers	1990	—	£8.50
L24	Birds of Britain	1994	—	£8.50
L6	Breeds of Cats	2000	—	£3.00
	Imperial Dog Collection			
L6	Airedale Terriers	1999	—	£3.00
L6	Border Collies	1999	—	£3.00
L6	Boxers	1999	—	£3.00
L6	Bulldogs	1999	—	£3.00
L6	Cocker Spaniels	1999	—	£3.00
L6	Dachshunds	1999	—	£3.00
L6	Dalmatians	1999	—	£3.00
L6	Dobermann	1999	—	£3.00
L6	German Shepherds	1999	—	£3.00
L6	Golden Retrievers	1999	—	£3.00
L6	Greyhounds	2000	—	£3.00
L6	Jack Russell Terriers	1999	—	£3.00

IMPERIAL PUBLISHING LTD. (Commercial) — cont.

Qty		Date	Odds	Sets
L6	Labrador Retrievers	1999	—	£3.00
L6	Pekingese	1999	—	£3.00
L6	Poodles	1999	—	£3.00
L6	Scottish Terriers	1999	—	£3.00
L6	Staffordshire Bull Terriers	2000	—	£3.00
L6	West Highland White Terriers	2000	—	£3.00
L6	Yorkshire Terriers	1999	—	£3.00
L20	Native North Americans	1995	—	£8.50
L48	Olympic Champions	1993	—	£12.00
L18	Snooker Celebrities	1993	—	£12.00
L24	The History of the Olympic Games	1996	—	£7.50

INDIA & CEYLON TEA CO. LTD.

24	The Island of Ceylon	1996	£4.00	—

IN LINE (Commercial, U.S.A.)

X6	Classic Motorcycles (Prototype Set)	1992	—	£3.00
X57	Classic Motorcycles Series 1 (including Hologram)	1993	—	£10.00

INKWORKS (Commercial, U.S.A.)

X90	The Adventures of Pinocchio	1996	—	£12.00
X90	The Phantom	1966	—	£14.00

INTREPID T.C. INTERNATIONAL (Commercial, Australia)

X100	ATP Tennis Tour	1996	—	£12.00

JOHN IRWIN SONS & CO. LTD. (Tea)

12	Characters from Dickens Works	1912	£16.50	—
6	Characters from Shakespeare	1912	£16.50	£100.00
8	The European War Series	1916	£14.00	£112.00

JF SPORTING COLLECTIBLES (Commercial)

X15	Australian Cricketers – 1930	1999	—	£10.00
X36	Battle of the Roses: Pre-War Personalities	2003	—	£25.00
L25	Boxers – World Champions	2000	—	£15.00
L40	Famous Footballers 1896-97	2000	—	£25.00
M36	Football Favourites 1940/50s, 1st Series	1999	—	£15.00
M36	Football Favourites 1940/50s, 2nd Series	1999	—	£15.00
M36	Football Favourites 1940/50s, 3rd Series	1999	—	£15.00
M36	Football Favourites 1940/50s, 4th Series	2000	—	£15.00
M36	Football Favourites 1940/50s, 5th Series	2000	—	£15.00
L24	Footballers in Action 1940/50s, 1st Series	2002	—	£16.00
L24	Footballers in Action 1940/50s, 2nd Series	2002	—	£16.00
L24	Footballers in Action 1940/50s, 3rd Series	2002	—	£16.00
L24	Footballers in Action 1940/50s, 4th Series	2002	—	£16.00
X24	Gentlemen v Players: Pre-War Personalities, 1st Series	2003	—	£15.00
X24	Popular Footballers 1919-1939, 1st Series	2000	—	£16.00
X24	Popular Footballers 1919-1939, 2nd Series	2000	—	£16.00

JF SPORTING COLLECTIBLES (Commercial) — cont.

Qty		Date	Odds	Sets
X24	Popular Footballers 1919-1939, 3rd Series	2002	—	£16.00
X24	Rugby League Stars 1940/50s	2002	—	£16.00
L24	Scottish Clan Tartans, 1st Series	2002	—	£15.00
X24	Speedway All-Time Greats, A Series	1999	—	£15.00
X24	Speedway All-Time Greats, 2nd Series	1999	—	£15.00
X24	Speedway All-Time Greats, 3rd Series	2000	—	£15.00
X24	Speedway Personalities in Action, 1st Series	2000	—	£15.00
X24	Speedway Personalities in Action, 2nd Series	2000	—	£15.00
L30	Stars of Football 1940s	2002	—	£21.00
L24	Uniforms of the Royal Regiment of Artillery	2003	—	£15.00
X28	Victorian Cricket Personalities	2000	—	£20.00
X15	Wembley Speedway Stars, A Series	1999	—	£8.00
X21	Wembley Speedway Stars, 2nd Series	2000	—	£15.00
L24	World Heavyweight Boxing Champions	1999	—	£15.00
L20	World Heavyweight Championship Contenders	2000	—	£12.00

JACOB & CO. (Biscuits)

D24	Banknotes that made History (with Album)	1975	—	£2.00
D32	Famous Picture Cards from History (with Album)	1978	—	£2.00
E16	Jacob's Club Circus	1970	£3.00	£48.00
M16	Nursery Rhyme Competition	1969	£1.25	£20.00
M30	School of Dinosaurs	1994	25p	£7.50
25	Vehicles of All Ages	1924	£2.50	£62.50
25	Zoo Series (Brown Back)	1924	£1.50	£37.50
25	(Green Back)	1924	£1.00	£25.00

M. V. JASINSKI (Commercial, U.S.A.)

X36	Flash Gordon	1990	—	£15.00
X36	Flash Gordon Conquers the Universe	1992	—	£10.00
X36	Flash Gordon's Trip to Mars	1991	—	£10.00

JESK (Confectionery)

25	Buses and Trams	1959	—	£17.50

JIBCO (Tea)

28	Dominoes (2 Printings)	1956	£3.25	—
K52	Miniature Playing Cards	1956	£3.25	—
K50	Puzzle Cards	1955	£4.00	—
K25	Screen Stars (2 Printings)	1955	£4.00	—
K25	Screen Stars, 2nd Edition	1956	£1.00	£25.00

JIFFI (Condoms)

M64	Kama Sutra	1989	—	£50.00

R. L. JONES & CO. LTD. (Drink)

24	Jet Aircraft of the World	1956	—	£4.00

JUBBLY (Drink)

Qty		*Date*	*Odds*	*Sets*
50	Adventurous Lives	1967	—	£5.00

JUNIOR PASTIMES (Commercial)

51/52	Popular English Players	1951	£3.00	£150.00
52	Popular Players (Footballers)	1951	£4.00	—
51/52	Popular Railway Engines	1951	£2.20	£110.00
L77/80	Star Pix	1951	£1.60	£125.00

JUST SEVENTEEN (Magazine)

T17	Posters	1986	—	£2.00

K. P. NUTS & CRISPS

12	Sports Adventure Series	1978	—	£11.00
20	Wonderful World of Nature	1983	60p	£12.00

KANE PRODUCTS LTD. (Confectionery)

36	ATV Stars (Packets)	1957	£3.00	—
50	British Birds and Their Eggs	1960	50p	£25.00
25	Cricket Clubs & Badges	1957	—	£3.00
L50	Disc Stars	1960	£2.20	£110.00
X50	Disc Stars	1960	£1.50	£75.00
50	Dogs	1955	£2.20	£110.00
X72	Film Stars (Plain Back)	1955	£1.50	£108.00
50	Flags of All Nations	1959	—	£10.00
25	Football Clubs & Colours	1956	—	£3.00
50	Historical Characters	1957	—	£5.00
25	International Football Stars	1957	£1.00	£25.00
30	Kings and Queens	1959	—	£8.50
X30	Kings & Queens	1959	25p	£7.50
25	Modern Motor Cars	1959	—	£15.00
50	Modern Racing Cars	1954	40p	£20.00
25	National Pets Club, Part I	1958	—	£5.00
25	National Pets Club, Part II	1958	£2.20	£55.00
25	1956 Cricketers, 1st Series	1956	£1.00	£25.00
25	1956 Cricketers, 2nd Series	1956	£1.00	£25.00
25	Red Indians, 1st Series	1957	£1.00	£25.00
25	Red Indians, 2nd Series	1957	£1.20	£30.00
25	Roy Rogers Colour Series	1958	£2.20	£55.00
25	Roy Rogers Series	1957	£3.40	£85.00
50	Space Adventure	1955	—	£30.00
50	20th Century Events	1955	£1.40	£70.00
K50	Wild Animals	1954	—	£4.00

KARDOMAH (Tea)

K?500	General Interest (Various Series)	1900	£3.25	—

KAYO CARDS LTD. (U.S.A.)

Qty		*Date*	*Odds*	*Sets*
X10	Heavyweight Holograms	1992	—	£15.00

M. & S. KEECH

15	Australian Cricket Team 1905	1986	—	£3.00
15	English Cricketers 1902	1987	—	£3.00

KEEPSAKE COLLECTIBLES (Commercial, U.S.A.)

X72	The Blue and The Gray	1997	—	£20.00
X72	Wild West	1996	—	£12.50

KEILLER (Confectionery)

KF?	Actresses & Views	1905	£8.00	—
F?	Actresses & Views	1905	£8.50	—
XF18	Film Favourites	1926	£10.00	—
25	Scottish Heritage	1976	—	£6.50

KELLOGG LTD. (Cereals)

16	A History of British Military Aircraft	1963	50p	£8.00
16	Animals (3D)	1971	£3.00	—
12	Famous Firsts	1963	20p	£2.50
L20	Gardens to Visit	1988	—	£6.00
12	International Soccer Stars	1963	£1.75	£21.00
M8	International Soccer Tips	1970	£4.00	—
40	Motor Cars (Black and White)	1949	£3.00	£120.00
40	(Coloured)	1949	£4.00	£160.00
X56	Playing Cards	1986	—	£4.00
8	Prehistoric Monsters and the Present	1985	£1.00	£8.00
16	Ships of the British Navy	1962	50p	£8.00
M6	Space (Surprise Gifts)	1989	—	£2.00
12	The Story of the Bicycle	1964	£3.25	£40.00
	The Story of the Locomotive, A Series			
16	(English Issue)	1963	£1.00	£16.00
12	(Irish Issue)	1963	£4.00	£48.00
16	The Story of the Locomotive, Series 2	1963	60p	£10.00
16	(Without Series 2)	1963	£2.75	£44.00
K8	Tony Racing Stickers	1988	—	£2.00
16	Veteran Motor Cars	1962	75p	£12.00

CANADIAN ISSUES

M150	General Interest, 1st Set	1940	£1.25	£187.50
M150	General Interest, 2nd Set	1940	£1.50	—
M150	General Interest, 3rd Set	1940	£1.50	—

KENT COUNTY CONSTABULARY

X24	England World Cup Squad 1982	1982	£2.75	—
X30	England World Cup Squad 1986	1982	£2.25	£67.50
X30	Olympic Athletes	1988	£1.25	£37.50

KENT COUNTY CRICKET CLUB

Qty		Date	Odds	Sets
51	Cricketers of Kent	1986	—	£7.50

KENTUCKY FRIED CHICKEN

L20	Star Wars Episode 1	1999	—	£6.50

KIDDYS FAVOURITES LTD. (Commercial)

52	New Popular Film Stars	1950	*£3.00*	—
50	Popular Boxers	1950	£2.20	£140.00
51/52	Popular Cricketers	1948	£3.20	£165.00
65	Popular Film Stars	1950	£3.00	—
51/52	Popular Footballers	1948	£3.00	£150.00
51/52	Popular Olympics	1948	£2.50	£127.50
52	Popular Players (Hearts on Front)	1950	£4.00	—
51/52	Popular Players (Shamrocks on Front)	1950	£2.75	£140.00
52	Popular Speedway Riders	1950	£3.00	—

KINGS OF YORK (Laundry)

25	Flags of All Nations (Silk)	1954	£2.00	£50.00
30	Kings & Queens of England	1954	—	£2.50

KINGS LAUNDRIES LTD. (Walthamstow, E. London)

25	Famous Railway Engines	1953	£3.80	£95.00
25	Modern British Warplanes	1953	£3.00	£75.00
25	Modern Motor Cycles	1953	£3.20	£80.00
25	Radio & Television Stars	1953	£3.00	£75.00

KING'S SPECIALITIES (Food Products)

26	Alphabet Rhymes	1915	£12.00	—
25	"Dont's" or Lessons in Etiquette	1915	£9.00	—
25	Heroes of Famous Books	1914	£8.50	—
25	King's "Discoveries"	1915	£8.50	—
25	King's "Servants"	1915	£8.50	—
25	Proverbs	1915	£9.00	—
37	Unrecorded History	1915	£8.50	—
100	War Pictures	1915	£11.00	—
25	War Series	1915	£10.00	—
25	Where King's Supplies Grow	1914	£8.50	—

KITCHEN SINK PRESS (Commercial, U.S.A.)

X90	The Crow	1996	—	£15.00

KLENE (Confectionery)

L144	Animals of the World	1954	85p	£122.50
L144	Birds of the World	1954	85p	£122.50
L292	Film Stars	1954	£1.75	—
L50	Footballers	1936	£30.00	—

KLENE (Confectionery) — cont.

Qty		Date	Odds	Sets
L48	Natural History Sketches	1954	£3.25	—
L72	Popeye	1954	£4.50	—
L50	Shirley Temple Cards (1-50)	1935	£5.50	—
L20	Shirley Temple Cards (81-100, Coloured)	1935	£6.00	—
L60	Shirley Temple Cards (101-160)			
	(Black Title)	1935	£5.50	—
	(Blue Title, Different)	1935	£5.50	—
L50	Shirley Temple Cards (161-210)	1935	£6.00	—

KNOCKOUT (Periodical)

20	Super Planes of Today	1956	—	£5.00

KNORR (Cheese)

T6	Great Trains of Europe	1983	£3.50	—

KRAFT CHEESE

12	Historic Military Uniforms	1971	—	£2.50

KYDD'S JAMS

20	Fruits and Recipes	1912	£7.50	—

LACEY'S CHEWING GUM

50	Footballers	1925	£26.50	—
?50	Uniforms	1923	£16.50	—

F. LAMBERT & SONS LTD. (Tea)

25	Before our Time	1961	—	£2.00
25	Birds and Their Eggs	1962	—	£15.00
25	Butterflies and Moths	1960	—	£2.50
25	Cacti	1962	—	£2.50
25	Car Registration Numbers, A Series	1959	—	£5.00
25	Car Registration Numbers, Second Series	1960	80p	£20.00
25	Football Clubs and Badges	1958	—	£3.00
25	Game Birds and Wild Fowl	1964	—	£7.50
25	Historic East Anglia	1961	—	£2.50
25	Interesting Hobbies	1965	—	£10.00
25	Passenger Liners	1965	—	£10.00
25	Past & Present	1964	—	£2.50
25	People & Places	1966	—	£5.00
25	Pond Life	1964	—	£7.50
25	Sports and Games	1964	—	£3.00

LANCASHIRE CONSTABULARY

24	Cop-a-Cards	1987	—	£7.50
D11	Cop-a-Cards, Series 3	1989	—	£2.00
X12	Motor Cars	1987	—	£5.00

LANCASTER REPRINTS (Canada)

Qty		Date	Odds	Sets
X9	The Seven Ages of Golf	1995	—	£4.50

HERBERT LAND (Cycles)

30	Army Pictures, Cartoons, etc.	1915	£32.50	—

LEAF BRANDS INC. (Confectionery)

X50	Cliff Richard	1960	£2.50	—
X50	Do You Know?	1961	20p	£10.00
X90	Famous Artistes	1960	£1.60	£144.00
X50	Famous Discoveries and Adventures	1962	£1.80	£90.00
X50	Footballers	1961	£1.80	£90.00
X40	The Flag Game	1960	40p	£20.00
X50	Totem Pole Talking Signs	1962	65p	£32.50

LEGENDS WALL OF FAME (London)

L20	British Rock Legends	1992	—	£9.00

LENG PAPERS

X18	Illustrated Songs	1915	£3.50	—

LEVER BROS. (Soap)

20	British Birds and Their Nests	1961	—	£2.00
F150	Celebrities	1900	£3.75	—
L39	Celebrities	1901	£6.25	£240.00
P24	The Life of Queen Victoria (Series 3)	1902	£9.00	—

PHILLIP LEWIS AGENCIES

X54	Poster Playing Cards – First World War	1999	—	£6.00
X54	Poster Playing Cards – Railway Travel	1999	—	£6.00
X54	Poster Playing Cards – Second World War	1999	—	£6.00

LEWIS'S LTD. (Store)

FX25	Real Photos of Wild Animals	1930	£8.00	—

LIEBIG EXTRACT OF MEAT CO. (see also Oxo)

This firm issued nearly 2,000 different sets throughout Europe between 1872 and 1974. Because inclusion of all these in this volume would be impracticable we have produced a separate catalogue of Liebig cards. See separate announcement for details. Some issues are included below as a sample of the scope of these series.

6	Ancient Egyptian Monuments	1931	—	£10.00
6	British Medieval Castles	1927	—	£15.00
6	Building a Transatlantic Liner	1932	—	£7.50
6	Carnivorous Plants	1933	—	£8.50
6	Celebrated Italian Generals	1911	—	£9.00
6	Chocolate	1929	—	£11.50

LIEBIG EXTRACT OF MEAT CO. (see also Oxo) — cont.

Qty		Date	Odds	Sets
6	Clocks	1905	—	£11.50
6	Corsica	1912	—	£11.50
6	Development of Commerce and Industry	1910	—	£9.00
6	Duelling	1900	—	£17.50
6	Episodes from Belgian History III	1907	—	£8.00
6	Equestrienne School	1938	—	£17.50
6	European Rustic Dwellings	1905	—	£9.00
6	Flourishing Cities of the Middle Ages	1907	—	£9.00
6	Fruit and Women in Costume	1900	—	£15.00
6	Great Conquerors II	1904	—	£9.00
6	Historic Carriages	1926	—	£12.50
12	History of Japan	1938	—	£15.00
6	In Venezuela	1907	—	£9.00
6	Iron I	1899	—	£15.00
6	Italian Lakes I	1904	—	£8.50
6	Italian Renaissance Art	1904	—	£9.00
6	Jerusalem Freed	1910	—	£9.00
6	Old Districts and Houses	1937	—	£11.50
6	Orders of Chivalry Open to Women	1905	—	£11.50
6	Orthoptera (Locust Family)	1947	—	£15.00
6	Plants used for Colours	1909	—	£9.00
6	Poisonous Fungi	1950	—	£11.50
6	Pompeii – As It Was and Now	1906	—	£9.00
6	Raphael	1905	—	£8.00
6	Samarkand, City of Tamerlane	1934	—	£9.00
6	Scenes of Africa	1906	—	£15.00
6	Scenes of Life in Spain I	1904	—	£8.00
6	Silk	1907	—	£8.00
6	Sport Round the World	1951	—	£25.00
6	Swiss Cantons	1898	—	£17.50
6	Termites	1937	—	£6.00
6	The Antarctic	1936	—	£15.00
6	The History of Italy X	1957	—	£3.50
6	The History of Our Provinces – East Flanders	1952	—	£4.50
6	The Hunter and His Dog	1951	—	£7.50
6	The Life and Works of Vittoria Alfieri	1964	—	£6.00
6	The Realm of Plants	1911	—	£11.50
6	The Rhine in History	1901	—	£9.00
6	Towers	1911	—	£9.00

LIEBIG EXTRACT OF MEAT CO. (see also Oxo) — cont.

Qty		*Date*	*Odds*	*Sets*
6	Tropical Butterflies and Beetles	1935	—	£11.50
6	War in the Alps	1926	—	£8.50
6	Water Utilisation in the Ancient World	1924	—	£12.50
6	Wedding Celebrations	1910	—	£9.00
6	Well Known Bridges	1899	—	£17.50

LIFEGUARD PRODUCTS (Soap)

25	British Butterflies	1955	—	£2.50

LIME ROCK CO. INC. (Commercial, U.S.A.)

X110	Dream Machines (Cars)	1991	—	£15.00

JOSEPH LINGFORD & SON (Baking Powder)

36	British War Leaders	1950	£1.50	£54.00

LIPTON LTD. (Tea)

48	Animals and Their Young (Canadian)	1991	50p	£24.00
60	Flags of the World	1967	—	£12.00
50	The Conquest of Space	1962	40p	£20.00

LITTLE CHEF (Restaurants)

M8	Disney Characters	1990	—	£12.00

LOCAL AUTHORITIES (School Meals)

5	British Sports Personalities	1997	—	£1.75

LONGLEAT HOUSE

25	Longleat House	1967	—	£2.00

LOS ANGELES FIRE DEPARTMENT (U.S.A.)

X4	Los Angeles Raiders	1985	—	£8.00

LOT-O-FUN (Periodical)

MF4	Sports Champions	1922	£5.50	£22.00

G. F. LOVELL & CO. (Confectionery)

36	British Royalty Series	1910	£27.50	—
36	Football Series	1910	£50.00	—
25	Photos of Football Stars	1926	£17.50	—

BRIAN LUND POSTCARDS

6	Rugby Union Six Nations 2000	2000	—	£1.00
6	Rugby Union Six Nations 2001	2001	—	£1.00
8	Rugby Union World Cup 1999	1999	—	£1.20

THE LYCHGATE PRESS

Qty		Date	Odds	Sets
10	Eloise	2001	—	£4.00
L25	Soccer Gallery	2000	—	£7.50
10	The Beatles	2002	—	£4.00
18	Tottenham 2000	2000	—	£6.50

J. LYONS & CO. LTD. (Ice Cream & Tea)

40	All Systems Go	1968	£1.20	£48.00
48	Australia	1959	20p	£4.00
M20	Banknotes	1974	—	£6.50
M12	Beautiful Butterflies	1974	—	£3.00
25	Birds and Their Eggs	1962	60p	£15.00
40	British Wildlife	1970	£1.00	£40.00
L16	Catweazle Magic Cards	1971	—	£8.00
M20	County Badge Collection	1974	—	£2.00
X12	Did You Know?	1983	50p	£6.00
40	European Adventure	1969	£1.25	—
40	Famous Aircraft	1965	40p	£16.00
40	Famous Cars	1966	£1.60	£64.00
40	Famous Locomotives	1964	£1.85	£75.00
48	Famous People	1966	80p	£40.00
D12	Farmyard Stencils	1977	—	£6.50
M14	Flowers (Cut-Out)	1976	—	£28.00
32	HMS 1902-1962 (Descriptive)	1962	25p	£8.00
32	(Non-Descriptive)	1962	—	£8.00
X12	Horses in the Service of Man	1984	—	£3.00
L35	Illustrated Map of the British Isles	1959	70p	£25.00
40	International Footballers	1972	£3.25	£130.00
40	Into the Unknown	1969	£1.20	£48.00
15	Jubilee	1977	£1.20	£18.00
X10	Junior Champs	1983	—	£2.40
M24	Kings of the Road	1977	*£1.00*	—
P6	150th Anniversary of Postage Stamps	1990	—	£2.00
50	100 Years of Motoring	1964	£1.00	£50.00
40	On Safari	1970	£1.00	£40.00
40	Pop Scene	1971	£2.00	£80.00
40	Pop Stars	1970	£2.25	—
L10	Pop Stars (Shaped)	1975	—	£3.50
K48	Quick Puzzle Cards	1955	£1.25	—
40	Soccer Stars	1971	£3.00	£120.00
40	Space Age Britain	1968	£1.20	£48.00
40	Space Exploration	1963	£1.30	£52.00
25	Space 1999	1976	£3.00	£75.00
25	Star Trek	1979	£4.00	£100.00
50	Train Spotters	1962	50p	£25.00
K100	Tricks & Puzzles	1926	£2.75	—
40	Views of London	1967	80p	£32.00
48	What Do You Know?	1957	20p	£4.00
24	Wings Across the World (Descriptive Back)	1962	20p	£4.00
24	(Non-Descriptive)	1961	—	£6.00
24	Wings of Speed (Descriptive Back)	1961	20p	£6.00
24	(Non-Descriptive)	1961	50p	£12.00

M.P. CARDS (Commercial)

L14	Nishikigoi (Koi Carp)	1997	—	£15.00
L12	Samurai Warriors	1996	—	£10.00
L12	The Geisha Collection	1997	—	£10.00

M.P.L. LTD. (Records)

Qty		Date	Odds	Sets
M5	Wings — Back to the Egg	1981	—	£12.50

MAC FISHERIES (Shops)

L12	Gallery Pictures	1924	£1.25	£15.00
L14	Japanese Colour Prints	1924	£1.10	£15.00
L12	Poster Pointers	1925	£1.00	£12.00
L12	Sporting Prints	1923	£3.50	£42.00

MACGIRR & CO. (Tea)

24	Birds & Their Eggs	1912	£8.00	—

JOHN MACKINTOSH & SONS (Confectionery)

15	Camping & Hiking Hints	1932	£14.00	—

MACROBERTSON (Confectionery, Australia)

24	Flags of All Nations	1916	£5.00	£120.00
24	Naval & Military Decorations	1916	£7.00	£168.00
24	Sons/Allies of the Empire	1916	£8.00	—
50	Sports of the World	1916	£3.20	£160.00

Wm. McEWAN & CO. LTD. (Brewers)

25	Old Glasgow	1929	£10.00	—

McVITIE & PRICE (Food)

8	The European War Series	1914	£15.00	£120.00

McVITIE'S (Biscuits)

M10	Superstars	1976	—	£20.00

MADISON CONFECTIONERY PRODUCTIONS LTD.

X16/32	Christmas Greeting Cards	1957	£1.25	—
X48	Disc Jockey, 1st Series	1957	£2.00	£96.00
X48	Disc Jockey, 2nd Series	1958	£1.50	£72.00
X50	Recording Stars	1958	£1.50	£75.00

THE MAGNET LIBRARY (Periodical)

MF15	Footballers	1922	£3.60	£54.00
MF6	Football Teams	1922	£4.00	£24.00
MF4	Football Teams	1923	£4.50	£18.00

SILKS

In the world of cigarette card collecting silks is the name given to all items woven in, or printed on, fabrics of all sorts, including satin, canvas, blanket and leather.

Many tobacco and a few other trade firms issued silks in the early part of this century. The best known of these are Godfrey Phillips in Britain, mainly with their B.D.V. brand, the American Tobacco Co. in the U.S.A. and the British American Tobacco Co. in the Commonwealth, usually under the names of their subsidiaries such as the I.T.C. (Canada) or United Tobacco Co. (South Africa). Among trade issues the majority were given away with magazines such as Happy Home and My Weekly. Noteworthy however are the series of cabinet size silks given with each Christmas number of 'The Gentlewoman' between 1890 and 1915.

In some cases the subjects on silks are repeats of card issues, such as 'Best Dogs of their Breed', but the majority are new subjects, and cover a very wide range of interests. These include Flags, Regimental Badges and Colours, County Cricket Badges, Famous Queens, Paintings, Red Indians, Great War Leaders, Dogs, Flowers and even Automobile Pennants. Manufacturers encouraged the smokers to use the satin issues to make cushion covers and the like — I.T.C. of Canada issued large centrepieces for this purpose, and Godfrey Phillips even issued a set of CARDS entitled 'Prizes for Needlework'.

Silks are often thought of as a specialised subject, but the general collector should consider some of these as an attractive addition to his album. We can supply an illustrated book listing all known British silks for £5.00 (post paid).

ERRORS & VARIETIES

In view of the enormous number of cards that have been produced, most of which have detailed descriptions, it is hardly surprising that mistakes occur occasionally. In some cases these were brought to light at an early stage, and a corrected card was also issued, but sometimes the error remained undetected until many years after the set appeared.

Some of the mistakes can best be described as 'Howlers', and among the best known are Carreras Figures of Fiction showing Uncle Tom with white feet, Pattreiouex Coastwise giving the date of the Battle of Trafalgar as 1812 and Player Sea Fishes with three versions of the Monk (or Angel) Fish, one of which states that it is inedible, while another describes its flesh as 'quite wholesome'. Gallaher, in its Great War Series, showed a Tommy with his rifle sloped on the wrong shoulder, and Carreras Britains Defence No. 47 can be found with the picture upside down. Most of these have been illustrated elsewhere, so we have shown here a different selection, with no comments other than – find the mistake for yourself.

Varieties occur as the result of deliberate changes by the issuer. Common examples of this are the updating of army ranks and decorations, new sports statistics, and changes of rank or title caused by a death. The most fruitful series for a study of varieties are probably in the series of Guinea Gold cards and also Wills Transvaal series, where over 250 different cards can be collected within the 66 numbers of the series.

Three books including all known British varieties are listed on page 12.

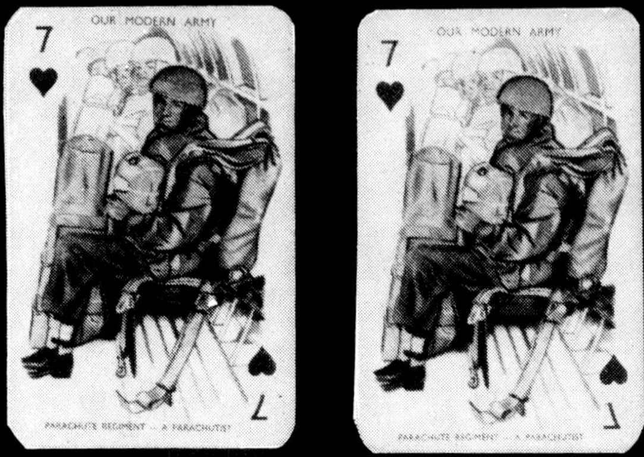

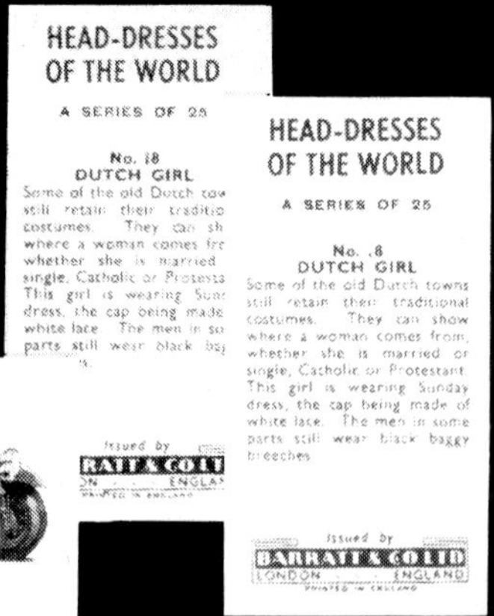

MANCHESTER EVENING NEWS (Newspaper)

Qty		*Date*	*Odds*	*Sets*
L30	Footballers	1976	£2.50	£75.00

MANCHESTER UNITED FOOTBALL CLUB

X26	Manchester United Footballers	1991	—	£15.00

MAPLE LEAF GUM

K75	Flag Tie Pins (Metal)	1960	65p	—
K90	Motor Car & Motor Cycle Badges (Metal)	1960	£1.00	—

R. MARCANTONIO LTD. (Ice Lollies)

50	Interesting Animals	1953	—	£4.00

A. T. MARKS (Commercial)

11	1892 Gloucestershire (Cricketers)	1990	—	£1.75
11	1892 Middlesex	1990	—	£1.75
11	1892 Surrey	1990	—	£2.75
11	1892 Sussex	1990	—	£2.75
12	1903 Middlesex	1990	—	£1.75
12	1903 Yorkshire	1990	—	£1.75
11	1912 Northamptonshire	1990	—	£2.75

MARLOW CIVIL ENGINEERING LTD.

25	Famous Clowns	1990	—	£30.00

MARS CONFECTIONS LTD.

25	Ceremonies of the Coronation			
	(Brown Back, Blue Caption)	1937	£1.00	£25.00
	(Brown Back, Brown Caption)	1937	£1.50	£37.50
	(Blue Back)	1937	£4.50	—
50	Famous Aeroplanes, Pilots & Airports	1938	£1.40	£70.00
50	Famous Escapes	1937	£1.00	£50.00
50	Famous Film Stars	1939	£1.30	£65.00
25	Wonders of the Queen Mary	1936	£1.40	£35.00

JAMES MARSHALL (GLASGOW) LTD. (Food)

30	Colonial Troops	1900	£32.50	—
1	Marshall's Products Illustrated	1926	—	£5.00
40	Recipes	1926	£4.00	—

MASTER VENDING CO. LTD. (Gum)

X25	A Bombshell for the Sheriff	1959	80p	£20.00
X50	Cardmaster Football Tips	1958	£1.20	£60.00

MASTER VENDING CO. LTD. (Gum) — cont.

Qty		Date	Odds	Sets
X16	Cricketer Series — New Zealand 1958	1958	£1.00	£16.00
X50	Did You Know? (Football)	1959	60p	£30.00
X100	Jet Aircraft of the World	1958	£1.50	£150.00
X100	Ditto (German Text)	1958	£1.50	—
X25	Taxing the Sheriff	1959	60p	£15.00
X36	Tommy Steele	1958	£3.00	—

J. JOHN MASTERS & CO. (Matches)

X12	Food from Britain	1987	—	£1.50

MATCH (Periodical)

X31	F.A. Cup Fact File	1986	—	£7.50

MATCHBOX INTERNATIONAL LTD. (Toys)

75	Matchbox Model Vehicles	1985	60p	£45.00

MAXILIN MARKETING CO.

25	Motor Cars	1951	—	£5.00

MAYNARDS LTD. (Confectionery)

12	Billy Bunter Series	1926	£22.50	—
?20	Football Clubs	1933	£30.00	—
18	Girl Guide Series	1921	£15.00	—
50	Girls of All Nations	1921	£4.50	£225.00
12	Strange Insects	1935	£4.00	£50.00
8	The European War Series	1916	£16.50	£132.00
12	Wonders of the Deep	1935	£5.50	£66.00
12	World's Wonder Series (Numbered)	1930	£4.50	£54.00
10	World's Wonder Series (Unnumbered)	1930	£5.50	£55.00

MAYPOLE (Grocers)

25	War Series	1915	£7.50	£187.50

MAZAWATTEE (Tea)

X39	Kings and Queens	1902	£4.00	£156.00

MEADOW DAIRY CO.

50	War Series	1915	£7.50	£375.00

J. F. MEARBECK (Printer)

30	Army Pictures, Cartoons, etc.	1915	£32.50	—

MELLIN'S FOOD

K2	Diamond Jubilee Coins	1897	£10.00	£20.00

MELOX (Dog Food)

Qty		Date	Odds	Sets
L50	Famous Breeds of Dogs	1937	£5.50	£275.00
M32	Happy Families (Dogs)	1929	£7.50	£240.00

MERLIN TRADING CARDS (Commercial)

X161	Premier Gold	1997	—	£16.00
X156	Premier Gold 98	1997	—	£30.00
X105	Premier Gold 2000	1999	—	£15.00
X20	Premier Gold 2000 - Club Badges	1999	—	£10.00
X20	Premier Gold 2000 - Top Scorer	1999	—	£10.00
X120	Premier League	1994	—	£15.00
X88	Premier League	1996	—	£12.50

MERRYSWEETS LTD.

X48	Telegum TV Stars	1958	£1.25	£60.00
X48	Tracepiks	1960	£6.00	—
X48	World Racing Cars	1959	£2.30	£115.00

GEOFFREY MICHAEL PUBLISHERS LTD.

40	Modern Motor Cars	1949	£1.25	£50.00
F48	Mystery Cards — Modern Motor Cars	1953	£5.00	—

MIDLAND CARTOPHILIC BRANCH

L24	Silhouettes of Veteran & Vintage Cars	1991	—	£6.00

MIDLAND COUNTIES (Ice Cream)

12	Action Soldiers (with Cadbury)	1976	—	£3.50
M20	Banknotes	1974	—	£12.50
D12	Farmyard Stencils	1977	—	£2.50
M24	Kings of the Road	1977	—	£6.50
X10	Steam Power	1978	—	£4.00

MILK MARKETING BOARD

P10	Milk Recipe Cards	1979	—	£2.50
25	Prehistoric Animals	1963	—	£6.50

MILLERS (Tea)

25	Animals & Reptiles	1962	—	£2.50

ROBERT R. MIRANDA (Confectionery)

50	150 Years of Locomotives	1956	—	£6.00
50	100 Years of Motoring	1955	—	£6.00
25	Ships through the Ages	1957	—	£7.50
50	Strange Creatures	1961	—	£4.50

MISTER SOFTEE LTD. (Ice Cream)

Qty		Date	Odds	Sets
12	Action Soldiers (with Cadbury)	1976	—	£6.00
M12	Beautiful Butterflies	1977	35p	£4.00
M20	County Badge Collection	1976	15p	£2.50
L12	Did You Know?	1976	35p	£4.25
25	Do You Know?	1961	£3.00	—
D12	Farmyard Stencils	1977	—	£4.00
M24	1st Division Football League Badges	1972	—	£6.50
M24	Kings of the Road	1977	30p	£7.50
E1	Map of the British Isles	1976	—	£2.00
15	Moon Mission	1962	£1.40	£21.00
M24	Pop Discs	1972	80p	£20.00
P24	Pop Parade	1969	—	£30.00
M10	Pop Stars (Shaped)	1975	85p	£8.50
X1	Secret Code Computer	1977	—	65p
D20	Sports Cups (Shaped)	1975	—	£10.00
M20	Stamp in a Million	1976	45p	£9.00
P12	Star Cards (Numbered, With Address)	1966	£1.50	£18.00
P12	Star Cards (Numbered, No Address)	1967	£1.50	£18.00
P24	Star Cards (Unnumbered)	1968	£1.50	£36.00
P24	Star Cards (Numbered)	1969	£1.50	£36.00
X24	Star Discs	1970	£1.50	£36.00
X10	Steam Power	1978	—	£3.00
M4	Super Human Heroes	1979	—	£3.00
P12	Top 10	1964	—	£7.00
P12	Top Ten (Address N.7.)	1965	£1.50	£18.00
P12	(Address W.6.)	1966	£4.50	—
20	Top 20	1963	80p	£16.00
25	T.V. Personalities	1962	£2.50	—
P12	Your World	1963	—	£4.00

MITCHAM FOODS LTD.

25	Aircraft of Today	1955	—	£3.00
25	Aquarium Fish, 1st Series	1957	£1.00	£25.00
25	Aquarium Fish, 2nd Series	1957	—	£3.00
50	Butterflies and Moths	1959	£1.20	£60.00
25	Footballers	1956	£2.00	—
50	Mars Adventure	1958	£5.50	—
25	Motor Racing	1960	£2.00	—

MIZZ MAGAZINE

P4	The Seasons	1986	—	£2.00

MOBIL OIL CO. LTD.

M30	Football Club Badges (Silk)	1983	£2.00	£60.00
X36	The Story of Grand Prix Motor Racing	1971	—	£14.00
25	Veteran and Vintage Cars	1962	£2.00	£50.00
24	Vintage Cars	1966	—	£5.00

MODERN WEEKLY (Periodical)

P3	Film Couples (Silk)	1928	£25.00	£75.00

MOFFAT B. & G. LTD. (Confectionery)

Qty		Date	Odds	Sets
D102	Money That Made History	1981	—	£10.00

MOFFAT BROS. (Confectionery)

L100	Cinema Artistes	1914	£12.00	—

THE MOLASSINE CO. (Dog Food)

50	Dogs (Full Length)	1963	£1.20	£60.00
50	Dogs (Heads)	1964	£2.00	£100.00
25	Dogs at Work	1970	—	£5.00
12	Dogs of All Countries	1925	£9.00	£108.00
50	Puppies	1967	£2.00	£100.00

MONTAGU MOTOR MUSEUM

M24	Veteran & Vintage Cars	1965	£3.50	£84.00

MONTY GUM

M98	Bruce Lee	1980	—	£25.00
L72	Daily Fables, 1st Series	1968	—	£25.00
X50	Elvis	1978	£2.25	—
M72	Flag Parade	1972	—	£9.00
M100	Flags of Ail Nations	1980	—	£5.00
X56	Footballers (P/C Inset)	1961	£2.50	—
M72	Kojak	1975	50p	£36.00
M54	Kojak (P/C Inset, Black Back)	1976	—	£22.50
M56	Kojak (P/C Inset, Red Back)	1976	—	£25.00
X56	Motor Cars (P/C Inset)	1956	£1.25	£70.00
M72	Starsky and Hutch	1978	75p	—
M100	The Cops, 1st Series	1976	50p	£50.00
M124	The High Chaparral	1970	—	£35.00
M100	T.V. Hits	1975	—	£25.00

MOORE'S TOFFEE

T50	The Post in Many Lands	1900	£22.50	—

MORNING FOODS LTD.

1	Advertisement Card	1953	—	*£5.00*
F25	British Planes (Numbered)	1953	£5.00	—
F25	(Unnumbered)	1953	80p	£20.00
F50	British Trains	1952	£5.00	—
25	British Uniforms	1954	—	£5.00
50	Modern Cars	1954	50p	£25.00
50	Our England	1955	—	£5.00
25	Test Cricketers	1953	£1.60	£40.00
12	The Cunard Line (Black Back)	1957	—	£3.00
12	(Blue Back)	1957	—	£4.00
25	World Locomotives (Black Back)	1954	—	£3.00
25	(Blue Back)	1954	—	£15.00

E. D. L. MOSELEY (Confectionery)

Qty		*Date*	*Odds*	*Sets*
M25	Historical Buildings	1954	—	£2.50

MOTOR CYCLE NEWS

L6	Motorcycle Classics	1995	—	£2.50

MOTORSPORT CHARITY MEMORABILIA

50	Formula 1 World Championship	2000	—	£9.50

V. MUHLENEN & CO. (Cheese)

M6	Swiss Views, Series III	1955	—	£9.00
M6	Swiss Views, Series IV	1955	—	£9.00

MURCO PETROLEUM

P28	English Counties	1986	—	£4.00
M50	World's Airlines	1978	—	£5.00

C. R. S. MURRAY & CO. LTD. (Chocolates)

1	The Caramel Chief	1930	—	£17.50

MUSEUM OF BRITISH MILITARY UNIFORMS

25	British Cavalry Uniforms	1987	—	£5.00
25	Military Maids	1987	—	£7.50
25	Warriors through the Ages	1987	—	£5.00

MUSICAL COLLECTABLES (Commercial)

26	The Gilbert & Sullivan Collection 1st Series (Player Reprint)	1994	—	£6.00
26	The Gilbert & Sullivan Collection 2nd Series (Player Reprint)	1994	—	£6.00

MUSGRAVE BROS. LTD. (Tea)

25	Birds	1961	—	£15.00
20	British Birds	1960	£8.00	£160.00
50	British Wild Life	1962	£6.60	£330.00
50	Butterflies of the World	1964	£5.50	—
25	Into Space	1961	—	£5.00
25	Modern Motor Cars	1962	60p	£15.00
25	Pond Life	1963	—	£7.50
25	Products of the World	1961	—	£2.50
50	Transport through the Ages	1966	£3.50	£175.00
25	Tropical Birds	1964	—	£3.00
25	Wild Flowers	1961	—	£10.00

MYERS & METREVELI (Gum)

Qty		Date	Odds	Sets
KF48	Film Stars	1953	£2.75	—
X48	Film Stars & Biographies	1953	£5.00	—
X60	Hollywood Peep Show	1953	£4.00	—
L50	Spot the Planes	1953	£4.00	—

MY WEEKLY (Periodical)

M9	Battle Series (Silk)	1916	£6.50	£59.00
M12	Floral Beauties (Silk)	1914	£5.50	£66.00
M15	Language of Flowers (Silk)	1914	£6.50	—
M54	Lucky Emblems (Silk)	1912	£8.25	—
M6	Lucky Flowers (Silk)	1913	£11.50	—
M12	Our Soldier Boys (Silk)	1915	£6.50	£78.00
M14	Soldiers of the King (Silk)	1914	£6.25	£87.50
M6	Sweet Kiss Series (Silk)	1913	£7.50	—
M6	War Heroes (Silk)	1916	£7.00	£42.00

NABISCO FOODS LTD.

M5	Aces in Action (Aviation)	1980	£4.00	£20.00
L24	Action Shots of Olympic Sports	1980	£1.75	£42.00
X4	Adventure Books	1970	£5.00	—
12	British Soldiers	1971	—	£1.50
P20	Champions of Sport	1961	£2.50	£50.00
P6	Eagle Eye Games	1979	—	£3.00
P8	England's Soccer Stars Tactic Cards	1980	£3.25	£26.00
12	E.T.	1983	—	£6.00
L24	Footballers	1970	£2.25	£54.00
G12	Freshwater Fishes of Britain	1974	—	£6.00
L10	History of Aviation	1970	£2.00	£20.00
D4	Johan Cruyff Demonstrates	1980	£5.00	£20.00
P10	Kevin Keegan's Keep Fit with the Stars	1978	—	£15.00
P10	Motor Show	1960	£2.75	£27.50
P6	Play 'n Score	1989	—	£7.50
L6	World Super Stars & Sporting Trophies	1980	£4.00	—

AUSTRALIAN ISSUES

32	Leading Cricketers (Crispies etc.)	1948	£3.50	£112.00
L24	United Nations in Action	1968	—	£10.00

EDWARD NASSAR & CO. LTD. (Coffee, Gold Coast)

25	Transport, Present & Future	1955	—	£2.50

NATIONAL SPASTICS SOCIETY

24	Famous County Cricketers	1958	£1.75	£42.00
24	Famous Footballers	1959	£2.00	£48.00

NEEDLER'S (Confectionery)

12	Military Series	1916	£21.50	—

PHILIP NEILL COLLECTABLES (Commercial)

Qty		Date	Odds	Sets
15	Arsenal – Double Legends of 1970/71	2002	—	£5.50
10	Bizarre Club Shirts	2001	—	£4.00
10	Brazilliant! (Pele)	2001	—	£4.00
20	British Internationals 1950-1952 (Soccer)	1999	—	£6.99
L7	Celtic '67	2003	—	£4.15
10	Classic Kits (Soccer)	2001	—	£4.00
L10	Elvis in Pictures	2003	—	£5.75
10	England's Top Goal Scorers	2002	—	£4.00
10	Football Heroes	2001	—	£4.00
10	Football in the Fifties	2001	—	£4.00
15	Football Stars of the Seventies	2002	—	£5.50
15	Football Stars of the Seventies, 2nd Series	2003	—	£5.50
15	Footballer of the Year	1999	—	£5.50
10	Greavsie	2001	—	£4.00
10	International Stars of Yesteryear	2000	—	£4.00
10	International Stars of Yesteryear 2	2001	—	£4.00
15	Kings of Europe (Manchester United)	1999	—	£5.50
15	Leeds United – The Revie Era	2002	—	£5.50
15	Liverpool Legends	2000	—	£5.50
15	Maine Road Heroes	2003	—	£5.50
10	Scottish Footballers	2000	—	£4.00
10	Scottish Internationals	2002	—	£4.00
15	70s Soccer Stars	2003	—	£5.50
10	Soccer 70 – The Year in Football	2002	—	£4.00
10	Soccer in the 60s Volume 1	1999	—	£4.00
10	Soccer in the 60s Volume 2	2000	—	£4.00
10	Soccer Stars of the 50s	2001	—	£4.00
10	Soccer Stars of the 60s	2001	—	£4.00
10	Ten of the Best – George Best	2000	—	£4.00
15	The Busby Babes	2002	—	£5.50
L7	Visions of Marilyn Monroe	2003	—	£4.15

NEILSON'S (Confectionery)

50	Interesting Animals	1954	—	£5.00

NELSON LEE LIBRARY (Periodical)

MF15	Footballers	1922	£3.40	£51.00
MF6	Modern British Locomotives	1922	£6.00	£36.00

NESTLE LTD. (Chocolate)

L12	Animal Bars (Wrappers)	1970	—	£2.00
24	Animals of the World	1962	—	£12.50
P12	British Birds (Reward Cards)	1900	£11.00	£132.00
49	Happy Families	1935	£1.00	£60.00
144	Pictorial World Atlas	1934	£2.50	—
100	Stars of the Silver Screen	1936	£1.40	£140.00
50	Stars of the Silver Screen, Volume II	1937	£2.00	—
136	This England	1936	80p	£110.00
T24	Wild Animals, Serie II	1910	£6.50	—
156	Wonders of the World, Volume I	1932	70p	—
144	Wonders of the World, Volume II	1933	70p	—

NEW ENGLAND CONFECTIONERY CO. (U.S.A.)

M12	Real Airplane Pictures	1929	£3.75	£45.00

NEW HOLLAND MACHINE CO.

Qty		Date	Odds	Sets
P12	Traction Engines	1960	£4.50	£54.00

NEWMARKET HARDWARE

L24	Some of Britain's Finest Bikes	1993	—	£6.00

NEWTON, CHAMBERS & CO. (Toilet Rolls)

P18	More Rhyme Time (19-36)	1934	£3.50	£63.00
P18	Nursery Rhyme Pictures (1-18)	1934	£3.50	£63.00

NEW ZEALAND MEAT PRODUCERS BOARD

X25	Scenes of New Zealand Lamb	1930	£2.80	£70.00

90 MINUTES (Magazine)

X56	Footballers (Playing Card Inset)	1993	—	£20.00

NORTHERN CO-OPERATIVE SOCIETY LTD. (Tea)

25	Birds	1963	£1.00	£25.00
25	History of the Railways, 1st Series	1964	—	£7.50
25	History of the Railways, 2nd Series	1964	—	£12.50
25	Passenger Liners	1963	—	£3.00
25	Then and Now	1963	—	£4.50
25	Tropical Birds	1962	—	£12.50
25	Weapons of World War II	1962	—	£11.50
25	Wonders of the Deep	1965	—	£2.50

NORTH WEST TOURIST BOARD

T40	Stockport	1995	—	£5.00
T40	Wigan	1992	—	£5.00

THE NOSTALGIA CLASSIC COLLECTION

Limited Edition reprints of rare sets

P4	Adkin – Games by Tom Browne	2001	—	£4.00
9	Allen & Ginter (U.S.A.) – Women Baseball Players	2001	—	£3.00
X50	Allen & Ginter (U.S.A.) – The World's Champions, Second Series	2001	—	£17.50
35	Ardath – Hand Shadows	2001	—	£7.50
25	A. Baker – Star Girls	2001	—	£6.00
20	Bradford – Boer War Cartoons	2001	—	£5.00
L16	Brigham – Down the Thames	2001	—	£6.50
25	B.A.T – Beauties, Blossom Girls	2001	—	£6.00
T6	Cadbury – Sports Series	2001	—	£3.00
10	Chappel – British Celebrities	2001	—	£3.00
30	Clarke – Cricketer Series	2001	—	£7.50
P7	Cope – The Seven Ages of Man	2001	—	£6.00
6	Empire Tobacco – Franco British Exhibition	2001	—	£2.00

THE NOSTALGIA CLASSIC COLLECTION — cont.

Qty		Date	Odds	Sets
25	Faulkner – Beauties (Coloured)	2001	—	£6.00
25	Globe Cigarette Co. – Actresses - French	2001	—	£6.00
17	Goode (Australia) – Prominent Cricketer Series	2001	—	£5.00
8	Hall (U.S.A.) – Presidential Candidates & Actresses	2001	—	£2.00
P12	Huntley & Palmer – Aviation	2001	—	£7.50
M20	James & Co. – Arms of Countries	2001	—	£7.50
50	Kimball – Champion of Games and Sports	2001	—	£10.00
15	Kinnear – Australian Cricket Team	2001	—	£4.00
50	Kriegsfield – Phrases & Advertisements	2001	—	£10.00
25	Kuit – Principal British Streets	2001	—	£6.00
50	Lacey's – Footballers	2001	—	£10.00
20	Lambert & Butler – International Yachts	2001	—	£5.00
20	J. Lees – Northampton Town Football Club	2001	—	£5.00
X6	Liebig (France) – Famous Explorers (S.1094)	2001	—	£5.00
25	Lusby – Scenes from Circus Life	2001	—	£6.00
15	Marburg (U.S.A.) – Beauties, "PAC"	2001	—	£4.00
35	Mayo (U.S.A.) – Prizefighters	2001	—	£7.50
13	National (Australia) – English Cricket Team 1897-8	2001	—	£4.00
50	Ogden – Cricketers & Sportsmen	2001	—	£10.00
X16	Old Calabar – Sports and Games	2001	—	£7.50
40	Orlando Cigarette Co. – Home & Colonial Regiments	2001	—	£8.50
30	Godfrey Phillips – Beauties, Nymphs	2001	—	£7.50
20	Godfrey Phillips – Russo Japanese War Series	2001	—	£5.00
20	Richmond Cavendish – Yachts (White Back)	2001	—	£5.00
6	E. Robinson & Sons – Medals & Decorations	2001	—	£2.00
25	E. Robinson & Sons – Regimental Mascots	2001	—	£6.00
16	S.D.V. Tobacco – British Royal Family	2001	—	£4.00
30	Salmon & Gluckstein – Music Hall Stage Characters	2001	—	£7.50
50	Singleton & Cole – Footballers	2001	—	£10.00
25	F. & J. Smith – Advertisement Cards	2001	—	£6.00
50	F. & J. Smith – Champions of Sport (Unnumbered)	2001	—	£10.00
10	Spiro Valleri – Footballers	2001	—	£3.00
12	Spratt – Prize Dogs	2001	—	£3.50
5	Taddy – English Royalty	2001	—	£2.00
20	Taddy – Royalty, Actresses & Soldiers	2001	—	£5.00
10	United Tobacconists – Actresses, "MUTA"	2001	—	£3.00
22	Henry Welfare – Prominent Politicians	2001	—	£6.00

NOSTALGIA REPRINTS

28	Baseball Greats of 1890 (USA Tobacco)	1991	—	£6.00
2	Baseball Stars (Ruth, Sisler)	1992	—	50p
50	Celebrated American Indian Chiefs (Allen & Ginter)	1989	—	£8.50
20	Clowns and Circus Artistes (Taddy)	1991	—	£6.00
50	Cope's Golfers	1984	—	£8.50
238	County Cricketers (Taddy)	1987	—	£32.00
15	Derbyshire	1987	—	£2.50
15	Essex	1987	—	£2.50
16	Gloucestershire	1987	—	£2.50
15	Hampshire	1987	—	£2.50
15	Kent	1987	—	£2.50
15	Lancashire	1987	—	£2.50
14	Leicestershire	1987	—	£2.50
15	Middlesex	1987	—	£2.50
15	Northamptonshire	1987	—	£2.50
14	Nottinghamshire	1987	—	£2.50

NOSTALGIA REPRINTS — cont.

Qty		Date	Odds	Sets
15	Somersetshire	1987	—	£2.50
15	Surrey	1987	—	£2.50
15	Sussex	1987	—	£2.50
15	Warwickshire	1987	—	£2.50
14	Worcestershire	1987	—	£2.50
15	Yorkshire	1987	—	£2.50
50	Cricketers 1896 (Wills)	1983	—	£8.50
20	Cricketers Series 1902 (Gabriel)	1992	—	£3.50
12	Cricket Terms (Faulkner)	1999	—	£2.50
50	Dickens Gallery (Cope)	1989	—	£8.50
25	Fishers (Duke)	2002	—	£6.00
12	Football Terms, 1st Series (Faulkner)	1999	—	£2.50
12	Football Terms, 2nd Series (Faulkner)	1999	—	£2.50
50	Fruits (Allen & Ginter)	1989	—	£8.50
25	Generals of the Late Civil War (Ellis)	1991	—	£6.00
12	Golf Terms (Faulkner)	1999	—	£2.50
12	Grenadier Guards (Faulkner)	1999	—	£2.50
25	Humorous Golfing Series (Berlyn)	1989	—	£6.00
25	Leaders (Kinney)	1990	—	£6.00
50	Military Series (Player)	1984	—	£8.50
12	Military Terms, 1st Series (Faulkner)	1999	—	£2.50
12	Military Terms, 2nd Series (Faulkner)	1999	—	£2.50
24	Motor Bike Cards (Thomson)	1993	—	£6.00
20	Motor Cycles (Thomson)	1993	—	£6.00
25	National Costumes (Wills)	1999	—	£6.00
25	Natives of the World (Taddy)	1999	—	£6.00
12	Nautical Terms, 1st Series (Faulkner)	1999	—	£2.50
12	Nautical Terms, 2nd Series (Faulkner-Grenadier)	1999	—	£2.50
25	Parrot Series (C.W.S.)	2001	—	£6.00
12	Policemen of the World (Faulkner-Grenadier)	1999	—	£2.50
12	Police Terms (Faulkner)	1999	—	£2.50
	Prominent Footballers (Taddy, 1907)			
15	Aston Villa	1992	—	£2.50
15	Chelsea	1998	—	£2.50
15	Everton	1998	—	£2.50
15	Leeds City	1992	—	£2.50
15	Liverpool	1992	—	£2.50
15	Manchester United	1992	—	£2.50
15	Middlesborough	1998	—	£2.50
15	Newcastle United	1992	—	£2.50
15	Queen's Park Rangers	1992	—	£2.50
15	Sunderland	1998	—	£2.50
15	Tottenham Hotspur	1998	—	£2.50
15	West Ham United	1998	—	£2.50
15	Woolwich Arsenal	1992	—	£2.50
4	Promotional Cards	1992	—	75p
12	Puzzle Series (Faulkner-Grenadier)	1999	—	£2.50
12	Sporting Terms (Faulkner)	1999	—	£2.50
18	Spurs Footballers (Jones)	1987	—	£2.50
12	Street Cries (Faulkner)	1999	—	£2.50

NUGGET POLISH CO.

X30	Allied Series	1910	£13.50	—
50	Flags of All Nations	1925	£5.00	£250.00
X40	Mail Carriers and Stamps	1910	£12.50	£500.00

NUMBER ONE (Periodical)

Qty		Date	Odds	Sets
P5	Get Fit and Have Fun	1991	—	£2.00

NUNBETTA (Grocer)

25	Motor Cars	1955	£8.50	£212.50

O.V.S. TEA COMPANY

K25	Modern Engineering	1955	—	£6.00

O'CARROLL KENT LTD. (Confectionery)

50	Railway Engines	1955	£4.00	£200.00

TONY L. OLIVER (Commercial)

25	Aircraft of World War II	1964	£3.50	—
50	German Orders & Decorations	1963	£1.25	—
50	German Uniforms	1971	—	£12.50
M25	Vehicles of the German Wehrmacht	1965	—	£25.00

ONLY FOOLS & HORSES APPRECIATION SOCIETY

L15	Only Fools & Horses	2002	—	£9.99

ORBIT ADVERTISING (Commercial)

28	Great Rugby Sides (N.Z. Tourists 1905)	1987	—	£3.00
16	New Zealand Cricketers 1958	1988	—	£5.00

OVALTINE BISCUITS

25	Do You Know?	1965	—	£8.00

OWBRIDGE'S (Pharmaceutics)

32	Happy Families	1914	£6.00	—

OXO LTD. (Meat Extract)

K47	Advertisement Series	1926	£5.50	—
K20	British Cattle	1934	£3.50	£70.00
15	Bull Series	1937	£2.40	£36.00
K24	Feats of Endurance	1934	£2.25	£54.00
K20	Furs and Their Story	1932	£2.50	£50.00
K36	Lifeboats and Their History	1935	£2.75	£99.00
K30	Mystery Painting Pictures	1928	£2.75	£82.50
P6	Oxo Cattle Studies	1930	£27.50	—
25	Oxo Recipes	1936	£2.30	£57.50

P. M. R. ASSOCIATES LTD. (Commercial)

Qty		*Date*	*Odds*	*Sets*
25	England, The World Cup, Spain '82	1982	—	£2.50

PACIFIC TRADING CARDS INC. (Commercial, U.S.A.)

X110	I Love Lucy	1991	—	£12.00
X110	The Wizard of Oz	1990	—	£12.50

H. J. PACKER & CO. LTD. (Confectionery)

K30	Footballers	1924	£45.00	—
50	Humorous Drawings	1936	£3.50	£175.00

PAGE WOODCOCK WIND PILLS

20	Humorous Sketches by Tom Browne	1902	£22.50	—

PALMER MANN & CO. LTD. (Salt)

24	Famous Cricketers	1950	*£20.00*	—
24	Famous Footballers	1950	*£18.00*	—
12	Famous Jets	1950	£10.00	—
12	Famous Lighthouses	1950	£10.00	—

PALS (Periodical)

MF27	Australian Sportsmen	1923	£8.00	£216.00
M8	Famous Footballers	1922	£8.00	£64.00
MF12	Football Series	1922	£3.75	£45.00

PANINI (Commercial, with Albums)

M240	A Team	1983	—	£20.00
M240	Auto 2000	1988	—	£20.00
X44	England Soccer Stars (No Album)	1996	—	£15.00
X190	The Royal Family	1988	—	£20.00

JAMES PASCALL LTD. (Confectionery)

48	Boy Scout Series	1912	£10.00	—
24	British Birds	1925	£2.75	£66.00
30	Devon Ferns	1927	£1.75	£52.50
30	Devon Flowers	1927	£1.75	£52.50
24	Devon Worthies	1927	£2.00	£48.00
18	Dogs	1924	£3.75	£67.50
10	Felix the Film Cat	1928	£22.50	—
30	Flags & Flags with Soldiers	1905	£13.00	—

JAMES PASCALL LTD. (Confectionery) — cont.

Qty		*Date*	*Odds*	*Sets*
30	Glorious Devon	1929	£1.75	£52.50
36	Glorious Devon, 2nd Series (Black Back)	1929	£1.75	£63.00
36	(Green Back)	1929	£2.00	£72.00
36	(Non-Descriptive)	1929	£5.00	—
2	King George V & Queen Mary	1910	£27.50	—
44	Military Series	1912	£16.50	—
20	Pascall's Specialities	1926	£16.00	—
12	Royal Naval Cadet Series	1912	£16.00	—
?	Rulers of the World	1916	*£27.50*	—
65	Town and Other Arms	1914	£11.00	—
50	Tricks and Puzzles	1926	£8.00	—
?13	War Portraits	1915	*£22.00*	—

J. PATERSON AND SON LTD. (Biscuits)

M48	Balloons	1960	£2.00	£96.00

PATRICK (Garages)

T24	The Patrick Collection (Cars)	1986	—	£15.00
P24	The Patrick Collection (With Coupons)	1986	—	£17.50

GEORGE PAYNE (Tea)

25	American Indian Tribes	1962	*80p*	—
25	British Railways	1962	—	£2.50
12	Characters from Dickens' Works (Numbered)	1912	£12.50	—
6	(Unnumbered)	1912	£15.00	—
25	Dogs Heads	1963	40p	£10.00
25	Science in the 20th Century	1963	—	£2.50

PEEK FREAN & CO. (Biscuits)

76 Page Illustrated Reference Book — £13.50

X12	English Scenes	1884	£10.00	£120.00
X4	Shakespeare Scenes	1884	£15.00	£60.00
X4	Views Abroad	1883	£12.50	£50.00

PENGUIN BISCUITS

E6	Farm Animal Series (Pairs)	1968	£2.25	£13.50
E6	(Singles)	1968	£2.50	—
E10	Home Hints	1974	£2.00	—
E12	Lake Nakuru Wildlife	1973	£2.25	£27.00
E10	Making the Most of Your Countryside	1975	£2.00	£20.00
E10	Pastimes	1972	£1.75	£17.50
E12	Playday	1973	£1.75	£21.00
E5	Zoo Animal Series (Pairs)	1969	£2.00	£10.00

PENNY MAGAZINE

MF12	Film Stars	1931	£4.00	£48.00

PEPSI COLA INC.

Qty		Date	Odds	Sets
L7	Star Wars Episode 1: Gamecards	1999	—	£5.00

PERFETTI (Gum)

40	Famous Trains	1983	£2.50	£100.00

PERIKIM CARDS (Commercial)

L7	The Boxer	2001	—	£3.00
L7	The Cocker Spaniel	2001	—	£3.00
L7	The Doberman	2001	—	£3.00
L7	The English Springer Spaniel	2001	—	£3.00
L7	The German Shepherd	2001	—	£3.00
L7	The Golden Retriever	2001	—	£3.00
L7	The Jack Russell	2001	—	£3.00

PETERKIN (Foods)

M8	English Sporting Dogs	1930	£13.00	£104.00

PETPRO LTD.

35	Grand Prix Racing Cars	1962	—	£8.00

PHILADELPHIA CHEWING GUM CORP. (U.S.A.)

X88	War Bulletin	1965	£1.30	£115.00

PHILLIPS (Tea)

25	Army Badges Past and Present	1964	—	£2.50
25	British Birds and Their Nests	1966	—	£35.00
25	British Rail	1965	—	£7.50

PHOTO ANSWERS (Periodical)

X12	Holiday Fax	1990	—	£2.00

FERD, PIATNIK & SONS (Austria)

X55	Masters of the Old Course – St. Andrews – Open Champions	1998	—	£7.00

STEVE PILKINGTON (Engineering)

X18	Central Lancashire Cricket League Clubs and Pavilions	1997	—	£7.00

PLANET LTD. (Gum)

Qty		Date	Odds	Sets
X50	Racing Cars of the World	1965	£2.40	£120.00

PLANTERS NUT & CHOCOLATE CO. (U.S.A.)

M25	Hunted Animals	1933	£3.20	£80.00

PLUCK (Periodical)

MF27	Famous Football Teams	1922	£3.20	£85.00

POLAR PRODUCTS LTD. (Ice Cream, Barbados)

25	International Air-Liners	1970	—	£12.50
25	Modern Motor Cars	1970	—	£17.50
25	Tropical Birds	1970	—	£12.50
25	Wonders of the Deep	1970	—	£10.00

H. POPPLETON & SONS (Confectionery)

50	Cricketers Series	1926	£25.00	—
16	Film Stars	1928	£8.00	—
?20	War Series	1916	£24.00	—
?12	Wembley Empire Exhibition Series	1924	£25.00	—

THE POPULAR (Periodical)

G26	Railway Locomotives	1922	£6.00	£156.00

POPULAR MOTORING (Periodical)

X4	P.M. Car Starter	1972	—	£2.00

POSTER STAMP ASSOCIATION

25	Modern Transport	1957	—	£2.25

PRESCOTT (Confectionery)

L36	Speed Kings	1966	80p	£29.00

PRESCOTT-PICKUP & CO. (Commercial)

50	Railway Locomotives	1980	50p	£25.00

PRESTON DAIRIES (Tea)

25	Country Life	1966	—	£2.00

PRICE'S PATENT CANDLE CO. LTD.

P12	Famous Battles	1910	£11.50	£138.00

W. R. PRIDDY (Antiques)

Qty		*Date*	*Odds*	*Sets*
80	Famous Boxers	1992	—	£7.50

PRIMROSE CONFECTIONERY CO. LTD.

24	Action Man	1976	£2.50	—
50	Amos Burke — Secret Agent	1970	—	£40.00
50	Andy Pandy	1960	60p	£30.00
50	Bugs Bunny	1964	*£1.20*	—
50	Burke's Law	1967	£3.25	—
25	Captain Kid	1975	£4.25	—
50	Chitty Chitty Bang Bang	1971	£1.20	£60.00
50	Cowboy	1960	—	£9.00
25	Cup Tie Quiz	1973	—	£2.75
25	Dads Army	1973	—	£9.00
50	Famous Footballers F.B.S.I.	1961	—	£20.00
25	Football Funnies	1974	—	£7.50
25	Happy Howlers	1975	—	£3.00
50	Joe 90	1969	£1.60	£80.00
50	Krazy Kreatures from Outer Space	1970	—	£7.50
50	Laramie	1964	£1.60	£80.00
50	Laurel & Hardy	1968	£2.50	—
M22	Mounties (Package Issue)	1960	£5.50	£121.00
50	Popeye	1960	£5.00	£250.00
50	Popeye, 2nd Series	1961	£5.00	£250.00
50	Popeye, 3rd Series	1962	—	£12.50
50	Popeye, 4th Series	1963	—	£12.50
50	Queen Elizabeth 2	1969	£1.00	£50.00
50	Quick Draw McGraw	1964	£2.50	—
50	Space Patrol	1970	—	£12.00
50	Space Race	1969	—	£4.00
12	Star Trek	1971	—	£5.00
50	Superman	1968	—	£16.50
50	The Flintstones	1963	60p	£30.00
50	Yellow Submarine	1968	£3.50	—
50	Z-Cars	1968	40p	£20.00

PRINCE EDWARD THEATRE

XF?4	Josephine Baker Cards	1930	£24.00	—

MICHAEL PRIOR (Commercial)

25	Racing Colours	1987	—	£6.00

S. PRIOR (Bookshop)

25	Do You Know?	1964	—	£15.00

PRIORY TEA CO. LTD.

50	Aircraft	1961	50p	£25.00
50	Birds	1962	60p	£30.00
24	Bridges	1960	—	£2.50
24	Cars	1958	£3.50	—

PRIORY TEA CO. LTD. — cont.

Qty		Date	Odds	Sets
50	Cars (Different)	1964	80p	£40.00
50	Cycles & Motorcycles	1963	£1.70	£85.00
24	Dogs	1957	—	£4.00
24	Flowering Trees	1959	—	£2.00
24	Men at Work	1959	—	£2.25
24	Out and About	1957	—	£3.00
24	People in Uniform	1956	£1.75	£42.00
24	Pets	1957	—	£3.00
50	Wild Flowers	1963	55p	£27.50

PRO SET INC. (Commercial, U.S.A.)

X100	Bill & Ted's Movie Cards	1991	—	£6.00
X100	Footballers and Fixture Lists	1991	—	£6.00
X100	Guinness Book of Records	1992	—	£6.00
X100	P.G.A. Tour Cards	1990	—	£13.50
X100	Thunderbirds	1992	20p	£9.00

PROPERT SHOE POLISH

25	British Uniforms	1955	—	£3.50

PUKKA TEA CO. LTD.

50	Aquarium Fish	1961	—	£45.00

PYREX LTD. (Glassware)

P16	Guide to Simple Cooking	1976	—	£2.50

QUAKER OATS

X12	Armour through the Ages	1968	£1.40	£16.50
M4	Famous Puffers	1983	£5.00	£20.00
M54	Historic Arms of Merrie England	1938	£1.00	—
X8	Historic Ships	1967	£4.00	£32.00
M6	Honey Monster's Circus Friends	1985	£2.50	—
15	Honey Monster's Crazy Games Cards	1985	£1.50	£22.50
M16	Jeremy's Animal Kingdom	1980	£1.25	£20.00
X4	Minibooks	1969	£2.75	£11.00
12	Monsters of the Deep	1984	£1.50	—
M6	Nature Trek	1976	40p	£2.40
X12	Prehistoric Animals	1967	£4.50	—
L8	Return to Oz	1985	£2.00	—
X12	Space Cards	1968	£4.50	—
X12	Vintage Engines	1967	£4.00	£48.00

PACKAGE ISSUES

12	British Customs	1961	60p	£7.50
L36	British Landmarks	1961	65p	—
12	Characters in Literature	1961	£1.50	—
12	Exploration & Adventure	1974	75p	£9.00
12	Famous Explorers	1961	£1.00	£12.00
12	Famous Inventors	1961	£1.50	£18.00
12	Famous Ships	1961	£1.00	—

QUAKER OATS — cont.

Qty		Date	Odds	Sets
12	Famous Women	1961	80p	—
12	Fascinating Costumes	1961	50p	£6.00
12	Great Feats of Building	1961	50p	£6.00
L36	Great Moments of Sport	1961	£2.25	—
12	History of Flight	1961	£1.25	£15.00
12	Homes and Houses	1961	75p	£9.00
L36	Household Hints	1961	65p	—
12	National Maritime Museum	1974	£1.25	—
12	National Motor Museum	1974	£1.50	£18.00
12	On the Seashore	1961	50p	£6.00
L36	Phiz-Quiz	1961	90p	—
L36	Railways of the World	1961	£1.75	—
12	Royal Air Force Museum	1974	£1.50	—
12	Science & Invention	1974	£1.00	£12.00
L36	The Story of Fashion	1961	65p	—
12	The Wild West	1961	£1.00	£12.00
12	Weapons & Armour	1961	£1.00	£12.00

QUEEN ELIZABETH LAUNDRY

45	Beauties	1912	£14.00	—

QUEENS OF YORK (Laundry)

30	Kings & Queens of England	1955	—	£30.00

QUORN SPECIALITIES LTD. (Foods)

25	Fish and Game	1963	£5.00	—

R. K. CONFECTIONERY CO. LTD.

32	Felix Pictures	1930	£30.00	—

RADIO FUN (Periodical)

20	British Sports Stars	1956	—	£5.00

RADIO REVIEW (Periodical)

L36	Broadcasting Stars	1936	£3.75	£135.00
E20	Broadcasting Stars	1936	£4.00	£80.00

RALEIGH BICYCLES

L48	Raleigh the All-Steel Bicycle	1957	£1.50	£72.00

REDDINGS TEA CO.

Qty		Date	Odds	Sets
25	Castles of Great Britain	1965	£1.60	£40.00
25	Cathedrals of Great Britain	1964	£1.60	£40.00
25	Heraldry of Famous Places	1966	£1.30	£32.50
48	Ships of the World	1964	--	£8.00
25	Strange Customs of the World	1970	—	£2.50
48	Warriors of the World	1962	£1.75	£84.00

REDDISH MAID CONFECTIONERY

50	Famous International Aircraft	1963	£3.00	£150.00
25	Famous International Athletes	1964	*£5.50*	—
25	International Footballers of Today	1965	£6.00	—

RED HEART (Pet Food)

P6	Cats	1954	—	£30.00
P6	Dogs, First Series	1953	—	£32.50
P6	Dogs, Second Series	1953	—	£35.00
P6	Dogs, Third Series	1954	—	£35.00

RED LETTER (Periodical)

P29	Charlie Chaplin Cards	1915	£12.00	£350.00
P?100	Fortune Cards (Playing Card Backs)	1932	£3.50	—
M4	Luck-Bringers (Silk)	1924	£15.00	£80.00
X72	Midget Message Cards	1916	£2.50	£180.00
X12	Red Letter Message Cards	1916	£3.00	£36.00
M100	The Handy Cooking Cards	1926	£1.00	—

REEVES LTD. (Confectionery)

25	Cricketers	1912	£27.00	£675.00

REFLECTIONS OF A BYGONE AGE (Fairs)

12	Nottingham Heritage Cards	1996	—	£2.00
6	Nottinghamshire Towns	2000	—	£1.00
6	Railways Around Nottingham	1996	—	£1.00
6	Steam Around Britain	2000	—	£1.00
12	Visitors to Nottingham Card Fair	1993	—	£2.00

REGENT OIL

T25	Do You Know?	1965	—	£2.50

RICHARDS COLLECTION (Commercial)

25	Soccer Stars of Yesteryear, Second Series	1997	—	£8.75
25	Soccer Stars of Yesteryear, Third Series	1997	—	£8.75
25	Soccer Stars of Yesteryear, Fourth Series	1998	—	£5.00

ESTEVE RIERA S.A. (Chocolate, Spain)

Qty		*Date*	*Odds*	*Sets*
X24	Costumes Through the Ages	1923	—	£30.00

RIDGWAY'S TEA

X20	Journey to the Moon (Package Issue)	1958	£6.25	—

RINGTONS LTD. (Tea)

25	Aircraft of World War II	1962	£1.40	£35.00
25	British Cavalry Uniforms of the 19th Century	1971	£1.25	—
25	Do You Know?	1964	—	£2.50
25	Fruits of Trees and Shrubs	1964	—	£2.50
25	Head-Dresses of the World	1973	—	£2.50
25	Historical Scenes	1964	—	£3.50
25	Old England	1964	—	£2.50
25	People & Places	1964	—	£2.50
25	Regimental Uniforms of the Past	1966	—	£5.00
25	Sailing Ships through the Ages	1967	—	£3.00
25	Ships of the Royal Navy	1961	—	£6.00
25	Sovereigns, Consorts & Rulers, First Series	1961	—	£7.50
25	Sovereigns, Consorts & Rulers, Second Series	1961	—	£7.50
25	The West	1968	—	£3.50
25	Then & Now	1970	—	£20.00
25	Trains of the World	1970	—	£2.50

RISCA TRAVEL AGENCY

25	Holiday Resorts	1957	—	£22.50

RIVERWYE PRODUCTIONS

X90	Laurel & Hardy	1997	—	£16.00
X72	Laurel & Hardy Millennium 2000 Celebrations	2000	—	£13.95
X72	Sherlock Holmes – Premiere Collection	2002	—	£19.95

D. ROBBINS & CO. (Bread, U.S.A.)

P24	Frontiers of Freedom	1942	—	£50.00
P24	Good Neighbors of the Americas	1942	—	£50.00
P24	Modern Wonders of the World	1942	—	£45.00
P23/24	Story of Transportation	1942	—	£45.00

ROBERTSON LTD. (Preserves)

1	Advertisement Gollywog	1962	—	£3.00
6	British Medals	1914	£20.00	—
L6	British Medals (Circular)	1914	£32.50	—
10	Musical Gollywogs (Shaped)	1956	£3.25	£32.50
10	Sporting Gollywogs (Shaped)	1955	£3.50	£35.00

ROBERTSON & WOODCOCK (Confectionery)

Qty		Date	Odds	Sets
50	British Aircraft Series	1933	£2.40	£120.00

CHRIS ROBINSON ATWORKSHOP (Commercial)

X16	The Pilgrims F.A.Cup Squad 1983-84	1984	—	£8.00

ROBINSON'S BARLEY WATER

X30	Sporting Records (with Folder)	1983	—	£5.00

ROBINSON BROS. & MASTERS LTD. (Tea)

25	Tea from the Garden to the Home	1930	£9.00	£225.00

ROB ROY CARDS (Commercial)

L20	Manchester United Series 1	1995	—	£15.00

ROCHE & CO. LTD. (Matches)

K49/50	Famous Footballers	1927	£8.00	—

THE ROCKET (Periodical)

MF11	Famous Knock-Outs	1923	£8.00	£88.00

ROCKWELL PUBLISHING

10	British Armoured Vehicles of World War II	2001	—	£4.50
L10	British Armoured Vehicles of World War II	2001	—	£7.00
10	British Fighting Jets	2003	—	£4.50
L10	British Fighting Jets	2003	—	£7.00
10	British Warplanes of the Second World War	2000	—	£4.50
L10	British Warplanes of the Second World War	2000	—	£7.50
10	Classic Football Teams Before the First World War (Sepia Borders)	2000	—	£4.50
L10	Classic Football Teams Before the First World War (Sepia Borders)	2000	—	£7.00
10	Classic Football Teams of the 1960s (Sepia Borders)	1999	—	£4.50
L10	Classic Football Teams of the 1960s (Sepia Borders)	1999	—	£7.00
L7	Classic Gunners (Soccer)	2001	—	£4.50
L7	Classic Spurs	2002	—	£4.50
10	Cunard in the 1950's	2003	—	£4.50
L10	Cunard in the 1950's	2003	—	£7.00

ROCKWELL PUBLISHING — cont.

Qty		Date	Odds	Sets
10	Early Allied Warplanes	2000	—	£4.50
L10	Early Allied Warplanes	2000	—	£7.00
X10	Early Allied Warplanes	2000	—	£7.50
10	Early Balloon Flight	2001	—	£4.50
L10	Early Balloon Flight	2001	—	£7.00
10	Family Cars of the 1950s	2000	—	£4.50
L10	Family Cars of the 1950s	2000	—	£7.50
X10	Family Cars of the 1950s	2000	—	£7.50
10	German Armoured Vehicles of World War II	2001	—	£4.50
L10	German Armoured Vehicles of World War II	2001	—	£7.00
X10	German Armoured Vehicles of World War II	2001	—	£7.50
10	German Warplanes of the Second World War	2000	—	£4.50
L10	German Warplanes of the Second World War	2000	—	£7.00
X10	German Warplanes of the Second World War	2000	—	£7.50
10	Hurricane Flying Colours	2002	—	£4.50
L10	Hurricane Flying Colours	2002	—	£7.00
10	Lost Warships of WWII	2002	—	£4.50
L10	Lost Warships of WWII	2002	—	£7.00
25	Olympic - Titanic - Britannic	2001	—	£8.50
L25	Olympic - Titanic - Britannic	2001	—	£10.00
10	Postcard Images of World War One	1999	—	£4.50
L10	Postcard Images of World War One	1999	—	£7.50
X10	Postcard Images of World War One	1999	—	£7.50
10	Solar System	2001	—	£4.50
L10	Solar System	2001	—	£7.00
10	Spitfire Flying Colours	1999	—	£4.50
L10	Spitfire Flying Colours	1999	—	£7.00
X10	Spitfire Flying Colours	1999	—	£7.50
10	The Great Heavyweights	2002	—	£4.50
L10	The Great Heavyweights	2002	—	£7.00
10	The Great Middleweights	2002	—	£4.50
L10	The Great Middleweights	2002	—	£7.00
25	The Titanic Series	1999	—	£9.00
L25	The Titanic Series	2000	—	£12.00
10	World War One Posters	2001	—	£4.50
L10	World War One Posters	2001	—	£7.00
10	World War II Posters – The Home Front	2001	—	£4.50
L10	World War II Posters – The Home Front	2001	—	£7.00
10	World War II Posters – The Services	2001	—	£4.50
L10	World War II Posters – The Services	2001	—	£7.00

RODEO BUBBLE GUM

M42	Western Stars	1953	£5.00	—

ROLLS ROYCE (Cars)

X25	Bentley Cars	1986	—	£50.00
X25	Bentley Cars, Second Edition	1987	—	£45.00
X25	Rolls Royce Cars	1986	—	£55.00
X25	Rolls Royce Cars, Second Edition	1987	—	£55.00

ROSSI'S (Ice Cream)

Qty		*Date*	*Odds*	*Sets*
M48	Flag Cards	1975	20p	£5.00
25	The History of Flight, 1st Series	1963	£1.00	£25.00
25	The History of Flight, 2nd Series	1963	£1.00	£25.00
25	World's Fastest Aircraft	1964	—	£20.00

DAVID ROWLAND (Commercial)

25	Association Footballers (Series 1)	1999	—	£7.50
25	Association Footballers (Series 2)	1999	—	£7.50
25	Association Footballers (Series 3)	1999	—	£7.50
25	Association Footballers (Series 4)	1999	—	£7.50
25	Association Footballers (Series 5)	1999	—	£7.50
20	Boxers (Series 1)	1999	—	£7.00

DAVID ROWLAND (Commercial) — cont.

20	Boxing Legends (Series 1)	1999	—	£7.00
25	Cricketers (Series 1)	1999	—	£7.50
25	Cricketers (Series 2)	1999	—	£7.50
20	Famous Footballers, Series 1	1999	—	£6.00
20	Famous Footballers, Series 2	1999	—	£6.00
20	Famous Footballers, Series 3	1999	—	£6.00
20	Famous Footballers, Series 4 (Managers)	1999	—	£6.00
20	Famous Footballers, Series 5	1999	—	£6.00

ROWNTREE & CO. (Confectionery)

K12	British Birds (Packet Issue)	1955	—	£24.00
25	Celebrities	1905	£24.00	—
X8	Circus Cut-Outs	1960	£5.50	£44.00
M20	Merry Monarchs	1978	—	£4.00
M18	Prehistoric Animals	1978	—	£7.50
L6	Punch & Judy Show	1976	£3.00	—
X42	Railway Engines (Caramac)	1976	—	£14.00
L2	Smartie Models	1976	—	£4.00
M10	Texan Tall Tales of the West	1977	£1.75	£17.50
48	The Old & The New	1934	£4.25	£212.50
120	Treasure Trove Pictures	1932	£1.75	—
24	York Views	1924	£11.00	—

ROYAL ARMY MEDICAL CORPS HISTORICAL MUSEUM

T16	Centenary Year RAMC Victoria Crosses	1998	—	£5.00

ROYAL LEAMINGTON SPA CORPORATION

25	Royal Leamington Spa	1975	—	£2.50

ROYAL NATIONAL LIFEBOAT INSTITUTION

Qty		Date	Odds	Sets
M16	Lifeboats	1979	—	£6.00

ROYAL SOCIETY FOR THE PREVENTION OF ACCIDENTS

24	Modern British Cars	1954	£2.00	£48.00
22	Modern British Motor-Cycles	1953	£3.25	£70.00
25	New Traffic Signs	1958	—	£6.00
24	Veteran Cars, First Series	1955	£2.00	£48.00
24	Veteran Cars, Second Series	1957	£1.50	£36.00

RUBY (Periodical)

T10	Famous Beauties of the Day	1923	£6.50	£65.00
T6	Famous Film Stars	1923	£9.00	—

RUGBY FOOTBALL UNION

50	English Internationals 1980-1991	1991	—	£12.50

RUGLYS

K22	English World Cup Rugby Squad	1999	—	£7.25
K22	Rugby World Cup All Stars	1999	—	£7.25
K25	Welsh Rugby World Cup Squad	1999	—	£8.20

S & B PRODUCTS (Commercial)

64	Torry Gillick's Internationals	1948	£8.50	—

S.C.M.C.C.

15	Stoke's Finest Hour (Soccer)	2002	—	£5.50

SAGION STUFFING

28	Dominoes without the Dot	1939	25p	£7.00

J. SAINSBURY LTD. (Groceries)

M12	British Birds	1924	£7.00	£84.00
M12	Foreign Birds	1924	£7.00	£84.00

SANDERS BROS. (Custard)

25	Birds, Fowls, Pigeons & Rabbits	1925	£6.00	—
20	Dogs	1926	£4.50	£90.00
25	Recipes	1924	£4.00	£100.00

SANITARIUM HEALTH FOOD CO. (Oceania)

Qty		*Date*	*Odds*	*Sets*
X12	Alpine Flora of New Zealand	1975	—	£2.50
X12	Alpine Sports	1986	—	£3.50
X12	Animals of New Zealand	1974	—	£4.50
L30	Another Look at New Zealand	1971	—	£3.00
L30	Antarctic Adventure	1972	—	£5.00
X25	Australian Bird Life	1963	—	£3.00
X12	Ball Sports	1989	—	£4.50
L20	Big Rigs	1983	—	£3.00
L20	Big Rigs at Work	1986	—	£3.00
L20	Big Rigs 3	1992	—	£3.00
X12	Bush Birds of New Zealand	1981	—	£3.00
L20	Cars of the Seventies	1976	—	£5.50
X12	Clocks through the Ages	1990	—	£5.00
L20	Conservation — Caring for Our Land	1974	—	£2.50
X12	Curious Conveyances	1984	—	£3.00
L20	Discover Indonesia	1977	—	£3.00
L20	Discover Science with the DSIR	1989	—	£2.50
L20	Exotic Cars	1987	—	£5.00
L20	Exploring our Solar System	1982	—	£3.75
L24	Famous New Zealanders	1971	—	£4.00
L20	Farewell to Steam	1981	—	£5.00
L30	Fascinating Orient	1974	—	£2.50
X12	Focus on New Zealand, Series 1	1979	—	£2.50
X12	Focus on New Zealand, Series 2	1982	—	£2.50
X12	Historic Buildings	1982	—	£4.00
X12	Historic Buildings 2nd Series	1984	—	£3.00
L20	History of Road Transport — New Zealand	1979	—	£5.00
X12	Horse Breeds	1990	—	£5.00
X12	Jet Aircraft	1974	—	£6.00
L20	Kiwis Going for Gold	1992	—	£3.00
L20	Looking at Canada	1978	—	£2.50
L20	Mammals of the Sea	1985	—	£2.50
X12	Man Made Wonders of the World	1987	—	£2.50
X12	Mountaineering	1987	—	£3.00
L25	National Costumes of the Old World (Different)	1968	—	£4.50
X12	New Zealand Disasters	1991	—	£2.50
X12	New Zealand Inventions and Discoveries	1991	—	£4.00
X12	New Zealand Lakes, Series 1	1977	—	£2.50
X12	New Zealand Lakes, Series 2	1978	—	£3.00
L30	New Zealand National Parks	1973	—	£5.00
L20	New Zealand Reef Fish	1984	—	£2.50
L20	New Zealand Summer Sports	1984	—	£3.50
L30	New Zealand To-Day	1974	—	£4.00
L20	New Zealand's Booming Industries	1975	—	£2.00
L20	New Zealanders in Antarctica	1987	—	£5.00
L20	New Zealanders on Top of the World	1991	—	£2.50
L20	'1990 – Look at How We've Grown'	1990	—	£2.50
L20	N.Z. Energy Resources	1976	—	£3.00
L20	N.Z. Rod and Custom Cars	1979	—	£5.00
X12	N.Z. Waterfalls	1981	—	£3.00
X12	Ocean Racers	1986	—	£3.00
L20	100 Years of New Zealand National Parks	1987	—	£2.50
X12	Our Fascinating Fungi	1980	—	£3.00
L20	Our Golden Fleece	1981	—	£2.50
L20	Our South Pacific Island Neighbours	1974	—	£4.00

SANITARIUM HEALTH FOOD CO. (Oceania) cont.

Qty		*Date*	*Odds*	*Sets*
L20	Our Weather	1980	—	£2.50
X12	Power Boats in New Zealand	1990	—	£3.50
L20	Saving The World's Endangered Wildlife	1991	—	£2.50
X12	Shipping in our Coastal Waters	1988	—	£2.50
X12	Spanning New Zealand (Bridges)	1992	—	£2.50
L20	Spectacular Sports	1974	—	£5.00
L20	Super Cars	1972	—	£6.00
X12	Surf Live-Saving	1986	—	£3.00
X10	The Hunchback of Notre Dame (Disney)	1996	—	£4.50
L20	The Many-Stranded Web of Nature	1983	—	£2.50
L20	The 1990 Commonwealth Games	1989	—	£4.00
L20	The Story of New Zealand Aviation	1977	—	£5.00
L20	The Story of New Zealand in Stamps	1977	—	£5.00
L20	The Wild South	1986	—	£2.50
M20	This World of Speed	1968	—	£3.50
L20	Timeless Japan	1975	—	£3.00
M20	Traditional Uniforms of the World	1969	—	£4.00
L20	Treasury of Maori Life	1980	—	£2.50
X12	Veteran Cars	1971	—	£5.50
L20	Vintage Cars	1973	—	£6.50
X12	Wild Flowers of N.Z.	1979	—	£3.00
X12	Windsports	1989	—	£3.00
L20	Wonderful Ways of Nature	1978	—	£2.50
X12	Wonderful Wool	1988	—	£2.50
L20	'World's Greatest Fun Parks'	1990	—	£4.00
L20	Your Journey through Disneyland	1988	—	£6.50

SAVOY PRODUCTS LTD. (Foods)

M56	Aerial Navigation	1926	£2.20	£120.00
M56	Aerial Navigation, Series B	1927	£1.80	£100.00
M56	Aerial Navigation, Series C	1928	£2.00	£110.00
M56	Famous British Boats	1928	£1.60	£90.00

SCANLEN'S (Gum, Australia)

X84	Cricket World Series	1990	—	£15.00
X84	International Cricketers	1989	—	£20.00
X90	World Series Cricket	1982	—	£20.00

THE SCHOOL FRIEND (Periodical)

L6	Famous Film Stars	1927	£9.00	£54.00
X10	Popular Girls of Cliff House School	1922	£10.00	£100.00
XF6	Popular Pictures	1923	£3.50	£21.00

THE SCHOOLGIRL (Periodical)

MF16	Zoological Studies	1923	£2.75	£44.00

SCHOOLGIRLS OWN (Periodical)

Qty		*Date*	*Odds*	*Sets*
12	Characters from Cliff House School	1932	£6.00	£72.00
F7	Film Stars (Anon.)	1929	£4.25	£30.00
12	Film Stars (Anon., Brown)	1932	£4.00	£48.00
12	The Royal Family (Anon., Brown)	1932	£3.75	£45.00

THE SCHOOLGIRLS' WEEKLY (Periodical)

F12	Famous Film Stars (Anon.)	1929	£5.25	—
XF1	HRH The Duke of York	1922	—	£6.00
XF4	Popular Pictures	1922	£3.75	£15.00

SCOTTISH DAILY EXPRESS

X24	Scotcards (Soccer)	1972	£6.00	—

THE SCOUT (Periodical)

L9	Birds' Eggs	1925	£5.50	£50.00
M12	Railway Engines	1924	£6.00	£72.00

SCRAPBOOK MINICARDS

27	Pendon Museum (Model Railway etc.)	1978	—	£2.00

SCREEN STORIES (Periodical)

F8	Film Stars (Anon.)	1930	£5.00	—

SECRETS (Periodical)

K52	Film Stars (Miniature Playing Cards)	1935	£1.50	—

SELF SERVICE LAUNDRETTES

50	150 Years of Locomotives	1955	£4.00	—

SELLOTAPE PRODUCTS LTD. (Adhesive Tape)

35	Great Homes and Castles	1974	40p	£14.00

A. J. SEWARD & CO. LTD. (Perfumes)

40	Stars of the Screen	1939	£10.00	—

SEYMOUR MEAD & CO. LTD. (Tea)

Qty		*Date*	*Odds*	*Sets*
24	The Island of Ceylon	1964	—	£2.00

SHARMAN (Newspapers)

T24	Golden Age of Flying	1979	—	£17.50
T24	Golden Age of Motoring	1979	—	£17.50
T24	Golden Age of Steam	1979	—	£17.50

EDWARD SHARP & SONS (Confectionery)

20	Captain Scarlet	1970	£6.00	£120.00
25	Hey Presto!	1970	—	£2.50
K53	Miniature Playing Cards	1924	£2.25	—
100	Prize Dogs	1924	£4.50	—

TONY SHELDON COLLECTIBLES PROMOTIONS

25	Famous Cricketers (Palmer Mann Reprint)	2001	—	£6.00
20	Kenyan Cricketers	1999	—	£7.25
20	Olden Goldies (Cricketers)	1998	—	£8.00
X18	Out of the Blue Into the Red (The Labour Cabinet)	1997	—	£6.75

SHELL (Oil)

M16	Animals (3-D)	1975	£1.00	£16.00
14	Bateman Series	1930	£7.00	£98.00
P20	Great Britons	1972	£1.50	£30.00
K20	Historic Cars (Medals) including Mount	1970	—	£20.00
K16	Man in Flight (Medals) including Mount	1970	£1.25	£20.00
M12	Olympic Greats (with Album)	1992	—	£3.00
M16	Wonders of the World (3-D)	1976	50p	£8.00

AUSTRALIAN ISSUES

M60	Beetle Series (301-360)	1962	50p	—
M60	Birds (121-180)	1960	45p	£26.00
M60	Butterflies and Moths (181-240)	1960	60p	—
M60	Citizenship Series	1965	30p	£18.00
M60	Discover Australia with Shell	1959	50p	£30.00
M60	Meteorology Series (361-420)	1963	30p	£18.00
M60	Pets (481-540)	1964	—	£24.00
M60	Shells, Fish and Coral (61-120)	1959	40p	£24.00
M60	Transportation Series (241-300)	1961	—	£24.00

NEW ZEALAND ISSUES

M48	Aircraft of the World	1970	—	£8.00
M60	Cars of the World	1970	—	£20.00
M48	Racing Cars of the World	1970	50p	£24.00
40	Vintage Cars (Transfers)	1970	30p	£12.00
L40	World of Cricket	1992	—	£10.00
P20	World of Cricket (Doubles)	1992	—	£15.00

SHELLEY'S ICE CREAM

Qty		*Date*	*Odds*	*Sets*
25	Essex-County Champions	1984	25p	£6.25

SHEPHERDS DAIRIES LTD.

100	War Series	1915	£8.00	—

SHERIDAN COLLECTIBLES (Commercial)

X12	Bobby Jones and St. Andrews	1995	—	£6.50
X1	Bobby Jones and St. Andrews, Promotional Card.	1995	—	50p
L7	Railway Posters – Golf	1996	—	£2.50
X1	St. Andrews, Advertisement Card	1995	—	50p
X12	The Bobby Jones Story	1993	—	£6.50
L6	The Golf Adventures of Par Bear	1994	—	£3.00
X25	The Players of the Ryder Cup '93	1994	—	£10.00
X12	The Tom Morris Story	1994	—	£6.50
X2	The Tom Morris Story, Substitute Cards	1995	—	£1.00
L7	"Underground Art" Football & Wembley	1996	—	£2.50
L7	"Underground Art" Rugby	1996	—	£2.50
L7	"Underground Art" Wimbledon	1996	—	£2.50
L7	"Underground Art" Windsor	1996	—	£2.50
L12	Winners of the Ryder Cup '95	1996	—	£6.50

SHERMAN'S POOLS LTD.

P8	Famous Film Stars	1940	75p	£6.00
P37	Famous Teams	1938	£4.00	£150.00
P2/37	Ditto (Aston Villa & Blackpool)	1938	—	£1.00
P38	Searchlight on Famous Players	1937	£4.50	—

W. SHIPTON LTD. (Commercial)

75	Trojan Gen-Cards	1959	80p	£60.00

SHUREY'S PUBLICATIONS LTD.

P?750	Views (Various Printings)	1906	£1.25	—

SIDELINES (Commercial)

L23	19th Century Cricket Teams	1988	—	£4.00

SILVER KING & CO. (Theatrical)

1	Advertisement Card	1905	—	£13.50

SINGER SEWING MACHINE CO.

52	Beauties (Playing Card Inset)	1898	£15.00	£780.00
P36	Costumes of All Nations	1892	£7.50	£270.00
P18	Costumes of All Nations (Different)	1894	£12.50	£225.00

SKETCHLEY CLEANERS

Qty		*Date*	*Odds*	*Sets*
25	A Nature Series	1960	—	£6.00
25	Communications	1960	—	£8.50
25	Tropical Birds	1960	—	£10.00

SKYBOX INTERNATIONAL (Commercial, U.S.A.)

X60	Babylon 5	1996	—	£17.50
X81	Babylon 5: Season 5	1998	—	£20.00
P60	Star Trek: First Contact (Widevision)	1996	—	£20.00
X96	Star Trek: TNG: The Episodes – Season 2	1995	—	£25.00
X108	Star Trek: TNG: The Episodes – Season 3	1995	—	£18.00
X108	Star Trek: TNG: The Episodes – Season 4	1995	—	£18.00
X108	Star Trek: TNG: The Episodes – Season 5	1996	—	£12.00
X108	Star Trek TNG Season 6	1997	—	£12.00
X100	Star Trek: 30 Years Phase	1995	—	£10.00

SLADE & BULLOCK LTD. (Confectionery)

25	Cricket Series	1924	*£60.00*	—
25	Football Terms	1924	£20.00	—
25	Modern Inventions	1925	£10.00	—
20	Now & Then Series	1925	£12.00	—
25	Nursery Rhymes	1925	£13.00	—
25	Science & Skill Series	1925	£12.00	—
25	Simple Toys & How to Make Them	1925	£12.50	—

P. SLUIS (Bird Food)

X30	Tropical Birds	1962	—	£15.00

SMART NOVELS (Periodical)

MF12	Stage Artistes & Entertainers	1924	£4.50	£54.00

JOHN SMITH (Brewers)

P5	Limericks (Beer Mats)	1976	—	£2.50

SNAP CARDS (Gum)

L50	ATV Stars, Series No. 1	1959	£1.80	£90.00
L48	ATV Stars, Series No. 2	1960	£1.50	£72.00
L50	Associated-Rediffusion Stars	1960	£1.80	£90.00
L50	Dotto Celebrities	1959	£1.20	£60.00

H. A. SNOW (Films)

12	Hunting Big Game in Africa	1923	£5.50	£66.00

SOCCER BUBBLE GUM

Qty		*Date*	*Odds*	*Sets*
M48	Soccer Teams, No.1 Series	1956	£2.00	£96.00
M48	Soccer Teams, No.2 Series	1958	£2.75	£132.00

SODASTREAM (Confectionery)

25	Historical Buildings	1957	—	£2.50

SOLDIER MAGAZINE

M24	The British Army - 1993	1993	—	£4.50

SOMPORTEX LTD. (Gum Vending)

X72	Adventures of Sexton Blake	1968	£2.00	—
L60	Famous T.V. Wrestlers	1966	£2.75	£165.00
L60	Film Scene Series, James Bond 007	1966	£5.50	—
L72	John Drake Danger Man	1966	£4.00	£290.00
L50	The Exciting World of James Bond 007	1965	£5.50	—
L72	The Saint	1967	£5.50	—
L71/72	Thunderball	1967	£2.25	£160.00
L72	Ditto	1967	—	£190.00
X73	Thunderbirds (Coloured)	1967	£5.50	—
L72	Thunderbirds (Black & White)	1967	£5.00	£360.00
X72	Thunderbirds (Black & White)	1967	£2.70	£195.00
X36	Weirdies	1968	90p	£32.50
26	You Only Live Twice (Film Strips)	1969	£10.00	—

SONNY BOY (Confectionery)

50	Railway Engines	1960	—	£9.00

SOUTH AFRICAN EGGS

L6	Oeufs Travel Collection	1988	—	£3.00

SOUTH WALES CONSTABULARY

X36	British Stamps	1983	—	£9.00
L36	Castles and Historic Places in Wales	1988	—	£10.00
X36	Merthyr Tydfil Borough Council	1987	—	£10.00
X37	Payphones Past and Present	1987	—	£25.00
X36	Rhymney Valley District Council	1986	—	£8.00
M32	Sport-A-Card	1991	—	£13.50
X35	The '82 Squad (Rugby)	1982	80p	£42.00

SPAR GROCERS

X30	Disney on Parade	1972	£4.00	—

SPILLERS NEPHEWS (Biscuits)

Qty		*Date*	*Odds*	*Sets*
25	Conundrum Series	1910	£18.50	—
40	Views of South Wales & District	1910	£17.50	—

SPORT AND ADVENTURE (Periodical)

M46	Famous Footballers	1922	£3.00	£138.00

SPORTING PROFILES (Commercial)

L16	AKA Cassius Clay	2002	—	£9.99
L17	FA Cup Final Programmes	2001	—	£7.50
L4	Heavyweight Champions of the 'Naughty '90s'	2001	—	£1.50
L40	Henry Cooper: A Career History	1997	—	£10.95
L23	Heroes of the Prize Ring	1993	—	£6.00
X25	Joe Louis	2000	—	£15.00
X11	John L. Sullivan Cradle to Grave	1997	—	£5.00
L30	Movies Idols – Humphrey Bogart	2003	—	£10.00
L30	Muhammad Ali – The Magazine Covers	2002	—	£9.00
L8	Rocky Marciano	2001	—	£3.00
L20	Steptoe & Son	2003	—	£.9.99
L50	The Greatest (Muhammad Ali)	1993	—	£12.00
L9	Tony Hancock – The Lad Himself	2002	—	£5.00

SPORT IN PRINT (Commercial)

M64	Nottinghamshire Cricketers	1989	—	£20.00

SPORT PHOTOS (Commercial)

96	"Smashers" (Soccer)	1950	£9.00	—

SPORTS TIME, INC. (Commercial, U.S.A.)

X100	Baywatch	1995	—	£10.00

SPRATTS PATENT LTD. (Pet Food)

K100	British Bird Series (Numbered)	1935	£4.50	—
K50	(Unnumbered)	1935	£3.50	£175.00
42	British Birds	1926	£5.00	£210.00
36	Champion Dogs	1926	£12.50	—
K20	Fish	1935	£11.50	£230.00
K100	Poultry Series	1935	£12.50	—
12	Prize Dogs	1910	£37.50	—
12	Prize Poultry	1910	£37.50	—
25	The Bonzo Series	1924	£6.00	£150.00

THE STAMP KING MANSFIELD

L7	Robin Hood	2002	—	£3.00

STAR JUNIOR CLUB

Qty		Date	Odds	Sets
10	Animals	1960	£1.00	£10.00
10	Sports & Games (Numbered)	1960	£2.00	£20.00
5	Sports & Games (Unnumbered)	1960	£2.00	£10.00

STAVELEY'S (Shop)

24	World's Most Beautiful Birds	1924	£5.50	—

STOKES & DALTON (Cereals)

M20	The Crimson Cobra	1950	£2.00	£40.00

STOLL (Films)

25	Stars of To-Day	1930	£7.00	—
25	The Mystery of Dr. Fu-Manchu	1930	£11.00	—

STOLLWERCK (Chocolate)

T144	Animal World	1902	£1.20	£175.00
F?100	Views of the World	1915	£5.00	—

THE SUN (Newspaper)

M134	Football Swap Cards	1970	50p	£67.00
M52	Gallery of Football Action	1972	£2.50	£130.00
M6	How to Play Football	1972	£3.50	£21.00
M54	Page 3 Playing Cards	1979	—	£10.00
160	Royal Album Stickers (& Album)	1989	—	£5.50
P50	3D Gallery of Football Stars	1972	£3.25	—

SUNBLEST (Bread, Australia)

M24	Sports Action Series	1975	—	£8.50
M25	Sunblest Explorer Cards	1975	—	£4.50

SUNBLEST TEA

25	Inventions & Discoveries, 1st Series	1960	—	£10.00
25	Inventions & Discoveries, 2nd Series	1960	—	£15.00
25	Prehistoric Animals, 1st Series	1960	—	£8.50
25	Prehistoric Animals, 2nd Series	1960	—	£8.00

SUNDAY EMPIRE NEWS

Qty		Date	Odds	Sets
48	Famous Footballers of Today (Durling)	1953	£3.75	£180.00

SUNDAY STORIES (Periodical)

M5	Flags (Silk)	1916	£12.00	—
M6	The King & His Soldiers (Silk)	1916	£12.50	£75.00

THE SUNDAY TIMES (Newspaper)

X100	Great Cars of the World (With Album)	1989	—	£8.00
40	Seaside Project (& Wallchart)	1989	—	£3.00
40	200 Years of Cricket (& Wallchart)	1989	—	£7.50
40	Young Persons Guide to the Orchestra (& Wallchart)	1989	—	£4.50

SWEETACRE (Confectionery, Australia)

48	Aircraft of the World	1932	£2.75	£132.00
36	Cricketers (Minties)	1926	£11.00	£400.00
24	Cricketers (Caricatures)	1938	*£22.50*	—
48	Favourite Dogs	1932	£4.25	£200.00
32	Prominent Cricketers (33-64)	1932	£4.00	£128.00
48	Sports Champions	1933	£3.50	£315.00
48	Steamships of the World	1932	£3.00	£144.00
32	Test Records (1-32)	1932	£4.00	£128.00
48	This World of Ours	1932	£3.25	—

SWEETULE PRODUCTS (Confectionery)

18	Aircraft (Packet)	1954	£5.50	£100.00
25	A Nature Series	1960	—	£2.50
25	Animals of the Countryside	1959	—	£2.50
25	Archie Andrews Jokes	1957	£7.25	—
25	Birds and Their Eggs	1954	—	£2.50
25	Birds and Their Eggs (Black Back)	1959	—	£5.00
25	(Blue Back)	1959	—	£5.00
25	Birds & Their Haunts	1958	£3.50	£87.50
52	Birds, Fish & Flowers (P/C Inset)	1961	—	£16.50
25	Birds of the British Commonwealth (Black Back)	1954	—	£2.50
25	(Blue Back)	1954	—	£2.50
M12	Coronation Series 1953 (Packet)	1953	£6.50	—
25	Do You Know?	1963	—	£3.00
25	Family Crests	1961	—	£2.25
25	Famous Sports Records	1957	—	£17.50
25	Football Club Nicknames	1959	—	£8.00
K18	Historical Cars & Cycles	1957	—	£10.00
18	Home Pets (Packet)	1954	£6.00	—
25	International Footballers (Packet)	1962	£6.50	£162.50
25	Junior Service Quiz	1959	—	£3.00
18	Landmarks of Flying (Packet)	1961	£5.00	£90.00
50	Modern Aircraft	1954	—	£6.00
25	Modern Transport	1955	—	£2.50
18	Motor Cars (Packet)	1952	£9.00	—
50	Motorcycles Old and New	1963	—	£75.00

SWEETULE PRODUCTS (Confectionery) — cont.

Qty		*Date*	*Odds*	*Sets*
30	National Flags & Costumes	1962	—	£16.50
25	Naval Battles	1959	—	£3.00
25	Products of the World	1958	—	£2.00
24	Racing Cars of the World (Packet)	1960	£8.00	—
18	Railway Engines — Past & Present (Packet)	1953	£7.00	£126.00
25	Sports Quiz	1958	—	£5.00
1	Stamp Card (Real Stamp Attached)	1962	—	35p
25	Stamp Cards	1961	—	£4.00
25	The Wild West (Black Back)	1960	—	£10.00
25	(Blue Back)	1960	—	£3.00
X30	Trains of the World	1960	£1.40	£42.00
25	Treasure Island	1957	—	£7.50
25	Tropical Birds	1954	—	£3.50
25	Vintage Cars	1964	—	£8.50
25	Weapons of Defence	1959	—	£2.50
25	Wild Animals	1958	—	£2.50
25	Wild Flowers	1961	—	£2.00
25	Wonders of the World	1956	—	£2.00

SWETTENHAM (Tea)

25	Aircraft of the World	1959	—	£12.50
25	Animals of the Countryside	1959	—	£2.00
25	Birds and Their Eggs	1958	—	£2.00
25	British Coins and Costumes	1958	—	£4.00
25	Butterflies and Moths	1958	—	£2.50
25	Evolution of the Royal Navy	1957	—	£2.50
25	Into Space	1959	—	£2.50
24	The Island of Ceylon (Conqueror Tea)	1964	£3.50	—
25	Wild Animals	1958	—	£5.00

W. SWORD & CO. (Biscuits)

25	British Empire at Work	1925	£11.00	—
20	Dogs	1926	£12.00	—
20	Inventors & Their Inventions	1926	*£12.00*	—
25	Safety First	1927	*£10.50*	—
25	Sports & Pastimes Series	1926	*£12.50*	—
25	Vehicles of All Ages	1924	*£11.50*	—
25	Zoo Series (Brown)	1928	£8.50	£212.50
25	Zoo Series (Coloured, Different)	1928	£10.50	—

SYMONDS CIDER & ENGLISH WINE COMPANY LTD.

M10	Sporting Greats (Early 1900s)	1998	—	£10.00

DES TAYLOR (Commercial)

L20	My Favourite Fish	2000	—	£7.50

TEACHER'S WHISKY

Qty		*Date*	*Odds*	*Sets*
X12	Scottish Clans & Castles (Circular Adv.)	1955	£4.50	—
X12	Scottish Clans & Tartans (Rectangular Adv.)	1955	£2.25	—

TEAMS LTD. (Commercial)

40	40 Years of Cards (Brooke Bond)	1994	—	£4.00

TEASDALE & CO. (Confectionery)

50	Cinema Stars (Anon.)	1935	£6.50	—
25	Great War Series	1916	£21.50	—

TESCO STORES

P6	Nature Trail Stickers	1989	—	£1.50

TETLEY TEA

48	British Birds	1970	£3.25	£156.00

TEXACO PETROL

12	Texaco Trophy Cricket Cards	1984	50p	£6.00

D. C. THOMSON & CO. LTD. (Periodical)

L30	Adventure Pictures	1929	£2.50	£75.00
M16	Badges of the Fighting Flyers	1939	£3.00	£48.00
P26	Battles for the Flag	1939	£5.00	—
K80	Boys of All Nations	1936	£1.20	—
20	British Birds and Eggs	1930	£2.65	£53.00
F11	British Team of Footballers	1923	£2.70	£30.00
L20	Canvas Masterpieces (Silk)	1925	£9.00	—
16	Catch-My-Pal Cards	1939	£1.25	£20.00
X12	Coloured Photos of Star Footballers	1927	£6.00	£72.00
64	County Cricketers	1955	£2.25	£144.00
16	Cricket Crests	1934	£8.25	£132.00
KF8	Cricketers	1923	£2.50	£20.00
X24	Cricketers	1924	£7.75	£186.00
P16	Cup-Tie Stars of All Nations	1962	£3.25	£52.00
12	Dandy Dogs	1928	£4.25	—
K28	Dominoes — School Caricatures	1936	£2.00	£56.00
20	Easy Scientific Experiments	1930	£2.40	£48.00
MF18	Famous British Footballers (English)	1923	£2.70	£48.50
K80	Famous Feats	1937	£1.20	—
24	Famous Fights	1935	£2.00	—
25	Famous Footballers	1955	£1.80	£45.00
24	Famous Footballers (Different)	1956	£1.75	£42.00
20	Famous Liners	1930	£3.25	£65.00

Qty		*Date*	*Odds*	*Sets*
L32	Famous Ships	1931	£3.50	£125.00
P12	Famous Teams in Football History	1961	£4.50	£54.00
P16	Famous Teams in Football History, 2nd Series	1962	£4.25	£68.00
16	Flags of All Nations	1934	£2.25	£36.00
K80	Flags of the Sea	1937	£1.00	—
KF137	Footballers	1923	85p	—
F18	Footballers	1923	£2.25	£40.00
X8	Footballers	1933	£6.00	£48.00
K52	Footballers — Hunt the Cup Cards	1934	£2.40	—
24	Footballers — Motor Cars (Double-Sided)	1929	£6.75	£162.00
MF22	Footballers — Signed Real Photos	1923	£2.00	£44.00
F40	Football Photos	1925	£5.00	—
48	Football Stars	1957	£2.00	£100.00
44	Football Stars of 1959	1959	£2.50	£110.00
K60/64	Football Team Cards	1934	£1.00	£60.00
64	Football Tips & Tricks	1955	75p	£48.00
L32	Football Towns and Their Crests	1931	£4.50	£144.00
T12	Great Captains	1972	£4.00	£48.00
12	Guns in Action	1938	£1.75	£21.00
M8	Hidden Treasure Clue Cards	1930	£12.50	—
P16	International Cup Teams	1964	£3.50	£56.00
6	Ju-Jitsu Cards	1925	£4.50	£27.00
24	Motor Bike Cards	1926	£5.50	£132.00
20	Motor Cycles	1930	£6.00	—
K100	Motor Cars	1934	£1.20	—
11	Mystic Menagerie	1925	£5.00	£55.00
36	1930 Speedway Stars	1930	£7.00	£252.00
K80	Punishment Cards	1936	£1.25	—
12	Queer Animals	1928	£2.50	£30.00
16	Queer Birds	1934	£2.50	£40.00
K80	Secrets of Cricket	1936	£2.25	—
36	Spadgers Monster Collection of Spoofs	1936	£2.50	—
48	Speed	1937	85p	£42.00
12	Speedsters of the Wilds	1928	£2.75	£33.00
48	Stars of Sport and Entertainment	1960	£1.75	£84.00
8/14	Star Footballers (Metal)	1932	£11.50	—
P22	Star Teams of 1961	1961	£3.25	£70.00
P16	The Great Stars of Football	1968	£3.00	£48.00
20	The Wireless Telephone	1930	£2.25	£45.00
32	The World's Best Cricketers (Green)	1926	£2.40	£75.00
36	The World's Best Cricketers (Mauve)	1930	£5.50	£198.00
72	The World's Best Cricketers	1958	£2.25	£162.00
X12	The World's Biggest	1937	£6.50	£78.00
30	This Seasons Latest Motor Cars (Metal)	1926	£16.00	—
K25	This Year's Motor Car Crests (Metal)	1926	£16.00	—
24	This Year's Top-Form Footballers	1924	£2.70	£65.00
P12	Top Cup Teams (Hornet)	1966	£4.50	£54.00
10	Vanguard Photo Gallery	1923	£11.50	—
96	VP Flips	1925	£1.25	—
24	Warrior Cards (Sectional Back)	1929	£2.25	£54.00
K28	Warrior Cards (Domino Back)	1936	£1.60	£45.00
K80	Warrior Cards	1937	£1.00	—
20	Why?	1930	£2.25	—
K28	Wild West Dominoes	1936	£1.75	£50.00
20	Wonders of the Rail	1930	£3.50	£70.00

D. C. THOMSON & CO. LTD. (Periodical) — cont.

Qty		Date	Odds	Sets
20	Wonders of the World	1930	£1.75	£35.00
64	World Cup Footballers	1958	£2.75	£176.00
M72	World Cup Stars	1970	£2.75	£198.00

THURMER & SYMES (Biscuits)

M96	Ocean Giants	1954	£2.40	—

TIMARU MILLING CO. (Cereals, New Zealand)

36	Focus on Fame	1948	—	£14.00
37	Peace & Progress	1947	—	£14.00
36	Victory Album Cards	1946	—	£20.00

TIMES CONFECTIONERY CO. LTD.

MF24	Roy Rogers — In Old Amarillo (Plain Back)	1955	—	£8.00
M24	(Printed Back)	1955	—	£16.00
MF24	Roy Rogers — South Of Caliente (Plain Back)	1955	—	£8.00
M24	(Printed Back)	1955	—	£16.00

TIP TOP (Ice Cream, New Zealand)

M10	Galactic Bar	1977	—	£10.00

TIP TOP SALES COMPANY (Malta)

M25	European Football Action, Series A	1932	£15.00	£375.00

TIT-BITS (Periodical)

K54	Pin-Ups (P/C Inset)	1976	—	£6.50
TF17	Star Cover Girls	1953	£4.00	—
T12	Tit-Bits Clubs	1977	£2.00	£24.00

CHOCOLAT TOBLER LTD.

50	Famous Footballers	1939	£8.50	—
T186	General Interest Series	1900	£1.20	£220.00

TOBY (Periodical)

24	Dogs (Anon.)	1926	£4.00	—
24	Dogs, 2nd Series (25-48, Anon.)	1926	£4.00	—
24	Sights of London (Anon.)	1926	£3.25	£78.00
24	Toby's Bird Series	1926	£3.25	—
24	Toby's Ship Series	1926	£3.50	£84.00
24	Toby's Travel Series	1926	£3.00	£72.00

TODAY (Newspaper)

Qty		Date	Odds	Sets
X14	Around Britain	1991	—	£2.50

TOMMY GUNN (Toys)

50	Medals (Plain Back)	1971	—	£4.00

TOM THUMB (New Zealand)

M24	Supercars	1980	—	£10.00

TONIBELL (Ice Cream)

12	Action Soldiers (with Cadbury)	1976	—	£3.00
M20	Banknotes	1974	20p	£3.00
M12	Beautiful Butterflies	1974	20p	£2.00
M20	County Badge Collection	1974	20p	£3.00
25	Did You Know?	1963	—	£2.50
L12	Did You Know? (Different)	1975	£1.25	—
X12	England's Soccer Stars	1970	£3.25	£40.00
D19	Famous Sports Trophies	1976	—	£8.00
D12	Farmyard Stencils	1977	—	£4.00
M24	1st Division Football League Club Badges	1972	£2.25	£54.00
X12	Horses in the Service of Man	1984	80p	£10.00
25	Inventions that Changed the World	1963	—	£2.50
X10	Junior Champs	1983	50p	£5.00
M24	Kings of the Road	1977	£1.00	£24.00
L24	Pop Star Cameos	1975	—	£8.00
K36	Team of All Time	1971	£1.75	£63.00
25	The World's Passenger Liners	1963	—	£2.50
25	This Changing World (With Line)	1963	—	£5.00
25	(Without Line)	1963	—	£6.00
25	Wonders of the Heavens	1963	—	£8.00

TOP FLIGHT (Confectionery)

25	Top Flight Stars (Sport)	1960	—	£65.00

TOPICAL TIMES (Periodical)

E8	Cricketers	1938	£14.00	£112.00
M6	Football Teams (Metal)	1924	£13.50	—
MF6	Football Teams	1924	£5.00	£30.00
MF10	Footballers (Pairs)	1924	£4.00	£40.00
E12	Footballers, Panel Portraits	1932	£4.25	£51.00
E24	Footballers, Panel Portraits	1933	£3.75	—
E14	Footballers, Panel Portraits	1934	£3.50	£49.00
E14	Footballers, Panel Portraits	1935	£3.50	£49.00
E16	Footballers, Panel Portraits (Coloured)	1936	£5.75	£92.00
E14	Footballers, Panel Portraits	1938	£3.50	£49.00
E16	Footballers, Panel Portraits	1939	£3.50	£56.00
E8	Footballers, Special Issue (Coloured)	1934	£6.00	£48.00
E8	Footballers, Triple Portraits	1937	£6.00	£48.00
L24	Great Players	1938	£2.75	£66.00
P24	Miniature Panel Portraits	1937	£2.75	£66.00
P24	Stars of To-Day	1938	£2.75	£66.00

TOP NOTE SLIDES

Qty		Date	Odds	Sets
P9	Pop Singers	1952	£5.50	—

TOPPS CHEWING GUM INC.

L80	A.L.F.	1988	—	£12.50
L88	American Baseball Stars	1988	—	£22.50
L88	American Baseball Stars	1989	—	£30.00
X99	Autos of 1977	1977	£1.50	£150.00
X98	Batman Returns (with Stickers)	1993	—	£4.00
X132	Battlestar Galactica	1979	20p	£26.00
X66	Bay City Rollers	1978	30p	£20.00
X49	Comic Book Heroes	1975	£2.00	£98.00
X99	Dick Tracy	1990	—	£10.00
X70	England 2002 (Soccer)	2002	—	£17.50
P18	England World Cup Supersquad	1990	—	£12.00
X220	Footballers (Red Back)	1975	£1.00	—
X88	Footballers (Scottish, Blue Back)	1975	£1.50	—
X330	Footballers (Blue Back)	1976	75p	£248.00
X132	Footballers (Scottish, Red Back)	1976	£1.50	—
X330	Footballers (Red Back)	1977	£1.00	—
X132	Footballers (Scottish, Yellow Back)	1977	75p	£99.00
X396	Footballers (Orange Back)	1978	25p	£100.00
X132	Footballers (Scottish, Green Back)	1978	90p	—
X396	Footballers (Pale Blue Back)	1979	£1.00	—
X132	Footballers (Scottish, Red Back)	1979	£1.00	—
X66	Footballers (Pink Back)	1980	£1.75	£115.00
X65	Footballers (Blue Back)	1981	80p	£52.00
X10/14	Footballers Stadium Club Promotion Cards	1992	—	£2.00
E18	Football Posters	1980	85p	£15.00
L41	Garbage Pail Kids, 1st Series A	1986	—	£15.00
L41	Garbage Pail Kids, 1st Series B	1986	—	£15.00
L42	Garbage Pail Kids, 2nd Series A	1986	—	£15.00
L42	Garbage Pail Kids, 2nd Series B	1986	—	£17.50
L55	Garbage Pail Kids, 3rd Series A	1987	—	£15.00
L70	Garbage Pail Kids, 3rd Series B	1987	—	£17.50
L48	Garbage Pail Kids, 4th Series A	1987	—	£15.00
L76	Garbage Pail Kids, 4th Series B	1987	—	£17.50
L60	Garbage Pail Kids, 5th Series A	1988	—	£15.00
L70	Garbage Pail Kids, 5th Series B	1988	—	£15.00
L44	Garbage Pail Kids, 6th Series A	1988	—	£17.50
L88	Garbage Pail Kids, 6th Series B	1988	—	£20.00
X77	Home Alone 2 (with Stickers)	1993	—	£3.00
X44	Home and Away	1987	—	£5.00
X110	Hook (with Stickers)	1991	—	£8.50
X99	Jurassic Park (with Stickers)	1993	—	£12.50
X49	Marvel Super Heroes	1980	£1.50	£75.00
X48	Monster In My Pocket	1991	—	£5.00
X66	Planet of the Apes	1974	£1.75	£115.00
X125	Premier Gold 2002	2002	—	£17.50
M75	Pro-Cycling	1988	—	£7.50
X72	Railway Quiz (See A. & B. C.)	1959	—	—
L264	Saint & Greavsie	1988	—	£20.00
P18	Scotland World Cup Supersquad	1990	£2.50	£45.00
X50	Shocking Laffs	1977	£2.00	£100.00
X66	Spitting Image	1990	—	£15.00
X88	Star Trek, The Motion Picture	1980	£1.75	£154.00

TOPPS CHEWING GUM INC. — cont.

Qty		Date	Odds	Sets
X66	Star Wars (1-66)	1978	£1.75	£115.00
X66	Star Wars (1A-66A)	1978	£2.75	—
X66	Superman The Movie, 1st Series (1-66)	1979	30p	£20.00
X66	Superman The Movie, 2nd Series (67-132)	1979	30p	£20.00
X77	Teenage Mutant Hero Turtles (T.V.)	1990	—	£7.50
X143	Teenage Mutant Ninja Turtles (Film)	1990	—	£7.50
M44	Terminator 2	1991	30p	£13.50
X88	The Black Hole	1980	40p	£35.00
X99	The Flintstones (with Stickers)	1994	—	£6.50
X66	Wacky Wrestling	1993	—	£5.00
X42	Wanted Posters	1978	60p	£25.00
U.S. ISSUES				
X154	Batman — The Movie (with Stickers)	1989	—	£20.00
X88	Buck Rogers in the 25th Century	1979	—	£18.00
X77	Close Encounters	1982	—	£25.00
P72	Dragonhearts (Widevision)	1996	—	£12.00
X99	Ghostbusters II (with Stickers)	1989	—	£17.50
X99	Greatest Olympians	1983	—	£10.50
X88	Gremlins 2	1990	—	£9.00
X59	Jaws 2	1978	—	£20.00
X99	Jurassic Park (with Stickers)	1993	—	£15.00
X33	Michael Jackson, 1st Stickers	1984	—	£12.50
X55	Mysteries of India	1967	—	£32.00
X66	Rambo	1985	—	£12.00
X22	Rambo (Stickers)	1985	—	£6.00
X99	Rocky II	1981	—	£10.00
X22	Rocky II (Stickers)	1981	—	£6.00
X66	Rocky IV	1986	—	£7.00
X11	Rocky IV (Stickers)	1986	—	£6.00
X50	Shocking Laffs	1976	£1.50	£75.00
G12	Smurf Tattoos	1983	—	£30.00
P80	Star Wars Episode 1 (Widevision)	1999	—	£19.50
P80	Star Wars Episode 1 Series Two (Widevision)	1999	—	£22.00
X66	Star Wars Series 3 (Yellow)	1977	—	£45.00
X66	Star Wars Series 4 (Green)	1977	—	£55.00
X66	Star Wars Series 5 (Orange)	1977	—	£55.00
X88	Superman II	1981	—	£25.00
X99	Superman III	1983	—	£20.00
X143	Teenage Mutant Ninja Turtles (Film)	1990	—	£10.00
X99	Teenage Mutant Ninja Turtles (T.V.)	1989	—	£7.50
X66	The 'A' Team	1983	—	£10.00
X86	The Goonies	1987	—	£17.50
X72	The X Files Season One	1995	—	£14.00
X72	The X Files Season Two	1996	—	£12.00
X72	The X Files Season Three	1996	—	£12.00
P72	The X Files Showcase (Widevision)	1997	—	£15.00
X55	Weird Wheels	1980	—	£10.00

JOHN TORDOFF & SON LTD. (Tea)

25	Safety First	1926	£8.50	—
25	The Growth and Manufacture of Tea	1926	£9.00	—

TOTAL PETROL

X25	Return to Oz	1985	—	£3.50

TOWER TEA

Qty		Date	Odds	Sets
24	Illustrated Sayings	1910	£22.50	—

TREBOR BASSETT LTD. (Confectionery)

48	Football 1991-2	1991	—	*£24.00*
48	Football 1992-3	1992	—	£8.00
48	Football 1995-6	1995	—	£20.00
P20	Jurassic Park (Slides)	1993	—	£8.00
48	Premier Players	1995	—	£8.50
48	Sonic the Hedgehog	1991	—	£6.00
48	World Beaters (Soccer)	1994	—	£12.00

TREBOR/SHARP (Confectionery)

25	Famous Pets	1972	—	£3.00
M48	Space Series	1964	£3.00	—
M48	V.C. Heroes	1964	£3.00	—

TRENOUTHS (Shop)

24	World's Most Beautiful Butterflies	1924	£5.25	—

TRIO BARS (Confectionery)

M6	Roland Rat Superstar	1990	—	£6.00

TRUCARDS (Commercial)

M30	Animals	1972	—	£2.50
M30	Battle of Britain	1972	—	£4.00
M30	Flowers	1972	—	£3.00
M30	History of Aircraft	1972	—	£3.00
M30	Sport	1972	—	£3.00
M30	Veteran & Vintage Cars	1972	—	£3.00
M30	World War I	1972	—	£3.00
M30	World War II	1972	—	£2.50

TUCKETT'S (Confectionery)

25	Photo's of Cricketers	1925	£27.50	—
50	Photos of Film Stars	1939	£5.50	—
25	Photos of Football Stars	1925	£20.00	—

W. & E. TURNER (Shoes)

20	War Pictures	1915	£14.00	£280.00

TWININGS TEA

Qty		Date	Odds	Sets
30	Rare Stamps	1960	50p	£16.00
30	Rare Stamps, 2nd Series	1960	—	£4.50
30	2nd Series (Red Overprint)	1961	—	£2.50

TYPHOO TEA LTD.

36 Page Illustrated Reference Book — £3.50

25	Aesop's Fables	1924	£2.80	£70.00
25	Ancient & Annual Customs	1922	£1.60	£40.00
T25	Animal Friends of Man	1927	£4.00	£100.00
T25	Animal Offence & Defence	1928	£1.50	£37.50
T25	A Tale of Two Cities	1931	£3.00	£75.00
24	British Birds & Their Eggs	1914	£9.00	—
T25	British Birds and Their Eggs	1936	£1.50	£37.50
29/30	British Empire at Work	1925	£1.20	£35.00
30	British Empire at Work Continuation Card	1925	£6.50	—
1	British Empire at Work Last Chance Card	1926	—	£8.00
25	Calendar 1934 (Dogs)	1933	£25.00	—
25	Calendar 1936	1935	£12.50	—
T1	Calendar 1937	1936	—	£8.00
T25	Characters from Shakespeare	1937	£1.40	£35.00
25	Common Objects Highly Magnified	1925	£1.00	£25.00
25	Conundrums	1915	£15.00	—
24	Do You Know	1962	—	£3.00
T25	Famous Voyages	1934	£1.20	£30.00
M20	Flags & Arms of Countries	1916	£12.50	£250.00
24	Great Achievements	1962	—	£24.00
T25	Historic Buildings	1936	£1.60	£40.00
T25	Homes of Famous Men	1934	70p	£17.50
T25	Horses	1935	£1.40	£35.00
T25	Important Industries of the British Empire	1939	50p	£12.50
T25	Interesting Events in British History	1938	50p	£12.50
T25	John Halifax, Gentleman	1932	£2.00	£50.00
T25	Lorna Doone	1930	£3.20	£80.00
10	Nursery Rhymes	1914	£20.00	—
24	Our Empire's Defenders	1916	£25.00	£600.00
48	Puzzle Pictures	1913	£27.50	—
T30	Robin Hood & His Merry Men	1928	£6.00	£180.00
M12	The Amazing World of Doctor Who	1976	£1.75	£21.00
T30	The Story of David Copperfield	1929	£2.50	£75.00
T25	The Swiss Family Robinson	1935	£1.60	£40.00
24	Travel through the Ages	1962	—	£3.00
T25	Trees of the Countryside	1938	60p	£15.00
T25	Whilst We Sleep	1928	£2.00	£50.00
24	Wild Flowers	1961	—	£2.00
T25	Wild Flowers in their Families	1936	90p	£22.50
T25	Wild Flowers in their Families, 2nd Series	1937	90p	£22.50
T25	Wonder Cities of the World	1933	£1.30	£32.50
M24	Wonderful World of Disney	1975	£2.75	£66.00
T25	Work on the Farm	1933	£3.00	£75.00
25	Zoo Series	1932	70p	£17.50

PACKAGE ISSUES

20	By Pond & Stream	1955	30p	£6.00

TYPHOO TEA LTD. — cont.

Qty		Date	Odds	Sets
20	Common British Birds	1955	30p	£6.00
20	Costumes of the World	1955	50p	£10.00
24	Do You Know	1962	30p	£7.50
20	Famous Bridges	1955	30p	£6.00
20	Famous Buildings	1955	20p	£4.00
24	Famous Football Clubs	1962	£1.50	£36.00
24	Famous Football Clubs, 2nd Series	1963	£1.50	£36.00
35	Football Club Plaques	1973	*£6.00*	—
24	Football Stars, New Series	1973	£2.50	£60.00
24	Great Voyages of Discovery	1962	40p	£10.00
24	International Football Stars	1967	£2.25	£54.00
24	International Football Stars, 2nd Series	1969	£2.50	—
24	100 Years of Great British Achievements	1972	50p	£12.00
20	Pets	1955	25p	£5.00
20	Some Countryside Animals	1955	25p	£5.00
20	Some Popular Breeds of Dogs	1955	80p	£16.00
20	Some World Wonders	1955	30p	£6.00
24	Travel through the Ages	1962	25p	£6.00
20	Types of Ships	1955	35p	£7.00
20	Wild Animals	1955	20p	£4.00
24	Wild Flowers	1961	50p	£12.00
PREMIUM ISSUES				
E24	Famous Football Clubs	1964	£12.00	—
E24	Famous Football Clubs, 2nd Series	1965	£8.00	£192.00
E24	Football Stars	1973	£7.50	£180.00
G24	Great Voyages of Discovery	1967	*£3.00*	—
E24	International Football Stars, 1st Series	1967	£7.50	£180.00
E24	International Football Stars, 2nd Series	1969	£7.00	£168.00
G24	100 Years of British Achievements	1972	—	£20.00

TYSON & CO. (Soap)

28	Semaphore Signals	1912	£14.00	£400.00

UNION JACK (Periodical)

MF6	Monarchs of the Ring	1923	£9.00	£54.00
M8	Police of All Nations	1922	£6.00	£48.00

UNITED AUTOMOBILE SERVICES

25	Castles (Series No. 1)	1925	£6.00	—
25	Churches (Series No. 2)	1925	£6.00	—
25	Places of Interest (Series No. 4)	1925	£6.00	—
25	"United" (Series No. 3)	1925	£6.00	—

UNITED CONFECTIONERY CO.

50	Wild Animals of the World	1905	£10.00	—

UNITED DAIRIES

25	Aquarium Fish	1962	—	£7.50
25	Birds and Their Eggs	1961	—	£15.00

UNITED DAIRIES — cont.

Qty		*Date*	*Odds*	*Sets*
25	British Uniforms of the 19th Century	1962	—	£15.00
25	The Story of Milk	1966	—	£7.50
25	The West	1963	—	£15.00

UNIVERSAL AUTOMATICS LTD.

X30	Trains of the World	1958	—	£20.00

UNIVERSAL CIGARETTE CARD CO. LTD.

15	Australian Cricket Team 1905	1986	—	£3.00
13	Car Registration Numbers (Irish)	1987	—	£4.00
15	English Cricketers 1902	1987	—	£3.00
25	Military Maids	1987	—	£4.50
25	People of the World	1987	—	£3.50

UNUSUALLY FUNNY FACTORY LTD. (Gum)

M40	Prehistorigum	1990	—	£6.50
M40	Team — Spirits	1990	—	£6.50

VAUXHALL MOTORS LIMITED

L25	Vauxhall Motor Sport Series	1993	—	£10.00
L25	Vauxhall's 90th Anniversary Series	1993	—	£8.50

VENORLANDUS (Commercial)

M48	World of Sport — Our Heroes	1980	—	£17.50

VERKADE'S FABRIEKEN N.V. (Biscuits, Holland)

T140	De Bloemen en Haar Vrienden	1933	—	£15.00
T140	De Boerderij	1935	—	£30.00
T138	Hans de Torenkraai	1936	—	£16.00
T132	Kamerplanten	1928	—	£27.50
T125/126	Mijn Aquarium	1925	—	£27.50
T126	Vetplanten	1926	—	£20.00

VICTORIA GALLERY (Commercial)

Officially Authorised Reprints of Imperial Tobacco Co. Series

P4	Advertisement Postcards (Wills)	1988	—	£5.00
50	Aeroplanes (Civil) (Player)	1990	—	£8.50
L25	Aviary & Cage Birds (Player)	1987	—	£8.50
50	Boxing Personalities (Churchman)	1990	—	£8.50
25	Characters from Dickens (Player)	1990	—	£6.00

VICTORIA GALLERY (Commercial) — cont.

Qty		*Date*	*Odds*	*Sets*
50	Derby and Grand National Winners (Player)	1988	—	£8.50
L25	Dogs (Wills)	1987	—	£8.50
25	England's Naval Heroes (Player)	1988	—	£10.00
L25	Famous Golfers (Wills)	1987	—	£8.50
50	Film Stars, Third Series (Player)	1989	—	£8.50
50	Fish & Bait (Wills)	1990	—	£8.50
L25	Game Birds & Wild Fowl (Player)	1987	—	£8.50
L25	Golf (Player)	1986	—	£8.50
50	Jockeys, 1930 (Ogdens)	1990	—	£10.00
L25	Lawn Tennis, 1931 (Wills)	1988	—	£8.50
50	Motor Cycles (B.A.T.)	1991	—	£8.50
25	Motors (Lambert & Butler 1908)	1992	—	£6.00
58	Musical Celebrities, Second Series (Wills)	1988	—	£9.50
25	Napoleon (Player)	1989	—	£6.00
L12	Prominent Golfers (Churchman)	1989	—	£6.00
50	Racing Greyhounds (Churchman)	1989	—	£8.50
L25	Racing Yachts (Player)	1987	—	£8.50
12	Recruiting Posters (Wills)	1988	—	£3.00
L25	Rigs of Ships (Wills)	1987	—	£8.50
	Original Issues			
L6	A Gathering of Spirits	1994	—	£2.50
L20	American Civil War Leaders	1992	—	£7.00
L20	Boxing Champions	1991	—	£10.00
L21	Boxing Champions, Second Series	1992	—	£7.00
L6	British Birds of Prey	1994	—	£2.50
L6	British Birds of Prey (Different)	1996	—	£2.50
L20	Caricatures of the British Army	1994	—	£7.00
L20	Caricatures of the British Army II	1994	—	£7.00
L1	Promotional Card	1994	—	50p
L6	Classic Motor Cycles (Harley Davidson)	1993	—	£2.50
L20	Endangered Wild Animals	1991	—	£7.00
L25	Hollywood Moviemen	1993	—	£8.50
L2	Promotional Cards	1993	—	60p
L20	Legends of Hollywood	1991	—	£7.00
L1	Promotional Card (John Wayne)	1991	—	50p
L25	Olympic Greats	1992	—	£8.50
L20	Partners (Cinema)	1992	—	£7.00
L20	Snooker Celebrities	1988	—	£7.00
L10	Spirit of A Nation	1991	—	£5.00
L25	The Ryder Cup, 1991	1991	—	£15.00
L12	The Twelve Days of Christmas	1992	—	£6.00
L20	Uniforms of the American Civil War	1992	—	£7.00
L24	Uniforms of the War of Independence	1993	—	£8.50
L48	Wild West	1993	—	£13.00

CHOCOLAT DE VILLARS

24	British Birds and Their Eggs	1926	£3.00	£72.00

VOMO AUTOMATICS

X50	Flags of the World	1965	75p	£37.50

JONATHAN WALES LTD.

Qty		Date	Odds	Sets
25	The History of Flight, 1st Series	1963	£8.00	—
25	The History of Flight, 2nd Series	1963	£8.00	—

WALES ON SUNDAY (Newspaper)

T36	World Cup Heroes (Rugby)	1995	—	£15.00
T24	World Cup Rugby Greats (With Album)	1999	—	£15.00

WALKER, HARRISON & GARTHWAITES LTD.

M15	Dogs	1902	£22.50	—

WALKERS SNACK FOODS LTD.

K50	Looney Tunes (Tazos)	1996	—	£7.50
K10	Wizard Monster (Tazos)	1996	—	£2.00
K20	World Tazos (51-70)	1996	—	£4.00

T. WALL & SONS (Ice Cream)

24	Do You Know	1965	—	£3.50
36	Dr. Who Adventure	1966	£2.75	£99.00
20	Incredible Hulk Records	1979	£2.25	£45.00
48	Moon Fleet	1967	—	£9.00
M6	Prehistoric Animals (Magicards)	1971	—	£3.00
P6	Sea Creatures	1971	—	£2.25
20	Skateboard Surfer	1978	—	£6.00
20	Time Travel with Starship 4	1984	£3.00	—

WALTERS PALM TOFFEE

50	Some Cap Badges of Territorial Regiments	1938	80p	£40.00

WAND CONFECTIONERY LTD.

X10	Chubby Checker — How to do the Twist	1964	*£7.00*	—
25	Commemoration Stamp Series	1963	£2.50	£62.50
X35	Pop D.J.'s	1964	£3.00	£105.00
25	They Gave Their Names	1963	—	£10.00
23/25	Ditto	1963	—	£2.00

WARNOCK & CO. (Tea)

24	The Island of Ceylon	1955	£3.60	£90.00

WARUS CARDS (Commercial)

10	The Abbey Road Series	1998	—	£4.25
10	The Beatles for Sale Series	1998	—	£4.25
10	The Hard Day's Night Series	1998	—	£4.25
10	The Help Series	1998	—	£4.25

WARUS CARDS (Commercial) — cont.

Qty		*Date*	*Odds*	*Sets*
10	The Let It Be Series	1998	—	£4.25
10	The Magical Mystery Tour Series	1998	—	£4.25
10	The Please Please Me Series	1998	—	£4.25
10	The Revolver Series	1998	—	£4.25
10	The Rubber Soul Series	1998	—	£4.25
10	The Sgt. Pepper Series	1998	—	£4.25
10	The White Album	1998	—	£4.25
10	The With the Beatles Series	1998	—	£4.25
10	The Yellow Submarine Series	1998	—	£4.25

WARWICK DISTRICT COUNCIL

30	England's Historic Heartland	1980	—	£2.50

WATFORD BISCUIT CO.

KF48	Cinema Stars	1952	£2.25	—

WEBCOSA & CO. (Gum)

X20	Trail Town	1963	£2.25	£45.00
M48	Victoria Cross Heroes	1964	£2.75	—

WEEKLY WELCOME (Periodical)

12	Lest We Forget Cards	1916	£9.00	£108.00

WEETABIX LTD. (Cereals)

XS25	Animal Cards	1960	60p	£15.00
T28	Asterix — His Friends & Foes	1976	£2.50	£70.00
T18	Batman and Wonderwoman	1979	£2.75	£50.00
XS25	British Birds Cards	1962	£2.00	£50.00
XS25	British Cars	1963	£3.00	£75.00
L25	Conquest of Space, Series A	1959	£1.80	£45.00
L25	Conquest of Space, Series B	1959	£1.80	£45.00
L4	Double Jigsaw	1991	—	£3.00
T24	Dr Who (Coloured Background)	1977	£4.50	—
T24	Dr Who (White Background)	1975	£5.00	—
T18	Flash Gordon	1981	£2.00	£36.00
T18	Huckleberry Hound	1977	£3.00	£54.00
T18	Mickey Mouse's Playmates	1978	£3.00	£54.00
XS25	Our Pets Cards	1961	60p	£15.00
T24	Robin Hood	1980	£2.00	£48.00
T18	Star Trek	1979	£4.00	£72.00
T18	Superman	1978	£2.50	£45.00
L25	The Western Story	1959	£1.20	£30.00
XS25	Thrill Cards	1960	£2.00	£50.00
P5	Weeta-Card	1989	—	£6.00
XS25	Working Dog Cards	1961	—	£8.50
T18	World of Sport	1986	£4.50	—

JAMES O. WELCH (Confectionery, U.S.A.)

Qty		Date	Odds	Sets
50	Comics	1950	£3.60	£180.00

WELSH RUGBY UNION

50	Great Welsh Rugby Players	1981	—	£4.00

JOHN WEST FOODS LTD.

M8	Famous Sea Adventurers	1972	—	£2.50

WEST LONDON SYNAGOGUE

50	Jewish Life in Many Lands	1961	—	£45.00
50	Jewish Symbols and Ceremonies	1961	—	*£50.00*
25/50	Ditto	1961	—	£3.00

WESTCO (Confectionery)

F60	Westco Autocards	1954	£7.00	—

WEST MIDLANDS COLLECTORS CENTRE

24	Busby Babes	1990	—	£6.00
30	England Captains	1997	—	£5.00
24	Golden Wolves	1989	—	£3.00
24	Vintage Spurs	1993	—	£5.00

WEST MIDLANDS POLICE

X24	Cop Card-Toons	1989	—	£6.50
X36	Pictorial History — Walsall & District	1986	—	£22.50
X8	Play Safe — Stay Safe (With Album)	1992	—	£1.75
X24	The Old Bill Collection (With Album)	1990	—	£6.50

WESTON BISCUIT CO. LTD. (Australia)

L24	Veteran & Vintage Cars, 1st Series	1961	—	£42.00
L24	Veteran & Vintage Cars, 2nd Series	1962	—	£8.50

WEST RIDING COUNTY COUNCIL

20	Health Cards	1924	£5.50	£110.00

WHAT CAMERA? (Magazine)

P12	Photocards	1989	—	£3.00

WHITBREAD & CO. LTD. (Brewers)

M1	Duke Without a Head	1958	—	£8.00
M50	Inn Signs, 1st Series (Metal)	1949	£2.60	£130.00
M50	Inn Signs, 2nd Series (Metal)	1950	£2.60	£130.00

WHITBREAD & CO. LTD. (Brewers) — cont.

Qty		*Date*	*Odds*	*Sets*
M50	Inn Signs, 3rd Series (Metal)	1951	£4.00	£200.00
M50	(Card)	1952	£2.80	£140.00
M50	Inn Signs, 4th Series	1953	£2.80	£140.00
M50	Inn Signs, 5th Series	1955	£3.00	£150.00
M25	Inn Signs, Bournemouth	1973	£4.50	—
M25	Inn Signs, Devon & Somerset	1973	£1.60	£40.00
M25	Inn Signs, Isle of Wight	1974	£4.00	—
M25	Inn Signs, Kent	1973	£4.50	—
M15	Inn Signs, London	1973	£2.50	£60.00
M10	Inn Signs, London (Different)	1974	£3.75	—
M25	Inn Signs, Marlow	1973	£3.50	£87.50
M25	Inn Signs, Portsmouth	1973	£5.00	—
M4	Inn Signs, Special Issue	1951	£4.00	£16.00
M25	Inn Signs, Stratford-upon-Avon	1974	£3.40	£85.00
M25	Inn Signs, West Pennine	1973	£3.40	£85.00
M25	Maritime Inn Signs	1974	30p	£7.50
M1	The Britannia Inn (Plain Back)	1958	—	*£30.00*
M1	(Printed Back)	1958	—	£45.00
M1	The Railway	1958	—	£6.00
M1	The Startled Saint	1958	—	£32.50

WHITE FISH AUTHORITY

25	The Fish We Eat	1954	—	£2.50

WHITEHAVEN LIBRARY

M6	The Port of Whitehaven	1978	—	£6.00

WHITEHEAD (Lollies)

X25	Kings & Queens	1980	—	£3.00

WIGAN POLICE

X24	Riversiders	1991	—	£8.00

WIKO (Germany)

50	Soldaten Der Welt	1969	—	£17.50

WILBUR-SUCHARD CHOCOLATE CO. (U.S.A.)

35/36	Flags	1918	£2.00	£70.00

WILCOCKS & WILCOCKS LTD. (Tea)

25	Birds	1965	£1.40	—
25	British Cavalry Uniforms of the 19th Century	1963	—	£10.00
25	Garden Flowers	1964	—	£6.00
25	Passenger Liners	1967	—	£15.00

WILCOCKS & WILCOCKS LTD. (Tea) — cont.

Qty		*Date*	*Odds*	*Sets*
25	People & Places	1966	—	£3.00
24	The Island of Ceylon	1955	£4.00	—
25	Tropical Birds	1965	—	£10.00
25	Wonders of the Deep	1965	—	£3.00
25	Wonders of the World	1971	—	£5.00

A.S. WILKIN LTD. (Confectionery)

25	Into Space	1960	—	£7.50

W.R. WILKINSON & CO. (Confectionery)

M25	Popular Footballers	1956	£35.00	—

ROBERT J. WILSON

L10	Traditional Lincolnshire Country Life	2002	—	£6.25
L10	Vintage Tractors	2002	—	£4.50

WIMPY (Restaurants)

M20	Super Heroes Super Villains	1979	85p	£17.00

WOMAN'S FRIEND (Periodical)

K52	Fortune Telling Cards	1925	£3.00	—

WOMAN'S OWN (Periodical)

F8	Film Stars	1955	£6.00	£48.00

E. WOODHEAD & SONS (Tea)

25	Types of British Soldiers	1916	£24.00	£600.00

WOOLWORTH (Stores)

M24	Fascinating Facts	1989	—	£4.00

WORTHINGTON (Brewers)

36	Sportsmen (Imperial Tobacco Reprints)	1992	—	£40.00

WRIGHTS BISCUITS LTD.

24	Marvels of the World	1954	—	£2.00
24	Mischief goes to Mars (Mischief Club)	1954	—	£6.50
24	(Wright at Side)	1954	—	£4.00
24	(Wright at Base)	1954	50p	£12.00

YOUNG BRITAIN (Periodical)

Qty		*Date*	*Odds*	*Sets*
MF15	Favourite Cricketers Series (In Pairs)......................	1922	£6.00	£90.00

SPECIAL INTRODUCTORY OFFER

The quality of our cards and of our service is second to none. In order to introduce ourselves to new clients, and as a 'Thank You' to existing customers, we are offering a 15% discount on any one order for complete sets of cards and odds, upon presentation of the original voucher below.

Just work out what you would like to order and sent us your list. Deduct the 15% and send us your name, address, cheque or Credit/Debit card details together with the voucher printed below. Orders for albums, pages, books and other accessories can be placed at the same time, but please remember that these must be at normal Catalogue prices. Please also note that this offer cannot be combined with any of our other current or future Special Offers.

You can order as little or as much as you like for this voucher offer. An order of £50 will cover the cost of this Catalogue and larger orders will result in considerable savings. For this reason we must restrict the offer to one voucher for each customer.

MONEY-SAVING VOUCHER

To: Murray Cards (International) Ltd., 51 Watford Way, Hendon Central London, NW4 3JH

Please send me the cards on my enclosed list. I wish to claim the 15% discount on all the complete sets and odd cards listed. This is the only voucher I have returned.

Name..

Address..

....

....

....

Tel No...Date.................................

Cheque enclosed OR

Credit/Debit Card No...

Start Date.......................... Expiry Date......................... Switch Issue Number.............

Offer valid 1st January to 30th September 2004.

PRINTED BY STOATE & BISHOP (PRINTERS) LTD. (01242) 236741